#34

The Concise Śrīmad Bhāgavataṁ

The Concise Śrīmad Bhāgavataṁ

Swami Venkatesananda

STATE UNIVERSITY OF NEW YORK PRESS

Published by
State University of New York Press, Albany

Printed in the United States of America

For information, address State University of New York
Press, State University Plaza, Albany, N.Y., 12246

Library of Congress Cataloging-in-Publication Data

Purāṇas. Bhāgavatapurāṇa. English.
The concise Śrīmad Bhāgavataṁ / [edited and translated by] Śwami
Venkatesananda.
p. cm.
Translation of: Bhāgavatapurāṇa.

ISBN 0-7914-0148-0. — ISBN 0-7914-0149-9 (pbk.)
I. Venkatesananda, Swami. II. Title.
BL 1140.4.B432E5 1989
294.5′925—dc20 89-4499
CIP

CONTENTS

PREFACE

This is a condensed version of a long Purana of 18,000 verses. By means of stories from the lives of avatars, sages, and kings, it popularized the teaching of the Vedas. To study it is the best of all ways to become acquainted with the living religion of India today. The nineteenth-century saint Ramakrishna said of the Bhagavatam, *"It is fried in the butter of Knowledge and steeped in the honey of Love."*

At regular intervals through the text, the chapters being condensed are designated by Book and Chapter numbers. Each interval is appropriate in length for a daily reading and there are 365 intervals.

Book One

Book One Chapter 1

Śaunaka and other sages said to Sūta: O sinless Sūta: We have assembled here in holy Naimiśāraṇya, to conduct this great sacrifice. We shall spend every spare moment in listening to discourses, for our own spiritual advancement and for the salvation of humanity.

In this dark age, blessed Sūta, people are short-lived. Yet even this short life-span is occupied by the pursuit of fleeting pleasures and consequent sufferings. Even when disgust for such pleasures arises in the heart of man, he is too dull-witted and lazy to apply himself to the scriptures that map out the path to liberation.

Beloved one, these scriptures are numerous, divergent in their message, conflicting in their conclusions, confusing and laborious. They have to be studied over a long period of time: but time destroys what it builds, leaving one running around in an endless circle, vainly endeavouring to put the fragmented personality and life into order.

Loving and benevolent Sūta! You are a master of all the scriptures and are therefore in the best position to help us. Give us the quintessence of these scriptures, equipped with which man will instantly be delivered from this ever-whirling cycle of birth and death. Instant integration of our whole personality and life is surely the only way to end the darkness of ignorance and the consequent sorrow.

We know, dear Sūta, that the Lord's descent on this earth (especially as Kṛṣṇa, the son of Vasudeva and Devakī) is intended for the protection and the prosperity of all beings: please explain this to us. Thus shall we remember him and his name. If one utters the Lord's name even unintentionally, one is instantly freed from fear; for fear itself is afraid of the Lord.

We are never tired of hearing of the Lord's incarnations and his countless exploits; therefore, narrate them to us. Through a succession of sages, these truths will reach all men for all time to come. Thus, contemplating the feet of the Lord while listening to his stories, man will instantly be freed from sin and sinfulness, and attain liberation. O Sūta! Sages who have enshrined the lotus feet of the Lord in their hearts are pure and perfectly peaceful; those who come into contact with them are instantly purified and their hearts are filled with peace.

In this dark age which has just commenced, when purity of heart is the first casualty in the conflict between the forces of light and the forces of darkness, association with sages and listening to this story of God narrated by them are the only means of liberation. This story captivates the mind and fills the heart of man with the love of God and thus effects an instant and integral transmutation of his whole personality.

We therefore bless the divine providence that has brought you to us at this vital juncture. Pray, commence your blessed discourse!

Book One Chapter 2

Sūta Ugraśravā said: Holy ones! Verily, your requests are highly praiseworthy, for they will inevitably lead to the narration of the glorious life of lord Kṛṣṇa. Man should constantly endeavour to do that which generates devotion to lord Kṛṣṇa—devotion which is motiveless, which knows no obstruction, and as a result of which one realises the all-blissful God.

Tradition grants man four goals—duty, wealth, enjoyment and liberation. A duty, however well performed, is but wasted labour if it does not generate eagerness to listen to God's glory. One should not perform one's duty for the sake of wealth alone. Wealth must be dedicated to a righteous life, and not be squandered on sensual pleasures. Sensual enjoyment is pleasure natural to living; it is not an end, or object to be pursued. Life itself is meant for the attainment of the highest knowledge, which is reality. It has been described as the absolute, the supreme self, and the Lord.

Now listen to the steps that lead one to this self-realisation. When one visits the holy places of pilgrimage, one meets and serves holy men. From them one hears the stories and the glories of lord Vāsudeva (Kṛṣṇa). The evil propensities in one's heart are thereby destroyed and in that pure heart there arises unwavering love for God. The Lord being pure satva, the base qualities born of rajas and tamas are eradicated altogether by such love. Without doubt and without delay one realises God as one's very self, the sole reality.

This reality or lord Kṛṣṇa is the very goal of all veda, all rites and rituals, all yoga, all spiritual activities, of all austerities, of righteousness, of the highest wisdom and of all life and activity. In fact, he alone exists. In the beginning he manifested his own nature, characterised by the three qualities (satva, rajas and tamas—purity, dynamism and inertia). Just as fire assumes different forms in accordance with the burning object, so lord Kṛṣṇa, who alone is all this, appears in infinite forms. He is the entire manifest creation, all the elements. He alone appears as the angels, human beings and the lower forms of creation; he alone is the creator (Brahmā), the protector (Viṣṇu) and the redeemer (Śiva). Yet, the supreme felicity and salvation of man are obtained through devotion to Viṣṇu alone, for he is pure satva, absolute purity.

Book One Chapter 3

Sūta said: O devout sages! When the Lord willed the creation into being, the cosmic consciousness (which is the unmanifested cosmic being) became the cosmic puruṣa, the manifest being. He had sixteen parts—the ten senses, the five elements and the mind. Simultaneously, as it were, myriads of forms were made manifest—human, subhuman, superhuman, vegetable and mineral. Hence the Lord is said to possess myriads of heads, eyes, feet, hands and mouths. The infinite was not exhausted by this infinite manifestation. Only a small part went into creation.

Lord Nārāyaṇa repeatedly descended into this creation to fulfil the divine purpose of creation. Listen to a few of such incarnations: The sanatkumārā (the eternally enlightened four brothers), the divine boar (who lifted up the earth), Nārada (who promulgated the code of worship), Nara and Nārāyaṇa (the eternal exemplars of penance), Kapila (the first metaphysician), Dattātreya (the foremost expounder of the science of the self), yajña (the spirit of self-sacrificing service), Ṛṣabhadeva (the first and foremost paramahaṁsa-ascetic), Pṛthu (who made the earth fruitful), the divine fish (which rescued the earth from the deluge), the divine tortoise (which helped in the production of nectar), Dhanvantari (who emerged with the nectar), Mohinī (who ensured that only the gods had the nectar and not the demons), the man-lion (who destroyed the demon Hiraṇyakaśipu), the dwarf (who assumed the cosmic form and redeemed king Bali), Paraśurāma (who routed unrighteous kings), Vyāsa (who edited the vedā and wrote the purāṇā or legends), Rāma (who exemplified in himself the ideal man), Balarāma and Kṛṣṇa (who re-established dharma), Buddha (the enlightened); and he who will come at the end of the present age, as Kalki.

Besides the above there are innumerable other incarnations of the divine such as sages and saints, and men of great power. All these are rays of the supreme being; but Kṛṣṇa is the Lord himself. All of them appear in order to protect the forces of light from the forces of darkness. He who recalls this morning and evening will be freed from all suffering.

Yet, O men of wisdom, it is wrong to conclude that the supreme being is born, lives and dies. The infinite forever remains infinite, even as space is never affected by the presence or absence of clouds. Creation is considered the 'sport of the Lord', because he who is ever full needs nothing, lacks nothing and desires to achieve nothing by this sportive activity. Yet, this has a purpose—to protect the forces of light. Only he who is ever devoted to the lotus feet of the Lord is able to comprehend the mystery of the Lord's incarnations.

Blessed ones, I myself heard the Lord's incarnations described by the renowned sage, Śukadeva. He heard it from his father Vyāsa and he imparted this great secret to king Parīkṣit who had been condemned to death.

Book One Chapter 4

Śaunaka asked Sūta: O blessed Sūta! You have whetted our appetite by what you have just told us. We wish to hear in detail the story of the Lord's incarnations and glories. When and why did the sage Vyāsa compose the scripture? You said that the sage Śuka learnt it from Vyāsa and then in his turn narrated it to king Parīkṣit. The sage Sūka was born with the highest wisdom of non-duality, living constantly immersed in the realisation of oneness.

It is said that once Vyāsa followed his son Sūka as the latter walked away. Śuka was naked and young; Vyāsa was aged and clothed. Yet, some women bathing in a roadside pond were unashamed when Śuka passed by but were ashamed when Vyāsa approached. When questioned, they revealed that whereas Śuka had risen above sex-distinctions, Vyāsa had not! Sage Śuka was wandering about as if mad, dumb and dull-witted. How could Parīkṣit and others recognise him as a sage?

O beloved Sūta! How was it that king Parīkṣit was condemned to death? He was so valiant and so good that he was invincible. He was beloved of his people. Why did he renounce his kingdom and its royal pleasures and sit at the feet of sage Śuka and listen to the stories and the glories of the Lord? Kindly enlighten us.

Sūta replied: O sages! During the age preceding this kali age, Vyāsa who could see the past, present and future, foresaw that during the kali age confusion of duties would set in, resulting in a decline of righteousness. So Vyāsa took upon himself the colossal task of editing the vedā, and he instructed four sages in four different branches of these. For those unable to learn and recite the vedā, Vyāsa composed the Mahābhārata which is considered the fifth vedā. However in spite of dedicating himself to the welfare of all people, the holy one was restless at heart.

Vyāsa mused: "I have studied the vedā, served the elders, worshipped the sacrificial fires, performed all the ceremonies and strictly adhered to the code of righteousness. I have perpetuated the study of the vedā and revealed their esssence in the Mahābhārata. Still my soul has not realised its oneness with the supreme being! Is it because I have not fully recounted the Bhāgavata Dharma, the path that leads to God-realisation, which is dearest to the paramahatmā, or holy men, and which is dear to the Lord himself?" While the sage Vyāsa was thus sitting dejected, sage Nārada appeared upon the scene. Vyāsa rose and welcomed Nārada, and worshipped the celestial sage whom even the gods adored.

Nārada's Previous Life
Book One Chapter 5

Celestial Sage Nārada said: O Vyāsa! You are a ray of the Lord. Through austerities and the practice of yoga you have plunged into self-knowledge and knowledge of the scriptures. You have elaborated the duties of man. These concepts of duty and the performance of ceremonies may still be misunderstood by unwary souls because they appear to grant reality to the ego and spiritual value to their egotistic actions. Only a few wise men will perceive that liberation lies in transcending these scriptural injunctions and being wholly devoted to the Lord.

O chief of sages! Only that speech, scriptural composition, wisdom or action is worthy which has the Lord's stories and glories for its content and which has the Lord himself as its subject and its object. One who is devoted to the Lord and from whom worldly duties have dropped away, even if he dies without reaching his goal or suffers a spiritual downfall, such a person is not touched by evil; whereas one who neglects devotion to the Lord on the pretext of 'worldly duties' achieves no purpose at all. Verily, the servant of the Lord does not return to this world of birth and death.

Hear now, O sage, the story of my past birth when I was the son of a maidservant of the brāhmaṇā. Once I happened to serve them and they were kind to me. Once a day I ate what was left of their dishes. All this purified my mind. At their feet I listened to the soul-absorbing stories of lord Kṛṣṇa. My heart longed for the Lord. I soon realised that this world, including heaven, is māyā, a product of my own ignorance. Constant hearing of the Lord's glories eradicated passion and ignorance from me. When the sages were about to depart, they imparted to me their most esoteric wisdom which they had gained directly from the Lord himself. Through this wisdom I realised the glory of lord Vāsudeva.

O Vyāsa! Ordinarily action leads to reaction, but when action is performed out of love of God, it leads to liberation. Hence, one should bow mentally to the Lord, uttering the mantra: "Obeisance to you, O lord Vāsudeva, we meditate on you. Obeisance also to Pradyumna, Aniruddha and Saṅkarṣaṇa." This mantra is the Lord's body. He is without form. He alone is a man of true insight who works and worships him uttering this mantra and constantly remembering him.

O Vyāsa, sing the Lord's glories and your heart will find supreme peace and eternal bliss. Your heart is restless only because you have failed to attain this so far.

Book One Chapter 6

The Celestial Sage Nārada continued: At that time I was five years old and was dependent on my mother who was greatly attached to me, her only child. She struggled hard to provide a comfortable living for me—but in vain. Who can transgress what is decreed by divine will? All are mere puppets in God's hands. It was out of regard for her that I continued to live in the village, though I was not attached either to it or to her. One night my mother was bitten by a snake; she died.

I welcomed this as a boon from the Lord though I had not wished it. So I wandered away until I reached a dense forest. There I began to practise meditation as I had been instructed by the holy ones.

As I contemplated the Lord's lotus feet, overpowered by love for him, he gradually appeared in my heart. I was thrilled. I experienced the bliss and the peace that passeth all understanding. But, alas, the vision disappeared and I became disconsolate. Then the Lord of mercy and love spoke: "In this birth you are not fit to realise me. It is possible to realise me only when one attains perfection in yoga and when all the impurities of one's heart have been burnt away. I revealed my form once in order to make you realise that one who desires to attain me is gradually freed from all the desires which are latent in his heart. Your service of the holy ones, even though it was for a short period, has fixed your heart on me. You will soon cast off this physical body and will then become one of my attendants. You will never cease to remember me. Even during the ensuing cosmic dissolution, by my grace you will not forget me nor your present existence." Thus spoke the Lord and I bowed to his will.

When the karma which had given birth to my physical body had been exhausted, death ensued. Immediately I became an attendant of the Lord himself. Soon after this there was the cosmic deluge. The entire creation, with its creator (Brahmā), was withdrawn into the Lord. I, too, entered his body. After a very long time the Lord willed creation into being once again, and Brahmā created me along with the other sages. Since then I have roamed freely throughout the universe, playing upon this vīṇā and singing his names and glories, and the Lord has revealed himself in my heart.

Singing the stories and glories of the Lord is the surest raft to cross this terrible ocean of worldly existence for those whose minds are disturbed by craving for sensual pleasures. Hence I commend that you recount the incarnations of the Lord.

Aśvatthāmā and Draupadī's Children
Book One Chapter 7

Sūta said: After sage Nārada's departure, Vyāsa sat in his hermitage and contemplated the Lord. Knowing that the love of lord Kṛṣṇa is the best cure for spiritual blindness which is the cause of all human suffering, he composed the Bhāgavataṁ. He who listens to this is filled with the love of lord Kṛṣṇa. This god-love instantly dispels grief, infatuation and fear. Kṛṣṇa is the supreme being himself; hence sages like Śuka who are established in non-dual consciousness, love him and listen to the Bhāgavataṁ. Having composed it Vyāsa imparted it to Śuka and other sages. I shall now narrate to you how Śuka imparted this knowledge to king Parīkṣit.

The great war of the Mahābhārata had concluded. Duryodhana lay dying on the battlefield. His friend Aśvatthāmā, a brāhmaṇa and son of Droṇa, unchivalrously murdered the young sons of the pāṇḍavā while they were asleep and offered their heads to Duryodhana (much to his distaste) as a parting gift! The infuriated Arjuna chased Aśvatthāmā, intending to kill him in revenge. In utter despair Aśvatthāmā released the mightiest missile, the brahma-śira. Bewildered, Arjuna prayed to Kṛṣṇa: "O Kṛṣṇa, you remove the fear of your devotees. You are the sole saviour of those who in this world of pain and death are scorched by the fire of sin and suffering. You have incarnated here to remove earth's burden and to provide your devotees with an object of constant meditation. Lord, I do not know what this dreadful fire is, which burns me from all sides." Kṛṣṇa revealed the nature of the missile and, impelled by Kṛṣṇa, Arjuna released a counter-missile. The two missiles seemed to burn the entire earth, but out of compassion for all living beings Kṛṣṇa now asked Arjuna to neutralise the missiles and then capture Aśvatthāmā alive.

Arjuna captured Aśvatthāmā. In order to fathom and to reveal Arjuna's devotion to righteous conduct, Kṛṣṇa urged him to kill the villain: "A noble man would not kill an enemy who is unguarded, asleep or tender of age. Aśvatthāmā did just that. It is proper to execute such a wicked person; or else he would persist in his evil." However, Arjuna did not kill him. In the pāṇḍava camp they discussed the punishment to be meted out to the war criminal. Some favoured execution but others favoured something less severe. Draupadī, although disconsolate at the murder of her innocent children, showed supreme wisdom and compassion. She pleaded that Aśvatthāmā, being a brāhmaṇa and the son of the preceptor, should not be killed in punishment, as the war had ended and peacetime justice should prevail. She reminded him, "This Aśvatthāmā is the son of your worshipful preceptor, Droṇa, who lives in his progeny. Let not his mother grieve for him, as I grieve for my children killed by him." However, Bhīma was impatient to kill Aśvatthāmā. Finally, Kṛṣṇa said: "He is a brāhmaṇa who should not be killed. But he is a villain who should be put to death. Draupadī and Bhīma should both be pleased. Do what is appropriate." Arjuna divined the Lord's intention. He cut off the gem on the brāhmaṇa's head along with the locks of hair, and let him go. This was tantamount to capital punishment.

Sūta continued: His mission accomplished, Kṛṣṇa was about to return to Dvārakā when Uttarā (widow of Abhimanyu, Arjuna's deceased son) ran screaming toward him, seeking his protection against a burning missile. Simultaneously the paṇḍavā were also afflicted by the most powerful Brahmā-missile released by the ungrateful and evil-minded Aśvatthāmā to destroy the very ones who had released him—even their unborn grandson in Uttarā's womb. Kṛṣṇa, however, surrounded the foetus with his grace. What evil power, however mighty, can defy it!

Kuntī, mother of the pāṇḍavā, was overcome by a great wave of devotion. She praised lord Kṛṣṇa:

"Lord, thou art the supreme being, but one with perverted vision cannot recognize you as such. Salutations, salutations unto thee. You protected us against all calamities, including the missile released by Aśvatthāmā. Yet, I pray thee, O master of the universe, may many calamities continue to befall us so that we may turn to you and, by doing so, be released for ever from the cycle of birth and death. They who are proud of their ancestry, power, learning and wealth do not even utter your name. You can be seen only by those who call nothing their own, and who have no sense of possession.

"Lord, thou art beginningless and endless time itself. Who can fathom your glory even when you manifest in human form? Thou art impartial, though the finite mind of man attributes diversity to you. Thou art the soul of the universe, the reality that appears as the universe. Thou art birthless, yet you assume numerous forms. Giant intellects advance various reasons for your incarnations. But you descend to earth to perform deeds which people will love to remember and to recount and which will bring them to thy lotus feet and confer upon them final liberation from birth and death.

"Lord, I take refuge in thy lotus feet. Cut asunder the ties that bind me and let my thoughts incessantly dwell only on thee. This is my heartfelt prayer, O Kṛṣṇa."

The Lord smiled and said: "So be it." Yudhiṣṭhira's turn came. He was inconsolable with grief and self-reproach for the destruction of so many warriors. "Even the declaration in the scriptures that a king does not incur sin by killing the enemies of the people in a righteous war does not satisfy me," he said.

Sūta said: Yudhiṣṭhira, son of the god of righteousness, was haunted by thoughts of war (which is always a source of unrighteousness) so he sought the presence of his grandfather, Bhīṣma. O sages, this was one of the rarest moments in history. Gods, angels and men assembled at the feet of Bhīṣma, the greatest warrior known to history, whose body had been pierced by so many arrows that when he fell to the ground his body did not touch the earth. He had the power to leave his body at will and was waiting for the sacred Uttarayana, or winter solstice, to do so. On this day the pāṇḍavā and lord Kṛṣṇa arrived.

Though on account of his loyalty to Duryodhana, Bhīṣma had fought against Yudhiṣṭhira in battle, Bhīṣma lovingly consoled Yudhiṣṭhira: "O king! I consider that whatever happened was brought about by that inscrutable power that directs events here on earth. What a wonder it is that where you, the embodiment of dharma, rule, with such warriors as Bhīma and Arjuna and with lord Kṛṣṇa himself as the supreme friend and well-wisher—even there such adversity could prevail! Know, therefore, that all this was the work of unseen and mysterious powers."

Bhīṣma continued: "Śrī Kṛṣṇa is God himself, though he lives incognito veiling his divinity with the power of illusion. He is the same to all. Yet, how compassionate he is to come to me just when I am about to leave the body! A yogi who casts off his body after entering his mind into the Lord, while reciting his names with his lips, is freed from cravings and karma (action-reaction chain)."

O sages, at Yudhiṣṭhira's request Bhīṣma then discoursed upon the duties of man in great detail, for Bhīṣma was the greatest among the knowers of truth. The sacred hour arrived. Bhīṣma looked at Kṛṣṇa with unwinking eyes and burst into rapturous hymn:

"At the hour of my departure I offer my mind to Śrī Kṛṣṇa, the supreme being, who assumes various forms for his own divine purpose. May my heart ever rest in Kṛṣṇa, whose radiant face is hallowed by hair laden with the dust of the battlefield, who volunteered to serve as Arjuna's charioteer, who taught him the Bhagavad Gītā, who protected the pāṇḍavā in numerous ways, and whose gaze fell on all those on the battlefield so that those who were killed (whether they were 'friend' or 'foe') would attain freedom from mortal existence and be endowed with a form similar to the Lord's."

Bhīṣma, the enlightened, became one with the absolute. Yudhiṣṭhira and the others, accompanied by lord Kṛṣṇa, returned to the capital, where Yudhiṣṭhira became king.

Sūta continued: Lord Kṛṣṇa rejoiced that the evil-doers had been conquered, and the righteous Yudhiṣṭhira had been crowned king. Yudhiṣṭhira had regained his equanimity and wisdom from Bhīṣma's discourses, and ruled the kingdom with love and justice. The gods rejoiced, for prosperity smiled on the country. Rid of evil and the fear of evil, people lived in peace, in physical and mental health.

Lord Kṛṣṇa obtained the permission of the pāṇḍavā to return to Dvārakā, his own capital (on the west coast of India). Parting was extremely painful and difficult. He who even listens to the stories of Kṛṣṇa longs to hear them without interruption. The pāṇḍavā were with him in person. How could they bear to live without him? Yet, it had to be.

The pāṇḍavā gave him a royal send-off. They went with him to the outskirts of their capital, Hastināpura. The simple, god-loving womenfolk of the country feasted their eyes on the Lord and sang his praises:

"Ah, my friend! Is this not the Lord himself who playfully creates, sustains and withdraws into himself the entire universe? Is this not the Lord whose glory is sung by saints and sages, by the vedā and scriptures? Indeed, he is the Lord himself whose lotus feet are realised by enlightened beings who have fully conquered their senses and have controlled their vital airs, whose minds yearn for his vision and whose hearts are thoroughly cleansed by unceasing devotion—for he alone can cleanse our hearts and fill them with purity. Whenever the rulers of the earth, their intellects clouded by tamas, live unrighteous lives and thus promote unrighteousness on earth, then he (who is purity itself) descends on earth in various forms, manifesting the divine attributes of omnipotence, omnipresence and omniscience and also truth, justice, compassion and divine activity. Blessed is Dvārakā, his own city; blessed are the people among whom he was born; blessed are the women espoused by him, who are the pride and glory of womanhood."

Lord Kṛṣṇa smiled—for these simple womenfolk, with pure love in their hearts had discovered the truth which had been veiled from the eyes of haughty kings and mighty warriors. After taking leave of the pāṇḍavā, lord Kṛṣṇa travelled through different states of central India and reached western India. Everywhere in this journey the people worshipped Kṛṣṇa.

Sūta continued: As he neared the outskirts of his capital city, lord Kṛṣṇa announced his return by blowing his conch. This signalled the commencement of the festivities. The city wore a festive appearance. People lined the main road to feast their eyes upon the ever radiant and beautiful face of the Lord. They welcomed him with words which expressed their love and devotion to him, their wisdom and reverence:

"O Lord, we bow down to your lotus feet, adored by the gods themselves, which are beyond the flux of change or becoming, and which are sought by those who aspire for liberation. You are our father, mother, our dearest friend, our preceptor and our supreme deity. Indeed we are the most blessed people on earth for we have been chosen to be close to you. Yet, such is your glory, O Lord, that even this familiarity augments our love for you. Every moment you are away seems an aeon!"

As the Lord passed through the flags and festoons, banners and buntings that adorned the roads to welcome him, there was a shower of flowers from above. The brāhmaṇā recited the vedā; muscians sang and women danced. There was great rejoicing in the air.

In the midst of all this, the Lord passed through the main thoroughfare of the city, bowing to all the people (even those who were considered low!), greeting them, clasping them to his bosom in great love and affection, holding their hands, smiling and casting endearing looks, granting them boons of their choice and blessing them. He himself received the blessings of the holy men and women, aged folk and others.

Lord Kṛṣṇa first entered the palace of his parents and bowed at their feet. Then he went into his own palace and was lovingly received by his wives who had been constantly thinking of him even in his absence. He had returned to them after witnessing the destruction of evil-minded people who had destroyed themselves by their mutual enmity. The same Lord now appeared as the husband of his consorts, though he is completely free from all taints of worldliness. How mysterious is the power of ignorance: ignorant people, finding the Lord engaged, like themselves, in various activities, regard him as a human being full of attachment! Such indeed is the divine glory of the Lord that though he seems to live like mortals subject to nature, he is not tainted by the qualities of nature, (satva, rajas and tamas). Even they who take refuge in him are untainted by the qualities of nature.

Book One Chapter 12

Śaunaka prayed: O Sūta, you said lord Kṛṣṇa protected the foetus of Uttarā. Tell us how Parīkṣit was born and what he did!

Sūta said: While being scorched by the fire of the great missile in the womb of his mother, the unborn son of Uttarā saw a being the size of the thumb, blue in colour, radiant and charming, clad in yellow robes that were brilliant like lightning and wearing a golden crown. It was lord Kṛṣṇa himself! The unborn child saw this being disperse the scorching rays of the missile with a divine weapon he wielded. When the fire had been quenched, this person vanished, even as the child looked on!

At an auspicious hour, Uttarā was delivered of the baby, the sole survivor of the pāṇḍavā clan. His grandfathers rejoiced greatly. Immediately after the birth, the king gave generously in charity.

Those well versed in the language of the stars predicted that the child would grow up to be a great and noble king. He would rule his subjects justly like Ikṣvāku, adhere to truth like Rāma, be charitable like Śibi, become famous like Bharata, be an archer like Arjuna, be heroic like the lion, enduring like the earth, forbearing like parents, a refuge like the Himālaya, even-minded like Brahmā, gracious like Śiva, protect all like Viṣṇu, possess excellent virtues like Kṛṣṇa, be generous like Rantideva, pious like Yayāti, firm like Bali and devoted to Kṛṣṇa as Prahrāda was. He would subdue the wicked.

In course of time, he would be subject to the curse of brāhmaṇā. Calmly awaiting his death by snake-bite, the king would renounce all worldly attachments and listen to the story of God narrated by the foremost among sages—Śuka himself. Thus established in the Lord, the king would cast off his mortal coil.

Since he was "protected at birth by lord Kṛṣṇa (Viṣṇu)" he would be known as Viṣṇu-rāta. Since he would continue to look throughout his life for the person whom he saw in his mother's womb, he would be known as Parīkṣit (one who is always looking for something).

Dhṛtarāṣṭra and Gāndhārī
Book One Chapter 13

Suta continued: At about the same time, O sages, Vidura (the younger brother of Dhṛtarāṣṭra) returned to Hastināpura from a long pilgrimage. After the whole family had joyously welcomed him back,

Yudhiṣṭhira enquired about Vidura's pilgrimage: "Blessed uncle, tell us what places you have visited. Surely places acquire sanctity when saints and god-men like yourself visit them."

Vidura gave a detailed account of his pilgrimage, excluding the destruction of the yādava-race which, he knew, would hurt them. Time passed by quickly. One day, filled with supreme love and concern for the ultimate good of his elder brother Dhṛtarāṣṭa, Vidura said to him: "Brother, why are you still leading a householder's life, attached to kinsmen and kingdom? Do you not see that all-powerful time is stealing days and months from our life-span? Don't you realise that soon we shall be overtaken by death? I consider him a hero who, having dedicated his whole heart and soul to the love of lord Kṛṣṇa, frees himself from worldly attachments, attains true knowledge and drops his body wherever it happens to fall—unknown, unwept and unsung". Hearing this Dhṛtarāṣṭra was awakened inwardly. He and his devoted wife, Gāndhārī, slipped away from the palace unnoticed and went to the forest.

When Yudhiṣṭhira discovered the absence of the royal couple, he was sorely distressed. Just then, the celestial sage, Nārada, arrived upon the scene. In answer to Yudhiṣṭhira's enquiry concerning his uncle and aunt, Nārada said:

"Grieve not for anybody, O king, for the entire world is in the control of God. All the worlds and their rulers adore the Lord. He himself brings people together and he brings about their separation. Whether you regard human beings here as the eternal spirit, as ephemeral living objects, as both eternal and ephemeral, or as neither eternal nor transient (as the indescribable and transcendent absolute), you should not grieve for them. Can one protect another in this world, O king? When one's own body is but a composition of the elements, and subject to disease, old age and death, how foolish it is to assume responsibility for others! Can one who is being swallowed by a python offer protection to another? O king, your uncle and aunt have gone to the forest and are spending their time in constant remembrance of the Lord, having completely gone beyond māyā and her three qualities. Shortly a fire will consume your uncle's body along with the hut in which he resides; and your aunt, devoted as she is to your uncle, will enter the burning hut. Hearing of this your other uncle Vidura will again leave on a pilgrimage. So, give up this meaningless sorrow."

As these words of wisdom, Yudhiṣṭhira regained his composure.

Sūta continued: Arjuna had gone to Dvārakā to ascertain lord Kṛṣṇa's welfare and that of other relatives. Several months had elapsed. Arjuna had not returned. The king grew anxious and began to notice bad omens.

The worst of these omens was that so soon after the Mahābhārata war in which all evil-doers had been killed, people had again taken to unrighteous living. Hypocrisy characterised their relationships. They were ruled by greed, anger and falsehood. There was hatred between friends and even between husband and wife. Yudhiṣṭhira feared that the dark age (kali) had set in. He said to Bhīma, his brother:

"Why has Arjuna not yet returned? May it be that lord Kṛṣṇa to whom we owe our fortune, our kingdom, nay our life itself, has left this world and ascended to his celestial kingdom? The strange behaviour of the animals, the way the seasons have changed and the throbbing of parts of the left side of my body, make me anxious. The horizon is smoky. The sun and the moon look dull. There are frequent earthquakes and violent thunderstorms accompanied by blinding lightning. There are strong winds which raise the dust and darken the whole earth. The sun has lost its brilliance. Heaven and earth seem to be set on fire. Rivers and lakes are agitated. There is gloom and sorrow in the very air. From these grave forebodings I infer that the earth has lost its charm, having been deprived of the touch of the feet of lord Kṛṣṇa."

One day as Yudhiṣṭhira was thus musing, Arjuna arrived. He collapsed at Yudhiṣṭhira's feet, which was quite unlike him. His face indicated terrible sorrow. This greatly aggravated the king's own grief and he questioned Arjuna:

"What is the cause of your agony, Arjuna? Are all our kith and kin in Dvārakā in good health? How is lord Kṛṣṇa himself? Why do you not talk? Why do you not answer? Why do you appear grief-striken? Is there something wrong with your health, O Arjuna? Were you insulted or ill-treated by somebody? Have you failed in your duty in any way: did you fail to offer protection to the needy—you who have never turned away anyone who sought your protection? Did you ever unwittingly eat before ensuring that the aged and the children who were hungry were fed? Or did you do anything at all unbecoming? Or—I shudder at the very thought—have you been separated from the most beloved Lord and intimate friend, śrī Kṛṣṇa? Kindly tell me."

Sūta continued: Arjuna, in a state of deep shock, replied to Yudhiṣṭhira, his voice choked with grief: "Brother, I had fallen prey to the Lord's deluding power. The Lord himself was with us as śrī Kṛṣṇa. It was he who enabled me and Bhīma to perform those heroic deeds admired even by gods. He saved us from several terrible pitfalls. It was by his grace I fought with lord Śiva and Indra, and later enjoyed a holiday in Indra's celestial abode. How can I describe the many mysterious ways in which he saved us, and particularly me, during the war! Seated in front of me in my chariot, he robbed all our adversaries of their strength and of their hearts, too! Seated safely behind him, I was immune to attack. But, alas, how foolish of me to have chosen the supreme Lord as my charioteer when sages of wisdom worship his feet in order to attain final liberation. He treated me as his friend: but, alas, I treated him as a friend, too, and took undue liberties with him. In his unlimited generosity, he tolerated such behaviour.

"Now I am deprived of him, the supreme Lord, dearest friend and companion: I have lost my heart; I am lifeless. I came to this shameful realisation when I was defeated by wicked and weak cowherds who attacked me and the Lord's spouses whom I was escorting! With him nothing was impossible; without him nothing is possible.

"O king, you asked about our kith and kin in Dvārakā. He had used the powerful yādavā to destroy the wicked ones; in the end, he brought about internecine hostility to destroy them. Having accomplished his mission he left, even as one extracts a thorn with another thorn and throws that away, too. Such are the Lord's mysterious ways that sometimes he appears to promote love and at others destruction."

As Arjuna uttered these words he recollected what Kṛṣṇa had taught him on the battlefield (the Bhagavad Gītā), and was instantly released from ignorance and grief. Hearing this terrible news and realising that the very day Kṛṣṇa left this earth, kali yuga (the age when unawakened people indulge in unrighteous actions) had set in, king Yudhiṣṭhira quickly crowned his grandson Parīkṣit as king, and renounced the world. By the laya yoga process of absorption he dissolved each element into its source, ultimately into cosmic nature which he merged in the supreme being. He then wandered in a northward direction like a deaf, dumb and dull man. His brothers followed his example. Vidura cast off his body near Dvārakā, the

Lord's own city. Draupadī concentrated her whole mind on the Lord and attained final liberation, or union with the Lord.

O sages, such in brief is the account of the ascension of the pāṇḍavā to heaven—which narrative bestows devotion and final liberation on the listener.

Book One Chapter 16

Sūta continued: In course of time, the devout and righteous king Parīkṣit married and begot four sons (Janamejaya and others). When he offered worship to the gods during the performance of three Aśvamedha rites, they manifested themselves to receive his offerings personally.

While the king was living in the kuru-jāṅgala region, he heard that kali (the dark age) had invaded his country in the form of unrighteous living. Deeply disturbed by this news the king made a tour of inspection of the whole kingdom. He was pleasantly surprised to hear people singing the glories and the glorious exploits of his grandparents (the pāṇḍavā) and of lord Kṛṣṇa. They even narrated the thrilling story of how lord Kṛṣṇa saved the king even while he was in his mother's womb. The village folk had woven these sublime episodes into sweet and inspiring songs. The king was highly pleased with these recitations and bestowed rich presents on the people who sang them, so that the history of Kṛṣṇa and the pāṇḍavā might never be forgotten.

Then, the king beheld an awe-inspiring spectacle. A bull, standing on one foot, was consoling a weeping cow. The bull was the embodiment of righteousness and the cow, of mother earth. As the king stood transfixed by this unearthly vision, the bull (dharma) asked the cow (earth) the cause of her grief: "Are you weeping because I am deprived of three legs and I stand on only one? Are you weeping because you, the earth, will soon come to be ruled by uncultured, unwise and unrighteous people? Or, are you sorry that spiritual knowledge has fallen into corrupt hands and that the men of learning and wisdom (brāhmaṇā) are selling it to gain wealth and political power?"

Earth (the cow) replied: "Dharma, you know the answers! Lord Kṛṣṇa by whose grace you had all your legs and by whose grace my burden was reduced, has left the world. Truthfulness, purity, compassion, forbearance, liberality, contentment, guilelessness, calmness, control of the senses, austerity, non-irritability, endurance, peace, knowledge, self-realisation, dispassion, lordship, heroism, majesty, strength, right judgment, independence, dexterity, loveliness, fortitude, gentleness, intelligence, modesty, amiability, quickness of mind, acuteness of the senses, bodily vigour, fortune, sobriety, steadiness, reverence, reputation, respectability and absence of egotism—these and other virtues which great men seek are present in him. Hence I am concerned for you and other divinities and the holy ones. In a godless world how can there be virtue? This is why I grieve—wicked people are a burden on me (earth)."

Book One Chapter 17

Sūta continued: The king Parīkṣit also beheld an uncultured and irreligious man in the guise of a king beating the bull and kicking the cow. Enraged, the monarch challenged the brigand, arrested him and then spoke to the bull. "Who are you, O bull, hopping along on one leg? Who cut off your other legs? How can such a thing happen in my kingdom? For it is said that the reputation, life-span, fortune and heavenly enjoyment of a king are destroyed if in his kingdom the people are oppressed by the wicked. Tell me who is the cause of your suffering and I shall destroy him!"

The wise bull, however, replied: "I thank you, O king, for your offer of protection. But how can I judge who is responsible for my suffering? Some say one is responsible for one's own suffering, others say it is providence, others say that it is the nature of the world, and yet others believe the cause to be beyond speech and intellect!" Interrupting the bull, the king said: "O bull, you are indeed dharma! You know that finding fault with evil is evil, too. In a former age you had four supports—austerity, purity, compassion and truthfulness. Unrighteousness has robbed you of the first three. Now kali, this dark age, is threatening the last leg. I know that the cow is mother earth bemoaning the departure of lord Kṛṣṇa."

Turning to the irreligious man (who was none other than kali), Parīkṣit said: "You have no quarter in my kingdom, O man of evil! Ever since you began to reside in the body of kings, unrighteousness has increased on earth. In my kingdom, however, lord Kṛṣṇa abides eternally, in the form of righteous actions and devotion to the Lord." Trembling before the king, Kali begged: "I pray to you: show me the places where I may abide without ever coming into conflict with you."

After deep thought, king Parīkṣit replied: "O Kali, you are the embodiment of unrighteousness and evil! Hereafter dwell in gambling dens, intoxicating drinks, lustful women, slaughter houses and gold. Residing in these five abodes, you will manifest as falsehood, intoxication, passion, slaughter and animosity."

O sages, a seeker after holiness should in every way avoid these five abodes of evil.

The king then restored to the bull the other three legs, comforted mother earth and returned to his palace.

A Sage Curses Parīkṣit
Book One Chapter 18

Sūta continued: O sages, king Parīkṣit was protected even before birth by the Lord. He fearlessly subdued the spirit of unrighteousness, kali, which had no quarter in his kingdom. Even when death knocked at his door, he faced it fearlessly. For, no confusion arises even at the hour of death in the hearts of those who constantly think of the lotus feet of lord Kṛṣṇa and speak about him. The water that touched his lotus feet is the holy river Gaṅgā that purifies the world and even the gods. The goddess of wealth and prosperity worships the dust of his feet.

Sages! I shall narrate to you how king Parīkṣit met with his mortal end. One day he was hunting in the forest. It was hot and he was extremely thirsty. He saw the hermitage of sage Śamīka, which he entered. The sage was seated in meditation. The king asked for water. The sage did not open his eyes. The thirsty king was annoyed, and for once in his life he entertained feelings of anger and hostility towards the holy ones. With the tip of his bow he picked up a dead snake lying there and threw it around the sage's neck as if to ask: "Are you really meditating, with mind and senses withdrawn, or are you merely trying to avoid me, on account of your arrogance?" Even then the sage did not open his eyes. The king went away.

The sage's son heard of the indignity perpetrated on his father and became exceedingly angry. "How dare these kṣatriyā (rulers) thus misbehave towards their masters! Their duty is to protect the holy men in all humility. These wicked kings misbehave like this because lord Kṛṣṇa is not here to chastise them. However, I shall myself punish the miscreant." The young man cursed the king: "May the terribly venomous snake, Takṣaka, bite the king seven days from now." He returned to the hermitage and wailed aloud. Śamīka's meditation was disturbed by this and he opened his eyes. The son told him all that had happened. Śamīka was not pleased! "O child! You have sinned against the king, who is lord Viṣṇu himself.

For a little error you have pronounced a terrible curse. If the king dies robbers will flourish, religion will decline and there will be confusion in society. All these sins arise from your rash action and will therefore assail us. Moreover, the devotees of the Lord never retaliate even when reproached, deceived, abused, disregarded or struck by others though they are capable of doing so. May the almighty Lord forgive the sin committed by this child of immature understanding!"

Book One Chapter 19

Sūta continued: As soon as the king's thirst was quenched, his temper cooled; he recalled with intense remorse his sinful conduct toward the holy hermit. He knew in his conscience that as a result of this misdemeanour shown to the holy man, who was the Lord himself, a great calamity would befall him. And, sure enough, he soon heard of the young brāhmaṇa's curse. He had anticipated it. He was ready for it. He welcomed it, as it would restrain him from further evil conduct. The curse awakened the intensest dispassion in him. Blessed was he that he knew the hour of his death seven days beforehand.

King Parīkṣit abdicated his throne in favour of his son, Janamejaya, and resolved to fast unto death on the bank of the holy Gaṅgā. When he sat down there, several holy sages reached the same spot. The king welcomed them, worshipped them, and told them of his noble resolve and the reason for it. He prayed to them to bless him: "To one such as I am, a sinful ruler of a kingdom, the young sage's curse is the grace of the Lord. Bowing to you, O holy ones, I pray: each time I take birth may I be endowed with devotion to the eternal lord Kṛṣṇa and the constant company of noble souls who are devoted to him, and may I also be blessed with friendship for all."

The sages applauded the king's decision and approved of his prayer. They resolved to spend the last week of his life in his company.

Meanwhile, sage Śuka arrived on the scene. He looked like a boy of sixteen. He had an extremely charming body, well built, well proportioned and perfect in every way. He was stark naked. There was no mark on the body to indicate to which caste he belonged (as he had gone beyond all castes) nor to which order of life (for he had reached the goal of life). Though he had the external appearance of a lunatic, the sages seated in the king's company recognised him and welcomed him.

Bowing to sage Śuka, king Parīkṣit greeted him. He considered himself supremely blessed to be visited by the sage. "Surely, lord Kṛṣṇa himself is pleased with me. That is why one who is awaiting death is granted the privilege of meeting a holy sage like you. Your very presence wipes out our sins. My Lord! Please tell me what should be done by a man who is about to die? Also, tell me what should be done by people in general—what should they listen to, recite, do, remember, resort to and avoid?"

Book Two

The Lord's Cosmic Form
Book Two Chapter 1

Sage Śuka said: A noble question, O king! Generally people who are attached to objects and persons related to these perishable bodies, which they foolishly believe to be their self, seek to know only that which brings them more pleasure. To be able to remember lord Kṛṣṇa (Nārāyaṇa) at the hour of death—this is the true goal of one's life, whether it is attained by knowledge of yoga or right living. The royal sage Khatvāṅga knew he had just one hour to live; and he renounced everything and merged himself in the Lord. What is the use of a long life to one who neglects his own salvation? At the approach of death one should cut off all attachments, even to the body. He should retire to a pure and secluded spot, and sit uttering the mystic word Oṁ. He should meditate on any of the limbs of the Lord's gross form with such love and devotion that he does not think of anything else. Such meditation destroys the impurities of his mind and floods it with the ecstasy of divine love or bhakti. He forthwith attains union with God.

I shall now describe to you the gross form of the Lord as an aid to your contemplation. It is the cosmic universal form wherein is seen this phenomenal universe (as it is, was and will be), the elements (earth, water, fire, air and space) as also the ego, intelligence and the fundamental essence of everything. In brief, the entire visible universe is nothing but the cosmic body of the Lord.

Meditate that the regions below earth (viz., pātāla, rasātala, mahātala, talātala, vitala, sutala and atala) are the Lord's soles, top of the feet, ankles, shanks, knees and the two thighs respectively. The earth (bhūloka) is his loins. The higher regions (bhuvarloka, svarloka, maharloka, janoloka, tapoloka and satyaloka) represent the Lord's navel, breast, neck, face, brow and head respectively. Māyā is his smile. Even so, the divinities are his sense-organs, the sky is his eye, the sun the sense of sight, night and day are the eye-lids. O king! Oceans are his abdominal cavity, mountains are his bones, rivers are blood vessels, trees are the hair on the cosmic person. The animals are also the different parts of his body, as are the human beings of the earth and the dwellers of heaven. In fact, there is nothing other than the Lord, O king! The entire universe is pervaded by lord Kṛṣṇa. And, you too, are in him.

Just as a dreamer creates various forms, including himself, in a dream, even so it is the one lord Kṛṣṇa who experiences everything through the intelligence of all. He is the storehouse of all existence and bliss. One should adore and cling to him alone, and to naught else—for elsewhere there is great downfall for oneself.

Book Two Chapter 2

Sage Śuka continued: I have described to you the contemplation with the help of which the creator (Brahmā) himself received from the Lord the power to create this phenomenal universe. The obstacle here is desire for pleasure and sense-gratification. However, a wise man should realise that sense-objects are snares which should be resorted to no more than is necessary for living. How little is really necessary! Earth is good to lie on, arms are good for pillows, the palms of the hands are the best receptacle for food and drink; rags on the roadside can serve to hide one's nakedness, the selfless trees provide food for all, rivers quench one's thirst, caves provide shelter; and the Lord protects all! Why should one beg at the door of the haughty rich?

I shall describe another method of meditation. In the lotus of your own heart visualise the beautiful form of lord Kṛṣṇa with four arms (bearing a lotus, a discus, a conch and a mace), as big as a thumb in height. He has a smiling countenance, with big beautiful eyes. He is clad in yellow and is decked in jewelry. Inwardly gaze at this charming form of the Lord till the mind is concentrated. Gaze at one limb of the Lord till it becomes perfectly clear and then go on to the next. Thus meditate on this form till the mind is thoroughly purified and you are able to meditate on the formless impersonal being which is the witness consciousness. Parīkṣit, I shall now describe how one should leave the body. Sitting in a meditative posture, he should practise control of the breath (prāṇāyāma) and then withdraw his senses from their objects. He should then control his mind and, through the process of negation of all that is not-self, arrive at steady contemplation. And finally, he should drop his body in the following manner:

Pressing the anus with his heels and overcoming languor he should raise the vital air up through the six centres of consciousness (cakras), from the maṇipūraka to the anāhata, and then with the help of reason he should push it to the root of the palate. Then closing the seven apertures (eyes, ears, nostrils and mouth) he should take the vital air to the middle of the eyebrows. If he does not wish to enjoy a visit to heaven he should offer himself to the Lord at the sahasrāra or the thousand-petalled lotus. He should leave the body through the crown of the head—brahmarandhra—and attain liberation here and now. If, however, he desires to visit heaven, he takes his mind with him and ascends by stages to the higher regions, dwells in the highest till the end of this world-cycle, and he will attain final liberation in due course. These are the two paths to liberation. He who has attained this divine goal does not return to this world of passing phenomena.

That alone, O Parīkṣit, is the highest virtue by which one is able to develop exclusive devotion to lord Kṛṣṇa.

Book Two Chapter 3

Sage Śuka continued: O king! I have told you what men should do when their end is near. However, people who have desires other than for liberation may worship other aspects of the Lord, e.g., Bṛhaspati for knowledge, Vasū for wealth, Aditi for food, the Ādityā for heaven, Aśvin for long life, Gandharvā for personal charm, Ūrvaśī for a lovely wife, Viṣṇu for renown and also for a pious life, the marut for bodily vigour and lord Kṛṣṇa for the cessation of all desires. They may worship Indra for enhanced sense-perception, māyā for prosperity, the god of fire for indefatigable energy, the rudrā for power, the two divine mothers for status and prestige, Brahmā for lordship over all, the yakṣā for protection against dangers, and Prajāpati for progeny. But a wise man, whether he is totally desireless, whether he seeks liberation or whether he has any other desire, should be intensely devoted to the supreme Lord. By such devotion, generated by listening to the stories and glories of the Lord, the seeker develops a distaste for sensual pleasures: for he who has developed a taste for listening to the Lord's glories longs for naught else!

Śaunaka said to Sūta: On hearing these inspiring instructions, what did Parīkṣit do? Parīkṣit was beloved of lord Kṛṣṇa. Śuka was the foremost among sages; he was intensely devoted to Kṛṣṇa. Their dialogue was bound to be saturated with devotion to the Lord. What is life worth if it is not dedicated to him? Trees live, bellows 'breathe', animals eat and procreate. That human being who has not heard the story of lord Kṛṣṇa is no better than a dog, a swine, a camel or a donkey. His ears are just holes! The tongue that does not utter his name is the tongue of a frog. The head that does not bow to him is a burden. The hands that do not worship lord Kṛṣṇa are those of a dead man. The eyes that do not gaze on the images of lord Viṣṇu are like the eyes on the peacock's tail. The feet that do not visit places sacred to the Lord are like roots of trees. A mortal who has not bathed himself in the dust of the feet of the Lord's devotees is a living corpse, and even so is he who has not devoutly pressed to his lips the tulasī (sacred basil) leaves offered at the feet of the Lord in worship. The heart which does not melt when the Lord's names are uttered is as hard as a stone: when the heart does so melt, the eyes shed tears of divine love and the hair stands on end. To live without the love of the Lord is evil.

Book Two Chapter 4

Sūta said: Sage Śuka's words of transcendental wisdom had begun to dispell Parīkṣit's nescience. He thirsted for more.

Parīkṣit asked Śuka: O sage! Even the few words that you have uttered so far have begun to dispel the gloom of my ignorance. Pray, tell me more and more about the glories of the Lord. Tell me how he creates the universe, protects it and redeems it.

Sūta said: Thus requested by the king, the noble sage bowed to the Lord and prayed for his benediction on the auspicious narration of his glories.

Śuka prayed: Salutations to that supreme being who playfully, effortlessly and motivelessly—but purposefully—creates the universe, sustains it and redeems it through his own threefold energy. Salutations to he who is the inner controller of all beings, and who is beyond reason and logic. Salutations to he who destroys the sorrow of the virtuous and who destroys evil in the universe; who is impartial and who grants to men of renunciation the liberation they seek. Salutations to the Lord who is near to his devotee but far from those who lack divine love. Salutations to the Lord: by singing his praises, thinking of him, seeing, saluting or adoring him, or by hearing of him, people are immediately purified of all sins. Salutations to the Lord by taking refuge in whom the wise attain liberation effortlessly. May the Lord who is the Lord of auspiciousness and prosperity, the Lord of all forms of worship, the Lord of all beings, the Lord of the intellect, the Lord of the universe and the Lord of the earth, be gracious unto me. May the Lord who is the Lord and the refuge of andhakā (blind, ignorant people), vṛṣṇī (angry, passionate, heretics) and sātvatā (noble worshippers of Kṛṣṇa)—in other words, the Lord and refuge of all humanity—who is yet the refuge especially of the holy ones, be gracious unto me. Meditation on the lotus feet of the Lord is samāḍhi which purifies one's heart and secures liberation. He and he alone evolved all created beings out of the primordial elements and entered into all beings as the indwelling presence: may he lend charm to my narration. I salute my guru, sage Vyāsa, my father. O Parīkṣit, this narrative was originally taught by the creator himself to the celestial sage Nārada. Listen attentively.

Creation
Book Two Chapter 5

Sage Śuka said: Sage Nārada asked the same question, in answer to which the creator Brahmā revealed the truth which I shall presently narrate.

Sage Nārada asked the creator, Brahmā: Lord, from the fact that even you practised penance and meditated, we infer that there is someone beyond you, the creater of all. Who is it that supports you and by whose power you have been able to create all this?

Brahmā, the creator, said: My son I welcome your question which enables me to sing the glories of the Lord, who is the real creator of the universe—not I! Foolish people think I am the creator: and foolish people speak of the body as the self and that which is associated with the body as 'mine'. In truth, nothing exists except lord Kṛṣṇa: there is no substance, no activity, no time, no nature nor a living soul! Only the Lord exists. The practice of yoga has Nārāyaṇa as its aim; even so, austerities and knowledge are directed to Nārāyaṇa; one's destiny leads to Nārāyaṇa. He is beyond the three qualities (satva or purity, rajas or activity, tamas or inertia). Yet, they bind the individual soul though it is essentially ever free, on account of the threefold illusion of "action, instrument and idea of I-am-the-doer" which is associated with the substance, intelligence and action.

When the Lord willed the creation of diverse beings, his māyā manifested time, activity and nature which were latent in him. Time disturbed the equilibrium of the qualities of nature (satva, ragas and tamas). From activity was evolved cosmic intelligence (mahat). From mahat, substance, knowledge and action emanated as the tāmasa transformation. This was ahaṁkāra (ego-principle) which again had three manifestations. From the tāmasa ahaṁkāra arose the five gross elements (space, air, fire, water and earth) with their corresponding faculties of sound, touch, sight, taste and smell. (Each succeeding element, however, inherits the faculties of the previous ones from which it is evolved.) From the sātvika ahaṁkāra evolved the mind, and the subtle deities who preside over the senses of perception and the organs of action. From the rājasa ahaṁkāra were evolved the five senses of perception and the five organs of action, as also the intellect, the faculty of action and the vital air (prāṇa).

All these together formed one cosmic egg which lay on the causal waters for a long time. Bursting open that egg, the cosmic person emerged. The worlds and the creatures formed his various limbs. The entire universe is nothing but the lord himself, O Nārada!

Book Two Chapter 6

Brahmā, the creator, continued: The entire creation now proceeded from the cosmic person. Fire and the organ of speech from his mouth; the sense of taste from his tongue; the vital airs and the element of air from his nostrils; all odours, food grains and the celestial physicians from his olfactory sense; colours and light from his sense of sight; heaven and the sun from his eyes; the cardinal directions from his ears; space and sound from his sense of hearing; the essence of all things and all loveliness from his limbs; touch, air and all kinds of sacrificial performances from his sense of touch; trees and plants from his hair; clouds from the locks of hair on his head and lightning from his beard; rocks and iron from his nails; guardian angels from his arms; protection from his feet (for lord Kṛṣṇa's feet are the source of protection and security; water and procreation from his generative organ; sexual enjoyment from his faculty of generation; the god of death and the excretory function from his organs of excretion; all destructive powers and hell from his anus; defeat, unrighteousness and also tamas from his back; large and small rivers from his arteries; mountains from his bones; the ocean, the origin and dissolution of all beings from his abdomen; mind from his heart; dharma and all of us gods from his citta (reasoning faculty). This is just an indication for you to meditate upon. Everything in this visible and manifest universe should thus remind you of the Lord. In fact, you and I, all these sages and all the gods, demons, human beings, animals, celestials, the planets, the stars, lightnings, clouds—the entire universe, past, present and future—are nothing but the Lord himself. No one can fathom his glory. The entire universe represents only a fraction of the manifestation of the supreme person: and it is where created beings reside. But immortality, security and freedom from fear are found on different planes of consciousness, above those of this mortal world. Scattered they were ineffective. God's will brought them together so that they could form the macrocosmic and the microcosmic bodies.

O Nārada, people belonging to the orders of celibates, anchorites and renunciates dwell in those higher planes, whereas the householders dwell in the mortal world. The latter are subject to death, insecurity and fear; the former are not.

Lord's Incarnations
Book Two Chapter 6

Brahmā, the creator, continued: Scriptures lay down two paths which people tread: the path of action and the path of meditation on God. The former (which is considered aviḍyā or ignorance) leads to sense-experience, and the latter (which is considered viḍyā or wisdom) leads to final beatitude. But both are established in God and both lead to God.

God himself is beyond all this, and beyond his own creation.

Soon after I was created by him, I wished to worship him, but could not find the materials with which to do so. He pervaded all; he was all. He was the sacrificial ground, the tent for conducting the worship, the vessels and other materials used in the worship, the sacred texts and the process of performing the worship—all indeed was he himself. I collected these materials which were the Lord himself and worshipped the same cosmic person! Later, the great sages also worshipped the cosmic person in a similar fashion. Then all beings— celestials, human and superhuman—adopted such worship of lord Nārāyana— realising that he alone is the worshipper, the worshipped, the materials used in the worship and the act of worship itself. There is neither a cause nor an effect, other than the Lord.

My son, I have held on to the feet of the Lord with a heart filled with devotion: hence, falsehood does not enter my words, my mind does not stray into false channels and my senses do not go astray either. Such is the case with the true devotee of the Lord.

The Lord's glory is immeasurable. Perhaps even he does not know the extent of his own māyā. He is infinite. How foolish, then, for the men of little intellect to try to fathom his glory and to judge him by their own standards! The unborn, eternal person himself creates, protects and dissolves himself within himself and by himself, again and again. Sages who have the body, mind and senses well under control realise him in their contemplation.

The first manifestation of the Lord is the cosmic person. Then come his other manifestations such as time, nature, the elements, all animate and inanimate beings. A man of wisdom should contemplate that whatever in this world is endowed with supernatural powers, glory, vigour, resolution, physical strength and forbearance, splendour, decorum, good fortune and intellectual acumen, is a manifestation of that supreme being. Such wisdom will lead him to the direct realisation of the Lord.

Book Two Chapter 7

Brahmā, the creater, continued: I shall describe to you in brief the Lord's incarnations in the world of man.

He assumed the divine form of a boar to uplift the earth by destroying the evil power of Hiraṁyākṣa. Incarnate as Hari he relieved the great distress of the world. As Kapila he blazoned the path to self-knowledge. As Datta he bestowed self-realisation on several kings. When I practised penance, it was he who as the Sanatkumārā proclaimed the truth that had been forgotten. As Nara and Nārāyaṇa he re-established the highest standard of asceticism and total conquest of lust and anger. He blessed Dhruva. As Pṛthu he exploited the subterranean treasures. As Ṛṣabha he exemplified the highest state of a sage (sanyāsi). As Hayagrīva he breathed out the vedā. As the divine fish he rescued the world and the vedā. As the divine tortoise he supported the mountain with which the celestials and the demons were churning the ocean. As Narasiṁha he dispelled the fear of the gods and redeemed Hiraṇyakaśipu. He redeemed the elephant Gajendra who had been caught by an alligator. As Vāmana, the dwarf, the Lord measured the earth and the heaven with his feet and blessed Bali, demonstrating that even the almighty can subdue the righteous only by supplication. As Haṁsa he taught the yoga of devotion to you, O Nārada. As Dhanvantari he protects all from disease, in response to the mere utterance of his name. As Paraśurāma he will quell the pride of wicked kings. As Rāma he will put an end to the haughty Rāvana. As Balarāma and Kṛṣṇa he will relieve the earth of its burden caused by wicked kings (the secondary incarnations of demons). As Vyāsa he will simplify the vedā for the comprehension of the dull-witted. When demons attempt to destroy the people from flying citadels of great velocity, the Lord will confound them. As Kalki he will destroy the evils of the kali age when people will fail to discourse upon the Lord's glories!

Such is the glory of the Lord's māyā. Only they can cross this māyā who are blessed by him as a result of their total self-surrender and only they will cease to consider the body (which is food for dogs and jackals) as the self. Only they will realise that all that exists is in fact the Lord himself. The Lord's māyā is overcome by sinful beings, nay even by sub-human beings (birds and beasts) if they develop true devotion to him—and of course by those who follow the teachings of the scriptures. O Nārada, I have thus told you in essence the Bhāgavataṁ which was revealed to me by the Lord himself; now you should expand and expound it. He who narrates this and he who listens to it are not deluded by māyā.

Book Two Chapter 8

King Parīkṣit asked sage Śuka: O holy sage! How did Nārada implement the command of Brahmā and expound the Bhāgavata-story? To whom did he impart this divine knowledge? I am eager to know. Tell me how I should fix my mind on the lotus feet of lord Kṛṣṇa at the time of my death, which is not far off.

For, the Lord himself soon enters the heart of the man who constantly listens to the stories and glories of the Lord. In his own mysterious ways the Lord enters the heart of the devotee through the cavity of his ears, and there rids the devotee of all sin and sinful tendency. He whose heart has thus been purified never abandons the lotus feet of the Lord, even as a fatigued traveller does not abandon the rest-house.

How does that which is unrelated to the elements get involved in them—is there a cause for this or is it accidental? What is bondage, what is liberation, and how does one remain established in one's own being?

When the Lord is spoken of as having limbs like any human

being, does it mean that he is just a human being? What is the true nature of the Lord, after he has discarded the appearance assumed by means of his illusory power or māyā?

Again, you mentioned that the different worlds are in his limbs, and again that they are his limbs. Can you clarify this apparent contradiction?

Tell me also in detail what is the length of the cycle of creation-preservation-dissolution. How do the worlds come into existence? How do living beings come into existence and how do they acquire their different characteristics?

Do the cyclical epochs have distinct characteristics? What are the duties of men of different sections of society and also of different stages of life? How should we worship the supreme person? How should we practise yoga? What is righteous living and righteous enjoyment?

Lord, you are the greatest among the knowers of truth, and you are therefore in the best position to enlighten me concerning all these. Others merely repeat what they have heard from others before them!

Sūta said: When Parīkṣit asked these questions, the sage Śuka began to narrate this noble story of God, which the Lord himself had revealed to Brahmā, the creator.

Book Two Chapter 9

Sage Śuka said: O king! The self which is consciousness itself can have no connection whatsoever with objects of this creation, except through the Lord's māyā or power of illusion—even as a man has no connection whatsoever with the objects perceived in his dream! Name and form are within māyā; 'I' and 'mine' are within māyā, too: they do not 'touch' the nameless, formless, infinite noumenon. I shall narrate to you how this truth was revealed to Brahmā the creator, by the Lord himself.

In the beginning, Brahmā the creator felt impelled to proceed with the work of creation, but was unable to do so. While he sat thus perplexed, he heard a voice which said, "Tapa" twice. Brahmā acted upon this invisible command to practise intense penance: he did penance for a thousand celestial years. This penance, which is the supreme wealth of men of renunciation, illumined everything—and at once the creator intuitively understood how to proceed with creation.

Pleased with Brahmā's penance, the Lord revealed his own domain to him. In it there is no affliction, confusion or fear. In it there is no rajas, tamas or even satva. There is no illusion (māyā) nor does time prevail there. Even the Lord's attendants look resplendent like the Lord himself. He is waited upon by countless sages and saints, yogī and devotees. All the divine qualities and prosperity are ever present there in their subtle embodiments.

The creator Brahmā then beheld there the supreme Lord himself, the omnipresent ruler of the whole universe, in all his indescribable glory and divine majesty. Adorned with supernatural ornaments, the Lord occupies the most excellent throne and is surrounded by the twenty-five natural powers— which are the ten senses, the five gross elements, the five subtle elements, the mind, the ego, the cosmic intelligence, nature herself and the spirit. And the Lord said to Brahmā: "I am pleased with your penance which I myself impelled you to perform. Man's righteous efforts culminate in my vision. Penance is my heart; I am the very soul of penance. It is by penance that I create this universe, by penance I maintain it and later absorb it. My power consists of penance. I am pleased with true penance; hypocritical yogī cannot please me. Ask of me, O Brahmā, any boon you choose: for I am the bestower of all blessings."

Bhāgavataṁ Revealed to Brahmā
Book Two Chapter 9

Sage Śuka continued: Brahmā prayed: Lord! You are the indweller and you know my heart. Yet, this I humbly ask of you: may I be blessed with an insight into your absolute aspect as the formless noumenon and the relative aspect as the supreme person. You are the transcendental being; and yet by your own mysterious power (māyā) you seem to appear as this universe, you yourself maintain it, and ultimately dissolve it—even as a spider weaves a web out of itself, plays with it and withdraws it into itself. May I be aware of this always: may I be a mere instrument in your hands in the work of creation, and may I never fall prey to the delusion that 'I create'.

The Lord said: I now bestow upon you, O Brahmā, the most esoteric knowledge, the truth about myself. By my grace, you shall be established in that knowledge, and you will be blessed with true insight into my essential nature as well as my manifestations.

Verily, O Brahmā! In the beginning I alone existed; naught else existed— neither existence nor non-existence in the relative sense.

Afterwards, too, I exist as all this and all that remains after all this has been created. The power that causes the perception of objects which do not exist in reality, in my being, is my own māyā or illusory power—it functions like a reflection, or like smoke veiling its own source (fire). Even as one may say that the gross elements enter or do not enter the bodies of living beings, depending upon the sense in which it is said, one may say that I have entered the bodies of living beings as the in-dwelling spirit or that I have not so entered, on account of my being infinite. The real seeker after truth should constantly seek the truth by the negative (not this, not this) method and the affirmative method (all indeed is Brahman).

And, the Lord withdrew the vision. Brahmā remained absorbed in meditation on the Lord. He practised self-discipline and contemplated the creation of the universe. In the meantime, Nārada approached Brahmā and asked him the very questions you have asked me: and I shall now narrate to you the *Bhāgavataṁ* (Story of God) which Brahmā revealed to Naradā in answer to his questions.

Book Two Chapter 10

Sage Śuka continued: This holy scripture deals with (1) the creation of the subtle cosmic elements and the disturbance of the equilibrium of the qualities of nature by the will of the Lord, (2) the creation by Brahmā of animate and inanimate beings, (3) the triumph of the Lord in the preservation of the universe, (4) the Lord's protecting grace, (5) stories concerning the world cycles, (6) the play of hidden tendencies leading to the bondage of human beings, (7) stories of the Lord's incarnations, (8) the cosmic dissolution when animate and inanimate beings are withdrawn into the Lord, (9) the emancipation of individual souls, and (10) the being which is the basis of all this. It is in order to make the tenth factor clear that the previous nine are dealt with in the scripture, for without the Lord as the basis the other factors have no existence and are meaningless.

When the cosmic person emerged from the cosmic egg he created water for his foothold. Since he lived in this water he was called 'Nārāyaṇa'. Then he proceeded to create. His divine will projected a threefold stream of his own divine power—subjective faculty (adhyātma) objective phenomena (adhibhūta) and the connecting intelligence (adhidaiva). When he stirred, strength and prāṇa were created. When he wished to eat, the palate and different flavours and the intelligence (deity) seeking and experiencing the taste were created: similarly created were the organ of speech, language, and the fire-god presiding over speech for speaking; nostrils, odour in objects, and the wind-god for smelling; eyes, colours, and the sun-god for seeing; ears, sound, and the deities presiding over space for hearing; the skin, the objects of tactile sense, and the divine being presiding over the tactile sense for touching; hands, the faculty of grasping and Indra (the presiding deity) for performing various acts; the feet, motion and Viṣṇu for moving about; the generative organ, copulation and the god Prajāpati for sexual intercourse; the anus, excretion and the god Mitra for excreting; the navel and the apāna-air, death and transmigration, and the presiding deity for passing from one body to another; the abdominal cavity and viscera, nutrition, and the deities presiding over them for eating; the heart and the mind, volition and desire, and the moon for contemplating the wonders effected by his own māyā. Thus were the macrocosm and the microcosm evolved by the Lord's will. The senses are all directed towards their objects by their presiding intelligence. The Lord himself creates and preserves this universe, appearing in the guise of animals, men and gods. But the gross and the subtle forms of the Lord are the work of māyā, the Lord's illusory power: hence the wise do not accept them. The Lord is not involved in action or creation: it is māyā that acts. The wise should realise that the Lord is beyond all descriptions of him.

Book Three

Book Three Chapter 1

Sage Śuka continued: O Parīkṣit, you know how the blind king Dhṛtarāṣṭra, blinded by infatuation for his wicked sons, tried even to destroy his own brother's children—the pāṇḍavā! They were lodged in a house of lac, and it was set on fire. When the pāṇḍavā escaped by the grace of the Lord, the kauravā (Dhrtarāṣṭra's sons) resorted to worse villainy, defeated the pāṇḍavā at gambling and dragged their consort Draupadī into open court. Even Draupadī's tears did not move the blind king. The pāṇḍavā were then banished to the forest. The kauravā refused to give them their share of the kingdom even after they had fulfilled the conditions of the exile and returned from the forest. When lord Kṛṣṇa himself went to the kauravā court as the pāṇḍavā messenger of peace, and pleaded with Duryodhana to deal justly with his cousins, he not only refused to listen but subjected the Lord to insolent treatment. Surely, that was a sign that his store of merit—which had won him sovereignty, royal pleasures and his life-span itself—had been exhausted! At this stage Dhṛtarāṣṭra invited his brother Vidura to his chamber to ask his advice.

O Parīkṣit, Vidura's counsel on this occasion was so full of wisdom that it has become a classic in ethics. He warned Dhṛtarāṣṭra that his own son (Duryodhana, whom he doted upon) was evil incarnate. That is why he antagonised the pāṇḍavā, who enjoyed the friendship of the Lord himself! Vidura's counsel only annoyed Duryodhana further. He insulted Vidura and wanted him to be banished from the capital. The wise Vidura was hurt, no doubt; but he saw the hand of the Lord in Duryodhana's insolence and voluntarily left on pilgrimage, leaving his weapons at the city gates. Roaming the land incognito, Vidura was able to enjoy to the full the mysterious grace of God. While Vidura was touring western India he heard of the great war and the destruction of the kauravā. Later, he met Uddhava, the closest friend and devotee of lord Kṛṣṇa. From Uddhava he enquired about the welfare of the people—his relations and the proteges of the Lord, as also the pāṇḍavā and Dhṛtarāṣṭra himself. "Uddhava, the Lord could easily have punished the kauravā then and there when they misbehaved towards him but he ignored their sinful conduct for a time and then, through them, exterminated all the arrogant rulers who were puffed up with the vanity of birth, wealth and learning. Mysterious are the ways of the Lord. He seems to incarnate and live here merely to subdue evil and to draw the good towards himself. Those who regard him as a mere human being are very easily deceived."

Book Three Chapter 2

Sage Śuka continued: O Parīkṣit, Uddhava was greatly devoted to the Lord. Even in his childhood he would forget food in his company. As he grew older this devotion grew more intense. Vidura's words evoked the profoundest devotion in him and for a time he lost consciousness of the outside world. With a voice choked with devotion,

Uddhava said: How tragic it is, O Vidura, that humanity (even those people close to him) should fail to recognise sri Kṛṣṇa as the supreme Lord while he was on this earth! They thought he was a human being like themselves. How gracious of the Lord that he thus appeared to common folk, from whom he has now veiled that form!

Vidura, how can I describe even his physical features which lent charm to the ornaments that adorned them. With that form he pretended to live like a human being and yet performed wonders which astounded all, including himself. At the Rājasūya ritual of Yudhiṣṭhira, those who beheld Kṛṣṇa felt that the creator had exhausted all his talents in fashioning that one physical form. In Vraja, women who saw him were completely lost in admiration. Though unborn, God who is the Lord of both the unmanifest and the manifest, was born with the qualities of the divine, just as fire assumes a form. He did this out of compassion for his own peaceful forms who were harassed by his own other forms.

It is a divine mystery, O Vidura, that the Lord, who thus became the son of Vasudeva and Devakī, appeared to be afraid of his enemies—Kaṁsa and Kālayavana. It moves me to tears to think of his telling his blessed parents: "Forgive me that I was unable to serve you on account of my dread of Kaṁsa". The human mind with its petty vanity is baffled at the very thought that he whose footstool is adored by the gods should stand before a mortal king and address him as 'My lord!' How merciful the Lord was: he conferred the great blessing of liberation even upon those who came to kill him (like Pūtanā), who hated him (like Śiśupāla) and upon those who fought in the great war and died on the battlefield gazing at his radiant countenance. I consider all of them devotees of the Lord; though they hated him, they had fixed their minds on him. Shall we foolishly resort to anyone else for protection?

Vidura, the Lord's childhood was full of wondrous incidents. In the house of his foster-parents in Vraja he appeared as a charming boy to the village folk, but at the same time he playfully rid the earth of terrible demons. By subduing the venomous Kāliya, by holding up Govardhana hill and by instituting the worship of cows, he promoted the prosperity of his kinsmen, and by his singing and dancing he brought great joy to the women of the village.

Book Three Chapter 3

Uddhava continued: While the Lord was yet a young boy, he returned to Mathurā and killed the wicked tyrant Kaṁsa. The omniscient Kṛṣṇa became Sāndīpani's disciple and learnt the vedā and other scriptures from him. At the end of the term, Kṛṣṇa brought back to life the dead son of the preceptor, as his 'fees'. Knowing that Rukmiṇī had chosen him for her husband, Kṛṣṇa boldly rescued her from the vicious kings who sought her hand. He won the hand of Satyā by taming seven wild bulls and in the ensuing combat with his rivals defeated several princes. He loved her so much that for her sake he took away a celestial tree growing in Indra's paradise! The Lord killed the wicked demon Naraka and rescued sixteen thousand princesses whom he had imprisoned. When they all wanted to marry him, the Lord multiplied himself into an equal number and duly married all of them. Through each of his wives he begot ten sons.

There were many demoniacal princes and others whom the Lord exterminated. Some he dealt with himself and he had others killed by his brother Balarāma. He also brought about their mutual destruction, as in the great war fought on the field of Kurukṣetra. A colossal number of people lost their lives in this war, all on account of the wickedness of Duryodhana who lent ear only to the counsel of his evil advisers. Even Kṛṣṇa's own kinsmen, the yadū, had grown too powerful and sinful. The Lord knew that if they got drunk and quarrelled among themselves, they would easily exterminate one another: and he brought this about.

The Lord placed Yudhiṣṭhira on the throne. He saved young Parīkṣit from Aśvatthāmā's missile even when he was in his mother's womb. And, the Lord enjoyed righteous pleasures of life during the period he reigned at Dvārakā, all the time remaining in a yogic state of detachment. He delighted this world and heaven, too, by his supernatural sports in Dvārakā, endearing himself to all by his friendliness, love and compassion. As he was thus enjoying life for many years, there arose in him a total non-attachment to the duties of household life. Such is the Lord's own example. How then can a man who wishes to follow that example delight in sensual pleasures, knowing that these—and indeed he himself—are under the control of providence!

Meanwhile, the lord's kinsmen had playfully offended a sage who cursed them! Soon after, these kinsmen bathed in the sea, performed the ritualistic worship, and gave plenty in charity to the brāhmaṇā.

Book Three Chapter 4

Uddhava continued: The yādavā ate and drank. Intoxicated, their intellects perverted by liquor, they began to fight among themselves till they were all dead. Then the Lord, his earthly mission fulfilled, decided to terminate the incarnation. He asked me to go to Badarikāśrama. And, he sat down at the foot of a peepul tree. Just then the enlightened sage Maitreya arrived there.

The Lord blessed me with endearing and encouraging words. He assured me that this was my last embodiment and revealed to me the holy Bhāgavataṁ. With folded palms and in an entranced state, I prayed to him: "Which of the four aims of life (virtue, wealth, pleasure and liberation) is difficult for those who are devoted to you! Yet, O unconditioned one, I crave for naught but to worship your feet. Your life and actions here are mysteries beyond human comprehension. You are omniscient, established in supreme wisdom. Yet, at times you sought the advice of people like me, as if you were ignorant and confused. This indeed is a great puzzle to me. Only you can reveal your own glory to us." After the Lord had revealed his real nature to me, I bowed to him again, and I am now proceeding to Badarikāśrama where Nara and Nārāyana are engaged in penance.

Vidura, who was greatly distressed by the news of the holocaust, prayed: "Please impart to me the revelation you received from the Lord."

Uddhava replied: O Vidura, the Lord revealed the truth to the sage Maitreya in my very presence. So receive it from him.

Sage Śuka said: Uddhava then spent a night on the bank of the river Yamunā and left that place the very next morning.

Parīkṣit asked: Tell me, O sage, how was it that only Uddhava survived the great holocaust which consumed the flower of the manhood of that time, when even the clansmen of the Lord had met with their end—and even after the Lord himself had departed?

Sage Śuka replied: This was in accordance with the will of lord Kṛṣṇa. Kṛṣṇa thought to himself: "When I terminate the incarnation, Uddhava, who is foremost among those who have attained self-realisation, will preserve the truth about me. In fact, he is not inferior to me in the least. He is fully self-controlled and is therefore best qualified to impart this knowledge to others in the world." While Uddhava went towards Badarikāśrama, the enlightened Vidura, with a heavy heart, reached the bank of the holy Gaṅgā and met the sage Maitreya.

Maitreya's Description of Creation
Book Three Chapter 5

Vidura met Maitreya at Haridvāra, and said to him: O Lord, people strive for happiness; but such striving does not bestow happiness or peace but only aggravates their suffering. I ask you: what must we do? Devotees of lord Kṛṣṇa roam the world in order to bless and redeem those unrighteous people who have turned away from lord Kṛṣṇa and are therefore miserable. What must one do, O blessed sage, to ensure that the Lord is enthroned in one's heart, illumining it with the highest wisdom? I long to hear, too, how the Lord creates the universe, sustains it and withdraws it into himself and how he incarnates in the world for the welfare of human, sub-human and superhuman beings, though he is actionless throughout.

I have heard from the sage Vyāsa all about the duties of people in this world. They do not interest me any more, for I know that the performance of such duties brings us momentary pleasure which is no pleasure at all. Insatiable is my longing to hear the stories and glories of lord Kṛṣṇa, sung by holy men like you, which, entering one's heart through one's ears, snap the bonds that bind one to this miserable ever-recurring mundane existence. I grieve for those who evoke the pity even of pitiable folk: namely, those ignorant people who have sinfully turned away from the stories and glories of lord Kṛṣṇa. Lord Yama (time, death) sunders their life-span wasted in useless thought, word and deed. Therefore, O Maitreya, narrate for my redemption the stories relating to the Lord's incarnation on earth.

Maitreya said: Well asked, O Vidura. You have placed mankind under a debt of gratitude by thus eliciting answers to your sublime questions. Listen:

Before creation the Lord alone existed. With his power latent (though consciousness was awake), he wondered: "Do I exist?" This power (which is called māyā) is both real (being his) and unreal (with no existence apart from him). Through this power the Lord created the universe. When the power stirred, the qualities latent in it were disturbed. The Lord himself entered into it as the puruṣa, the self. From this as yet unmanifest māyā the cosmic intelligence evolved with the entire cosmos hidden in it, when it was revealed by the Lord or consciousness. From the mahat-tatva (cosmic intelligence) the ego (aham) was evolved. The ego is the cause of the gross elements, sense-faculties and the mind. The ego is threefold—sātvika, rājasa, tāmasa. From the sātvika ego evolved the mind and the intelligence presiding over the senses. From the rājasa ego evolved the organs of knowledge and of action. From the tāmasa ego were evolved the source-elements—space, air, fire, water and earth—each one serving as the cause of the next and inheriting the qualities of its predecessor in addition to its own. The deities presiding over these categories are indeed rays of lord Viṣṇu. But, when they found themselves unable to function, on account of their diversity, they prayed to the Lord.

Book Three Chapter 5

The Gods said: We salute your lotus feet, O Lord, that pacify the burning sorrow of those who take refuge in them, and sitting at which sages discard the miseries of mundane life. The living beings in this world, O Lord of the universe, are stricken by threefold torment, and so do not enjoy peace of mind: hence we resort to the shade of your feet which are the source of wisdom. We surrender to thy feet which are sought by sages who recite the vaidika mantrā in seclusion and which are the source of the purifying waters of the holy river Gaṅgā. With their hearts purified by devoutly listening to your stories and glories, and endowed with wisdom and dispassion, your devotees are able to control their minds by contemplating thy foot-stool; we take shelter in it. O Lord, you have descended into matter for the purpose of creating, sustaining and dissolving the universe. We surrender ourselves to you; only such self-surrender bestows freedom from fear upon your devotees. We adore your lotus feet which are inaccessible to those who are attached to their body and home with the feelings of 'I'ness and 'mine'ness, though in truth you dwell in all. O supreme Lord, they who on account of their sinful tendencies have been robbed of their minds by the objects of enjoyment, do not see the glory of your devotees who enjoy looking at your feet. On the other hand, they who, by drinking the nectar of your stories have grown in love for you (which love is characterised by dispassion and wisdom) soon reach your abode. There are others, too, who enter into you, after conquering the powerful māyā by means of yoga samādhi: these heroes tread the difficult path, not they who are your servants.

O Lord, we have been created by you for the purpose of bringing the universe into existence. Yet, since we are all unrelated and unintegrated, we are unable to do so. Pray, confer upon us your divine vision and your creative energy, in order that we may have an insight into our real nature and your divine will.

Book Three Chapter 6

Sage Maitreya said: Thereupon, the Lord as the power of time, entered into the twenty-three deities presiding over the twenty-three categories (mahat and others) and thus he united them and roused them to activity. These independent faculties now became integrated parts of the divine cosmic body. This cosmic being remained unmanifest for a thousand celestial years in the shape of a cosmic egg. He is the first avatāra or incarnation of the Lord. He manifested himself as one (heart), ten (the prāṇā or vital forces) and three (the ten senses and the mind, the objects of senses, and the connecting intelligence).

The Lord illumined these potentialities. Spontaneously the universe was created. The jīva (individual soul) was endowed with various faculties (the senses of perception, the organs of action, the mind, the intellect, the discriminating intelligence and the ego); their corresponding objects were created; and the intelligence that determines the correspondence between the objects and the faculties came into being.

In this cosmic being also appeared the citta, the domain of Brahmā, and the intellect which enables the jīva to discriminate right from wrong. From his head evolved the heaven, the earth from his feet and the atmosphere from his navel. Divine sātvika beings dwell in the heaven, human and sub-human beings on earth because of their rājasa nature, and spirits and ghosts with a tāmasa nature roam in the atmosphere.

From the mouth of the cosmic being were created the vedā (Brahmā), and the brāhmaṇa, the guru. From the arms sprang the ruling class, the kṣatriya, and their calling as the protectors of society. From the thighs of that being were born agriculture and allied occupations, and the farmer who grows food for all beings. From the feet of the cosmic being issued the vocation of service, which is indispensable to all, and the sudra whose very occupation pleases the Lord. The Lord is best adored by each of these by the due performance of his duties.

Who can fully expound the glory of this cosmic being? It is true that to sing his glories is our best and only worthwhile occupation. Yet, even the creator cannot do justice to them. Nay, the māyā of the Lord is so powerful that it deludes even those who possess such powers. Perhaps even the Lord himself does not know the course of his own māyā—what shall we say of others! Salutations to the Lord who is beyond speech and mind, beyond the comprehension of sages like me and even of the gods.

Book Three Chapter 7

Vidura asked: How can it be said that the Lord created the universe playfully? The child is moved to play by a desire for pleasure or for companionship. The Lord has no desire and he is the sole infinite being! If it is said that the Lord does it all through māyā, how can this māyā affect him? He alone dwells in all; then how can he suffer and be subjected to karma and so on? Pray enlighten me.

Sage Maitreya said: That the Lord should appear to become bound is truly against all logic. Yet, such is the power of māyā that the jīva appears to be bound, even though such bondage does not exist in reality, just as one sees his head chopped off in a dream. Vidura, when the surface of water is agitated, the 'moon in the water' (reflection) seems to quiver. This is due to false identification. When the jīva identifies itself with the body, which is subject to birth, death, hunger, thirst, etc., it attributes these conditions to itself. That false identification gradually vanishes by the grace of lord Kṛṣṇa, which is earned by turning away from worldy life and by the practice of devotion to the Lord. When devotion arises in the heart of man all sufferings come to an end, as in the case of a man in deep sleep.

Vidura said: O lord, my doubts have been dispelled. In this world the most ignorant man and the man of wisdom who has transcended the mind and the intellect are both free from cares, while the others suffer. It is clear that the objective world does not exist; the illusion of its appearance seems to arise in the self: I shall get rid of even this misconception through the devout service of your divine feet. Only through service of sages like you does one develop devotion to the lotus feet of the Lord, which puts an end to the cosmic illusion. Such devotion is not granted to those who have not practised intense austerities.

Now, O lord, tell me all about the Lord's glories. Tell me of the various paths to god-realisation. And tell me even those truths which I may not have asked of thee. O holy one, the recitation of the vedā, performance of sacrifices and penance and the giving of gifts do not equal even a fraction of the merit of rendering one jīva free from fear.

Brahmā's Manifestation
Book Three Chapter 8

Maitreya replied: The whole of your dynasty is blessed for this noble question of yours, in answer to which I shall now narrate the Bhāgavata Purāṇaṁ which was originally revealed by the Lord himself and has since been handed down through a succession of sages.

Prior to creation, the Lord was engrossed in yoga nidrā (conscious sleep) on the primeval waters, absorbed in his own bliss. The subtle bodies of all the beings who had existed in the previous cycle were within the Lord in their atomic state. Only time was awake and time had been endowed with the power to arouse the creative faculties within the Lord at the time allotted by him.

When this moment arrived, time illumined the nature of all the beings resting in the Lord in their atomic state. The Lord saw countless worlds within his own being. These worlds were stirred by the quality of activity, impelled by time. The subtle matter which issued from the navel of the Lord as a result of this stirring looked like a lotus, and it illuminated the primeval waters like the sun. The Lord himself entered this lotus; and the creator (Brahmā) appeared on it. Brahmā looked around in the four directions and thus came to have four heads. He asked himself: "Who am I? What is my support? Who supports this lotus which seems to be my support?"

Brahmā dived into the primeval waters, looking for his own source. A long period of time elapsed. Time is the Lord's discus (sudarśana) and frightens people by consuming their life-span. Brahmā gave up the search and returned to his own abode to practise deep meditation. After a hundred years of deep meditation the light of wisdom dawned in him and he saw.

On the primeval waters in which the whole universe was submerged lay the Lord on the body of Śeṣa (the residue of the previous cycle, visualised as a serpent). He shone with a splendour that had no comparison. The worlds with all their animate and inanimate objects were hidden within him. He was inaccessible even to the sun, moon and stars; his own divine weapons devoutly went around him. At that very moment the creator, intent on bringing the universe into being, beheld the lotus which supported him, the primeval waters, the cosmic blast, space and himself. He then fixed his mind on the Lord and began to praise him.

Book Three Chapter 9

Brahmā prayed: O Lord, it is after long penance (lit: burning that illumines the truth) that I behold the reality that you alone exist. You are unclouded by ignorance, unsullied by desire. When the equilibrium of the three forces that constitute your own māyā is disturbed, you yourself appear as many. You have assumed this divine form, O Lord, as the first of many forms in which to descend into the world of mortals, on account of your compassion for your devotee, to make yourself easily accessible to him. He who takes refuge in your lotus feet is not deluded by your māyā and is freed from fear. On account of wealth, house and friends one is subjected to fear, sorrow, attachment, ignominy and inordinate greed, and one clings to a false sense of possession which is the source of great sorrow till one grasps your feet which confer fearlessness. Constantly taking part in activities connected with your worship and listening to and singing your glories one develops love for your feet, and this leads to self-forgetful union with you. On account of the distracting and deluding power of the senses, and as long as one feels totally different from you, so long will he revolve in this unending cycle of birth and death, which, though false, is yet the source of great sorrow.

How gracious you are, O Lord, for you yourself reveal the path which leads to you! By hearing your glories this path is discovered. You dwell in the hearts of your devotees which are purified by devotion to you. What is more, in whatever manner they conceive of you in their consciousness, that very form you assume, to bless them! You are easily pleased O Lord, with the love of those who are compassionate to all beings, and not with pompous rituals of ambitious people. For, you have yourself assumed the various forms of beings here. I bow to you, the very self of animate and inanimate beings. May I, while playing my role as the creator of the world, not be tainted by the vain feeling that I am the creator!

The Lord said: It was through my grace that you practised penance, O Brahmā. When you searched for me, you were baffled and I revealed myself in your own heart. He who sees me in all beings is freed from delusion. When he realises that the self is devoid of the elements and the senses, but that it is the innermost reality, he is liberated. He realises that all forms of public service and all spiritual practices are directed towards me. Shake off lassitude and confusion and begin the work of creation as already ordained by me.

Book Three Chapter 10

In response to Vidura's request, Maitreya described creation: When the Lord disappeared, Brahmā once again practised penance for a hundred celestial years. Then he saw that the lotus on which he was seated and the cosmic waters around it were tossed by wind. He consumed both wind and water. He decided to bring the universe into manifestation with the help of the lotus. He entered the lotus and split it into three parts: these three 'worlds' are the abodes of jīvā for working out their karma. The other, higher, worlds are for those who are unselfish and virtuous.

The universe, which existed as none other than God, was then evolved by the Lord through time, which in itself is unmanifest, which has no beginning nor end but which brings about the metamorphosis of elements. Ninefold is this creation, the tenth is the creation of both God's nature and the creator's transformation. The first six proceed from God's nature. The next three were created by Brahmā, though ultimately even these are part of the Lord's own playful creation. They are: (1) the cosmic intelligence-energy called mahat; (2) the ego or aham; (3) the subtle elements which give rise to the gross elements; (4) the indriyā, viz., the senses of perception and the organs of action; (5) the deities presiding over these and the mind, born of the sātvika ego; (6) tamas or the principle of nescience or ignorance which clouds understanding veils the truth; (7) the sixfold immobile creation, viz., trees which bear fruit without flowering, annual plants which die after fruition, creepers that climb, plants with a hard bark, creepers that do not climb and trees which bear fruit after blossoming, all of which draw their nourishment from below and are almost insentient; (8) animals or horizontal beings without a sense of time, irrational and instinctual, which depend upon senses alone, but are ignorant at heart. Of these there are twenty-eight varieties—the cloven-hoofed beasts, the whole-hoofed beasts, beasts that have five claws, and the birds of the air; (9) the human beings, with an abundance of restless dynamism, who derive pleasure from sense-enjoyments which are rooted in pain and sorrow; and (10) sages, Sanaka and others, jointly created by God's nature and by Brahmā.

In addition, God's creation consists of: gods, manes, demons, celestial musicians, the celestial nymphs, yakṣā and rākṣasā, siddhā with supernatural powers, celestial bards, vidyādharā, ghosts, spirits and fiends, and also kinnarā, kimpuruṣā and aśvamukhā.

Do not forget, O Vidura, that it is the Lord who projects himself as all these beings!

Book Three Chapter 11

Maitreya continued: I shall now describe to you the universe, its evolution and dissolution.

The minutest material substance which continues to remain stable without mixing with other atoms to form other substances is called paramāṇu. Man, however, deludedly imagines that these paramāṇū combine to form other substances. The entire undifferentiated material substance, before it undergoes transformation is the aviśeṣa, great and infinite. The smallest unit of time is that in which light traverses the minutest; and the longest measure of time is that in which light traverses the largest. Time and space are two modes of a single phenomenon.

Two paramāṇū form the primary atom (aṇu); three atoms combine to form the trasareṇu. The time taken by light to traverse three trasareṇu is the smallest conceivable measure of time called truṭi, which is a fraction of a wink! When you multiply this measure you get successively a minute, hour, day, month, year and so on. The year is reckoned in several ways, such different reckonings based upon the 'movement' of the sun, of jupiter, or of the moon, or upon the year divided into months of 30 or 27 days. Salute the sun whose power makes food grow, whose light removes the delusion of men and who promotes commonweal in various ways.

A cycle of four epochs (yugā) is reckoned to be 4,320,000 human years. Beyond the three worlds which constitute our galaxy, one thousand revolutions of the four yugā constitute daytime and an equal length of time constitutes night-time. During this night the creator 'sleeps', and as the next day dawns the universe is re-created as before. During the daytime of the creator, fourteen cosmic rulers rule the universe: they are called manū, who are verily the part-manifestations of the Lord himself. At the close of the day the creator assumes an iota of inertia and, refraining from his work, remains quiet. By the power of time (in due course) the whole creation merges into him. The sun and the moon disappear; the three worlds get dissolved into him. As the divine energy consumes the three worlds, the sages ascend to a higher region. Oceans swell and the 'worlds' are submerged. The Lord alone remains, 'asleep' on his couch called 'Śeṣa' (the remnant).

That was one day of Brahmā. Brahmā's life-span is one hundred such years. Half of that life-span is called a parārdha. We are living in the beginning of the second parārdha. Interminably long as they are, even two parārdha, or the creator's full life-span, are but as the twinkling of an eye for the Lord, who is beyond time which spans all else—from the minutest material substance to the life-span of the creator.

This vast universe is but a paramāṇu in that cause of all causes which comprises myriads of such universes: that cause is lord Viṣṇu, the supreme person.

Book Three Chapter 12

Maitreya continued: The creator proceeded with his work. To begin with, the diversity of creation needed the principles of darkness that promote diversification, viz., ignorance of self, identification with the body, craving for pleasure, anger and fear of death as the end of life. Not pleased with these negative factors, Brahmā then created the four sages (Sanaka and others) and urged them to propagate mankind. But they were not interested! Brahmā tried to suppress his anger at his sons' effrontery; but it sprang out from the centre of his eye-brows, as a boy. This boy cried: "What is my name and what is my abode?" Brahmā christened the crying boy 'Rudra' (besides other names) and assigned to him his abodes (the heart, senses, vital air, the elements and penance) and also his consorts (Rudrāṇī). Rudra became a prajāpati (progenitor) and begot numerous destructive beings! Brahmā forthwith restrained him and sent him away to engage himself in penance.

The creator himself brought forth the ten sages from his various limbs. Nārada from his lap, Dakṣa from his thumb, Vasiṣṭha from his breath, Bhṛgu from his skin, Kratu from his hand, Pulaha from his navel, Pulastya from his ears, Angirā from his mouth, Atri from his eyes and Marīci from his mind. Dharma issued from the creator's right breast; and adharma (unrighteousness) from his back. Even so the god of love issued from his heart, the god of anger from his brows, and the god of greed from his lower lip. Vāk, the goddess of speech, sprang from his mouth.

The creator fell in love with Vāk. His sons, however, remonstrated and prayed to the Lord: "Salutations to the Lord who manifested this universe which was already hidden in him! May he protect righteousness!" The creator cast off his body which floated away as a dark cloud. From his four mouths now issued: the four vedā, the four scriptures dealing with duty; the four sciences (warfare, medicine, music and architecture); the epics and legends, the sacrifices, the four pillars of virtue (knowledge, charity, austerity and truthfulness); the four stages of life and the duties prescribed for each (the celibate-student, the householder, the recluse and the man of renunciation) and the four mystical formulae and metres. From him issued the alphabets and the seven musical notes.

Yet, the creator saw that his progeny was not multiplying! Instantly his body became twofold: one part male and the other female. The male was Svayaṁbhu manu and the female was Śatarūpā. From this time creation multiplied by copulation. Manu begot two sons (Priyavrata and Uttānapāda) and three daughters (Ākūti, Devahūti and Prasūti). The three daughters helped populate the earth.

The Divine Boar
Book Three Chapter 13

Maitreya continued: Svayaṁbhu manu bowed to his father, the creator, and said: "Pray, tell me what my duty is so that by its due performance I may attain fame here and a good destiny hereafter." This conduct pleased Brahmā who enjoined his son to rule the earth and govern her people virtuously, assuring him that the Lord would be pleased if he did so. However, the earth had sunk into the ocean. Manu prayed that it might be salvaged so that he might govern it.

The perplexed creator contemplated the Lord: "Let the Lord who created me devise a plan to salvage the earth." At once a tiny boar no bigger than the thumb issued from the creator's nostril. Immediately it grew as large as an elephant and as solid as a rock. Brahmā and his sons began speculating about the identity of this mysterious being. The boar had now assumed the size of a mountain, and roared. This removed their doubt and they recognised the Lord disguised as a boar (warthog).

The Lord, whose very person represented all the forms of sacrifice and worship, went about sniffing to locate the earth; he had fearful tusks but looked with love and compassion at the sages. He dived into the water. He discovered the earth in the depths of the ocean. As he was hauling it up to the surface of the water, a demon named Hiraṇyākṣa intercepted him. But the Lord quickly disposed of him and planted the earth firmly on the surface of the water.

Brahmā and the others then sang his praises: "Victory, victory to you, O invincible Lord! You promote the spirit of sacrifice. Your body is composed of knowledge (vedā) and your actions are acts of worship and sacrifice. Hail, hail to thee: you yourself are the mantrā used in worship, you are the worship and the deities invoked during the worship. Uplifted on the tip of the gleaming tusks, the earth shines resplendent, and this form of yours is as awe-inspiring as a huge mountain. You, O Lord, are the abode of the wonder of wonders, and hence it is no wonder that you have been able to salvage the earth which had sunk deep within the ocean. Who can fathom your immeasurable glory! We pray: please establish the earth firmly so that it may become the habitation for all beings."

Soon after, the Lord, who had assumed the form of a boar (or warthog) for the purpose of salvaging the earth, disappeared, having accomplished his mission. The Lord is highly pleased with those who listen to this marvellous story with faith and devotion. Of his own accord the Lord confers the highest state of liberation on those whose mind and heart are fixed exclusively on him.

Vidura asked: How did the Lord come to encounter the demon Hiraṇyākṣa? O sage, tell me more about the origin of the demon.

Maitreya said: Diti was one of the daughters of Dakṣa, son of the creator. She was married to Kaśyapa, the son of Marīci, one of the sages. All her twelve sisters had also married Kaśyapa and had children: only Diti had none. At dusk one day Diti approached Kaśyapa and urgently solicited him, passionately desirous as she was of offspring.

Kaśyapa conceded the reasonableness of the demand but pointed out that the time was inauspicious. He said: "I shall presently gratify your desire. I know that the wife is the foundation of household life. And, the householder crosses the ocean of sorrow carrying the people belonging to other stages of life, even as a man crosses the ocean in a ship. That is made possible because the wife shoulders almost the entire burden of household life. We menfolk cannot repay the debt we owe to you, the goddess of the house, even during a whole life-time, nor in lives to come. The wise men who wish to pierce the veil of ignorance sing of the blameless actions of Rudra. There is none even equal to him and he is the goal of the righteous. Yet he behaves as though he is a fiend! Dusk is the period when lord Rudra roams about, followed by fearful ghosts and goblins. So let this, his hour, pass."

Diti, however, could not control herself. Bowing to the inevitable, Kaśyapa gratified her passion, bathed again and continued his evening prayers. Her appetite having been appeased, Diti realised her folly and once again prayed to Kaśyapa: "May my offspring not be subjected to lord Rudra's wrath! I bow to lord Śiva the invincible, who removes the sorrows of his devotees and confers boons upon them, who wields the rod (to punish the wicked) though he is perfectly non-violent, and who is the personification of anger." Kaśyapa consoled her saying: "Since you transgressed the bounds of lord Rudra, two terrible demoniacal beings will be born to you. Yet, since you are repentant and remorseful, they will have the good fortune to be slain by lord Hari himself." Diti dreaded the first part of the prophecy, but was consoled by the second part of it. Kaśyapa continued: "Since you are devoted to lord Hari, lord Śiva and myself, one of the children born of one of your sons will shine as the greatest among the devotees of the Lord and will win undying fame in this world."

Maitreya continued: Afraid that her demoniacal sons would harm the gods, Diti retained the foetuses within her for a hundred years. Nevertheless, on account of the potential calamity, the worlds lost their lustre and the gods lost their splendour. The gods went to Brahmā, the creator, and enquired of him concerning the source of this dark force, and its remedy.

Brahmā explained: O gods, once upon a time my sons Sanaka and his three brothers went to Vaikuṇṭha, the abode of lord Viṣṇu. In Vaikuṇṭha the Lord dwells in his personal form, made of purest light itself. This realm is the centre of the entire creation, and all the galaxies revolve around it, paying homage to it, as it were. In that realm everything is celestial, divine, pure and supernatural. Divine bards sing the Lord's glories, seated in aerial vehicles made of precious stones and gold. The minds of those who dwell in this realm are so saturated with the love of lord Kṛṣṇa (Viṣṇu) that no undivine thought can taint them. Lakṣmī, the goddess of wealth, abides in it in her personal form, worshipping the Lord with holy basil leaves. Only they who are totally absorbed in their devotion to lord Viṣṇu, and who thus are saturated with goodness, can enter that realm: not they who waste their time in useless talk.

The sages entered that realm. Undeterred by anyone they passed through six gates, or doors. The seventh doorway was guarded by two shining beings who had the actual form of lord Viṣṇu himself. When the sages tried to enter this doorway these two shining guards barred their entrance. This effrontery angered the sages, who said to the guards: "The entire universe abides in the Lord's abdomen, and hence the dwellers in his kingdom do not perceive diversity at all! How is it that you, though endowed with divine bodies similar to the Lord's, betray fear born of diversity and bar our entrance?" The sages felt that these two guards should, in order to rid themselves of this grave defect, be born into the mortal world. The guards (Jaya and Vijaya) shuddered on hearing this and, while accepting the justice of such a pronouncement, prayed that they might not forget the Lord during their sojourn in the lower regions.

Hearing of his guards' misbehaviour towards the sages, lord Viṣṇu himself came out. The delighted sages glorified the Lord. "Lord, though you had already entered our hearts as a description of your divine secret by our father Brahmā, our eyes rejoice to behold your form in front of us today. Though you dwell in the hearts of all, the evil-minded people fail to behold you. You are the highest spiritual truth realised, by your own grace, by sages who are totally free from egotism and lust. Whatever be our future, may our minds take constant delight in dwelling at your feet."

Book Three Chapter 16

Brahmā continued: When the sages had offered their prayer, the Lord said: These two attendants of mine, Jaya and Vijaya, are guilty of an unpardonable offence, since they have offended you, and, therefore, offended me. As it is popularly held that the master shares his servant's guilt, I offer you my apologies for their conduct. You, sages, are my deities. If I am glorified in the universe and if my glories purify the hearts of those whose ears they enter, it is because my glory is sustained and sung by you. Because I am devoted to you the dust of my feet is considered capable of destroying all sins, and the water with which my feet are washed sanctifies the three worlds: hence people sprinkle it on their heads. Yet, I bear on my head the dust of sages' feet. The twice-born, cows and all helpless beings are my own bodies. They who, blinded by ignorance, treat them as different from me, are torn to pieces by the gods of punishment appointed by me. On the other hand they who love and serve the sages as my own self delight my heart. These two servants of mine have offended you—the sages—and hence deserve the fate appointed by you. Bless them so that they may soon return to my domain.

The Sages said: O Lord, being a friend and well-wisher of sages, it is natural that you look upon them as your deities. The eternal religion (sanātana dharma) is from you and is preserved by your own manifestations. You alone are the secret and immutable goal of dharma. In fact, you alone are manifest from age to age as dharma. We pray to thee, cleanse our hearts of all impurities. Your glorification of sages is the playful way in which you fulfil your role as the protector of dharma. Be pleased, then, O Lord, to do as you would with these servants of yours and with us who sought to punish your attendants.

The Blessed Lord, however, said: What you did was in perfect accord with my will. These attendants will be born in demoniacal forms and be intensely devoted to me through hate, and will soon return to my domain.

Brahmā concluded: O gods, the sages prostrated to the Lord and departed. The Lord said to Jaya and Vijaya: "Fear not. You will be absolved of the sages' curse when you concentrate all your mind and heart on me with hate. You will soon return to me." It is those two attendants of the Lord who have entered the womb of Diti. All this has taken place in accordance with the Lord's will, which even the masters of yoga find difficult to understand.

Birth of Hiraṇyakaśipu and Hiraṇyākṣa
Book Three Chapter 17

Maitreya said: Satisfied with Brahmā's words the gods returned to their abodes. A full hundred years after conception, Diti was delivered of twin sons. At the hour of their birth it looked as though cosmic dissolution was about to take place. Parts of the earth shook, the horizon appeared fiery, meteors and thunderbolts rained on the earth. Gales hissed fearfully and uprooted trees, clouds screened the sky and the earth lay shrouded in dense darkness. The oceans were rough and the aquatic creatures were terror-stricken. There were solar and lunar eclipses again and again. Animals were panic-stricken. Certain (malefic) planets shone brightly whilst others lost their lustre.

The two sons of Diti were born powerful, with adamantine frames the size of mountains. Their crowns scraped the sky and the earth trembled under their feet. The father, sage Kaśyapa, named them Hiraṇyakaśipu and Hiraṇyākṣa.

They gained boons from the creator which made them almost invincible. Hiraṇyakaśipu conquered the three worlds and brought even the deities under his subjection. Hiraṇyākṣa was very fond of war and roamed the earth looking for a fight. He had unequalled strength of mind and body and he was puffed up with pride. No one could stop his movements. Even the gods hid themselves from him in terror. This added to his vanity and he roared aloud and challenged everyone to a duel.

Finding none, he jumped into the ocean which became greatly agitated. Even large and powerful ocean-dwellers avoided a confrontation with him. For several years Hiraṇyākṣa moved about in the ocean and eventually reached the abode of Varuṇa, the deity persiding over the ocean.

Hiraṇyākṣa fell at the feet of Varuṇa, with the intention of ridiculing and insulting him, and mockingly invited him to a duel. "You are a great god who has conquered many gods and demons. And, you have even celebrated your victory by performing the rājasūya ritual. Come, fight with me, O lord," he said. Varuna was angry. Knowing the will of the Lord he restrained himself and replied: "I am too old to fight with you. And I do not see anyone other than the ancient person who will be able to satisfy your thirst for a fight. You are skilled in warfare. Therefore, O chief of the dark forces, approach him who is glorified even by heroes like you." Varuṇa, of course warned Hiraṇyākṣa that the Lord would quell his pride, defeat him in battle, and that it is for this purpose that the Lord assumed forms again and again, though he is formless in his essential nature.

Hiraṇyākṣa's Redemption
Book Three Chapter 18

Maitreya continued: The demon accepted Varuṇa's challenge but did not heed his warning. He found out the whereabouts of lord Viṣṇu from sage Nārada, who told him that the Lord had just rescued the earth from the depth into which it had fallen and was rushing up to establish it on the surface of the waters. The demon looked at the Lord disguised as a boar (or warthog) and laughed: "Ah, an amphibian beast!"

Hiraṇyākṣa spoke to lord Viṣṇu: "We are the owners of the earth, O god disguised as a boar! You cannot take her away without our sanction. You have little prowess except the power of deception (māyā). I shall kill you easily." The demon, who had golden locks on his head, followed the Lord as the latter brought the earth up to the surface, shouting derisively: "Are you not ashamed (to steal the earth from us and to run away from a challenging adversary)?"

The Lord placed the earth securely on the surface of the waters and invested it with his own power so that it might not swerve from its orbit. The demon stood looking at him. Brahmā and the other gods showered flowers upon the Lord. He then taunted the demon in his turn. They joined in battle. When the demon came to hit him with his mace, the Lord dodged the blow, even as yogī dodge death. With his mace the Lord struck the demon, who intercepted it with his own mace.

Thus the fierce battle continued. Brahmā and the sages witnessed the battle between the demon Hiraṇyākṣa and the supreme being, who had assumed the form of a boar, but who was in fact the personification of the highest spirit of self-sacrifice. The demon and the Lord were fighting for the sake of the earth.

Brahmā prayed to the Lord: "O Lord, having obtained a boon from me, this demon has become haughty enough to offend the gods themselves. Please do not delay his destruction any further, for soon twilight will set in and demoniacal creatures wax in strength in darkness. This fool has, luckily for us all, come to you of his own accord. Kill him speedily and thus protect us all and establish peace on earth."

Book Three Chapter 19

Maitreya continued: The Lord listened to the prayers of Brahmā, the creator, and smiled approvingly. He hit the demon with his mace. However, when the demon returned the blow the Lord's mace slipped from his hand. Such was the chivalry even of the demon that he would not take undue advantage of his adversary's unarmed state. The Lord admired the demon's chivalry, and summoned his cakra (revolver) which immediately appeared in his hand. The gods witnessing this battle prayed for the Lord's victory over the demon.

The demon (who also had terrible tusks) sprang into the air and hit the Lord with his mace. The Lord playfully knocked it down with his left foot, even though it came toward him with the force of a tempest. The next time the demon hurled the mace, the Lord caught it with ease.

Then the demon took up a flaming trident and hurled it at the Lord. As it flew through the sky, it shone extremely brightly. The Lord broke it into pieces with the cakra. The enraged demon then hit the Lord with his hard fist, but this produced no impression on the Lord. The frustrated demon now began to use conjuring tricks: there arose fierce gales and dust-storms which darkened the horizon, there was a shower of stones from every side and the celestial bodies were hidden by thick clouds which rained filth to the accompaniment of lightning and thunder. Mountains discharged destructive weapons. However, the Lord's cakra dealt effectively with these diabolical tricks and they disappeared at once.

The demon now tried to get a strangle-hold on the Lord with his strong arms: but as he tried to clasp him, he discovered that the Lord could not be so encompassed. The Lord struck Hiraṇyākṣa below his ear, and the demon fell dead. The gods were happy but they also marvelled at the demon's good fortune. For, struck by the foot of the Lord—whom yogī meditate upon seeking final liberation—and gazing on the face of the Lord, this hero among demons discarded his body! Verily, that is because the demon was the Lord's own attendant before and will soon regain his post. The gods offered a prayer of thanksgiving to the Lord, who returned to his domain.

Sūta said: He who listens to or narrates this episode of the Lord's encounter with Hiraṇyākṣa enjoys wealth, fame, longevity and all the objects of his desire, and is freed from the worst of sins.

Book Three Chapter 20

In answer to Vidura's further questioning concerning creation, sage Maitreya continued: You know how Brahmā the creator appeared on the lotus which had sprung up from the navel of the Lord, and how, entering into Brahmā's heart, the Lord himself enabled him to perceive the plan of the creation as it existed in previous world-cycles. Brahmā at first created five-fold ignorance which causes diversity. He did not like his own creation and discarded that body. This became 'night' and the forces of darkness (yakṣā and rākṣasā) took possession of it. They were the sources of hunger and thirst and even tried to eat the creator himself!

Then Brahmā created the divinities with the quality of satva (purity, light) predominant in them. Brahmā dropped that form, too, when it had accomplished its purpose. It became 'day' and the gods took charge of it.

From his hind part Brahmā evolved the demons, who are ever lustful. In fact they were so lustful that they solicited Brahmā himself! He prayed to the Lord, who commanded him to discard that body, too. This body, when it was discarded, took the form of 'twilight' which appeared to the demons as a ravishingly beautiful girl. The deluded demons were infatuated by her.

Brahmā laughed heartily at this. He evolved out of his own loveliness the celestial musicians (gandharvā) and the nymphs (apsarā). His body from which these were evolved became 'moonlight'. He discarded that, too, and these celestials took possession of it.

From his own slothfulness, Brahmā evolved the ghosts and fiends of fearful forms. He discarded that body with a yawn, and the ghosts and fiends took hold of it. They manifest as yawning and sleep. They possess impure people and cause insanity.

The invisible beings called sādhyā and the manes were then evolved by Brahmā's body, full of vigour and energy. It is through this body that oblations are offered to the manes. By this faculty of remaining hidden, Brahmā evolved the siddhā and vidyādharā and they took possession of that body. When Brahmā admired his own form reflected in water, the kinnarā and kimpuruṣā were created. Brahmā then lay down in a sullen mood and the hairs that dropped from his body became snakes.

Lastly, he created the manu and gave them his own form, the human form. Seeing this, all those who had been created before were happy and they said: "O creator! We are glad. You have done well. Since the spirit of sacrifice is well established in this human form, we shall get our share." Having equipped himself with penance, yoga and samādhi, Brahmā evolved the ṛṣi to whom he gave a part of his own body endowed with meditation, supernatural power, austerity, adoration and dispassion.

Kardama and Devahūti
Book Three Chapter 21

Sage Maitreya continued: The creator commanded the ten sage-progenitors (prajāpatī) to populate the earth. One of them, Kardama, practised penance for ten thousand years, during which he constantly lived in a spirit of total surrender to the Lord who showers instant blessings upon his devotees with the help of kriya yoga combined with samādhi. The Lord revealed his glorious form to the sage, who fell at his feet and extolled him with a heart full of joy and supreme love.

"O Lord! Your lotus feet enable us to cross the ocean of mundane existence in an instant; only ignorant people will worship them for the fulfilment of sensual and worldly desires. Your true devotees, however, turn away from worldly pleasures and live a life of god-intoxication. They know that the wheel of time, which you have set in motion, constantly shortens the life-span of mortals. You fulfil your devotee's wishes; and I wish to marry in order to fulfil the creator's command. May I, O Lord, be married to a girl of a pious disposition, who is devoted to you."

The Lord said: "O lord of created beings, know that a prayer addressed to me never goes in vain. I was aware of the wish that arose in your heart even before you expressed it. I have already granted it. Emperor Svayaṁbhu manu will soon give you his daughter in marriage. You will be blessed with nine daughters. Living an unselfish and egoless life, you will realise your oneness with me after you have fulfilled the duties allotted to you by me. You will be compassionate to all beings and attain self-realisation. Not a single living creature will fear you, and you will realise that you and the entire universe are one with me. I shall myself be born as your son and expound the truth." The Lord then returned to his abode. Kardama was still in an ecstatic mood.

Kardama's hermitage on the shores of the divine lake Bindusarovara enjoyed all the blessings of earthly scenic beauty, an atmosphere charged with divinity and supreme peace. It abounded in wonderful trees and lovely birds. The lake got its name from a tear drop that fell from the Lord's eyes when he was overcome with joy at seeing Kardama's supreme love for him.

On the appointed day, Svayaṁbhu manu came to Kardama's heritage with his daughter Devahūti. Kardama welcomed the monarch, saying: "Surely, a king tours his territory for the protection of the good and to curb evil. For the king is a part manifestation of the Lord himself, who promotes righteousness and subdues unrighteousness. If you do not thus keep in close touch with the people of your kingdom, the evil-doers will have a free rein and unrighteousness will flourish. O king, kindly reveal the purpose of your visit and tell me what I can do for you."

Book Three Chapter 22

Sage Maitreya continued: The first king and law-giver of the world, Svayaṁbhu manu, was embarrassed to hear himself thus praised by sage Kardama, and returned the compliments in suitable terms: "The Lord evolved you, the holy brāhmaṇa, out of his mouth. You are rich in penance, knowledge and yoga and uninterested in the pleasures of the senses. For your protection, he created us from his arms. That is why sages and kings protect each other: because they are parts of the one being. It is the Lord, therefore, who protects, and who is protected; for both are parts of his one being. I consider it a great good fortune that I have been able to see you and bow at your feet. Now listen to my prayer! My daughter, princess Devahūti, has set her heart on you since the day she heard of you from the celestial sage Nārada. As you have not taken the vow of life-long celebacy, I pray that you will accept her hand."

Kardama replied: "Certainly I wish to marry to fulfil the creator's command to populate the world. Only they who have worshipped the lotus feet of the Lord can even see Devahūti, your daughter and the sister of Uttānapāda. I therefore consider it a good fortune to marry her. I shall certainly accept her hand in marriage but on one condition, and that is that I shall remain with her only until she bears me a son. After that I shall observe the rules of a sanyāsī (as revealed by the Lord himself) which are praiseworthy, being based on non-violence." Having said this the sage remained immersed in contemplation of the Lord.

After clearly and explicitly ascertaining the opinions of both the queen and the princess Devahūti herself, Svayaṁbhu manu gave his daughter away in marriage to Kardama, who was an abode of virtues: and it was a perfect match. After the wedding manu tearfully took leave of his daughter and son-in-law and returned to his kingdom, where a truly royal welcome awaited him.

Ruling over the kingdom from the capital Barhiṣmati, Svayaṁbhu manu, the first king of the world, promulgated the first and most ancient code of morals (manu smṛti) laying down the duties of people belonging to the various professions and stages of life. He ruled for a whole manvantara (which consisted of seventy-one rounds of the cycle of four epochs or yugā) every moment of which was spent in pursuits connected with the lord Vasudeva, chanting his names and worshipping him in various forms and ways.

Book Three Chapter 23

Sage Maitreya continued: Devahūti, who was devoted to her husband and could read his thoughts, served him with one-pointed devotion. Without the least trace of lust, deceit, hate, greed, vanity or sin, by ever vigilant and active service, she satisfied her spiritually radiant husband through her fidelity, purity, nobility, self-control, service, affection and sweet speech.

Time fled by. She had become weak and emaciated. The sage noticed this and expressed his admiration in the following words: "I am pleased with your great devotion and service. I bless you with supernatural vision. Behold the blessings I have earned by my penance, which are yours, too, on account of your devotion to me." Devahūti replied: "My lord, I know that you have yogic powers. It is my great good fortune to have you as my husband and to serve you. I pray that you may fulfil your promise to bless me with your offspring."

Kardama exercised his supernatural powers and created a flying mansion which was of supernatural construction and shone with supernatural beauty. Then he asked Devahūti to bathe in a divine lake which would grant all one's wishes. As she entered the water, she beheld celestial damsels who said they were her servants! They bathed, dressed and decked her with ornaments. She thought of her lord and was immediately transported to his presence. The sage saw that she had been restored to her former state of youthful charm.

Kardama then made her ascend in the flying mansion and took her round the world. They roamed in all directions and visited all the countries of the world. They spent some time in the best pleasure-gardens of the world. All this was made possible by Kardama's devotion to the Lord and Devahūti's devoted service to her husband. Then they returned to the sage's hermitage.

Then the sage decided to fulfil Devahūti's desire for progeny. Regarding her as his own self, the sage of self-realisation impregnated her, making himself ninefold. The very same day Devahūti gave birth to nine daughters. However, she found that Kardama was about to leave the hermitage to take to a wandering life of a sanyāsī. She pleaded that she had not yet been blessed with a son! "O sage," said she: "your daughters will all leave me when they get married. When you leave the household life there should be someone to look after me. I have had enough of worldly pleasure. Yet, I have found the attachment to the ignorant binds one to the wheel of birth and death, whereas attachment to a holy man is liberating. I seek liberation from the bondage of mundane life. Bless me with freedom from fear."

Kapila
Book Three Chapter 24

Sage Maitreya continued: Kardama recalled the Lord's promise and reassured Devahūti that the Lord would most certainly fulfil her holy wish. She, for her part, continued to adore the Lord with her entire being. After a considerable time the Lord entered the energy of the sage Kardama and manifested himself through her, even as fire manifests in firewood. This most auspicious birth of the Lord was hailed even by the gods. The creator, Brahmā, named the Lord 'Kapila'. Commanded by Brahmā the sage Kardama gave his nine daughters in marriage to nine sages—Kalā to Marīci, Anasūyā to Atri, Śraddhā to Aṅgira, Havirbhū to Pulastya, Gati to Pulaha, Kriyā to Kratu, Khyāti to Bhṛgu, Arundhatī to Vaśiṣṭha, and Śānti to Atharva. All of them took leave of Kardama soon afterwards and went to their new homes.

Kardama now turned to the Lord, who had been born as his own son, and said: "Seekers of truth and devotees realise you only after many lifetimes of devotional practice; and the wicked do not realise you at all till their hearts have been thoroughly purified. Yet, how gracious of you, O Lord, that you have chosen to appear in the house of an ordinary man like me, unmindful of possible popular criticism. It only demonstrates your supreme grace. Indeed, you have done so to redeem your promise, to enhance the glory of your devotees and to propound the knowledge of the self. Lord, you are truly beyond all forms, but you assume the forms that your devotees love. I take refuge in Kapila, the supreme being, who rules over cosmic intelligence and cosmic life-principle, who is the Lord of time and all the elements, who creates them and then absorbs them into himself, being the consciousness that underlies all of them. Having fulfilled the promise I gave my father, and having all my desires fulfilled in you, I seek your permission to renounce this life and take to the mendicant life."

The Lord said: "I have appeared in this world in order to expound the knowledge of the self. I allow you to go from the household life. By adoring me with all your actions you will be freed from death. By beholding me in your heart you will be freed from all sorrow and fear." Thus blessed by the Lord who was his own son, sage Kardama took to the homeless life, with his mind fixed on the Lord whom he saw as his very self and the self of all beings. In this manner Kardama attained final liberation from the wheel of birth and death.

Book Three Chapter 25

Sage Maitreya continued: When Kardama had thus left for the homeless life of a sanyāsī, Kapila continued to live in Bindusarovara, looking after his mother. One day Devahūti said to Kapila: "O perfect one! I am thoroughly convinced of the futility of sensual life. And, I have in you the divine eye to look through the veil of ignorance. You are the Lord, the sun that dispels all illusion. It is only by your grace that the feeling of 'I' towards the body, and 'mine' towards what is associated with the body can be removed—for they are the manifestations of your own māyā or illusory power. I bow to you, eager as I am to know the truth."

The Lord Kapila said: O blessed mother, in my opinion the path of final beatitude is yoga, whereby one is freed from sorrow and pleasure. I shall expound that yoga to you. Know that mind is the cause of bondage and liberation. When it seeks the objects of pleasure it is bound, and when it is devoted to the Lord the soul is liberated. It is the pleasure-seeking mind that generates lust, anger, greed and hatred. When it grows indifferent to pleasure it regains its equipoise and purity. Then the soul pierces the veil of ignorance and the perception of diversity, and sees the self alone as the all: even natural urge (the instinctual drive) is greatly weakened.

For the seeker after this glorious goal of self-realisation, devotion is the best path. The same love which leads to bondage when directed towards sensual objects, frees the soul when it is directed towards holy men. These holy men are forbearing, compassionate, friendly towards all beings and peaceful, and have goodness as their ornament. They have no enemies in the world. They are firmly rooted in their devotion to me. For my sake they have renounced all selfish activities and all kith and kin. I am their sole refuge. They listsen to and narrate stories concerning me. They are never touched by any affliction whatsoever. Attachment to such holy men is beneficial, for they are the best antidote to all attachment. In their company you will develop, by stages, supreme love for God and total aversion to pleasure. Through the practice of yoga you will realise him here and now.

Motiveless devotion to the Lord is excellent. It is superior even to final beatitude; the devotee is not interested in anything but me. Such devotion dissolves all the sheaths that veil the soul. Without even aspiring for it, these devotees attain my own domain. They who take me as their only refuge and who consider me as their all-in-all are never deprived of a place in my domain. Time has no jurisdiction over them. I liberate them from the terrible fear of birth and death. This is the greatest good for man in this world: a mind that has been offered to me in total devotion.

Book Three Chapter 26

Lord Kapila continued: Devotion is not the enemy of understanding nor vice versa, but they are inseparable friends. Hence, I shall now describe the nature of knowledge which frees one from bondage. The self, the indweller, is eternal, is beyond all description and beyond matter. He is the self-effulgent presence in all hearts, and the universe is revealed to us by this light. This omnipresent reality, or the self, though for ever independent of all materiality, yet permitted matter to form in him. This matter, originally extremely subtle and unmanifest, is of the nature of three qualities.

This association of the spirit with matter is like the imagination or dream of the individual. The self, or the spirit, which is eternally free from materiality, succumbs to the charm of matter, as it were, and gets involved in it, just as the spectator of a play might get emotionally disturbed by the events on stage. The substance of the universe (matter) is ever changing in form. This constitutes the events of history! The self is the eternal witness, really and truly unaffected by these 'events'; yet, it assumes doership on account of this self-imposed ignorance—or false identification with matter.

This assumption of doership automatically brings about birth and death, pleasure and pain. In fact, prakṛti (or matter of nature) is the 'cause' of the self's involvement in the natural events: for nature functions in the light of the self. But, then, experience of pleasure and pain would be absent if the self or puruṣa did not to some extent imagine that what happens to matter happens to him. This imagination is of course not real and it happens only in the self's self-imposed ignorance.

I shall describe prakṛti to you. It is also known as praḍhāna. It is made up of three qualities or three forms of energy—satva, rajas and tamas (nuclear, electromagnetic and gravitational?). Prakṛti is its own cause and effect (both the hen and the egg). Change is the only unchanging attribute of nature or prakṛti. There is constant evolution and involution, composition and decomposition, birth and death. The twenty-four categories (the five gross elements, the five subtle elements, the four-fold internal sense, the five senses of perception, the five organs of action) are evolutes or praḍhāna. Kāla, or time, is really the power of God (or puruṣa or ātmā). The Lord himself is kāla or time. Praḍhāna evolves the elements, the senses and matter. The Lord abides in all beings as the puruṣa or ātmā, and outside them as kāla, or time, which is the twenty-fifth category.

The direct realisation of these twenty-five categories frees one from the delusions of doership and enjoyership, and hence from sin and sorrow.

Book Three Chapter 26

Lord Kapila continued: When the Lord (who is consciousness) thus actively witnessed the play of prakṛti, the power in intelligence (cit-śakti) was released. Cit-śakti is the potentiality of manifestation and individuation. When this cit-śakti (or power of intelligence) stirred, the equilibrium of nature (matter or praḍhāna) was disturbed and the principle of cosmic intelligence was born. This cosmic intelligence (known as mahat tattva) is of the form of light; and this light dispelled the dense darkness that prevailed during the previous cosmic dissolution.

What mahat is in the macrocosm, citta (the mind-stuff) is in the microcosm. It is characterised by satva, it is pure, tranquil, the seat of the Lord, and it is known as Vāsudeva. From the mahat, as it underwent transformation, evolved the ahaṁkāra (ego) which is threefold, viz., sātvika, rājasa and tāmasa. From this threefold ahaṁkāra are evolved the elements and the mind, and it is therefore symbolised as the thousand-headed serpent, Ananta, and is also known as Saṅkarṣana (the second of the four names of the Lord). It is this ego that assumes doership and also appears as the instrument as well as the countless effects (actions and results).

From the sātvika ahaṁkāra the mind was evolved. The mind is known by the name of Aniruddha (the fourth of the four forms of the Lord), the ruler of the senses, and is to be meditated upon by the yogī as having the colour of a blue lotus.

From the rājasa ahaṁkāra the principle of buddhi (understanding) was evolved. It is buddhi which understands the nature of substances and enables the senses to function. It is also known as Pradyumna, the third of the four names of the Lord. Doubt, wrong knowledge, conviction, memory and also sleep are the five functions of this buddhi. The senses of perception, the organs of action and prāṇa (or the life-force) were also evolved out of the rājasa ahaṁkāra.

From the tāmasa ahaṁkāra the gross elements, the subtle senses and the principles of hearing, touch, colour, taste and smell were evolved. First came the principle of space, distance and sound (which is nothing but sound). Space gives space for things to grow, gives rise to ideas of inside and outside and serves as the abode for life. Then came the principle of touch, the tactile sense and air, as also the functions of air. Then the principle of colour, the sense of sight and fire, as also the functions of fire in the world. Then the principle of taste, as well as the different flavours through the sense of taste, water and the functions of water. Then the principle of smell and the olfactory sense, earth as also the functions of the earth (e.g., to be the firm support for all living beings).

Book Three Chapter 26

Lord Kapila continued: From space arose air, from air fire, from fire water, and from water the earth. That cause exists in the effect as well, and so each of these elements shares the characteristics of the preceding ones, in addition to its own special characteristic. All these characteristics are therefore found in earth.

The five gross elements, the mahat and the ahaṁkāra were disunited. Hence the lord Nārāyaṇa entered them along with his own potency called time, as well as the destiny of all the souls who had not attained final liberation during the previous cycle, and the qualities of nature (prakṛti). The seven principles were at once roused to activity. And, there appeared the cosmic egg (viśeṣa) from which emerged the cosmic being (virāṭ).

This shining cosmic egg, which was insentient, was surrounded by the elements, the ego and the mahat. The Lord entered this cosmic egg and set in motion the process of evolution. The subtle senses were now evolved from the elements in the cosmic egg and knitted together into one unit, as they were all part of the cosmic being.

The mouth appeared in the cosmic being along with the organ of speech and the god of fire. Then the nostrils appeared and along with them the sense of smell and prāṇa. Then a pair of eyes and the sense of sight, followed by the sun-god. Then there appeared the ears, the sense of hearing, followed by the deities governing space. There then appeared on the cosmic being the skin and its hairs, and with them herbs and plants and the deities presiding over them. The organ of generation then evolved in him, with it the procreative faculty and the god presiding over the waters. Then came the anus, the faculty of defecation and the god of death who presides over this function. Similarly the hands evolved, the faculty of grasping and the presiding deity Indra. Then the feet, locomotion and Viṣṇu. Then blood vessels and the rivers, then ocean and the abdomen and hunger. Then the heart and the mind, as well as the moon. Then the buddhi and Brahmā, ego and Rudra, and lastly the citta and the inner controller. All the senses tried to rouse the cosmic being—one after the other—but failed. Only when the inner controller who presides over the citta tried, did he wake up. Hence one worships that inner controller with devotion, dispassion and spiritual understanding acquired through the practice of yoga.

Book Three Chapter 27

Lord Kapila continued: Though the inner controller or the spirit dwells in the body, it is not tainted by the latter's experiences (pleasure and pain). It is devoid of doership and is beyond the reach of the three qualities of nature (prakṛti). It is but a totally free witness of nature. Yet, on account of the spell cast by the play of these qualities of nature, the self imagines that he is the doer of actions, he loses his peace of mind on account of this delusion, and in that self-imposed state of ignorance undergoes birth and death. The objects do not exist as such, except in the imagination of the subject; yet so long as one thinks of these objects and is attached to them, he cannot escape the wheel of birth and death, just as even non-existent events cause unhappiness to the dreamer.

Therefore, one should practise the yoga of devotion and gradually bring the mind under control. One should equip oneself with the following qualities: the yama (non-violence and so on), love for listening to my stories, equal vision, freedom from attraction and repulsion, freedom from hostility, continence, the vow of silence, devotion to one's duty performed in a spirit of dedication to God, contentment with whatever is got by chance, moderation in eating etc., love of seclusion, tranquillity, friendliness, compassion, self-control, non-identification of the body with the self brought about by the clear perception of the distinction between matter and spirit, and seeing God in all. The intellect thus purified, the spiritual aspirant at once perceives the self directly. It is not deluded by appearances. Just as the reflection of the sun in a pot of water in the house is discovered by the light shining on the wall, the reflection of the light of the self in the ego is discovered in the functioning of the mind and the senses.

Devahūti asked: The soul was originally deluded by nature. Even if it then perceives the self, there still exists the danger of it being deluded again. How can I remove even the root of delusion, so that this may not happen again?

Lord Kapila replied: When one practises intense devotion to me day and night over many life-times, he develops a distaste for the world and is not tempted even by the highest heaven and psychic powers. He is not deluded again, even as one who has awakened is not deluded by a nightmare which frightened him while asleep. By my grace he realises the self, his doubts are dispelled by the vision of the self and he attains to that state known as kaivalya (total independence) from which there is no return.

Book Three Chapter 28

Lord Kapila continued: I shall now describe the yoga of meditation to you, O mother. By this the mind gains composure and flows along the path to God. To the best of one's ability one should do one's duty and refrain from unrighteousness, be contented with the gifts of providence, worship holy men, cease from worldly activities and yearn to attain liberation, be moderate in eating and seek a secluded and secure dwelling, practise non-violence and truth, refrain from theft and greed, observe continence, lead an austere life, be pure, worship the Lord, observe the vow of silence, acquire mastery over bodily posture and life-force, withdraw the senses from the objects of pleasure and direct them together with the mind, towards the Lord seated in the heart. He should, with the help of the mind, fix the life-force at any one of the mystical circles (cakras) within, constantly dwell on the stories and glories of lord Viṣṇu and thus find inner tranquillity. By these and other methods one should control the mind, the senses and the life-force.

If this foundation has been well and truly laid with the help of understanding and wisdom, meditation becomes easy, natural and almost effortless. One should then sit in a comfortable posture in a pure spot and practise prāṇāyāma which consists of inhalation, retention and exhalation of breath (and the retention can be after inhalation or after exhalation) in order to steady the mind. Prāṇāyāma purifies the mind. Sins are destroyed by concentrating the mind. Pratyāhāra, or withdrawal of the senses, burns up attachment. Meditation destroys all that is undivine within oneself. When the mind is thus purified he should, with his gaze fixed on the tip (or root) of the nose, contemplate the divine and celestially beautiful form of the Lord.

The Lord's countenance is radiantly blissful. His body is sky-blue in colour. His four hands hold the conch, the discus, the mace and the lotus. Around his waist is a garment of yellow silk. On his chest is a brilliant gem and around his neck a never-fading garland. This ever-youthful form stands on the lotus of the devotee's heart. One should meditate on this form till the mind ceases to wander. Then one should contemplate the form, part by part, for more intimate awareness—the lotus feet, the knees, the waist, the chest, the four hands, the face, the eyes and the lips of the Lord, The divine beauty of the Lord frees the devotee from the desire to see anything else.

The devotee's heart melts in love of God. Even the mind which was used to thinking of the Lord is now withdrawn. Thought ceases and the mind is dissolved in him. The yogī now experiences cosmic consciousness. He knows that pleasure and pain (and the like) do not touch the self, but they pertain to the ego which is a product of ignorance. He sees the one self in all beings. He has transcended māyā (illusion) and thus the fragmentation of the supreme being into 'I', 'you' and 'he'. He rests in his own true being. He does not identify the self with the body, which continues to live as prompted by the destiny that created it.

Lord Kapila continued: The yoga of devotion is manifold and its practice differs in accordance with the difference in the nature, quality and the chosen method of the devotees. Yet, broadly speaking, he is a tāmasa devotee whose heart is full of violence, hypocrisy and jealousy; he is a rājasa devotee who worships me for selfish and worldly ends; he is a sātvika devotee who worships me for the destruction of his sins and offers his activities to me, regarding my worship as his duty. All of them, however, consider themselves as distinct from me. Bhakti yoga is truly the uninterrupted flow of the mind-stuff towards me.

The true lover of God is not interested in any worldly gain, nay, not even in the five types of beatitude which are his unsought; namely, sālokya (residence in my realm), sārṣṭi (having the same powers as I have), sāmīpya (close proxmity to me), sārūpya (having my form) and sāyujya (oneness with me). He performs his duties without the least selfish interest, he worships me in and through the images and other symbols, he sings my glories, he adores holy men, he is full of compassion for the afflicted and friendly towards all, he is an abode of noble virtues (the yama and the niyama), he is devoted to hearing my stories and glories, he rejoices in the company of my devotees and he is egoless. The devotee who is established in these divine qualities experiences a great surge of love for me the moment he hears my name and glory.

However, he who worships me in the images but who shows contempt for the least of my creatures in whom I abide is a hypocrite; he derives no benefit. I am ever present in all beings. My devotee should worship me in images only so long as he does not realise me as the presence in his heart, as well as in the hearts of all beings. That devotee who is full of vanity hates me if he hates any being; if he regards me as distinct from himself and bears malice towards any living creature, he can find no peace. Therefore, my devotee should propitiate me by loving all beings and by being kind and charitable. Knowing that I am the inner controller dwelling in the bodies of all beings, my devotee should bow to all with great and genuine respect.

I have described to you both the yoga of meditation and the yoga of devotion. By following either of these a man attains the supreme being, who manifests as prakṛti (nature) and puruṣa (Lord) and is yet beyond them, who is providence and also the universal time-spirit, for fear of whom the cosmic elements perform their allotted functions.

Lord Kapila continued: Kāla (or the time-spirit) is death to the ignorant individual who is tossed about in the stream of birth and death. But his whole being is so dull that he does not know of this tragedy, and (even if he does) how to get out of it. Yet, if he is alert he will discover the truth. For whatever the individual acquired after a lot of pain and struggle in order that he might be happy, is destroyed by the time-spirit, and the foolish man grieves. Alas, on account of delusion, he regards as permanent the impermanent body and the things related to that body (house, property and wealth).

The foolish jīva, ignorant of its real nature as the unconditioned self, loves every embodiment (human or subhuman) and is reluctant to part with this perishable body. Strange is the Lord's māyā that even though the individual is subjected to almost constant and interminable suffering here, he still clings to the embodied existence, trying to find petty and fleeting pleasures here. He counts wife, children, house, cattle, wealth and relations as blessings, so perverted has his intelligence become. He is terribly attached to the family life, though he sees that it is full of misery; and if through righteous or pious activity he is able to postpone the evil even a little, he considers himself fortunate and blessed.

Through wealth earned by fair means and foul he pleases his family, but when he loses this wealth that very family treats him with contempt. Yet, the old man clings to it, awaiting his death. As the agony of death grips him he becomes unconscious. The terrible messengers of death invest him with a subtle body and escort him to hell to undergo various tortures there. In hell he suffers the penalty for all his unrighteous actions done during his life on earth. O mother, it is the opinion of some sages that heaven and hell are here on earth itself, for one sees here on earth all manner of terrible sufferings to which its inhabitants are subject.

The body, the family that is related to that body and the wealth earned in order to support that body and family are all left behind. The jīva takes only the bundle of sins that he has earned here with that body on account of that family and that wealth. Having been subjected to terrible tortures in hell for the expiation of the sins, and having passed through the subhuman births in order to purify oneself—the jīva after a long time becomes a human being again on this earth.

Lord Kapila continued: The soul destined to be reborn as a human being enters the womb through the semen of a man. In one night the sperm is united with the ovum. In five days it grows into a little bubble. In ten days it grows to the size of a plum. In a month the head is formed, and in two months hands, feet and other limbs appear. In three months the other parts of the body are formed. In four months the essential ingredients of the body (such as blood and flesh) are formed. During the sixth month the foetus begins to move. It is nourished by the food and drink of the mother. In the seventh month it is endowed with consciousness. By the grace of the Lord it remembers its past births and prays to the Lord:

"I take refuge in the Lord who has placed me here in accordance with my own karma. I bow to him who is beyond delusion and who appears in my own heart as unconditioned consciousness. In that consciousness I realise that though I am bodiless, birthless and deathless, I appear clothed with a body etc., on account of ignorance. It is through his grace that I recall my own past and the present predicament. It is through your grace, O Lord, that I am able to extol your glories in this manner. Though life in the womb is full of troubles, I dread the prospect of being born in the world; for then one is immediately enveloped by māyā and, forgetting the true self, falls prey to the false notion of the ego. I shall, therefore, enthrone the lotus feet of lord Viṣṇu in my heart, and, preventing all distractions of the mind, I shall quickly redeem myself from ignorance, so that this great sorrow of birth may not be my lot again."

At the appointed time, the baby is delivered into this world. The agony of birth deprives him of the memory of the past and even of his resolve. Reduced to the pathetic plight of a large worm and wallowing in the filth, the baby cries aloud. He grows, fed by people but unable to communicate with them, harassed by insects and crying almost incessantly. He grows up into youth experiencing its diversions and frustrations. He falls an easy prey to the Lord's māyā in the form of woman. (He or she who aspires for self-realisation should avoid the company of the opposite sex as he would avoid the gate of hell.)

Thus, the soul revolves on the wheel of birth and death, reaping the fruits of its actions. The coming together of the subtle body and the physical body is regarded as birth and when they cease to function as one organism, it is regarded as death. A wise man does not view death with horror nor does he cling to life. He moves about in this world free from attachment, regarding the physical body as a part of this world.

Book Three Chapter 32

Lord Kapila continued: I shall now describe to you, mother, the different paths that individuals take on leaving this world. One who is full of selfish desires worships the different deities. Devoted to them and devoted to his ancestors, he takes the lunar path and returns to the earth-plane. They who perform their duties unselfishly and unattached to them and offer them to me, and who are therefore peaceful and pure at heart, they who tread the path of renunciation, egoless and free from the sense of possession and whose minds are purified by the fulfilment of their duty, reach the omnipresent Lord through the luminous solar path. There are yet others who meditate on the manifest deity, considering him to be non-different from the supreme. When the creator Brahmā enters the Lord at the end of the world-cycle, these yogī who have controlled their breath and their minds, who are not completely free of the ego yet have identified themselves with the manifest deity, merge in the supreme Lord, along with Brahmā. They who have even the least trace of a sense of doership are reborn at the beginning of the next world-cycle (or creation) as sages, yogī and perfect ones, and are the first teachers of yoga.

Therefore, O mother, worship the Lord with all your being. It is only when the entire being is devoted to the Lord that dispassion for worldly and heavenly pleasures—and the spiritual wisdom that enables one to see unreality as unreal and thence to realise the truth—arise in one's heart. When the devotee, though living in this world with his senses responding to the stimuli of their objects, ceases to be attracted to or repelled by these objects, he is freed from bondage. He realises that it is the Lord alone who appears in the diverse forms of the seer, the sight and the seen. Brahman is infinite and Brahman himself appears as the diverse objects of the universe, because of the outgoing tendency of the mind and the senses. Only he experiences unity who is devoted to the Lord and diligent in his daily practice of yoga.

I have thus expounded the wisdom of the absolute and the paths that lead to truth. The Lord is one and he alone is attained through the different paths. He who listens to this even once with his mind fixed on me will surely attain to my state. This wisdom should be imparted only to a devotee, a meek and humble spiritual aspirant, not to the arrogant, selfish and wicked man who is thirsting for sensual pleasures.

Book Three Chapter 33

Maitreya continued: Devahūti was enlightened by the Lord's discourse. She bowed to him with a heartfelt prayer of thanksgiving. She said: "Even the creator Brahmā perceived you only with his mental eyes. You are beyond all action; yet your powers are inconceivable. You are the Lord of the universe; and you yourself appear to perform the functions of creation, preservation and dissolution through the qualities of your nature. Into you the universe returns at the end of the world-cycle. Yet, how is it that you condescended to be born of my womb? Nay, you assume a personality for the protection of righteousness and for the removal of unrighteousness. Such is your glory, O Lord, that by occasionally hearing or repeating your name even men of low upbringing (those who eat the flesh of dogs) gain the venerable status of brāhmaṇā. He who sees you is no doubt instantly liberated from this mundane life. Though you have appeared as my son Kapila, you are indeed the supreme being."

Kapila once again assured his mother Devahūti that by following his instructions she would attain the state of liberation; and then taking leave of her, Kapila went away in the north-easterly direction and entered the ocean, where he resides even now in all his divine radiance.

Devahūti applied herself to the practice of yoga with all her being. She renounced the celestial house in which she had spent the best years of her life with her lord Kardama—the house which was furnished with beds of ivory with mattresses soft and white as foam of milk; whose walls were made of transparent crystal, illumined by jewelled lamps borne by statues of women; and which was surrounded by gardens of incomparable beauty. She practised meditation as instructed by her son. She meditated upon the omnipresent being as her very self, through the uninterrupted flow of devotion, dispassion and the wisdom born of the due performance of yoga, which gives rise to self-knowledge. Her mind was established in Brahman, the Lord, and she was freed from the false notion of individuality and therefore from sorrow. She rose above body-consciousness. Her body had been transmuted by (or into) austerity and yoga, and was protected by the Lord. She did not even notice that her hair was dishevelled and that her garments had fallen away.

Her consciousness had entered into lord Vāsudeva. The sacred place where she attained final liberation is known as Siddha-pada. As the mortal coil fell it was transformed into a river.

Such is the glorious story of Kapila, which confers love of God on its listener.

Book Four

Book Four Chapter 1

Lord Maitreya said: I have told you, O Vidura, the story of one of manu's daughters, (Devahūti). Of his two other daughters (Akūti and Prasūti) he gave Akūti to Ruci. They propitiated the Lord with supreme concentration of mind, with the result that lord Viṣṇu himself was born as their son, along with his consort Lakṣmī. In that incarnation Viṣṇu was known as Yajña (the spirit of sacrifice), and Lakṣmī as Dakṣiṇā (the gift). In course of time Yajña married Dakṣiṇā and begot twelve sons: Toṣa, Pratoṣa, Santoṣa, Bhadra, Sānti, Iḍaspati, Idhma, Kavi, Vibhu, Svahna, Sudeva and Rocana (representing the fruits of sacrifices or of worship if duly performed with appropriate gifts). They were collectively known as tuṣitāḥ.

Of Devahūti's nine daughters, Kalā bore Kaśyapa and Pūrṇimā. Pūrṇimā gave birth to Viraja, Viśvaga and Devakulyā, the last of whom later became Gaṅgā. The sage Atri who had married Devahūti's daughter Anasūyā, engaged himself in intense penance, standing on one foot for a hundred years praying that he might be blessed with offspring resembling the Lord himself! Pleased with his penance, the trinity (creator, preserver and redeemer) appeared before him and said to him: "O sage, as you willed it, precisely so shall it be, not otherwise. We are that which you have meditated upon. And, part of us shall be born as your sons, enhancing your glory and establishing theirs." The ray of the creator Brahmā was born as the moon-god, that of the preserver, Viṣṇu, as Dattātreya, and that of the redeemer, Śiva, as sage Durvāsā.

The sage Aṅgirā and Śraddhā had four daughters and two sons, Utathya and Bṛhaspati. The sage Pulastya and Havirbhū had the sage Agastya and the great ascetic Viśravā (who begot Kubera the god of wealth, and, by another wife, Rāvaṇa, Kuṁbhakarṇa and Vibhīṣaṇa). Pulaha and Gati had Karmaśreṣṭha, Varīyān and Sahiṣṇu. Kratu and Kriyā had sixty thousand sages known as Vālakhilyā. Vasiṣṭha and Ūrjā had seven sons (Citraketu, Suroci, Virajā, Mitra, Ulbana, Vasubhṛdyāna and Dyumān). Atharva and Śānti had Dadīci. Bhṛgu and Khyāti had two sons Dhātā and Vidhātā, and a daughter Śrī, and also Kavi. He who listens to this recitation of Kardama's progeny is freed from sins.

Manu's daughter, Prasūti, was given to Dakṣa, who begot sixteen daughters. To Dharma, Dakṣa gave thirteen of his daughters viz., Śraddhā, Maitrī, Dayā, Śānti, Tuṣṭi, Puṣṭi, Kriyā, Unnati, Buddhi, Medhā, Titikṣā, Hrī and Mūrti, who in turn bore Śubha, Prasāda, Abhaya, Sukha, Mud, Smaya, Yoga, Darpa, Artha, Smṛti, Kṣema, Praśraya, and the sages Nara-Nārāyaṇa, who later were born as Arjuna and Kṛṣṇa. Dakṣa's other daughter Svāhā was given to the fire god Agni. Another daughter was given to the manes. Dakṣa's last daughter Satī was given to lord Śiva, but died while she was still young.

Dakṣa and Śiva
Book Four Chapter 2

Sage Maitreya continued, in answer to Vidura's query concerning the untimely end of Satī's life: Once, the sages and the gods attended a grand religious rite performed by the prajāpatī, the lords of creation. Dakṣa, one of the prajāpatī, entered the assembly. At his entry all those assembled stood up in recognitioin of his prowess, except his own father Brahmā and lord Śiva. Dakṣa was enraged at the latter's disrespectful behaviour. He thundered: "Listen, O sages and gods, to what I say neither out of ignorance nor out of spite, but in order to set forth right conduct. This haughty and impure person, who appears like a mad man and is besmeared with the ashes of the dead, who associates with goblins and behaves like one, is my own son-in-law and so is almost a son to me. Alas, it was a terrible blunder to let him marry my noble daughter, at the instance of my father. Today he has insulted us all by flagrantly violating the principles of right conduct and not showing the respect due to me. Hence, I declare that he, Śiva, shall no longer get a share in offerings to the gods in religious rites." Having said this, in spite of the remonstrance of some sages, he walked out.

Nandī, the foremost among the devotees of lord Śiva, put a terrible curse on Dakṣa and the brāhmaṇā who were guilty of acquiescence in Dakṣa's insulting behaviour towards Śiva: "This fool who mistakes his body for the self and is therefore attracted to sensual pleasure and pompous and showy rituals, is no better than an animal; hence his face shall be turned away from truth and his head shall be that of a goat. He and those who follow him shall be born again and again in this world. These brāhmaṇā who revel in learning and in the performance of rituals for their livelihood, who eat what they like, who live with their faith pinned on the flowery utterances of the vedā and hate lord Śiva, shall wander in this world as beggars."

Hearing Nandī's curse upon the entire community of brāhmaṇā, the sage Bhṛgu uttered a counter-curse: "The followers of lord Śiva shall be regarded as heretics, for they have chosen the path of impiety, denounced the authority of the vedā and the brāhmaṇā, and they wear matted locks and smear themselves with ashes and indulge in intoxicating drinks. The vedā lay down the path approved of by lord Viṣṇu himself. Since you denounce the vedā, you are all to be regarded as heretics."

Hearing this curse, lord Śiva walked out of the assembly hall with his formidable retinue.

The prājapatī carried on the ritual for a thousand years, and returned to their homes after the ceremonial bath.

Book Four Chapter 3

Lord Maitreya continued: A long time passed. Dakṣa had been elevated to the office of the doyen to the prajāpatī, or lords of beings. He grew more vain. He had successfully completed the Vājapeya rite, and he had commenced the even grander Bṛhaspati Sava rite.

From the abode of lord Śiva, Satī (Śiva's wife and Dakṣa's daughter) saw sages, seers and gods flying in their aerial vehicles to attend Dakṣa's rite. Overwhelmed by an intense desire to participate in the ceremony which would be attended by all her sisters and their spouses, Satī approached lord Śiva for permission to go, pleading that it is right to go to the house of the husband, preceptor, parents and other relatives uninvited. "The whole creation is within you, O Lord," Satī said, "yet my feminine nature asserts itself and I wish to see my sisters and mother. I do not wish to be left out of this spectacular rite. I wish to go there, along with you."

Lord Śiva smiled at Satī's demonstration of ignorance and replied: "It is indeed true that one does not need an invitation to visit one's parents, etc. But, that applies only when there is no malice in the latter's hearts. Knowledge, penance, wealth, physical appearance, age and ancestry enhance the nobility of the noble, but aggravate the wickedness of the wicked. Hence it is unwise to resort to the company of the wicked even if they appear to possess these virtues, and even if they are one's own relations. To be insulted by one's relations is worse than suffering an injury at the hands of an enemy. The latter heals; the former does not. If you go, your father will ignore you because you are my wife, despite the fact that you were his favourite daughter. He who is attached to his body, regarding it as his true self, hates exalted souls and does not want to understand them. He fails to see that these exalted souls, who do not so identify their body with the self, respect everybody by bowing to all with their whole inner being, and not just with their bodies, knowing that the Lord dwells in the hearts of all. The pure mind is itself Vāsudeva. In it the pristine glory of the Lord is revealed. I adore the Lord always in the purity of my mind. What have you to do with one who insulted me, though I had not wronged him? If you go, disregarding my advice, you will suffer. For to suffer indignity at the hands of one's beloved relations and friends is itself death."

Book Four Chapter 4

Lord Maitreya continued: Satī was annoyed with lord Śiva. Thwarted desire manifested as grief and anger which clouded her wisdom. She left for her parents' home accompanied by Nandī and other attendants of Śiva. When she entered the hall where Dakṣa was performing the religious rite, none of the sages or gods greeted her, for fear of incurring the wrath of Dakṣa: only the womenfolk welcomed her. She saw that lord Śiva had not been allotted a share of the ritual offerings. On account of pride in his status and learning, Dakṣa had blasphemously ignored lord Śiva. Satī angrily denounced Dakṣa.

Satī said: People like you, O brāhmaṇā, only see faults in the virtues of others. There are others who do not. The greatest of the noble ones, however, greatly magnify even small virtues in other people. Alas, you hate lord Śiva of immeasurable power and glory. Yet, the mere utterance of the two syllables of his name destroys sin. You called him inauspicious! How utterly senseless is such an accusation! Do not even gods like Brahmā adore his feet? Would they do so if he were inauspicious? I must not be here. For, one should cut off (if one can) that vile tongue of unrighteous men who insult the Lord, and then give up one's own life; if one is powerless to do so, one should close one's ears and leave that place. This is proper conduct.

I do not condemn your religious ceremony: for there are those who adhere to the injunctions of the vedā and there are sages for whom they are of less importance than self-realisation. The two paths are different. One should adhere to one's own dharma, but not go out of one's way to decry another's. Lord Śiva, being identical with the supreme being, is beyond all duties. You have behaved unbecomingly towards him. I shall not retain the body that was born of you.

Having said this, Satī sat down and decided to leave the body in a yogic way. She united the prāṇa and the apāna in the solar plexus. With the help of the udāna she raised this force to the region of the heart, where she united it with the mind-stuff of consciousness. After passing through the throat centre, she raised it to the eye-brow centre. She contemplated the lotus feet of the Lord, and the fire of yoga consumed her body.

The celestials denounced Dakṣa. Lord Śiva's attendants who were witnesses to this rose to kill Dakṣa. The sage Bhṛgu saved the situation by quickly performing a magic rite, as a result of which thousands of beings emerged from the ritual fire to defend it. These beings (known as ṛbhū) drove away the attendants of Śiva.

Book Four Chapter 5

Sage Maitreya continued: Sage Nārada informed lord Śiva of these happenings—how Satī had burnt herself by the fire of yoga and how his attendants had been routed by the ṛbhū invoked from the holy fires by sage Bhṛgu. In great rage lord Śiva tore a matted lock from his head and dashed it on the rock in front of him. The lock instantly turned into a mighty being, Vīrabhadra, with a thousand arms, three eyes and fearsome teeth.

Vīrabhadra bowed to lord Śiva and prayed for instructions. Lord Śiva commanded him: "You are a manifestation of a ray of myself; go forth and destroy Dakṣa and his rite." Vīrabhadra again bowed to the Lord and proceeded towards Dakṣa's abode, followed by the hosts of lord Śiva's attendants.

In Dakṣa's abode there was great commotion. Everyone noticed clouds of dust raised in the north. Everyone had a dreadful foreboding of evil. Dakṣa's wife and the other women felt that it was retribution for Dakṣa's wicked action which resulted in Satī's self-immolation.

Even as they were brooding thus, lord Śiva's attendants swarmed into the hall where the rite was being performed and began systematically to destroy everything connected with it. Maṇimān, one of the attendants of lord Śiva, bound sage Bhṛgu; Vīrabhadra similarly bound Dakṣa; Caṇḍīśa dealt with the god Pūṣa and Nandī caught hold of Bhaga. The others ran in all directions.

Vīrabhadra forcibly pulled out the moustache and beard of sage Bhṛgu, for the latter had offered oblations into the fire holding the ladle in one hand and proudly twirling his moustache with the other. He knocked down Bhaga and pulled his eyes out: Bhaga had mischievously winked when Dakṣa was insulting the Lord. He then knocked out the teeth of Pūṣa who had laughed arrogantly when Dakṣa was uttering curses against the lord. Then he proceeded to behead Dakṣa, but he could not. However, when he offered Dakṣa's life as a sacrifice unto the Lord in the manner in which the animal is offered in sacrifice, Dakṣa's head fell off. Vīrabhadra and the Lord's attendants then returned to Kailāsa. All the evil ones had been punished in the appropriate manner.

Book Four Chapter 6

Lord Maitreya continued: The defeated sages and gods waited on the creator Brahmā and told him all that had happened. Brahmā replied: "Go at once to holy Kailāsa and take shelter at the lotus feet of lord Śiva, whom Dakṣa and all of you have offended by denying him a share in the ritual offerings. There is no other way. Neither I, nor lord Yajña (Viṣṇu), nor the sages and gods know his nature and power, nor can we placate one (Śiva) who is independent."

Accompanied by all the gods and the sages, Brahmā went to mount Kailāsa, lord Śiva's domain. In Kailāsa dwell divine beings endowed at birth with supernatural powers, as well as those who have acquired such powers by other means—like drugs, penance, mantra or the practice of yoga. The mountain peaks dazzle with precious stones and minerals. The mountain slopes are lush with the best among tropical and sub-tropical trees. They echo and re-echo with the sounds of different birds and peacocks. They abound in deer, tigers, lions and other wild animals. There the celestial city of Alakā is girded by the rivers Nandā and Alakanandā. The city is inhabited by noble men and is crowded with aerial vehicles made of precious metals and studded with jewels.

The gods and Brahmā gazed admiringly for a while at this enchanting scene. They saw a huge banyan tree at a distance. Under it lord Śiva was seated, completely tranquil and spiritually radiant. He who is the friend of all beings is constantly engaged in penance and the practice of yoga for the welfare and prosperity of all beings. He was attended upon by great sages and yogī and he was instructing sage Nārada, who was eagerly listening. With their palms joined in humble salutation, the gods and Brahmā bowed to lord Śiva, who was in the highest state of superconsciousness. Lord Śiva quickly got up to greet Brahmā and the brāhmaṇā sages: such indeed is the glory of the truly great, that they are truly humble.

Brahmā said to lord Śiva: O Lord, I know that you are one with the supreme being though you playfully carry on the work of creating, sustaining and dissolving the universe through your dual aspect as Śiva and Śakti. It is you who established the institution of the ritual and you have fixed the rules of the rite. You confer beatitude on the good and mete out just punishment to the wicked. I know, O Lord, that anger does not approach even they who are devoted to you, for you are beyond the reach of lord Viṣṇu's māyā which deluded Dakṣa and the others. They were helpless against it, and deserve your compassion. Pray, let them all be revived and resume their original forms. And, let the religious rite commenced by them come to a successful conclusion. The sages, for their part, will ensure that you are allotted your due share of the offerings.

Book Four Chapter 7

Lord Śiva said: No one offends me. Those who are deluded by the Lord's māyā come under the rod of corrective punishment. Let Dakṣa, whose head has been burnt in the ritual fire, be given the head of a goat. Sage Bhṛgu shall have the beard and the moustache of a goat, too. Bhaga can look through the eyes of Mitra; and Pūṣa can eat through the mouth of the one who performs the rite. The other gods shall also be revived, now that they have duly allotted me my share of the offerings.

Sage Maitreya continued: The sages and the gods busied themselves to carry out lord Śiva's instructions. When they joined the goat's head to Dakṣa's body, he was revived. With a voice choked with emotion he saluted the Lord and said: "By thus punishing me, you have done me a great favour, O Lord. You have created the brāhmaṇā out of your own mouth. You protect them in your own mysterious way even if it appears to be painful." With Brahmā's permission the ritual was recommenced. For the purification of the place they propitiated lord Viṣṇu. When they contemplated him, O Vidura, he manifested himself in their midst in his supremely radiant form. They rose and, standing with their palms joined in devout salutation, they adored him in appropriate language. Dakṣa extolled him as both the transcendental being and the immanent jīva, beyond māyā and at the same time appearing to be subject to māyā. The chief priests confessed to him that they only knew him as Yajña, the sacred rite, and so resorted to the ritual. The other priests confessed that they were all clinging to the wheel of transmigration and to the ephemeral pleasures of life, instead of taking refuge in the Lord's feet. Brahmā said: "You are the very ground of knowledge, not that which the jīva perceives through his mind and senses." The siddhā rejoiced that since they were immersed in the nectar of the Lord's stories and glories they were not affected by pain or pleasure. The masters of yoga declared that he who was established in non-duality was dearest to the Lord. The brāhmaṇā affirmed that the Lord himself is the rite, the performer, all the instruments used and the Lord of the rite. The others present glorified him in appropriate terms.

Lord Viṣṇu said: I am the creator Brahmā and the redeemer Śiva. I am the cause of the universe. I am the self, Lord and supervisor of all, self-effulgent and unqualified. Entering into my own māyā I create, protect and dissolve the universe. The ignorant man sees diversity in that non-dual Brahman, the ever-free supreme self. He, however, who does not see such diversity attains everlasting peace.

Thus blessed by the Lord, Dakṣa worshipped him and concluded the rite. Satī was reborn as the daughter of Himavān and Mena, and was reunited with her Lord.

He who listens to this story attains renown and longevity and is freed from sins.

Dhruva
Book Four Chapter 8

Lord Maitreya continued: Priyavrata and Uttānapāda—the two sons of Svayaṁbhu manu—ruled the world righteously. Uttānapāda had two wives, Sunīti and Suruci. Suruci, the younger, was dearer to her husband than the elder wife, Sunīti.

One day when the king Uttānapāda was seated on the throne with Suruci's son Uttama on his lap, Dhruva (born of the first wife

Sunīti) approached the king, eager to have his share of paternal love. Suruci intervened and rebuked the boy harshly: "Though the king is your father you were not born of me, and therefore you shall not aspire for the throne. Pray to the Lord that you may be reborn of me if you wish to ascend the throne."

Weeping, Dhruva sought his mother's company and consolation. Sunīti consoled him: "Do not entertain uncharitable thoughts towards others; for man reaps what he has sown; the pain he has inflicted on others returns to him in due course. Retaliation perpetuates the vicious circle of cause and effect: whole-hearted worship of the Lord wipes out sorrow from your heart in an instant. It was by such adoration of the Lord that your great-grandfather Brahmā became the creator and your grandfather manu enjoyed supreme bliss."

Strengthened by his mother's words of wisdom, Dhruva left the place and proceeded towards the forest. The sage Nārada met him on the way, and in order to assess the depth of sincerity and strength of will that the boy-devotee possessed, he explained to Dhruva the difficulties that beset the latter's path: "Even sages fail in their attempt to obtain his vision," he said. Dhruva politely informed the sage that his warning, though well-meant, made no impression on his young heart and that he was determined to go ahead.

Pleased with the young boy's firmness, the sage showered his blessings on Dhruva. He said: "Go and find a secluded place on the bank of the holy river Yamunā. Bathe in the river thrice daily, and, having seated yourself firmly and purified your senses and mind by the practice of prāṇāyāma, meditate on the ever-blissful form of the Lord who is the abode of virtue, auspiciousness and beauty. I shall now instruct you in the most secret of all sacred formulae—Om namo bhagavate vāsudevāya—which, if repeated for seven nights, enables one to see the celestials moving about in the sky. Worship an image of the Lord made of stone or other substance, by using this very mantra. Thus adored, the Lord will confer upon you the desired boon."

Nārada then went to king Uttānapāda who was grief-stricken at the way in which his second wife had treated his first-born son. He assured the king of Dhruva's safety and future glory.

Dhruva engaged himself in unprecedented penance. Constantly meditating upon the Lord, for a month he lived on fruits eaten every third day, the next month on withered grass every sixth day, and the third month taking water every ninth day. The fourth month he was inhaling air every twelfth day, and by the fifth month he abandoned even this, his whole being completely absorbed in the Lord, whom he saw as his very self. As he thus held his breath, the gods were agitated for they could not breathe! They prayed to the Lord to protect them.

Book Four Chapter 9

Sage Maitreya continued: The Lord, upon whom the young Dhruva had meditated in the lotus of his heart, stood in front of him. When the inner vision was withdrawn Dhruva opened his eyes and beheld him. He wanted to sing his praises, but lacked the talent and the diction. The Lord mercifully touched Dhruva's cheek with his conch, and Dhurva burst forth in an ecstatic hymn: "Salutations to the omnipotent Lord, who from within me enlivens my power of speech, my hands, my feet, my hearing, the sense of touch and the rest. Lord, I know only your grossest form, which is the world of matter with its animate and inanimate inhabitants, but not your transcendental aspect which is beyond description. You are the source of all faculties, even the apparently contradictory ones. You are the all. I take refuge in you."

The Lord blessed him: "You will occupy a position never before occupied by anyone, which will shine even when the worlds are destroyed at the end of the day of Brahmā, and which serves as the pivot around which the entire stellar sphere revolves. Here on earth you will reign as king for a very long time." And the Lord withdrew his manifestation.

Dhruva was overjoyed at having had the Lord's blessings in person, but was stricken with remorse at not having obtained the greatest boon of final liberation from him. He repented of the jealousy aroused in his heart at seeing his half-brother on the throne, which betrayed ignorance of the truth that all beings were his own self. Reflecting thus, Dhruva returned to the palace.

When the king heard from sage Nārada that Dhurva was returning home, he was thrilled. It was as if Dhruva had returned from the abode of death. Surrounded by brāhmaṇā and elders, ministers and friends, he went forth in a golden chariot to welcome Dhruva. Both the mothers and Uttama, Dhruva's half-brother, also went. When the king met Dhruva just near the garden, he jumped out of his chariot and embraced the boy with tears of joy. Dhruva bowed to his mothers. Suruci was filled with happiness: surely, the whole world loves one who has received God's blessings and who is friendly to all. Sunīti, Dhruva's mother, bathed him in her tears of joy. The people of the kingdom congratulated the king on thus regaining the beloved prince who had been lost for many months.

The royal procession wended its way through the city, which wore a festive appearance. In course of time the king installed Dhruva on the throne, as he found that the ministers and the people loved him. The king retired to the forest, intent on spending the rest of his life in contemplation of the Lord.

Book Four Chapter 10

Lord Maitreya continued: Dhruva (lit: the unmoving) married Bhramī (lit: the revolving, moving) and was blessed with two sons named Kalpa (lit: a world-cycle) and Vatsara (lit: year). He had another wife Ilā and through her a son Utkala and a daughter. Uttama, Dhruva's half-brother, died a bachelor and his mother, Suruci, died heart-broken.

Uttama had been killed by a yakṣa during a hunting expedition in the Himālayā. Enraged by this, king Dhruva challenged the yakṣā to battle. He marched towards the capital of the yakṣā, named Alakā, and blew his conch as a sign of invitation to war.

Soon the yakṣā, who are demigods, rushed in great numbers towards the valiant king Dhruva. Dhruva, skilled in the art of warfare, hit each one on the forehead with three arrows (lit: 'bāṇa' could mean bomb or bullet). Thus surprised, the yakṣā applauded the enemy's skill and proceeded to rain upon him a volley of various warlike weapons, almost submerging the hero Dhruva. However, Dhruva emerged from this and with counter-missiles destroyed their missiles.

The battle grew fiercer. Dhruva's weapons rained death upon the enemy and the battlefield was strewn with the heads and headless trunks of countless yakṣā. Others had been maimed. However, the few surviving enemy warriors used their black arts. Knowing their prowess in black magic, Dhruva did not enter their capital city.

Simultaneously, from different directions there appeared clouds, thunder and lightning. And, the clouds rained filth. This was followed by the appearance of a magic mountain and a mysterious shower of all kinds of weapons, as if from nowhere. Though the oceans were far away, the conjurers were able to 'create' oceans on the battlefield, which made it look as though the oceans would deluge the entire world.

Seeing the noble Dhruva in such an impossible situation, the sages prayed: "O Dhruva, may the Lord who wields the Sārṇga bow and who destroys the sorrow of the afflicted, destroy your enemies. By uttering or hearing his name people easily overcome even death, which is so difficult to conquer."

Book Four Chapter 11

Lord Maitreya continued: The sages' prayer reminded Dhruva of the most terrible missile invented by Nārāyaṇa himself. As he seized it, the hallucinations generated by the conjurers vanished, even as ignorance and its offspring vanish at the dawn of wisdom. From this most powerful missile golden and white-hot tongues of flame flew towards the enemy with terrifying noise. Mad with rage, the enemy rushed towards Dhruva, only to be cut down by him.

Svayaṁbhu manu, the great-grandfather of Dhruva, felt that it was time to intervene and so arrived upon the scene of battle.

Svayaṁbhu Manu said to Dhruva: Enough of this unbecoming rage, my child. It is the gateway to hell. You are killing these innocent beings because you think that one of the members of this community was responsible for your brother's death. Killing is not righteous, inasmuch as it is based upon the erroneous idea that the body is the self. When your brother's body died, he did not die. Nor are you killing these yakṣā when you slay their bodies. All this is a product of ignorance.

You propitiated the Lord even when you were very young and by his grace you have attained a status of unparalleled eminence in the universe. You are in a position to instruct others on righteous conduct, yet you are yourself indulging in sinful conduct. The Lord is pleased when you acquire forgiveness, compassion, friendliness and equal vision towards all beings. Then there is freedom from limitation (jīva) and union with the absolute. These followers of Kubera, the god of wealth, were not the slayers of your brother: it is the will of God that is responsible for the birth and death of a person. He creates the universe, and he protects and ultimately destroys it. Yet, because he is not egotistic about it, he is not tainted by the activities of the qualities of nature. The Lord's energy has the power to create, preserve and to destroy. Moved by this energy, male and female unite to reproduce their likeness. Moved by this energy, the individual body is destroyed through the agency of some other being: and the destroyer is destroyed by death.

Therefore, dear child, give up the idea of 'I' and 'mine' and adore the Lord with all your heart. A wise man who seeks to become fearless should not come under the influence of anger, which makes people fear and avoid him. You have committed a great offence against lord Śiva himself, for Kubera is his friend and you have killed his followers. Therefore, adore him with all your heart.

Book Four Chapter 12

Lord Maitreya continued: The lord of wealth, Kubera, was pleased to learn that Dhruva's anger had subsided. He went to Dhruva, blessed him, and consoled him with the words: "The yakṣā did not kill your brother nor did you kill them in retaliation. Death (the spirit of time) puts an end to their embodiment. None can escape death; the circumstance is an excuse. Birth and death are as unreal as the events of a dream. It is ignorant feelings of 'I' and 'mine' towards the perishable body and its relations that give rise to a sense of bondage and the consequent suffering. Give up these feelings and adore the Lord. In the meantime, ask of me any boon you wish." The noble Dhruva prayed for the only boon worth asking for: "May my heart be ever devoted to lord Vāsudeva." Kubera granted it.

Dhruva ruled the country for a long time, with his heart constantly devoted to the Lord. Totally devoid of ego-sense, he exhausted his karma (past merit) by enjoyments and past demerit by self-restraint. In due course he installed his son Utkala on the throne and left for Viśāla to devote himself exclusively to the Lord.

There Dhruva engaged himself in the practice of yoga. Firmly seated in the yoga posture he practised prāṇāyāma, followed by pratyāhāra or withdrawal of the senses. Then he meditated upon the gross form of the Lord till the distinction between the meditator and the object of meditation was lost in samādhi. He became aware of a space vehicle approaching him. From it stepped two divinities, resplendent and richly adorned. Dhruva bowed to them. They said: "We are the attendants of lord Vāsudeva upon whom you are meditating and whom you have propitiated. Come, ascend this space vehicle and we shall transport you to the celestial pole where you shall reside, receiving the homage of the entire universe which will revolve around you." As he was about to ascend the vehicle he thought of his mother, Sunīti, but the Lord's attendants revealed to him that she was in another vehicle, going ahead of him. Dhruva placed his foot on the head of Death and ascended into space. He flew on, past the planets and the stars to the abode of Viṣṇu, which is inaccessible to those without compassion for all beings but which is accessible to those who constantly do good to others. They who are tranquil, who look upon all with equal vision, pure at heart, devoted to the welfare of all beings and who befriend the Lord's devotees, reach his realm.

Nārada sang the glory of Dhruva. This auspicious story of Dhruva confers on one who recites it or hears it, all auspiciousness, wealth, fame and longevity, and most important of all, devotion to the Lord which uproots and destroys the tree of sorrow.

Book Four Chapter 13

Lord Maitreya continued: Utkala, Dhruva's son, was also endowed with discrimination and dispassion from his very birth. He had attained self-knowledge. His unconventional behaviour gave others the impression that he was mad, deaf, dumb and blind. Hence, the elders in the royal court enthroned his younger brother Vatsara as king.

Vatsara (year) married Svarvīthi (milky way): and they had six sons— Puṣparṇa, Tigmaketu, Īśa, Ūrja, Vasu and Jaya. Puṣparṇa married Prabhā (daylight) and Doṣa (night). Prabhā gave birth to Prātaḥ (morning), Madhyandina (noon) and Sāyaṁ (evening). Doṣa gave birth to Pradoṣa (nightfall), Niśītha (midnight) and Vyuṣṭa (dawn). In this line of succession was born the king Aṅga.

Aṅga was pious and noble. Once he performed the royal rite known as aśvamedha. Although all the rules regulating this rite had been scrupulously observed, the gods did not arrive to receive the offerings. The officiating sages divined the reason, which was that Aṅga, as a result of a sin committed in a previous birth, had no son. They, therefore, advised him to perform another rite, as a result of which he was blessed with a son.

This boy, Vena, however, proved to be anything but a blessing. He was a devotee of Mṛtyu (death) and therefore of adharma or unrighteousness. He was aggressive, destructive and vicious. People were literally frightened of him. He would strangle any animal or child who dared to go near him. His father, Aṅga, did his best to restrain him and to lead him along the path of righteousness. All his efforts failed miserably.

In the end he gave up the whole thing as hopeless. He even regretted having prayed for a son. "Blessed indeed are they that do not have children, for they do not have to endure the pain caused by a wicked son's misdemeanour," he thought. Again, he reflected over it and came to the conclusion: "It is perhaps better to have a wicked son than to have a good son. For, a good son causes one to cling to him and through him to the world! A wicked son at least creates disgust in the heart of the father!" And he concluded: "A wise man will not value that bondage known as a son who involves his parents in sin, hostility and disgrace." Suddenly he left the palace for an unknown destination.

The people and the authorities were distressed when they found out that their king had left the kingdom. They searched for him everywhere but could not find him. Thereupon they informed the elders that the whereabouts of the king were unknown.

Vena
Book Four Chapter 14

Lord Maitreya continued: The sages saw that the kingdom without a king was becoming a fertile ground for lawlessness and unrighteousness. With the consent of the queen, therefore, they crowned Vena king. Though this had the immediate effect of subduing the evil-doers who were terribly afraid of the cruel Vena, it placed on the throne a haughty dictator and totalitarian monarch. Soon Vena realised the dread in which people held him and the power he had over them and forbade all religious practices. The sages grieved at heart: with and without Vena, unrighteousness seemed to be inevitable. They decided to talk to him.

The Sages said: O king! Listen to our counsel which is conducive to your own good. When a man does his duty with his body, mind, speech and intelligence, he attains to the realms free from sorrow. Yours is the sacred duty of ensuring the peace, prosperity and security of your people. Pray, do not abandon it. The king in whose kingdom the people are devoted to religious activities enjoys the blessings of the Lord, and the people enjoy peace and prosperity. People worship the Lord and thus ensure your welfare; therefore, it is but proper that you should promote their welfare and thus win their affection. The Lord will be highly pleased with you and confer many boons upon you.

The wicked Vena replied: "O fools, why do you prattle of a Lord whom people are supposed to propitiate by ignorant religious practices, when you have before you one in whom all the gods dwell—your king, myself! Know that I am the only one fit to be worshipped by you."

That was indeed too much and Vena's wickedness had exceeded all bounds. He had already forfeited his right to live by his despotism, his cruelty and finally his hostility to the Lord himself. When the enraged sages uttered "Huṁ", Vena fell dead. The sages went away to sing the glories of the Lord who is their very life and soul. Vena's mother, however, preserved the body of her wicked son by a magical process of embalming.

Bereft of a king, the evils of anarchy prevailed once again in the kingdom. The sages who had been responsible for Vena's installation as king and later for his death, now took counsel among themselves. The welfare of the whole of mankind is their concern. If the brāhmaṇā and the sages ignored the afflictions of the people and remained unconcerned, they would lose their spiritual energy. Reflecting thus, they churned with great velocity the thigh of Vena's corpse and out of it issued a dark dwarf, who asked them: "What shall I do?" To which the brāhmaṇā replied: "Sit down". From this command, he came to be known as Niṣāda. He had inherited his 'father's' sinful nature, and his descendants became the niṣāda, the tribes who dwelt in dense forests.

Pṛthu
Book Four Chapter 15

Lord Maitreya continued: Once again the sages churned the corpse of Vena, but this time it was the arm. Great energy was released. It manifested as a divine couple in close embrace. The sages were happy, for they knew that the male was a part manifestation of the supreme being himself, incarnate to rule and to protect the world, and the female was a part manifestation of the goddess of beauty, bliss and prosperity, who is forever inseparable from her Lord and whose bounties only they who are devoted to him enjoy. The sages called the male Pṛthu and the female Arci. Pṛthu was in fact the first ruler of the world, in as much as it was he who established an empire, made the earth yield her treasures and enabled man to enjoy them in order and harmony.

The gods and the men rejoiced when Pṛthu was incarnated. They and the celestials sang, danced and paid him homage. Knowing that Pṛthu was part manifestation of the Lord himself, all the gods appeared before him and symbolically surrendered their insignia to him as a token of their recognition of his sovereignty. The brāhmaṇā (priests) officiated at the coronation ceremony. The deities presiding over the holy rivers themselves brought the holy water for the rite. King Pṛthu and queen Arci, seated on the throne, shone with divine radiance.

The god of wealth presented Pṛthu with a throne. Varuṇa, the god presiding over waters, presented an umbrella. The wind-god gave him fans. The god of virtue gave him a garland of fame. The ruler of gods gave him a crown. The deity presiding over mortality and morality gave him a sceptre. The creator gave him a coat-of-arms made of knowledge which is the best protective armour. Lord Viṣṇu presented him with a discus. Lakṣmī blessed him with inexhaustible prosperity. Rudra presented him with a sword and Durgā gave him a shield. The moon-god gave him horses. Tvaṣṭā gave him a chariot. The fire-god presented him with a bow and the sun-god gave him radiant arrows. The earth gave him wooden sandals. The celestial beings imparted the knowledge of fine arts to him. The sages gave him the blessing that his words would always come true. When the minstrels wanted to sing his praises the king tried to restrain them with the words: "Noble ones! It is not desirable that a mortal man should have his glories sung in his very presence, for he may still fall from glory and become an object of ridicule. You are free to sing the glory of God. Good people do not encourage self-glorification even if their conduct deserves it. And, as for us, we are yet unknown to the world and as yet there is no justification whatsoever for our praises to be sung."

Book Four Chapter 16

In spite of these remonstrances, the Minstrels sang: How can we describe your glory, O Lord? You have descended into this world clothed in your own illusory power called māyā. To all external appearances you have sprung from the arm of Vena. But in fact, you are lord Viṣṇu himself, temporarily bearing the name Pṛthu. We are singing your glory, not because it does you good, but because it is good for us—for we are eager to extol the Lord whose manifestation you are.

Lord you manifest in yourself the most exemplary qualities which a ruler should possess.

Our lord Pṛthu is the greatest among righteous men, who also inspires others to be righteous. Through him the gods that protect mankind carry on their appointed role. He levies reasonable and light taxes on the people, only to give this wealth back to them in their time of need. Our Lord is extremely forgiving and he protects even those who wrong him. At his command the clouds rain. He has immeasurable love for his people, who rejoice at the very sight of his radiant face. A glance or a smile from him removes all the anxieties of his people. No one can fatham his glories. He is perfectly contented and ever blissful.

He is like the sun that evaporates water on the earth and returns it as rain: he collects taxes and returns the wealth to the people. He is like the earth: his patience and forbearance are limitless. He is like the moon, gladdening the people's hearts. He is like the ocean, mysterious, unfathomable, inscrutable and all-containing.

Like the supreme being whose ray he is, he is easily accessible to all yet beyond any one's reach, and therefore cannot be influenced or corrupted. Like the indweller of all, he knows the ins and outs of all his people. His justice is unvarying and he knows neither fear nor favour. He punishes those who deserve to be punished, even if it be his own son, but not one innocent person is punished in his realm.

King Pṛthu is a true rājā (king) for he pleases (rājate) all. He does not swerve from his promise and adheres strictly to the path of truth. He is devoted to the welfare of all, particularly the aged and the poor. He is the supreme person, the Lord of the three worlds, the indwelling presence, who has incarnated by a ray of himself: he is the one infinite being in whom ignorant people perceive diversity.

Our Lord will conquer and rule the whole world. At his command the earth will yield her riches. He will crush mountains, level the ground, and make the earth a safe and comfortable habitation for his subjects. His might will know no opposition.

Book Four Chapter 17

Lord Maitreya continued: Those brāhmaṇā who had installed Pṛthu on the throne had become emaciated; and they submitted to the king that there was famine on the earth and they were all starving. The king reflected for a while and understood the cause, which was that the earth was not yielding its treasures.

The king took his weapons and marched out of his palace: he had to make the earth yield food. It was as if he would burn the whole earth with his anger. He was ready to blow up the earth (with explosives?) so that the earth would become fit for cultivation of foodgrains. In whichever direction he turned, he saw the earth (symbolically in the form of a cow); but she had hidden (in bushes and forests?) her own precious potentialities. His weapons followed her wherever she ran: he cut down trees and had the ground ploughed.

The earth pleaded: "You know what is right, O king. Protect me in order that your subjects may live. Do not destroy me. Deal gently with me, as you would deal with a lady. I have been created to support mankind; what will you gain by ruthlessly cutting me down and blasting me?"

The monarch, however, replied: "It is true that you are the support of mankind, O earth. But, ignoring my command, you refuse to yield the herbs and the foodgrains whose production was ordained by the creator. I shall break you with my bāṇa (bomb?) and thus bring you under the plough to appease the hunger of my people." The king also added: "It is not a sin for a king to kill the wicked man or woman who is heartless and is the cause of people's misery. On the contrary it is his duty." He was determined to crush the earth into tiny pieces the size of sesame seeds in order to make her yield food.

Terror-stricken, the earth glorified and prayed to king Pṛthu: "I salute the supreme being who, through his various potencies creates, sustains and dissolves the universe. I see before me the same creator who brought me into being by his own power, standing with uplifted weapons, intent on protecting the animate and inanimate beings that he has created. Lord, you once lifted me up from the cosmic waters. And, today you yourself stand upon me with uplifted weapons in order to protect your creatures. Hail, hail to you."

Book Four Chapter 18

Lord Maitreya continued: After thus extolling king Pṛthu, the earth felt that it was time to reveal her secret and also to surrender her wealth to him. She said: "Lord, it is verily by the use of proper and appropriate methods which have been discovered and established by sages that anything is gained. He who abides by the laws of the wise reaps a rich harvest. The foolish one who ignores these laws and resorts to selfish, egotistic and violent methods does not obtain the desired end. I noticed that your predecessors on the throne were not righteous; and so I withheld my riches lest the wicked ones wax stronger by consuming them. You can of course milk the riches in my depths in a wise manner."

Accepting this proposal, the king proceeded to 'milk' the earth, the milch-cow (giver of all one desires). Each class of beings placed the best of their own at the head to serve as the calf, 'milked' what they most needed from the earth, and gathered this wealth in a suitable vessel. With Svayaṁbhu manu as calf, the king himself drew from the earth all the annual plants and herbs. The sages, with their preceptor as the calf, drew sacred knowledge into the vessel of their senses of hearing, speech and mind. The gods, with Indra as calf, obtained the nectar called soma. The evil ones obtained wines and intoxicants. The celestial musicians got sweetness of song and beauty. The manes got their food, kavya. The siddhā got various mysterious powers. The ghosts obtained in a skull the beer of blood. The snakes received poison. The herbivorous animals obtained grass; and the carnivores got flesh to eat. The trees obtained sap; and the mountains obtained minerals. Thus every class of beings received the object of their wish from the inexhaustible mother earth. Pleased with this turn of events, the king adopted earth as his own daughter.

The king did not stop with 'milking' the earth. He began to organise the people of the earth, creating towns, villages, cities, castles and forts, cattlesheds etc., and commenced mining operations to extract precious metals from the earth. He also laid out farms and provided houses for farmers. This was the first time in the world that such civic organisation was attempted. On account of this wise organisation, the people of the earth lived in peace and security.

Book Four Chapter 19

Lord Maitreya continued: King Pṛthu now embarked upon the greatest of all royal rituals—the performance of one hundred aśvamedha rites. He who successfully completed the hundred rites became Indra, the ruler of heaven. The then Indra had himself qualified for the post in this way. Hence, when Pṛthu had completed ninety-nine, he became jealous and invented ways and means of preventing the successful completion of the hundredth.

Indra stole the chief symbol of the rite, the horse. As he was speeding along the skies, one of the officiating priests noticed it and asked Pṛthu's son to give him chase. Indra disguised himself as a religious mendicant of a heretic order. Pṛthu's son desisted from killing him. But, the priest Atri urged him on: "Have no mercy on him who tried to prevent this religious rite." As Pṛthu's son pursued Indra again, the latter abandoned the horse and hid himself. The boy returned with the horse and earned the title 'Vijitāśva'.

But soon Indra returned to his old game. Again the horse was stolen and Indra was disguised as a religious mendicant of a strange sect; and again, the sage Atri had Vijitāśva pursue the god, to recapture the horse and bring the rite to a successful conclusion. Once again Indra gave up the horse and his disguise, remaining invisible. Incidentally, these actions on the part of Indra were giving rise to a cult of heretics whose perverted judgment regarded unrighteousness as righteousness and therefore the obstruction of a religious rite as meritorious. This naturally angered the noble king Pṛthu. He got up to fight with Indra himself.

The sages who saw this were disturbed. They restrained him, assuring him that by offering a most potent oblation into the sacred fire they would destroy Indra's position. When they were about to do this the creator appeared before king Pṛthu and pleaded: "Indra whom you thus seek to harm, is also a part manifestation of the Lord. Yet, O brāhmaṇā, look at the unrighteous manner in which he has endeavoured to obstruct this noble rite. He is consumed by fear and jealousy. He will repeat the same obstructive manoeuvre again and again. O king! What need have you for the throne of Indra? Both of you are part manifestations of lord Viṣṇu. Why then, need you be angry with your alter-ego? The mind which seeks to do something against the will of the gods gets enraged. Listen to our advice. Let this rite remain one short of completion and let Indra retain his throne. Thus will you put an end to this feud and schism which might give rise to heretical pseudo-religious cults." King Pṛthu did as Brahmā advised and terminated the ritual without completing the hundredth one, to the satisfaction of all concerned.

Book Four Chapter 20

Lord Maitreya continued: Pleased with Pṛthu's admirably self-sacrificing gesture, lord Viṣṇu appeared before him, along with Indra.

The Lord said: Indra, who unbecomingly interfered with your religious rite, tenders his apology, O king. It behoves you to forgive him. Noble souls in this world bear no ill-will at all towards their fellows. Ill-will is an indication that one recognises diversity, and diversity is born of wrong indentification of the body with the self. He who knows that the omnipresent, unborn and undying self is distinct from the three guṇā (qualities of nature), and is not deluded by māyā, is not tainted by activities that give birth to sin and suffering. This self is realised by him whose mind is purified by duties performed unselfishly, as acts of my worship. His mind gradually turns away from worldliness and becomes established in supreme peace, which is my own formless state. To such a one there is no further birth. Therefore, perform your duty, O king, in the right spirit. To protect his people is the foremost duty of the king. This enables him to share the merit earned by his subjects. If the king neglects this duty, he lives in sin. I am pleased with you, O king; ask any boon of me.

His eyes bedimmed with tears of love and gratitude and his voice choked with devotion, Pṛthu said: "O Lord, what boon shall I ask of you, the Lord of the universe, who can instantly bestow the final beatitude upon anyone? I do not crave even for final beatitude. I do not care for anything that is not drenched with the nectar that flows from your lotus feet. Give me ten thousand ears, O Lord, with which I might constantly listen to your stories and glories. I long to share the good fortune of goddess Lakṣmī who is devoted to your lotus feet and who serves you constantly. But I may evoke her jealousy, just as I evoked the jealousy of Indra. You are transcendent. You rest in your own bliss, and have nothing to do with even Lakṣhī. The words 'Ask any boon of me' are words of your own māyā! Unless a man falls into the snare of a separate individuality, how can he ask any boon of you? You are ever showering the highest good upon us all, even as a loving father showers his attention and affection upon his children unasked."

The Lord was highly pleased with Pṛthu's prayer and attitude. He heartily granted him the greatest boon of devotion to his lotus feet. Indra and Pṛthu embraced each other. The king duly honoured all the gods, sages and celestial beings. They and lord Viṣṇu returned to their respective abodes. The king returned to his palace.

Book Four Chapter 21

Lord Maitreya continued: The people gave a royal reception to their king as he reentered his capital and his palace. He ruled his subjects with great wisdom and statesmanship for a long period and on leaving this world attained to the highest abode of the Lord.

In answer to Vidura's question asking for a detailed description of the king's good works, lord Maitreya said: O Vidura, hallowed is the land that lies between the two holy rivers, Gaṅgā and Yamunā. Living there king Pṛthu discharged his royal duties, enjoying the pleasures that his own past karma brought him, unsought and undesired. He held absolute sway over all his subjects, except over the holy ones, whom he revered. Once the king convened an assembly. He worshipped the elders and addressed the gathering. He was a majestic figure, O Vidura, and since he was unadorned with jewelry his own natural charm was arrestingly manifest. As he spoke, his words were full of sweetness, culture, courtesy and soul-force, and reflected his own experience.

King Pṛthu said: To me has been assigned the task of punishing the wicked and restraining them, and of protecting the people in general. By discharging my duty I shall earn the pleasure of the Lord.

The king who levies taxes on the people without instructing them in dharma earns their sins and forfeits his own good fortune. I pray to you: with your mind fixed on the lotus feet of the Lord, do your own duty. You will thereby earn for me the grace of the Lord.

The great ones of the past—Manu, Uttānapāda, Dhruva, Priyavrata, Brahmā, Śiva and my own grandfather Aṅga, Prahrāda, Balī, and the like—have proclaimed with one voice that the unique goal of our lives is to adore bhagavān Nārāyaṇa. Alas, there have been others who have voiced a contrary view: they are to be pitied. By adoring the Lord your sins are wiped out instantly. So worship him with your body, mind and speech, and with whatever you do to earn your livelihood.

The Lord himself is the worship, the worshipper and the worshipped. May the ruling class never oppress the brāhmaṇā (the knowers of Brahman, the infinite) who are endowed with purity, faith, austerity and restrained speech. May the dust of their feet ever adorn my forehead.

The holy ones applauded the king's speech. His spiritual eminence had redeemed his wicked father Vena, even as Prahrāda's devotion had redeemed his demoniacal father.

Book Four Chapter 22

Lord Maitreya continued: As the people were thus glorifying him the sanatkumārā (the four eternally youthful sons of the creator) appeared. The king worshipped them and said: "It is out of place to enquire about your welfare, for you are ever established in the self. Blessed is even the poorest man who is able to welcome you and offer you a seat and a little water. Pray, tell me: how can one attain salvation in this birth?"

Sanatkumārā applauded the question addressed to them for the welfare of all and replied: Contact with holy men is good for both parties, for then the right questions are asked and the right answers given for the good of all. O king, total non-attachment to the not-self and absolute devotion to the self have been declared to be the means to salvation. This is easily cultivated by faith, dedication of one's actions to the Lord, devotion to the yoga of knowledge, worship of the Lord, listening to his stories and glories, avoidance of worldly company by resorting to seclusion (except when his devotees assemble to sing his glories), by practising the yama and niyama, by abandoning all selfish activity and cultivating devotion to him. He who is firmly established in these should seek a guru, and with his help dissolve the subtle body that stands as a veil between him and the self. Perception of diversity exists only when one is under the sway of the subtle body (mental conditioning); just as the diversity of substance and image exists only when there is a reflecting medium such as water or a mirror. When the senses dwell on sense-objects the mind is distracted, discrimination is lost and wisdom is lost. Hence, he who is intent on salvation should beware of being distracted by sense-objects. Of the four 'goals' of life only liberation is of permanent value; righteousness, enjoyment of pleasure and acquisition of wealth are subject to termination. Therefore, O king, resort to the lotus feet of the Lord: sages cut asunder the knots of egoism by merely contemplating the splendour of his toe-nail. Great is the travail of those who endeavor to cross this ocean of samsara, beset by the crocodiles of the six categories (the five senses and the mind; or desire, anger, greed, vanity, delusion and jealousy). Therefore, be devoted to the lotus feet of lord Nārāyaṇa and thus cross this ocean of samsāra.

The delighted king offered himself and all that belonged to him at the feet of the sanatkumārā, saying: "Only men of knowledge are fit to wield political and military power, and to rule the world." Thus adored by the king, the sanatkumārā rose to their abode. Thus enlightened by them, the king ruled his kingdom without the slightest attachment to the world. He did what had to be done, at the right time and place, in the right way, to the best of his ability and resources. In due course he was blessed with five sons—Vijitāśva, Dhūmrakeśa, Haryakṣa, Draviṇa and Vṛka. Truly he was a rājā because he delighted the hearts of his people by his thought, word and deed (which is what the word 'rājā' means). His glory echoed and re-echoed throughout the world.

Book Four Chapter 23

Lord Maitreya continued: Realising that he was growing old, king Pṛthu entrusted the affairs of the kingdom to his son and retired to the forest along with his wife. This mighty ruler of the world practised the traditional austerities during the three seasons. In summer he engaged in 'the austerity of the five fires' (surrounding oneself with fires in addition to remaining exposed to the hot sun above). In the rainy season he stood in pouring rain. During the winter he stood neck-deep in freezing water. He practised the threefold austerity of body, speech and mind. Through these he had exhausted his karma. In his purified heart there arose unalloyed devotion to the Lord.

Through worship of the Lord he developed wisdom, characterised by dispassion. The light of this wisdom dispelled the wrong identification of the self with the body, etc. Freed from egotism and ego-born cravings, he transcended that wisdom, too, and became devoted to the stories and glories of lord Kṛṣṇa. For, such whole-souled devotion alone is the best safeguard against any backsliding.

One day he decided to give up his body. Seated in the siddhāsana with his heel pressed against the anus, he raised his prāṇāśakti from the base to the psychic centres at the navel, the heart, the throat and the space between the eyebrows successively. Then taking it up to the crown of the head he merged the elements that constituted his body in the corresponding cosmic elements. Then he proceeded to unify them. He dissolved earth in water, water in fire, fire in air and air in space. He merged the mind in the senses and the senses in the subtle elements. He withdrew all of them and merged them, along with the ego, in the mahat tattva (or cosmic intelligence). He merged this in the jīva, which is truly the infinite conditioned by māyā. By supreme wisdom Pṛthu realised this conditioning as unreal and thus transcended the jīva. He had attained cosmic consciousness, nirvāṇa or liberation.

Arci, Pṛthu's queen, saw that her lord had ceased to live and prepared to perform his funeral rites. Then she bathed herself in the river and with great love and devotion went round the burning pyre, which she ascended, determined to cast off her mortal body along with her husband's. The divinities who witnessed this great self-sacrifice, sang of her glories. "This queen served her husband with great love during his life-time. On account of that she has already gone beyond our regions. Surely, she will be with her husband in the abode of the Lord. This indeed is the goal of all human beings, but fools neglect it."

Such is the story of the first monarch of the world, O Vidura. Whoever reads or listens to this becomes like Pṛthu. He will fulfil all his desires. He who listens to this daily will develop devotion to the Lord and thus easily cross this ocean of birth and death.

Pracetās
Book Four Chapter 24

Lord Maitreya continued: When Pṛthu's son Vijitāśva became king-emperor, he divided his dominion into four quarters and gave a quarter each to his brothers—to Haryakṣa, the eastern quarter; to Dhūmrakeśa, the southern quarter; to Vṛka, the western; and to

Draviṇa, the northern quarter. Vijitāśva (who was also known as Antardhāna because he had the power to vanish at will) begot three sons by his wife, Śikhaṇḍinī—Pāvaka, Pavamāna and Śuci (fire-gods who were born as humans on account of a sage's curse, and who regained their original status through yoga), and by his other wife, Nabhasvati, he begot Havirdhāna. Vijitāśva handed the reins of his kingdom to Havirdhāna and engaged himself in ceaseless performance of religious rites, as the royal duties of punishing, taxing and dominating others were repugnant to him. At the same time he fixed his mind on the lotus feet of the Lord and thus earned for himself a place in the Lord's kingdom.

Havirdhāna begot six sons (Barhiṣad, Gaya, Śukla, Kṛṣṇa, Satya and Jitavrata) by his wife Havirdhānī. In course of time Barhiṣad became the ruler. He was well versed in vaidika rituals. He was continually engaged in these rites and earned the name Prācīnabarhi. He married Śatadrutī and begot ten sons. It is said that Śatadrutī was so beautiful that the gods who came to witness the wedding (even Agni, the god of fire himself) fell in love with her. The sons were collectively known as the pracetā.

Commanded by their father to marry and beget children, the pracetā sought to perform tapas. On their way they met lord Rudra and learned from him a sacred hymn. They then entered a lake and recited this hymn for a period of ten thousand years.

(In answer to Vidura's question, Maitreya narrated how the pracetā met lord Rudra.) As the pracetā wended their way in a westerly direction, intent on performing tapas, they beheld a big and beautiful lake. They heard celestial music, and as they stood transfixed by that music, lord Rudra emerged from the lake in front of them, surrounded by celestials.

Lord Rudra said: O pracetā, I know your heart's desire. I appeared here only to bless you and to impart to you a secret and sacred hymn. You are dear to me because you have taken refuge at the lotus feet of lord Viṣṇu. He who is devoted to his dharma for a hundred lifetimes attains the abode of the creator; then after a period of time he comes to me. But the devotee of lord Viṣṇu, on leaving this world, goes straight on to the kingdom of Viṣṇu which even we can reach only after the end of this world-cycle. Now hear from me the sacred hymn which is conducive to final beatitude.

Book Four Chapter 24

Lord Rudra said: Salutations to lord Vāsudeva, the self-luminous controller of the subtle elements and the senses. Salutations to lord Saṅkarṣaṇa the destroyer of the material universe. Salutations to lord Pradyumna who is the inner self of all and who awakens the universe. Salutations to lord Aniruddha the controller of the senses and the mind. Salutations to the sun, the paramahaṁsa, who is ever full. Salutations to the fire, the door to heaven and to liberation. Saluations to the Lord who, as the essence of everything, bestows satisfaction on all creatures. Salutations to space inside and outside all things, which conveys sound, the symbol of meaning. Salutations to secular and spiritual activity which lead respectively to the world of the manes and that of the gods; salutations to death which is the fruition of unrighteousness and the source of suffering. Salutations to the Lord who ordains the fruit of action. Salutations to lord Kṛṣṇa of infinite wisdom, the lord both of self-knowledge and yoga. Salutations to lord Rudra, the lord of the ego endowed with threefold faculties or powers. Salutations to the lord of knowledge and activity. Hail to the supreme being who has assumed all forms.

Grant us thy vision—for we are eager to behold thee who are held in great esteem by your devotees; let us behold that form which is most dear to thy devotees and which delights even the senses. It is perfect in every detail— with four graceful arms, a charming countenance, lotus-like eyes with the outer corners ever smiling, a beautiful abdomen rhythmically moving with inhalation and exhalation, a pair of radiant feet that drive away the darkness of our ignorance by the light of their nails, the entire form richly adorned with rare jewels and fine garments.

One should constantly medidate upon this form of thine, O Lord. Thus shall one be freed from fear. Thou art easily attained by one who is devoted to thee; not by others. All-devouring death does not touch one who has taken shelter at thy feet. A moment spent with thy devotee is infinitely superior even to heavenly enjoyment. May we enjoy the company of those who have immersed their hearts in thy glories and their bodies in the Gaṅgā issuing from thy feet; grant us this boon. Even they who are devoted to the vaidika rites should worship this form for their salvation, for thou art the indweller of all beings. Thy true nature cannot be directly perceived, but can only be inferred. O all-pervading being, thou art our only refuge.

This hymn is called yogādeśa. Repeat it constantly. The creator himself taught us this hymn. Rising before dawn he who listens to or recites this hymn with devotion and faith is freed from all karmā, and attains whatever he desires.

Lord Maitreya continued: The pracetā went into the lake and commenced their penance, reciting the hymn taught by lord Rudra. In the meantime, sage Nārada visited their father Prācīnabarhi and gently admonished him: "You cannot end sorrow by ceaselessly performing these rituals, O king. Remember the animals that you have sacrificed at these rites, by their thousands? They are eagerly waiting for the day when you will reach the other world. They will then tear you angrily with horns of steel. Listen, I shall tell you a story:

"Once upon a time there was a king of great renown called Purañjana. He had a friend known as Avijñātā the Unknown. The king went in search of a suitable home. One day he beheld a city like Bhogavatī (pleasure centre) which had nine gateways. In that city he saw a bewitching damsel surrounded by ten attendants with a powerful captain and guarded by a five-hooded serpent. Smitten with love, the king approached her and enquired who she was.

"The girl replied: 'I do not know who my father is, or for that matter, who anyone's father is. I only know that I am here. I do not know who built this city. These are my companions. And, this serpent is awake, even when I sleep, guarding this city. Welcome to this city! With the help of my friends I shall give you all the pleasures you seek, for a hundred years, since you are a brute, utterly ignorant, unwise and unmindful of a future life. Whom else can I thus indulge? It is here in this city that one can earn riches, sensual pleasure and religious merit'.

"Greatly pleased with the consent that he had thus obtained, the king entered the city with the girl as his wife. The city had nine gates, seven of which were on an elevation and two lower down. Five of these gates opened towards the east, two to the west, one to the north, and one to the south. Through two of these gates the king travelled to Vibhrājita, accompanied by his friend Dyumān. Through two other adjacent gates he travelled to Saurabha, accompanied by Avadhūta. Accompanied by two other friends, Rasajña and Vipaṇa, the king went out through another gate known as Mukhya, to the lands of Apaṇa and Bahūdana. Through the gates Pitṛhū and Devahū to the north and the south, the king accompanied by Śrutadhara, went to north Pāñchāla and to south Pāñchāla. Accompanied by Durmada, the king went out of one western gate, Āsurī, to Grāmaka. Accompanied by Lubdhaka he went out of the other western gate to Vaiśasa. Two gates led to blind alleys, through which he engaged in diverse activities.

"The king was thoroughly infatuated with his wife. All his actions and experiences were exactly the same as those of his wife—so deluded, unmindful and forgetful of his own nature, had he become!"

Book Four Chapter 26

Sage Nārada continued: One day the king went hunting. He was armed with a mighty bow equipped with an inexhaustible quiver of arrows; his car was drawn by five horses, and it had two shafts, two wheels and one axle, three flagpoles, five cords, a single rein, one driver or conductor, a single seat, two poles to which the yoke was fixed, five recesses and sevenfold protection. It was capable of five functions. The king was extremely fond of hunting; and in his eagerness to go to the forest he did not take his wife with him.

It has been ordained that a king may hunt wild animals within the bounds of necessity. This applies to life itself. He who performs necessary actions (called duty) which spring from wisdom, is not bound or tainted. The egotist who acts otherwise falls into the stream of the qualities of nature, and having lost his wisdom descends the ladder of evolution.

The king hunted mercilessly, needlessly and heedlessly. The animals thus tortured by him died in agony. Having hunted to his diabolical heart's content, the king was overcome by fatigue. He returned home, refreshed himself with a bath and rested. His mind was disturbed by passion for his wife and he sought her company. However, he could not find her. He therefore asked the ladies-in-waiting where the queen was. "That house is not pleasant and comforting where a man does not enjoy the company of a fond mother or of a wife who regards her husband as God himself," he said. "Therefore, tell me the whereabouts of my wife, who consoles me when I am unhappy and inspires and illumines my heart at every step."

The ladies-in-waiting thereupon pointed to where the queen lay as if unhappy and displeased. The king, profoundly shaken by this unusual sight, knelt beside her, touched her feet, placed her on his lap, caressed her and did everything his infatuated mind could think of to pacify her. He asked her: "Who has offended you, O beautiful lady? Tell me, and I shall punish him if he is not a holy one or a devotee of the Lord. He who has committed an offence ought to deem it a favour to be punished for his crime; for such punishment is an act of supreme grace and love. Be gracious to me, your loved one. I have offended you by not taking you with me to the forest on this hunting expedition. Ah, never before have I seen your face so cheerless. Pray, accept my love and forgive the offence."

Book Four Chapter 27

Sage Nārada continued: When the queen discovered that she had quite enslaved the king, she rose, bathed, dressed and decked herself and sought his eager company. Thoroughly infatuated by her amorous play the king spent his life, not noticing the passage of time, not knowing whether it was night or day. Passion for pleasure had completely robbed him of all wisdom and discrimination. He begot, by his wife, eleven hundred sons and one hundred and ten daughters. He had them all duly married, and was happy to see their progeny multiply. He engaged himself, as you are doing now, in rites and rituals which involved slaughter of innocent animals. While he was thus leading a useless life disregarding that which was conducive to his true spiritual welfare, senility crept upon him.

O king! Caṇḍavega is the name of a chief demi-god (Gandharva). He has a destructive force of three hundred and sixty dark men and an equal number of fair women. They attack every city as soon as it is built: some fall sooner and others later. When they began to attack Purañjana's city, the serpent Prajāgara defended it. In course of time, however, this defender grew weak and weary. The king was distressed; but fear of the impending calamity did not arise in his mind.

Kāla, the time spirit, has a daughter whose terrible nature has earned for her the title Durbhagā (misfortune). She sought a suitable husband. Puru, the son of Yayāti, accepted her as his wife for some time. Then she sought to seduce me; and when I resisted, she cursed me: "May you wander for ever". She then approached Bhaya (fear) and courted him. She praised his infallible power over mankind. She counselled: "People's hope in you never goes in vain (where there is hope, you unfailingly respond). He is a fool who refuses to give or take an offer." And also: "This is manliness—to relieve human distress" and thus tried to persuade him to accept her hand.

Bhaya saw in her approach the hidden will of the gods themselves—to bring about the death of living beings—and smilingly replied to her: "O lady, you are disliked by everybody in the world. But do not despair. I have a worthy husband in mind for you. Moreover, you may move about unperceived with my army and enjoy the whole creation, bound as it is by karma. Marry my brother Prajvāra (fatal fever) and let me be a brother to you. We three, helped by four hosts, shall hold sway over the whole of mankind."

Book Four Chapter 28

Sage Nārada continued: Happily wedded to Prajvāra and followed by the forces of Bhaya, the daughter of Kāla, the time spirit, afflicted the world. One day they attacked the city of Purañjana. Seized by the daughter of Kāla, Purañjana became powerless. The armies of Bhaya entered the city and all its inhabitants suffered manifold agonies. Purañjana's mind was still enmeshed in worldly pleasures and attachments. Reluctantly, he was compelled to abandon the city. At that moment, Prajvāra entered the city and it began to burn. This caused indescribable suffering to Purañjana. The guardian serpent Prajāgara made one last bid to defend the city; and when this failed he prepared to leave. Haunted by the notion that the city was himself, and his wife and children were his, Purañjana grieved for them. Bhaya bound him and began to drag him away. Alas, even at that moment the king failed to recognise his old friend Avijñātā. Yonder the sacrificial animals were waiting to torture him.

At heart the king was still attached to his wife. He was therefore reborn as the beautiful daughter of the ruler of Vidarbha. In course of time, Malayadhvaja, the ruler of Pāṇḍyā, married her; they begot a lovely daughter and seven sons. The daughter was espoused by the sage Agastya. Entrusting his kingdom to his sons, Malayadhvaja retired to the forest, accompanied only by his wife. There he purified his body and his mind by intense austerities and meditation on lord Kṛṣṇa. He attained union with the supreme being following the teaching of the Lord, his preceptor. He had risen above the pairs of opposites and realised that he was the self which is a silent witness of the activities of the body and the mind. Thus meditating upon the Lord for a great number of years, this self-realised sage left his body! The devoted queen who had emulated his noble example in austerity and who served him day and night, discovered one day that his feet were no longer warm. Greatly agitated and stricken with sorrow, she built a funeral pyre on which she laid her husband's body. She was ready to ascend it when a brāhmaṇā intervened.

He reminded her: "Do you not recognise me? I am your closest friend and companion, Avijñātā. Long ago, you left me and went in search of a dwelling. You were caught in the snares of a woman, in your desire for carnal pleasure. You dwelt in the mansion with five gardens, nine gates, one guard, three walls, six families of merchants and five markets. It was built of five materials, with a lady as the chief. You forgot your divine nature and therefore, after passing from that body, you were reborn as the daughter of Vidarbha. I am you and you are I. The difference is the difference that you notice when look at your reflection in a mirror or in the pupil of someone's eyes. You and I are the blessed swans (haṁsā) that dwell eternally in the lake of cosmic consciousness." Listening to this, she too attained cosmic consciousness.

Book Four Chapter 29

Explaining the spiritual message of the allegory, sage Nārada said: Purañjana (the maker of a city) is the jīva which, forgetting its eternal and only friend, God (Avijñātā—the unknown—in the story), seeks an abode for itself. The jīva feels that the human body is the best abode, with its two hands and two feet and nine orifices. The young woman is the intellect; the ten senses are her male companions and their functions their female counterparts, and the eleventh mighty warrior (captain) is the mind. The kingdom of Pāñchāla in which this nine-gated city is situated is the field of sensual enjoyments, which is offered to Purañjana by Purañjanī.

The nine gates are: the two eyes, the two nostrils, the two ears, two organs of excretion and the mouth. The different directions into which they open are obvious! Through these the indweller goes out, seeking the different kinds of pleasure. In these excursions he is accompanied by companions, who are the sense-organs or faculties that reside in these apertures. Through the eyes he sees, through the nostrils he smells, through the mouth he speaks and also tastes food, through the right ear he hears scriptures dealing with worldly activity and religious rites, through the left ear he hears scriptures relating to the attainment of inner peace and devotion to God, through the organ of generation he experiences sexual pleasure and through the anus he defecates.

The two gates leading to blind alleys are the hands and feet with which the entity performs various actions. The inner apartment in which he enjoys the company of his wife is the heart. Here the jīva identifies itself with the qualities of the intellect or the mind. Though the jīva is truly free and undisturbed, on account of this foolish identification it considers itself the doer, the enjoyer and the sufferer.

I told you that the king went hunting. The body is the chariot with the senses of perception as horses. Good and evil deeds are its wheels. The three guṇā are the flagpoles. The five prāṇā are the cords. The mind is the rein, the intellect the charioteer, the heart is the seat for the indweller, the pairs (like pain and pleasure) are the poles to which the yoke is fixed, the sense-objects the recesses, the seven components of the body the protective sheaths and the five organs of action are the five kinds of motion. In this vehicle the jīva roams, enjoying sensual pleasures. Such enjoyment has been likened to the slaughter of animals.

Book Four Chapter 29

Sage Nārada continued: In this allegory the year is described as the caṇḍavega. The days and nights have been spoken of as the dark males and fair females. Senility is the terrible woman, the daughter of Time. Mortal fear took her as his sister, and fatal fever is her spouse. Her attendants are the mental and the physical ailments. All these, so to say, begin to afflict the jīva from the moment of its birth! Prāṇa (life-force) resists these destructive forces for a time, but eventually it succumbs.

Even though tormented in innumerable ways, the jīva loves to live in the body, if possible for a hundred years! Though essentially independent and free, it deludes itself into a false identification with the intellect and through that with the body, etc. It gets involved in the three guṇā of nature. Sometimes it performs sātvika or good actions; sometimes rājasa and tāmasa actions. In accordance with these actions it is reborn—sometimes as a god, sometimes as a human being (male or female or neither), sometimes as a subhuman being—always as determined by past action. Alas, its fate is like that of a dog going from door to door, here getting some food, there getting kicks; the jīva, in the grip of lust, indulges in good and evil actions, reaps welcome and unwelcome harvests and ascends and descends the ladder of evolution.

Here in saṁsāra the jīva cannot hope to be free from suffering. In fact, the very effort to get rid of suffering involves suffering, and gives rise to more suffering eventually. Just as a man carrying a heavy load shifts his burden from one shoulder to another without lightening it, so the jīva continues to suffer one type of pain after another, the remedy often proving to be worse than the disease. Mere action cannot end suffering. Freedom from ignorance, alone is the cure. This freedom arises in the heart which is full of devotion to the Lord and to the guru. Such devotion to lord Vāsudeva generates both dispassion and wisdom.

Religious rites cannot bring about this wisdom, O king! That alone is the right action or ritual which promotes devotion to the Lord in your heart. Hence give up the performance of rituals involving the slaughter of innocent creatures and listen to the stories and glories of the Lord. Take refuge in him. You will be freed from all suffering, like hunger and thirst, fear and grief and so on.

Book Four Chapter 29

Sage Nārada continued: O king, thus have I answered your question. Now consider a deer that is nibbling grass in a delightful garden, pleasantly distracted by friends and by the music of the bees, totally oblivious to the hungry wolf in front and the deadly hunter behind! This deer is yourself, O king! Give up this worldly life fraught with a million sorrows and haunted by the hunter called death. Take shelter at the lotus feet of the Lord.

King Prācīnabarhi said: "O sage, by the light of your wisdom the darkness of my delusion has vanished. Even sages find it hard to reveal the truth which is beyond the domain of the senses. I have heard it said that the jīva performs good and bad actions here and reaps their results hereafter. But, such actions come to an end and are not seen anymore!"

Sage Nārada replied: Life continues, O king, even beyond the event called death. In that life one enjoys the fruits of past actions, in another body similar or dissimilar to the previous one. Karma and the consequent rebirth are the result of the feelings of 'I' and 'mine'. If you study the functioning of the senses and the mystery of their co-ordination, you realise the existence of a mind. In the same manner, by studying the characteristics and the tendencies of the mind you realise that there was existence prior to birth. Again, you sometimes think of a thing which you have neither seen nor heard of in this life-time: this points to that thing having been seen or heard of in a previous life-time, for the mind cannot conjure up an object or an event it has not previously experienced, though it can bring about new combinations of old facts.

The wrong notions of 'I' and 'mine' do not cease whilst the subtle body exists. The subtle body is composed of sixteen categories—the five prāṇā, the ten senses and the mind. When these conjoin consciousness, the same subtle body is called a jīva. It is on account of this subtle body that the jīva takes birth and dies, suffers and enjoys. Mind alone is the cause of birth and death of all beings. It is the thought of the pleasure enjoyed in worldly objects that impels the jīva to seek a repetition of those pleasures; and thus get bound. Birth and death and bondage to the wheel of cause and effect will not cease till spiritual ignorance and actions performed in ignorance, cease. In order to overcome the ignorance and the bondage, worship the Lord, O king, viewing this universe as being one with him.

(Having thus instructed king Prācīnabarhi, Nārada went on his way. Entrusting state affairs to his sons, the king retired to the forest and attained God-realisation. He who reads or listens to this sublime story is freed from his subtle body.)

Pracetās
Book Four Chapter 30

In answer to Vidura's question, sage Maitreya narrated the manner in which the Lord, pleased with their penance, blessed them: Standing in the waters of the lake, the pracetā propitiated the Lord by reciting the hymn which lord Rudra had taught them. After ten thousand years, the Lord appeared in front of them in all his peaceful radiance and glory. His form was beautiful and soothing to behold.

The Lord said to the pracetā: I am highly pleased with the brotherly love that has enabled you all to engage yourselves in a single undertaking, with singleness of purpose and total harmony. He who remembers you every day will grow in brotherly love towards his brothers and love for all beings. On him who adores me with the hymn of lord Rudra, I will confer any boon he desires.

You will soon be blessed with an illustrious son, O pracetā. The sage Kaṇḍu begot a lovely girl by a celestial maiden who abandoned her in the forest. The trees sheltered the baby and rājā Soma (the moon-god) fed her with nectar. Marry her, and she will also pursue the same path as you all do. The household state is not bondage for those who perform right action and spend their time listening to my glories. Thus listening to the great knowers of truth they will experience ever-new light in their hearts, and thus attaining me, they will neither be deluded, grieve nor give way to sensuous delight. You too will eventually reach me, with your hearts thoroughly purified.

The pracetā answered with a prayer: Salutations to the one on whom the finite mind falsely superimposes diversity! Salutations to lord Hari who is pure satva, who is Vāsudeva, Kṛṣṇa, the Lord of devotees, who liberates all from saṁsāra. Salutations to the Lord in whose navel is a lotus, who is adorned with a garland of lotuses and whose feet and eyes resemble lotuses. We ask you only one boon: as long as we revolve in this wheel of saṁsāra, may we enjoy the company of your devotees. This indeed is the greatest of all blessings. The fact that a moment with your great devotee, lord Śiva, yielded the supreme blessing of your vision is the best proof of this.

The Lord granted the boon and vanished. When the pracetā emerged from the lake they were annoyed that the trees around the lake were so high as to obstruct their vision of the heavens. The pracetā began to burn them down. The distressed trees (as advised by the creator) begged of the pracetā to desist, and offered their foster-daughter to them. The pracetā married her and begot by her Dakṣa—the same Dakṣa who had been killed by Śiva in a previous incarnation. The creator appointed him the lord of created beings, with the duty of furthering the work of creation.

Book Four Chapter 31

Lord Maitreya continued: After many years, the pracetā recalled the words of lord Viṣṇu, and wisdom dawned in their hearts. Entrusting their wife, Māriṣā, to the care of their son Dakṣa, they left their home. Intent on realising the self they practised control of their breath, of speech and of mind, in which they became quite proficient. In the meantime sage Nārada happened to go there. The pracetā confessed to him that they had almost forgotten the knowledge imparted to them by lord Śiva and lord Viṣṇu. They prayed to Nārada to re-kindle that knowledge.

Sage Nārada said: O pracetā! Nothing that you do in this world is of the least value unless it is directed towards lord Hari, who bestows himself on his devotee. The self is the culmination of all that is blessed and worthy: lord Hari is the very self of all beings, and therefore extremely dear. Even as the branches, the leaves and the stem of a tree are nourished by watering the root, when the Lord is propitiated all beings in the whole universe are propitiated. Know this as the truth, O pracetā: the Lord alone exists and the universe stands in relation to him as sun's rays do to the sun itself. Just as clouds appear and disappear in space, so the world of matter comes into being, remains and dissolves in the absolute. It has no independent existence apart from the absolute. Therefore, knowing that the Lord is your own self, worship him at all times.

But how? By compassion towards all beings, by contentment with what comes unsought and by the quiescence of all the senses. The Lord is easily pleased by these. The Lord is imprisoned in the heart of the devotee who has banished from it all cravings for sensual pleasure. The Lord loves those whose only wealth is the Lord himself; and therefore he does not relish worship offered to him by those who are proud of their learning, wealth, family or works, and who maltreat the poor devotee. The goddess of wealth herself is in constant attendance upon the Lord; yet, he is at the beck and call of his devotee. No man of wisdom should fail to adore him with all his being.

Having thus instructed the pracetā, sage Nārada returned to his abode. Contemplating the Lord, the pracetā attained liberation.

Sage Śuka said: Vidura heard this sacred story from the lips of lord Maitreya. He bowed to the sage's feet and went to Hastināpura. O Parīkṣit! He who listens to this story of the kings who were devoted to the Lord shall attain wealth, glory, longevity, all happiness in this world and final liberation.

Book Five

Priyavrata
Book Five Chapter 1

Sage Śuka continued: O king, they who have once tasted the nectar of the Lord's feet will not abandon them, even if their devotion is temporarily interrupted. Priyavrata, the son of Svayaṁbhu Manu, having heard from sage Nārada of the glory of whole-souled devotion to his feet, was about to abandon the world. In the meantime the creator, accompanied by sages and celestials, approached the prince. Svayaṁbhu Manu and Priyavrata worshipped the creator, after which he said:

"Listen dear child, all of us (even the gods) are bound by the word of God and three guṇā or qualities of his nature. Thus we do what is ordained by his inexorable will. No embodied being can undo the Lord's will, whether by penance, knowledge, power of yoga, intellectual power, wealth or righteous life, either by one's self-effort or with another's help. Even a liberated soul continues to live in this world till the momentum of his past action is exhausted. True, he who has not controlled his senses is subject to birth and death even if he dwells in a forest; but, if one's mind and senses are controlled, one is not tainted by leading the householder's life. You have controlled them and should therefore rule the world."

The creator departed. Manu appointed Priyavrata as ruler of the globe and then renounced the householder's life. Priyavrata married Barhiṣmatī, the daughter of Viśvakarma, and by her begot ten sons (all of whom bore the name of an aspect of fire) and a daughter. Of the sons, three (Kavi, Mahāvīra and Savana) adopted the life of perpetual celibacy, in order to attain self-realisation. By another wife, Priyavrata had three sons—Uttama, Tāmasa and Raivata—who in their turn became rulers of the globe for a whole epoch.

The emperor Priyavrata appeared to have lost the sense of direction and to have been caught up in worldly life. Observing that the sun only illumines half the globe while the other is plunged in darkness, he tried to convert night into day by illumining the dark side of the earth with a radiant space vehicle or satellite, in which he circled that side seven times every night. In his time the earth was divided into seven continents—and he appointed each of his seven sons as ruler over one of them. Very soon he recovered his wisdom and one day, with his discrimination and dispassion fully awakened, he abandoned the householder's life and once again pursued the path of renunciation.

The following verses are sung in his glory: "Without the grace of the Lord who can do what Priyavrata achieved—he attempted to dispel darkness from the face of the earth, divided the earth into seven continents for administrative convenience, ultimately renounced the pleasures of the three worlds and dedicated his life to the service of the servants of the Lord."

Book Five Chapter 2

Sage Śuka continued: While Priyavrata was engaged in whole-souled devotion to the Lord, his son Āgnīdhra ruled Jambūdvīpa justly and wisely. A householder ought to propitiate his ancestors by begetting a worthy son in order to carry on the family's religious tradition. Towards this end the king meditated upon the Lord, creator of all, in order to earn his grace. The creator thereupon sent a celestial damsel by the name Pūrvacitti to where Āgnīdhra was meditating.

Pūrvacitti came to mount Mandara where Āgnīdhra sat absorbed in deep meditation, and began to sport there. The setting was highly romantic, with birds singing and bees humming, and a gentle breeze wafting the fragrance of the lotus and other flowers in the pleasure-garden. The king gently opened his eyes and beheld the celestial nymph. Smitten with love, he spoke to her:

"Who are you thus roaming this forest? Are you a sage? I see you have on your face two bows (the brows): are they for self-protection or for hunting defenceless prey like me? At whom are those arrows of sidelong glances aimed? I see that the bees hovering around you are singing vaidika hymns in praise of you, their preceptor. You are not wearing the traditional ascetic robes made of the bark of trees, but you are clad in lovely yellow garments. I admire those two horns that have grown on your chest: what is hidden in them? I would like to be better acquainted with your native place which gives birth to people who carry on their chest a strange pair of organs that agitate the mind of undisciplined people like me. Surely, you are a ray of lord Viṣṇu, the protector of the universe.

"You confound my mind. The ball with which you are playing so gracefully, distracts me. Even the breeze seems to aggravate the situation by blowing your garments away. Tell me, what austerities did you practise in order to get such a lovely form which distracts the austerities of others? I cannot live without you, O lady who has been sent to me by the Lord, the creator himself. Take me where you please."

Pūrvacitti, too, fell in love with the king, and so became his queen. In course of time she gave birth to nine sons—Nābhi, Kimpuruṣa, Harivarṣa, Ilāvṛta, Ramyaka, Hiraṇmaya, Kuru, Bhadrāśva, and Ketumāla. She then returned to the abode of Brahmā. The sons, who were strong, were allotted their share of the kingdom by their father. The king, however, was not sated with sensual enjoyments, and so meditating constantly upon Pūrvacitti, he ascended to the realm of the manes to be with her. Then, the nine sons of Āgnīdhra married the nine daughters of Meru.

Ṛṣabha
Book Five Chapter 3

Sage Śuka continued: King Nābhi had married Merudevī, the daughter of Meru. They had no issue for some time and therefore resolved to perform a special ritual to invoke the blessings of the Lord. Even before the conclusion of the rite (known as pravargya) the Lord's heart was moved by supreme compassion, and with his characteristic longing to fulfil the wish of his devotee, the Lord, in his most resplendent form, appeared before the king and the assembled devotees. The king and the officiating priests bowed their heads to the Lord, and the priests offered the following prayer, in sublime prose:

"O supreme being, how can we sing thy ineffable glories? It is only because the wise ones realised the inadequacy of language and human intelligence that they commanded us to worship you with the single word 'namaḥ'. O Lord, you are easily pleased with any prayer said by your devotee in a voice faltering with love, offering at the same time just water, basil leaves and sprouts of durva grass. You are the very goal and embodiment of the highest aspirations of the human being; and yet we worship you for small selfish ends. Surely, you have appeared to us today to teach us this lesson: that you are ever intent on showering your redeeming grace on all, even if you have not been approached properly and unselfishly. You have nothing to gain from our worship and glorification. Yet, you appear in our midst as if you are eager to be glorified, though in fact you confer on us the supreme blessing of thus contemplating your glories. To sing your glories incessantly is our only duty. Therefore, we humbly pray that while stumbling, sneezing, falling down and yawning, when we are in distress and so on, and even while suffering from fever and on our death-bed, when we are likely to be helpless and powerless to remember you, your sin-destroying and soul-redeeming name may appear on our tongue. Now, this royal sage Nābhi is desirous of having a son like you. Forgive our ignorance in that we ask of thee, supreme Lord, such a petty boon! But grant him the boon."

The Lord replied: "O sages, you have placed me in a difficult position. For, there is no one like me in the universe! There cannot, therefore, be a son like me. Yet, you brāhmaṇā are my own mouth, and your word is my word. Hence, your words cannot prove false. I shall therefore be born of Nābhi, with a part of myself."

Soon afterwards, the Lord descended into the palace of king Nābhi in a divine form, entirely pure and unmixed with rajas and tamas, with a view to bless the king and also to teach mankind the highest form of renunciation.

Book Five Chapter 4

Sage Śuka continued: On the person of this divine child the people noticed signs of divinity. His nature was divine from his very birth. He was born with control of the mind and senses. Even his infant mind turned away from pleasure. He was exceptional in every way. And, therefore, his father Nābhi gave him the most appropriate name Ṛṣabha (the foremost).

Indra, the king of heaven, was jealous of Ṛṣabha. He therefore withheld rain from Nābhi's kingdom. Knowing this, Ṛṣabha laughed aloud and with the powers at his command he sent a heavy shower of rain all over the land. In spite of all this, overcome by the Lord's māyā, the king regarded Ṛṣabha as his beloved son.

In course of time the king discovered that all the people of his kingdom loved Ṛṣabha greatly. On an auspicious day he crowned him king, in accordance with the wishes of his subjects. Nābhi then retired to the place known as Viśāla, along with his wife, and engaged himself in adoration of the Lord in his form as Nara and Nārāyaṇa, and attained union with him.

Lord Ṛṣabha lived and ruled in such an exemplary manner that he embodied the very best aspects of life. First he lived with a preceptor to exemplify the life of an ideal student. Having granted the preceptor the boons he asked, the divine student then entered the householder's life. He married the girl Jayantī, bestowed upon him by Indra himself; and through her he begot one hundred sons. The eldest of these was known as Bharata, who was a great master of yoga; it is after him that this country is known as Bhārata-varṣa. Of the others, Kavi, Hari, Antarikṣa, Prabuddha, Pippalāyana, Āvirhotra, Drumila, Camasa and Karabhājana, were great devotees of the Lord. Eighty-one other sons of Ṛṣabha were pious and noble in their conduct and so they became brāhmaṇā, though they were kṣatriyā by birth.

Lord Ṛṣabha was a wise statesman and an ideal householder who, through his own example, taught the people the long-forgotten dharma. During his reign there was no unrighteousness in his kingdom; no-one even thought of covetting others' property. All the people vied with one another in their love and devotion to lord Ṛṣabha. On one occasion, he addressed his own sons as follows.

Book Five Chapter 5

Lord Ṛṣabha said: This human birth should not be wasted on sensual pleasures, but utilised in austerities for the realisation of the absolute. The service of the great ones is the door to liberation, whereas the company of the sensuous is the gate to hell. The great ones are calm, free from anger, compassionate and pious, with their hearts totally dedicated to me. They have no selfish interest in the world and they maintain their bodies for my sake alone. Selfish and sensuous action binds the jīva, who wallows in ignorance. In ignorance man regards his body as himself, and wife, house, etc., as his. When this conditioning of the mind is removed the truth about these dawns in him. Freed from the ego and the consequent bondage, he reaches the supreme. By the adoration of the Lord, by the perception of the truth that all life is tormented by sorrow, by the cultivation of virtues and the firm restraint of the mind and the senses, and above all, by constant vigilance, one should cut the knot of the ego. Thus the storehouse of karma is destroyed. Thenceforth one should desist from even such endeavour.

The foremost duty of a king, a father or a guru is to communicate this wisdom to those in his charge, without imposing it upon them and without rebuking them if they are not mature enough to understand the message and to act upon it. One who does not thus endeavor to save the other from birth and death is neither a guru, kith and kin, father, mother, deity nor husband.

With a pure mind look upon all animate and inanimate beings as my abodes: this is the best way in which you can worship me. Serve the eldest amongst you—Bharata—who is a great and noble soul.

Sage Śuka continued: Having thus instructed his sons and, through them, all his subjects, Ṛṣabha abandoned the householder's life, and roamed the land incognito and naked, like one possessed by a spirit, or demented. The reactions of the people were varied. His fine figure attracted the attention of the women, but his uncouth appearance repelled many. His peculiar behaviour thoroughly veiled his spiritual glory, and the people behaved contemptuously towards him, subjecting him to every sort of indignity. Yet, he remained unmoved, for he saw that all the indignity was directed towards the body which was not the self. Firmly established in the self, Ṛṣabha adopted the mode of life of a bull, a deer, a crow and a python in succession. He exemplified the different states of an advanced yogi. He lived in constant oneness with lord Vāsudeva and therefore did not even take notice of supernatural powers that sought him.

Book Five Chapter 6

King Parīkṣit asked: Ṛṣabha was established in the self and the seeds of karma had been completely burnt in him. Why did he then renounce the world and wander about as if mad or possessed by a demon?

Sage Śuka replied: Indeed, lord Ṛṣabha had freed himself from all bondage. But, wise men do not relax their vigilance lest a moment's heedlessness should lead to a great downfall. The wise say that one should never trust one's mind, which can be deceptively quiet, treacherously waiting for an opportune moment to lead one astray. Indeed, even so have the austerities of many great ones been disrupted. Just as an unfaithful wife does not hesitate to allow her paramour to enter the house and murder her husband, the wicked and fickle mind of a non-vigilant man allows lust, anger and other evils to enter and destroy spiritual knowledge and wisdom.

Lord Ṛṣabha's glory is indescribable. Yet, the people could not recognise his divinity, as he was roaming about as if demented. Having exemplified in himself the conduct of a yogi of the highest spiritual attainment, the Lord wished to show them how to leave the body. He had completely dissociated himself from the subtle body; the physical body then continued to roam about due to past momentum, sustained by a trace of the Lord's māyā. He wandered thus in the regions known as Konka, Venka, Kūṭaka and Dakṣiṇa Karnāṭaka. One day, as he was walking in the Kūṭaka mountains, there arose a forest fire, kindled by the rubbing of bamboos against one another. The fire consumed the forest and the body of lord Ṛṣabha, too.

Ṛṣabha's conduct is not for imitation. Yet, people will imitate his external behaviour, walk about naked, make themselves unpresentably filthy, and revile the vedā, the sages and lord Viṣṇu, pretending to be established in a transcendental state. This is the height of ignorance and foolishness.

People extol the land of Ṛṣabha's birth thus: "Of all the countries in the world, Bhārata is exceptionally holy, inasmuch as in that country people extol the glories of lord Viṣṇu." Salutations to the glorious lord Ṛṣbhadeva, for ever established in self-realisation, who illumined the path of self-knowledge for the salvation of people deluded by attachment to their body, etc.

He who listens to or recites this story of lord Ṛṣabhadeva develops great devotion to the Lord.

Bharata
Book Five Chapter 7

Sage Śuka continued: Ṛṣabhadeva had expressed the wish that Bharata should become the ruler of the kingdom after him. So, when Ṛṣabha left for the forest, Bharata became king. Such was the glory of his rule that the country came to be known after him—Bharata.

Bharata married a daughter of Viśvarūpa, named Pañcajanī, in order to fulfil the will of the Lord. The couple gave birth to five sons—Sumati, Rāṣṭrabhṛt, Sudarśana, Āvaraṇa and Dhūmraketu.

Bharata, too, was an exemplary ruler, even as his father and his grandfather had been before him. He was greatly devoted to duty. He possessed a thorough knowledge of the scriptures and their injunctions. He also worshipped the Lord in the prescribed manner, through the sacred rites and rituals. However, when the priests presiding over the rites were engaged in their performance, Bharata visualised that the Lord himself was the fire, the oblation, the rite and the performer of the rite. Though the vaidika mantrā invoked several deities during the performance of the ritual, Bharata intuitively knew them all to be the limbs of the one cosmic being. Above all, he was totally free from any desire for any kind of earthly or heavenly reward, and so the performance of these rites purified his heart and mind.

When Bharata's mind had thus been purified, devotion to the Lord arose in it. One day, after ruling the country for a long time, Bharata decided that it was the Lord's will that he should retire from the kingly duties. Thereupon he went to the āśrama of sage Pulaha on the bank of the river Gaṇḍakī, in which sacred stones called sāligrāma (symbols of lord Viṣṇu) are found.

In that āśrama, Bharata engaged himself in the ceaseless adoration of the lord Vāsudeva. With the mind and the senses completely controlled, he worshipped the Lord with holy basil leaves. As he recited the names of the Lord, his hair stood on end, tears rolled down his cheeks and he lost consciousness of the outside world. In such a state he even forgot to complete the ritual worship he had undertaken, and remained immersed in the consciousness of the Lord's presence in his heart.

Clad in nothing but a deer skin, with his matted locks wet on account of repeated ablutions, Bharata meditated upon lord Nārāyaṇa, manifest as the orb of the sun, reciting the following hymn:

"The light of the sun, beyond darkness and the taint of materiality, is the dispenser of the fruits of our actions. All this was created by his mind. Entering all this, he protects the jīva, with the power of his consciousness. We take refuge in that light which illumines our intellect."

Book Five Chapter 8

Sage Śuka continued: One morning, having completed his ablutions, Bharata was seated on the bank of the holy river Gaṇḍakī, repeating the praṇava (Oṁ). Meanwhile a doe came to the river to drink, when suddenly a lion roared in the forest nearby. The frightened doe leapt across the stream. The exertion, the fear and the advanced state of her pregnancy caused the doe to deliver prematurely and die.

The compassionate Bharata adopted the orphaned fawn. Considering it his foremost duty ordained by providence, which brought this helpless creature to him, he nourished it with great care. Very soon the bond of deep affection which grew between them made Bharata neglect his religious duties and even worship of the Lord. He bagan to think constantly of the misfortune of the fawn, reaffirming every time that it was his duty, privilege and blessing to care for it. He asked himself: "Do not the great ones give up their own self-interest in order thus to show compassion to helpless creatures?"

The fawn became his constant companion, and throughout the day his mind was preoccupied with thoughts concerning its welfare, joy, pleasure, security and protection. Nay, if it did not come to his side early in the evening he felt miserable, wondering what had happened to it. He recollected again and again how the fawn would tease him when he closed his eyes pretending to meditate. He remembered with satisfaction how, when the fawn unknowingly defiled the sacred articles and when he scolded it, it would immediately sit in a corner like a hermit. Bharata was so thoroughly infatuated with the fawn that he blessed the earth for being trodden by his pet which he treated as his own son.

How mysterious it is that the heart of one who had renounced great wealth, status and pleasure should fall a victim to attachment to a creature belonging to the sub-human species! However, in course of time, Bharata's end approached. Even at the hour of death, Bharata was looking at the deer and thinking of it. He and the deer died at the same time; and Bharata was reborn as a deer.

Yet he remembered his previous birth and lamented: "What a pity that, even after renouncing the world to adore the lotus feet of lord Vāsudeva in the seclusion of the forest, I should have slipped from the spiritual path through love for a deer." Remembering all this, he ran away from his herd to the hermitage of Pulaha, and lived there as an ascetic till he shed that body.

Book Five Chapter 9

Sage Śuka continued: One brāhmaṇa descendant of the sage Angirā had two wives: by his first wife he begot nine sons, and by his second wife he had twins, a boy and a girl. They say that the boy was Bharata reborn. Even as a child he remembered both of his previous incarnations. Therefore, great vigilance characterised his behaviour. The father felt that it was his duty to educate and train his son. To this end, he invested Bharata with the sacred thread and taught him the holy gāyatrī. But Bharata, his mind totally absorbed in the absolute and therefore not interested in worldly affairs, did not seem to learn anything.

In the meantime the father died and the second wife ascended the funeral pyre with him, entrusting her children to the care of the first wife. Bharata's half brothers soon abandoned the futile task of educating their younger brother, whom they considered a congenital idiot. But, however much they insulted him, their ill-treatment did not affect him in the least. He did whatever work he was told to do; he ate whatever was given to him. He had risen above the pairs of opposites, such as pain and pleasure, honour and dishonour. And, he roamed about freely.

At that time the chief of a band of robbers had vowed to offer human sacrifice to the goddess Bhadrakālī. Their chosen victim had escaped. They were looking for another. And, they chanced upon Bharata who was then working as a watchman guarding a farm. Finding him stout and strong, healthy and whole, they tied him and took him to the temple of the goddess, to be sacrificed. Absorbed as he was in the infinite, he was totally unmindful of what was done to the body. They bathed it, adorned it, fed it and prepared it for the sacrifice. However, just as he was about to be beheaded, the goddess Bhadrakālī emerged from the image and lopped off the heads of the robbers. Thus indeed does evil aimed at the great ones recoil upon the evil-doer. Nor is it a wonder that the Lord, with his ever-vigilant protective weapons, rescues his devotee from every danger—the devotee who is free from the deluded identification of the body with the self and who, free from malice, is the friend of all beings.

Book Five Chapter 10

Sage Śuka continued: While Bharata was wandering like this, a king named Rahūgaṇa, (the ruler of Sindhu and Sauvīra) was journeying from his kingdom to the sage Kapila's hermitage, to seek spiritual instruction from him. The king was borne in a palanquin. The palanquin bearers were looking for one more to assist them. They happened to see Bharata nearby and quickly asked him to join them. He consented without question, unmindful of what work was allotted to the body. Yet, as he carried the palanquin, he had his eyes fixed on the ground, mindful as he was, not to hurt any living creature. This resulted in the palanquin being jolted repeatedly, causing discomfort to the royal occupant.

Hearing from the other bearers that the new bearer was not behaving well, the king at first taunted him: "Ah, you fat and strong fellow, are you tired already?" And then rebuked him, saying: "If you don't do your duty properly, I, your master, will punish you in order to teach you a lesson."

At this, Bharata replied gently: "Fatness, leanness, mental and physical ailments, hunger and thirst, fear, conflict, desire, old age, sleep, sense-enjoyment, anger, vanity and grief pertain to one who is born with the body, not to me. You can only command a servant if you are his master. But the words 'servant' and 'master' are not real and final designations of anyone. They have only conventional usage. Can you really teach me? And, what will you gain by teaching me?" Bharata continued to walk, bearing the palanquin on his shoulders.

Hearing these words, Rahūgaṇa descended from the palanquin and, placing his head at the feet of Bharata, questioned: "Who are you, wandering about incognito? Are you the sage Kapila whom I seek? You make a distinction between one who is born with the body, and the self. In the case of cooking rice, the pot, the water in the pot and the outer and the inner portions of the rice all get heated on account of their contact with fire. In the same way does not the self experience hunger, thirst, etc., on account of its contact with the body? Again, does the king not propitiate the Lord by performing his duty—to command and instruct his subjects in their duties? Kindly forgive my insolent behaviour, O sage; for one who insults a holy man soon perishes. And, kindly enlighten me."

Book Five Chapter 11

Bharata, the knower of Brahman, replied: Though unwise, you talk as if you are wise. The wise do not confuse mundane problems with spiritual enquiry into truth. The revelations of the scriptures (which are indispensable) are a sealed book to the ignorant man who is not awake to the fact that worldly life and religious rituals are as unimportant as dream life and dream activity.

The mind that is conditioned by the three guṇā leads one to good and evil action and their consequences. The mind, which is one of the sixteen components of the subtle body, is agitated by the guṇā and is therefore vulnerable to lust, anger, greed, etc. In fact it dons various forms and takes birth in higher or in lower species. It is only so long as the mind functions thus that one experiences the waking and the dream states with their corollaries such as pleasure, pain, etc. Hence have the wise declared that the mind is the cause of bondage and liberation, of evolution and degradation. A mind that is attached to modes and moods is subject to sorrow; that mind which has risen above them attains peace and bliss. The lamp whose wick is attached to oil emits flame and smoke, whereas if it is free from the oil, the flame returns to its own state, (which is nirvāṇa). Even so, the mind that is distracted by the modes of nature is bound by different actions; but, when it is free of them, it rests in truth.

There are principally eleven states or modifications of the mind. When the mind-stuff flows out through the five organs of perception and thus experiences the objects, and when it flows through the five organs of action and functions in this world, and when it entertains false notions of 'mine' towards the body etc., through the ego-sense—these are the eleven states which ramify into numerous modifications. But, these states of the mind have no existence of their own, nor are they generated by one another. There is only one reality underlying them all—the witness consciousness (kṣetrajña). This witness is never involved in the modes of nature nor moods of the mind. For, this kṣetrajña is eternal, self-luminous, unborn and supreme, Nārāyaṇa and bhagavān Vāsudeva who by his own will dwells in all beings as their inner controller. It is only when a man conquers his worst enemies (such as lust and anger), when he frees himself from the conditioning of his self (which is known as the mind) and when he worships the lotus feet of the Lord and his guru, that he is liberated.

Book Five Chapter 12

Rahūgaṇa said: O holy one! You are indeed a great yogi of self-realisation. The nectarine words that have flowed from your lips have brought great relief to me, for I had been poisoned by misunderstanding concerning the self. But, I am unable to grasp clearly the meaning of your statement that though actions and their effects are valid in relation to worldly life, they cannot stand the test of any enquiry into their reality.

The holy brāhmaṇa, Bharata, replied: O king, all bodies here on earth are verily the products of the earth (food, etc.). One lump of earth rides in the palanquin, and another lump of earth bears the palanquin. Vainly thinking that you are one of these lumps and that you are a king, etc., you ill-treat others—the poor people whom you have employed to carry your palanquin— instead of sympathising with them. The false notion of the least usefulness of action in this world will be dispelled the moment you see that all beings are but the products of the earth, to which they return with all that they have done on earth! What we call earth is itself made up of subtle atoms. And, we postulate their existence and their combination to form molecules and substances, because our reason demands such explanations: but this reason is a manifestation of ignorance. Therefore, all such explanations are ignorance. All descriptions such as lean, fat, small, big, animate and inanimate, substance, nature, time, action, etc., which imply duality, are the products of ignorance and are false. The truth, however, is that consciousness alone exists, without inside or outside, perfect and supremely peaceful; it is known as Bhagavān and the sages call him Vāsudeva. Rahūgaṇa, this cannot be known by penance or religious rites, by going away from the household state nor by the recitation of the veda, nor even by the worship of water, fire and sun; no, it cannot be reached except by bathing oneself in the dust of the feet of the great ones, in whose company all worldly topics cease and the stories and the glories of the Lord alone are sung.

I was a king named Bharata once. On account of an unfortunate attachment to a deer I was born a deer. By the grace of God and on account of the worship of the Lord and the company of holy men, I did not forget my former life even when I was an animal. Hence, in this birth I move about veiling my real nature. Therefore, O king, resort to the worship of the Lord and to holy company, severing all attachment to the world by the sword of wisdom.

Book Five Chapter 13

The holy brāhmaṇa, Bharata, continued: A company of merchants, wandering in search of wealth, enters the forest of mundane existence. Six dacoits rob them. They are harassed by wolves and insects. They behold a city in the clouds. They cling to their houses, wealth, etc. When hungry they eat from unholy trees or beg from one another. They run to a mirage or a waterless pool to quench their thirst. They are scorched by forest fires. Upon losing their wealth, they swoon. They want to climb a hill; but they give up the attempt, their feet sore with thorns. Assailed by a boa constrictor, they lose consciousness. Sometimes, losing their sight, they remain lying down. They try to extract honey from beehives and are stung by the bees. If they do get some honey others snatch it from them. They trade with one another, and on account of their greed, become enemies. They covet one another's wealth, get frustrated when they cannot get it, and sometimes enter into marital relations for the sake of it. Leaving behind dead companions, they carry the new-born ones and proceed on their journey, which is goal-less and interminable. Even they who have strong minds, and who have conquered the whole world, lie on the earth, having falsely clung to it with the feeling

"This is mine'. They have hated one another for the sake of the earth. They do not reach the destination of those who have given up hate. They become attached to some places where the birds chirp sweetly. They befriend some animals; later, abandoning them, they befriend a monkey. Sometimes they fall into a ravine; they cling to a creeper and climb back. Thus walking the forest path, they do not find the supreme object of their life. Rahūgaṇa, you have been placed on this forest path; now give up violence and be the friend of all; in the spirit of non-attachment be devoted to lord Hari, and, wielding the sword of wisdom, reach your destination.

The king then bowed to the sage, all his doubts having been dispelled by the company of the sage for just one hour. The holy sage, having thus instructed the king who had earlier insulted him, continued to wander the earth as before. Rahūgaṇa, his ignorance dispelled, shed the false notion that he was the body and lived a life of enlightenment.

Book Five Chapter 14

Requested by king Parīkṣit to explain the parable, sage Śuka continued: The world of sense-experiences is like the forest path into which, on account of māyā, the individual strays. He busies himself in different activities, even as merchants engage themselves in business to earn wealth. Though he meets with repeated failures, he fails to see that he is on the wrong path and to turn to the right one. On this path he is waylaid by robbers (i.e., the senses, which in fact rob him of his wisdom). Only that is wealth which promotes dharma; only that is dharma which involves worship of the Lord. Only such dharma is conducive to happiness in this world. However, worldly men are led in a contrary direction by the senses which rob them of this wealth (dharma).

In the forest called worldly life, even they whom a man regards as wife and children prove to be robbers: they rob him of his wealth. Even the religious actions of a householder are powerless to secure lasting peace or happiness, for the weeds of evil grow on the field of his life again and again (like the weeds growing on a field, even though it is ploughed) until the roots are destroyed. He pursues sense-pleasures as an ingnorant man runs after a mirage in a desert. He deludedly runs after gold, which is the root of all evil. Attached to his home, wealth and so on, he runs about blindly in this fleeting and perishable world, thus wasting a precious human birth. Embraced by a woman, he gives way to lust, totally oblivious of the fact that the all-seeing eye is watching him from all directions.

Occasionally, he realises for a moment the illusory nature of these sensual pleasures. But he is soon sunk in ignorance once again and he pursues the same pleasures. When the merits of his past births come to an end, and there is an end even to this transitory happiness, he seeks the protection and help of other men instead of turning to God and to dharma. He even embraces a heretic creed, misled in his own deluded state by these vile men and thus suffers untold misery here and hereafter.

He clings to wealth. When it is lost, he is ready to rob his own parents or children. Stripped of its affluence, his home appears to be a burning forest. And, when the king levies taxes and thus deprives him of his dear wealth, he despairs and behaves as if he is dead.

Book Five Chapter 14

Sage Śuka continued: Sometimes the worldly man undertakes scripturally-ordained rituals, which is like lifting a huge mountain! Sometimes suffering dishonour and calumny, he is robbed even of his sleep. Seeking small pleasures in this life, in the midst of endless suffering, he lays his hands on wealth and women belonging to others: instead of gaining pleasure, he is subjected to greater pain by the officers of the law or the husband of the woman. Even if this does not happen and he does get the wealth or the woman, this gain does not stay with him for long: someone else robs him of the wealth, which changes hands frequently and never stays with one person in this world. Even when he engages in lawful business he incurs the displeasure of his rivals, who become his enemies.

Such are the innumerable obstacles that one encounters along the path of worldly life. Yet, the foolish man who has no self-control at all falls an easy prey to the temptations of a woman, who is the Lord's own creative energy or māyā. He slaves for her and is deluded by the attention of his children and their wives and so on.

Living in this fool's paradise the man does not notice the passage of time. He clings to heretic beliefs. When these heretic beliefs are unmasked and their falsity exposed, he turns to the right belief. Still he does not keep the company of wise and holy men, but loves to befriend other worldly men. He is still interested only in sex and wealth.

Fortunes alternate in his life. Now he is wealthy. Now he is poverty-stricken and does not even have a bed to sleep on. To counteract this poverty he sometimes enters into matrimonial alliances but later he dissolves them. In this worldly life if someone dies, people no doubt cry and express grief, but they bury the dead and carry on the same old pattern of life with the living. Only a good man turns to the right path, takes to the discipline of yoga and strives to attain the exalted state which sages, who are tranquil in their innermost being and who have turned away from worldly life, reach easily. Even kings prefer to die fighting others in the hope of conquest. Clinging to the creeper called karma they revolve on this wheel of transmigration.

What a sublime life king Bharata led! Even when he was a deer he was devoted to lord Hari. Whoever listens to or narrates this story of the royal sage Bharata will attain health, long life, wealth, happiness and final liberation.

Book Five Chapter 15

Sage Śuka continued: Bharata's son Sumati (who followed in the footsteps of Ṛṣabha) begot Devatājit. Here is a list of his descendants: Devadyumna, Parameṣṭhī, Pratīha, Pratihartā (and two others), Aja and Bhūmā, Udgītha, Prastāva, Vibhu, Pṛthusena and Nakta: and Nakta begot Gaya.

Gaya was a part manifestation of the Lord himself. By performing all his duties with the utmost unselfishness, his heart and mind were purified. He protected his subjects in every way—from external enemies, from hunger and thirst, and from their own internal enemies—by punishing them when they committed a crime and by humouring and instructing them when they gave way to depression or wrong thinking. By offering all his actions as devout worship at the feet of lord Viṣṇu, who is none other than the absolute, he freed himself from bondage to the wheel of transmigration. Truly he lived in a state of god-consciousness, and being totally free from the false notions of 'I' and 'mine' he ruled the country and the people in an exemplary manner. Of him the wise ones sing:

Which king in the world can rival Gaya, who was actively devoted to the Lord, who had great knowledge, who was the defender of dharma, whom prosperity befriended, who was the leader of assemblies and the humble servant of the holy ones? On his coronation day the daughters of Dakṣa and the deities presiding over the sacred rivers, themselves anointed him. Enthralled by his goodness and his greatness, mother earth yielded her riches to his subjects. The vaidika rites yielded their greatest fruits to him, unsought. Other kings paid him tribute and the holy ones blessed him. The Lord himself was highly pleased with the devotional practices of Gaya: the Lord by propitiating whom all beings—divine, human and subhuman—are propitiated, from the creator to the blade of grass.

Gaya's son was Citraratha; after whom came in succession—Samrāṭ, Marīci, Bindumān, Madhu, Vīravrata, Manthu, Bhauvana, Tvaṣṭā and Viraja, who begot a hundred sons (the eldest of whom was Śatajit) and a daughter, Viraja, by his knowledge and conduct, brought great glory to the dynasty of Priyavrata.

Book Five Chapter 16

King Parīkṣit said: I wish to know the extent of the division of the earth-plane in detail, for I feel that by contemplating this, the gross material form of the Lord, one will eventually be able to arrive at a knowledge of his essential nature.

Sage Śuka said: O king, it is impossible even for a man of very long life to grasp by thought, or to express in words, the full extent of the display of the Lord's māyā. Therefore we shall describe the name, form, extent and characteristics only of the most important aspects of this earth-plane.

The dvīpa in which we live is the centre of the seven dvīpa; if you visualise the whole as a lotus, it is the pericarp. There are nine varṣā in this dvīpa, divided by eight mountain ranges. In the centre is the Ilāvṛta, in the middle of which is situated the mountain range called Meru which is entirely golden. To the north of Ilāvṛta lie the three mountain ranges Nīla, Śveta and Sṛṅgavān and the varṣā (continents) of Ramyaka, Hiraṇmaya and Kuru— every exterior range being slightly shorter in length than the interior range. To the south of Ilāvṛta stand the three mountain ranges—Niṣadha, Hemakūṭa and Himālaya, and the continents Harivarṣa, Kimpuruṣavarṣa and Bhāratavarsa. To the west of Ilāvṛta is the mountain range Malayavān, and to the east the Gandhamādana—extending up to the Nīla mountain in the north and the Niṣada mountain in the south. They are the boundaries of Ketumālā and Bhadrāśva continents respectively.

There are four mountains around the Meru, named Mandara, Merumandara, Supārśva and Kumuda. On these four are four big trees, the mango, jambu, kadamba and banyan respectively. There are also four lakes with milk, honey, sugar-cane juice and fresh water as their 'waters'; the gods and others who drink of these acquire psychic powers. There are also four supernatural gardens named Nandana, Caitraratha, Vaibhrājaka and Sarvatobhadra. The juice of the fruits falling from the mango trees irrigates the country. The banks of the river carrying the juice of the jambu fruit undergo a chemical change that transmutes clay into gold. From the kadamba tree, honey flows in five branches. From the banyan innumerable streams flow. They who partake of the blessings that flow from these streams enjoy health, happiness and long life.

Near the foot of the Meru there are twenty mountains. To the east are two mountains. To the west, north and south, similarly there are two mountains each. On the very top of mount Meru is situated the city of the creator Brahmā, surrounded by other cities for the gods that guard the different directions.

Book Five Chapter 17

Sage Śuka continued: When lord Viṣṇu (as Trivikrama) lifted up his left foot to measure the heavens after having measured the earth with his right foot, his big toe-nail pricked a hole in the celestial sphere. Through this hole flows the stream (of cosmic rays) which goes by the name Bhagavatpadī, bearing the richest blessings acquired by contact with the lotus feet of the Lord. This blessed stream is received by Dhruva (the pole star) on his head, and then by the seven sages circling Dhruva (the ursa major) who adore this stream. Descending further, this blessed and divine stream washes the stellar sphere and the lunar sphere before it reaches the city of Brahmā on mount Meru.

From there it branches into four streams and flows in four directions: Sītā flows eastwards, Cakṣu flows west, Bhadrā flows north and Alakanandā flows south to the peaks of the Himālayā and joins the ocean in the south. One who bathes in this river easily obtains the fruits of the great vaidika rituals.

Of these continents, Bhārata-varṣa alone is the one where one can work and shape his own destiny; the other eight are considered to be continents to which souls return from heaven to work out the merits left. In those countries the people are long-lived and healthy, they have prolonged youthfulness and extraordinary sexual power; yet, during their long life their womenfolk conceive only once, and that too towards the close of their child-bearing period. And, here there are serene and sacred hermitages of sages and saints.

Lord Nārāyaṇa, the supreme being, manifests himself even now in all the nine continents for the purpose of redeeming the people.

In Ilāvṛta, lord Śiva (who is the only male inhabitant, all others having been rendered female by a curse) adores the supreme being known as Saṅkarṣaṇa, with the following hymn:

"O adorable Lord, you are the abode of all auspicious qualities. You bless your devotees with your vision, which puts an end to their transmigration. Your vision is uncoloured by the sense-objects and by the activities of the mind, though you are aware of all these as their controller; therefore, he who wishes to gain self-control naturally adores you. You preserve the world for the sake of the others so that they, too, might evolve into your devotees. Yet, you are above creation, preservation and dissolution. Your first-born was the mahat-tattva which goes by the name Brahmā and I am his son. We, the gods, carry out thy will under your control and are unified by you. Salutations to you."

Description of the Cosmos
Book Five Chapter 18

Sage Śuka continued: On the continent of Bhadrāśva, Bhadraśravā and his people adore lord Vāsudeva's own dear manifestation as Hayagrīva with the following hymn: "Salutations to lord Dharma who purifies the self. How mysterious it is that intelligent and thinking beings fail to realise that death is waiting to devour all, and that soon after cremating their father or even their son, they indulge in carnal pleasure! You are beyond illusion and therefore beyond all action; yet you are everything, beyond all conditioning. Salutations to Hayagriva."

On the continent of Harivarṣa, the gods, men and demons adore the Lord as Narasiṁha, reciting the following hymn: "Salutations to lord Narasiṁha, the light of lights! O Lord, you have strong claws and strong teeth; reveal yourself fully. Burn the storehouse of our karma. Swallow up the darkness of our ignorance. Oṁ. Svāha. Grant us fearlessness. Oṁ kṣrauṁ. May all beings be happy, and may the wicked people become good. May all have goodwill for one another. May our minds be focussed upon you, the friend and sole treasure of the poor devotee; may our heart not stray into sensual channels which lead us away from the path of virtue. Alas, neglecting the lotus feet of the Lord, the life of our life (like water for fish), people run after possessions, which are the cause of our suffering and bondage. One who renounces these and adores Narasiṁha is freed from all fear."

On the continent of Ketumālā, the Lord dwells as the lord of love, Pradyumna, delighting the heart of goddess Lakṣmī and the sons and daughters of Samvatsara (the year). Lakṣmī, along with these sons and daughters, adores the Lord with the following hymn: "Oṁ hrām hrīm hrūm. Salutations to the Lord of the senses, who is different from all the qualities of nature, the ruler of all senses and understanding, complete with all the sixteen aspects of perfect being, personification of the vedā, of food, immortality, indeed of everything. Salutations to one who is strength, power and magnetism. Oh, what a pity that the people who worship you should ask for other boons, rather than for that of having you as their sole Lord. I pray, kindly place thy lotus hand on my head and bless me."

Book Five Chapter 18-19

Sage Śuka continued: In the Ramyakavarṣa, Satyavrata adores the Lord's form as the fish, with the following prayer: "Salutations to the Lord who is the foremost, who is pure satva, who is the life-force and ojas, and who is strength of mind and body."

In the Hiraṇmayavarṣa, Aryamā adores the Lord as the tortoise with the following prayer: "Salutations to the Lord as tortoise who is pure satva, whose position is indeterminable, and who is the most ancient and cosmic being, the support of all."

In the land of the northern Kurū, earth adores the Lord as the boar with the following hymn: "Salutations to the Lord who is known through the mantrā, who is sacrifice, who is the supreme person, whose actions are pure and who is triyuga."

On the Kimpuruṣa continent, Hanumān, who is the foremost devotee of the Lord, adores lord Rāma. He listens to the story of the Lord sung by the celestials, while repeating the mantra: "Salutations to the Lord who is disciplined and has ideal qualities. Devoted to his people, he is the exemplar of goodness, he is the great one and the great king, and for whom the holy man is like god." Hanumān further extols Rāma in the following words: "The Lord's life on earth was meant to teach mankind, not just to subdue the demons. In his great love for Sītā he exemplified the ideal husband. In every one of his actions he exemplified the ideal king and the ideal man. He held up devotion as the only means to attain him, by extending his friendship even to devoted animals."

On the continent known as Bhārata, the Lord dwells as Nara-

Nārāyaṇa, performing perpetual austerities in order to bless the people and to set an example of a life of dharma, enlightenment, dispassion, divinity, self-control and selflessness, which lead to liberation. The sage Nārada and the people adore the Lord with the mantra: "Salutations to the Lord who is devoted to self-control, free from the false notion that the body is the self, who is the treasure of the poor, the foremost among sages, the paramahaṁsa, the supreme guru of all. Lord, the glory of yoga lies in giving up false identification with the body. Hence all spiritual effort is useless if one is afraid or reluctant to give up this useless body! The sole remedy for that fear is devotion to your lotus feet."

Book Five Chapter 20

Sage Śuka continued: Jambūdvīpa is surrounded by a salty ocean, beyond which is the Plakṣadvīpa. In that dwells the god of fire with seven tongues. Priyavrata's son Idhmajihvā divided this dvīpa into seven continents—Śiva, Yavasa, Subhadra, Śānta, Kṣema, Amṛta and Abhaya. There are seven rivers and seven mountain ranges in this dvīpa. There are four classes of people: Haṁsa, Pataṅga, Ūrdhvāyāna and Satyāṅga. The inhabitants of this dvīpa live long—a thousand earth-years. They worship the sun with the following prayer: "We adore the sun who is the visible form of Viṣṇu, and who is the very self of ṛtam (natural order) and truth, immortality and death."

Plakṣadvīpa is enclosed in an ocean of sugar-cane juice. Beyond that is the Śālmaladvīpa (which in its turn is surrounded by an ocean of wine). Śālmalī is the silk cotton tree, which is the abode of the divine bird Garuḍa. Priyavrata's third son Yajñabāhu divided this dvīpa into seven continents— Surocana, Saumanasya, Ramaṇaka, Devavarṣa, Pāribhadra, Āpyāyana and Avijñāta. There are seven mountain ranges and seven rivers. The four classes of people there are known as Śrutadhara, Vīryadhara, Vasundhara and Iṣandhara. They worship the moon-god with the following hymn: "May the moon-god, who nourishes all beings by day and by night, be our ruler and protect us."

Beyond that is the Kuśadvīpa which is surrounded by an ocean of ghee (clarified butter). Hiraṇyareta, the fourth son of Priyavrata, divided this dvīpa into seven continents—Vasu, Vasudāna, Dṛḍharuci, Nābhigupta, Stutyavrata, Vivikta and Vāmadeva. In them are seven mountain ranges and seven rivers. This dvīpa is inhabited by four classes of people, known as Kuśala, Kovida,

Abhiyukta and Kulaka. They worship the god of fire with the following hymn: "You carry our offerings to the Lord whose limbs are the divinities and thus propitiate the Lord."

Beyond that is the Krauñcadvīpa, surrounded by an ocean of milk. Priyavrata's son Ghṛtapṛṣṭha divided it into seven continents—Āma, Madhuruha, Meghapṛṣṭhā, Sudhāmā, Bhrājiṣṭha, Lohitārṇa and Vanaspati. There are seven mountain ranges and rivers in it. The four classes of people (Puruṣa, Ṛṣabha, Draviṇa and Devaka) worship the lord Varuṇa, thus: "Oh God, you possess the energy of the Lord, capable of wiping out our sins. Purify our bodies."

Book Five Chapter 20

Sage Śuka continued: Beyond that is the Śākadvīpa which is enclosed by an ocean of liquid curds. Medhātithi, the sixth son of Priyavrata, divided it into seven continents—Purojava, Manojava, Pavamāna, Dhūmrānīka, Citrarepha, Bahurūpa and Viśvadhara. There are also seven mountain ranges and seven rivers in this dvīpa. The four classes of people (Ṛtavrata, Satyavrata, Dānavrata and Anuvrata) practise prāṇāyāma and worship the god of wind with this prayer: "May he the inner controller, who having entered all beings protects them, protect us."

And, lastly there is the Puṣkaradvīpa, surrounded by an ocean of fresh water. In that stands a great lotus with hundreds of millions of gold petals. It is the seat of the creator. In the centre of that dvīpa there is just one mountain called Mānasottara. On this dvīpa there are the four cities of the god of gods, Indra. Over it revolves the wheel of time, turning one full round in one divine day. The first ruler of this dvīpa was Priyavrata's seventh son Vītihotra, who appointed his two sons—Ramaṇaka and Dhātaki—to rule the two continents on this dvīpa, and retired to the forest, following the example of his six brothers. The people of this dvīpa worship the creator, Brahmā, with the following hymn: "Salutations to the Lord who is reached through meritorious actions, who enables us to know the supreme being, who is non-dual and peaceful."

Beyond this is another plane, equally wide. Beyond that there is a plane which has a surface of gold, where whatever is dropped is not found again— wherefore it is shunned by all. This is called 'Lokāloka'—and it is a boundary between the sun-illumined spheres and the spheres not illumined by the sun.

The vast distance from mount Meru to the Lokāloka mountain

covers but one-fourth of the terrestrial sphere. Beyond that mountain are the four 'elephants' appointed to guard the quarters—Ṛṣabha, Puṣkaracūḍa, Vāmana, and Aparājita. Beyond the Āloka (a plane non-illumined and therefore non-perceivable) is the region or plane which only the lords of yoga can reach.

The sun who illumines the planes that are perceived, is in their centre; and he is the very self of all beings.

Book Five Chapter 21

Sage Śuka continued: That was the revelation of the extent of the earth plane. Thus do the knowers of truth succinctly describe the whole by describing one half—between the two is space. The sun placed in the centre of this plane illumines the heavens, the earth and the intervening space.

During the summer solstice the sun 'moves' northward and days become longer than nights. During the winter solstice the sun 'moves' southward and nights become longer than days. When the sun traverses Aries and Libra, days and nights are equal.

They say that the circumambulation of the Mānasottara mountains is a journey of 95,100,000 yojanā. There are on that mountain four cities—that of Indra in the east, that of Yama in the south, that of Varuṇa in the west, and that of Soma in the north. When the sun traverses these cities, we experience sunrise, midday, sunset and midnight respectively. But, for those who dwell on the mount Meru, it is perpetual day. As the sun sets it sends the world to deep sleep. And, when it rises in the opposite direction, it torments the people, making them perspire.

Wise men speak of a chariot of the sun, symbolically, as having a year for its wheel, twelve months for spokes, six seasons for its segments and a hub of three pieces. Its axle (gravitational field) is fixed to mount Meru on one side and to the Mānasottara on the other. Fixed in this manner, the wheel revolves over the Mānasottara mountain. There is another axle, one-fourth the dimension of the first one, which is fixed at one end to the first axle and the other to the pole star.

The chariot itself is 3,600,000 yojanā long and 900,000 yojanā broad. Aruṇa (the dawn) is the charioteer. Seven horses are yoked to this chariot. As the chariot moves forward sages and saints, celestials and the denizens of the nether world sing the glories of the Lord who is the sun-god.

Sage Śuka continued: Though it is believed that the wheel of time constitutes the sun, moon and so on, in fact it is different from and independent of them, even as the potter's wheel is distinct from the ants that may be crawling on it. In fact it is lord Nārāyaṇa himself who, for the welfare of all the worlds and for the purification of all actions, has divided himself, so to speak, into the three (the three vedā, viz., ṛk, yajus and sama; or the three periods of time, viz., past, present and future; or the three paths of jnana, bhakti and yoga), and into the twelve (months) and the six (seasons—spring, etc.), so that all beings may reap the fruits of their actions. Therefore, they who with faith and devotion follow the path of the three vidyā, who follow the doctrines of the varṇāśrama dharma (whether they are considered 'high' or 'low') whether they perform ritualistic action or practise yoga, attain to the state of blessedness.

The same Lord, who is the very soul of all beings, enters the sun and transits through the twelve signs of the zodiac. They say that two fortnights make a month, during which the sun traverses two and a quarter constellations. One sixth of the year is a season (ṛtu); and half of the year is an ayana. The moon which is at a distance of one hundred thousand yojaña moves faster than the sun, and therefore transits the twelve signs of the zodiac in two fortnights' time. The moon is the nourisher of all living beings and presides over mind and food.

Three hundred thousand yojanā beyond the moon are the twenty-eight constellations (including Abhijit). At a further two hundred thousand yojanā beyond them is Venus, which is an auspicious planet as it brings rain and is considered to have a neutralising effect on the influence of planets like Mars.

Two hundred thousand yojanā beyond Venus is Mercury, an offspring of the moon, which is normally beneficient. If, however, it outstrips the sun, it forebodes ill, bringing storm or drought. At a distance of another two hundred thousand yojanā is Mars, an inauspicious planet which portends evil. Two hundred thousand yojanā beyond that is Jupiter. Two hundred thousand yojanā beyond Jupiter is Saturn, the slow-moving malefic planet. One million and one hundred thousand yojanā beyond that is Ursa Major revolving around the pole star, wishing for the welfare of all the worlds.

Book Five Chapter 23

Sage Śuka continued: One million and three hundred thousand yojanā beyond Ursa Major is the pole star, known as the highest abode of lord Viṣṇu, where Dhruva dwells constantly and to whom the gods and other celestials pay homage.

All these heavenly bodies revolve, fixed as they are to the wheel of time by the Lord himself, so that the countless living beings (which are the products of the conjunction of matter and spirit) might reap the fruits of their past actions and work out their destiny.

Some say that the stellar sphere can be meditated upon as the Lord himself in the form of the body of a dolphin, which lies coiled with its head downwards. At the tail end of this dolphin is the pole star. On the tail are located four stars representing Kaśyapa, Agni, Indra and Dharma. At the root of the tail are Dhātā and Vidhātā. At the hip is Ursa Major, representing the seven sages. On the right side of the dolphin are the fourteen constellations of the northern hemisphere; and on the left side are the other fourteen. At its upper jaw is Agasti and at its lower jaw is Yama. Mars is at the mouth, Saturn is at its generative organ, Jupiter on the hump, the sun at the chest, Nārāyaṇa in the heart, the moon in the mind, Venus at the navel and the Aśvini Kumārā at the breasts. Mercury is located in the breath. Rāhu is at the neck; and the Ketū (comets) are throughout the body. All other stars are rooted in the hairs of this divine dolphin.

Every day at sunrise and sunset one should contemplate this divine form of lord Viṣṇu which is composed of all the divinities, and, devoutly waiting upon the Lord, utter the following prayer: "Salutations to the supreme being, the wheel of time, the ruler of gods. Thus we meditate upon him." He who repeats this prayer thrice daily is freed from all sins; the sins of one who contemplates this divine form are immediately wiped out.

Book Five Chapter 24

Sage Śuka continued: Ten thousand yojanā below the sun is Rāhu. The presiding deity of this planet was a demon, who by the grace of God became an immortal, but who has a grudge against the sun and the moon because they betrayed him. (The story itself will be narrated later.) Rāhu causes the solar and the lunar eclipses.

Ten thousand yojanā below Rāhu are the abodes of demi-gods known as siddhā, cāraṇā, and vidyādharā; below these are the playground of ogres, goblins and other spirits, whose realm extends to the limits of violent winds and clouds. A hundred yojanā below this aerial region is the earth which has already been described.

There are seven subterranean regions in which dwell beings known as daityā and dānavā, and the reptiles. These subterranean regions are richly endowed with mansions of precious gems. The dwellers in these regions are not haunted by the distinctions of day and night, and the different seasons. They have great strength and are long-lived.

In Atala lives the demon Bala, son of Maya the founder of sorcery and conjuring tricks. Once when he yawned three types of vicious women issued from his mouth: svairiṇī, kāminī and puṁscālī, who are excessively lustful. They administer hāṭaka to the man entering Atala to make him potent, and enjoy him at will. Thus intoxicated, the man deludes himself that he is all-powerful!

In Vitala resides lord Śiva (with his retinue of ghosts and goblins) and his consort. He is known as Hāṭakeśvara, for he is the source of the river Hāṭaka, whose froth condenses into gold known as hāṭaka and which is worn by the demons and demonesses.

In Sutala dwells Bali, the son of Virocana. We shall narrate later how this Bali was robbed of the three worlds by the Lord who wanted to please Indra. Bali was delighted with this blessing! For, he realised that the sovereignty of the three worlds that Indra gained was nothing compared to the blessing of service to the Lord, that Bali enjoys! The Lord who is the self of all bestows himself on his devotee, whereas being the king of heaven only makes one forget him.

In Talātala resides the demon Maya, the master conjurer, who possessed the three cities which were reduced to ashes by lord Śiva.

In Mahātala live the serpents known as Krodhavaśā, the chief of whom are Kuhaka, Takṣaka, Kāliya and Suṣeṇa.

In Rasātala dwell powerful demons, the enemies of the gods.

And, finally, in Pātāla dwell the lords of the realm of nāgā (serpents) with many heads. The jewels that shine on their heads dispel the darkness of these subterranean regions.

Book Five Chapter 25

Sage Śuka continued: Thirty thousand yojanā below Pātāla resides lord Ananta (lit: endless) who is a part manifestation of the Lord. He is also known as Saṅkarṣaṇa (he who draws together), who is the deity presiding over the ego. The earth held up by one of his thousand heads, looks like a mustard seed. The Lord looks extremely charming and radiant. He is adored by all the hosts of serpent demons of the nether regions, who are all reflected on the toe nails of the Lord. Clad in blue garments, wearing a waist-band of gold, with one of his hands holding a plough and in one of his ears an ear-ring, he dwells there, his destructive wrath restrained, for the welfare of all beings.

When a seeker hears of the above description from the lips of his preceptor and then meditates upon lord Saṅkarṣaṇa, the knot of his ignorance is cut asunder.

The glorious sage Nārada thus extols him in the court of the creator Brahmā:

"No one can conceive of and describe the glory of that supreme being who is the ultimate cause of creation, preservation and dissolution of the entire universe. He is eternal, the causeless cause of everything; he is one and yet bears in himself the diversity of all creation. That same being, out of supreme compassion for us, has now taken a form, clothing himself in pure satva, in order to redeem us by attracting us to himself. One who hears his name or utters it by chance or on account of suffering or when he has fallen down or while prattling, is freed from all his sins without residue (aśeṣaṁ); whom else than that lord Śeṣa, need a seeker after liberation resort to for his refuge? No one—even if endowed with a thousand tongues—can adequately describe the glories of lord Ananta, the infinite, who playfully supports everything in the universe—himself remaining supportless."

O king Parīkṣit, thus have I described to you the regions to which men who perform various actions with a desire to earn manifold blessing, go. What else would you like to hear from me?

Book Five Chapter 26

In answer to the king's request to describe the diversity of creation and the whereabouts of the hells, sage Śuka said: The hells lie within this universe, on the southern side. There is the abode of lord Yama (the deity presiding over death and retribution) who is the son of the sun-god. On the jīva being brought to him, Yama ordains appropriate punishment in accordance with the divine law. This punishment is undergone by the jīva in one of the twenty-eight hells.

He who robs another of his wealth, child or wife is thrown by the messengers of Yama into the hell known as tāmisra. He who deceives another person and enjoys another's wife, etc., is hurled into andhatāmisra where greater darkness prevails, as it does in the heart of the deceiver.

He who, motivated by his infatuated love for his wife, children etc., supports them while exploiting and hating others for their sake, is sent to a hell named raurava. There he is tormented by creatures called rurū which are more deadly than snakes. There is another hell called mahāraurava where another class of rurū called kravyādā (who are carnivorous), eat the flesh of the man who lived a selfish life and indulged in feeding only his own body.

He who cooked birds and beasts alive is consigned to kumbhīpāka where he is fried in oil by the servants of lord Yama. He who is inimical to his father, a holy man or the scriptures, is sent to a hell call kālasūtra where he is made to live on a red hot copper sheet.

The heretic who abandons his own dharma and embraces another creed or faith is thrown into the hell called asipatravana. The leaves of the trees in that place are all sharp-edged swords. The man running about that place is tormented by them and whipped by the messengers of Yama. A king or an officer of the state who punishes the innocent is thrown into sūkaramukha where his limbs are crushed by powerful hands.

He who inflicts pain on others, knowingly, is consigned to andhakūpa where he is tormented by those very beings whom he tormented, and does not even obtain sleep or rest. He who eats what he gets in this world without sharing it with others, falls into the worst of all hells called krimibhojana, where he is eaten by worms.

He who robs a holy man of what belongs to him (except in an emergency) is taken to sandamśa where he is tortured with red-hot balls. The immortal man or woman who indulges in forbidden sex relations is made to embrace a red-hot iron image of the sinful partner, in the hell known as taptasūrmi. He who has indiscriminate sexual relations here is placed on a silk-cotton tree full of thorns in the vajrakaṅṭakaśālmalī.

Book Five Chapter 26

Sage Śuka continued: Those rulers who transgress the bounds of dharma fall into the river vaitaraṇī, full of filthy substances, where they are tormented by aquatic creatures. They who live with a prostitute, disregarding dharma, are also thrown into a filthy pond called puyoda.

In prāṇanirodha, the messengers of Yama pierce with arrows those brāhmaṇā and others who hunt and kill animals. In viśasa hell they who slaughter animals in sacrifice are hacked to pieces. In lālābhakṣa, he, who forced his wife to drink his seed, is thrown into a river of the generative fluid. In sārameyādana, dogs with sharp and powerful teeth tear to pieces those robbers, rulers or their servants who loot villages or caravans. In the hell called avīcimat, they who gave false evidence and they who cheated others in business, are thrown from a mountain top and their bodies are shattered.

In ayaḥpāna, the brāhmaṇa or anyone else who, though observing a sacred vow, drinks wine, or a ruler or a tradesman who drinks the soma juice, is made to drink molten iron. In ksārakardama, that man who does not respect and honour his elders and other respectable persons, and who is therefore considered dead though alive, is hurled headlong into the hell.

In rakṣogaṇabhojana, the men who offer human sacrifices by Bhadrakālī or Bhairava are cut into pieces, their blood drunk by the very persons whom they killed, who then sing and dance as their earthly tormentors did before. In śūlaprota, they who bait animals, inviting them to come close only to kill them, or, who delight in torturing animals in various ways, are impaled by the servants of Yama. In daṇḍaśūka, those men, as fierce as serpents by nature, who torture living beings, are devoured by serpents. In avātanirodhana, they who imprisoned others in dark cells are themselves confined to a dark hole full of fire and poisonous smoke. In paryāvartana, the eyes of that sinful man who looks with anger at strangers and visitors are plucked by crows, vultures, etc. In sūcīmukha, the vain rich man who distrusts others and hoards his wealth has his body stitched all over.

Like these, there are hundreds and thousands of hells to which the sinful go; and even so the righteous go to heavenly worlds; with some residue, they are reborn in the mortal world.

Both the path of renunciation and the gross form of the Lord consisting of the fourteen worlds, have been described to you. He who reads or hears this description reaches the supreme being, with his heart and mind purified.

Book Six

Ajāmila
Book Six Chapter 1

King Parīkṣit asked: O blessed one, kindly tell me how one can avoid going to hell.

Sage Śuka replied: If before death one realises that one has sinned and atones for the sins, one will not go to hell, which is otherwise inevitable.

King Parīkṣit asked again: O lord, a man commits sins only because he has lost self-control. One who has no self-control repeats such sinful actions again and again. How is it possible for him to desist from sin and atone for his past sins? Even if he does atone for them, as he has no control over himself he may commit the sin again, which makes a mockery of atonement.

Sage Śuka replied: You are perfectly right. The act of atonement is not sufficient to counteract the act of sin. A disease may be suspended by taking a medicine, but it is cured only by avoiding its cause, such as wrong food. One who eats wholesome food does not become ill. By the practice of divine virtues (like charity, continence, truthfulness) and of religious observances one overcomes the sinful tendencies themselves. But one who is devoted to lord Vāsudeva at once destroys all the accumulated sins and their roots, which are the sinful tendencies. For a sinner there is no purifying agent better than the service of the Lord's devotees and servants.

Other methods of self-purification are defective in one way or the other; but devotion is the best, surest and infallible way. In fact, if one who resorts to other methods is not devoted to lord Nārāyaṇa, his efforts are vain and futile. They who have entered their mind into the lotus feet of lord Kṛṣṇa even once in their life-time here, do not see the messengers of death even in their dreams, as they have atoned for all sin. In this connection, the wise relate the following story:

There was once a brāhmaṇa in Kanyākubja known as Ajāmila. Against all codes of right conduct this brāhmaṇa was cohabiting with a woman of easy virtue. They had ten children. To maintain them this fallen brāhmaṇa fell still further by resorting to robbery, murder and other sinful actions. Thus he lived till he was eighty-eight years of age.

He did not even realise that he would die. But on the appointed day the messengers of death came to him in their fearful forms. Attached as he was to his last son named Nārāyaṇa, the old man called out his name. As he uttered the name of the Lord, his servants from heaven rushed to the scene and drove away the messengers of death who were trying to drag Ajāmila away.

Book Six Chapter 1

Sage Śuka continued: The messengers of Yama (death) questioned the Lord's servants: "Who are you, O shining beings, who interfere with the execution of the authority of Yama?"

The Lord's servants smilingly answered the question with another question: "If you are the messengers of Yama, can you tell us who is punished after death, and how?"

The Messengers of Yama answered thus: The scriptures determine which are virtuous and which are sinful actions. In this world the elements themselves, the sun and the moon, time and space are all witnesses to the actions of man. Man has free-will to be virtuous or to be vicious. To the extent a man does virtuous or vicious actions here, by him and to that extent is their harvest reaped in the hereafter. Therefore, the good, evil and mixed actions performed by a man here earn him good, evil and mixed fortunes in the hereafter: for the omniscient lord Yama witnesses all.

However, in one condition the jīva is oblivious of the nature of his existence in the previous condition: even as while a man is dreaming, in that dream state he is unaware of his living conditions in the waking state.

The jīva identifies itself with the subtle body—composed of the ten senses, the five vital forces and the mind—and, in ignorance, superimposes on itself their actions and experiences. Thus attached, it is led by this subtle body from one birth to another. Egoistic attachment to the subtle body is the cause of sorrow, but the ignorant jīva does not realise this truth; on the contrary, it deludedly tries to push the sorrow away by more action. This perpetuates the chain reaction. This ignorant false identification compels everyone to act; no one can remain inactive for an instant. It is this subtle body which, with the help of the sperm and ovum, builds the physical body. This helpless state of the jīva's bondage is due to the identification with matter; and it ceases when the jīva turns to and is devoted to God. Such is the law of karma.

Ajāmila was a pious brāhmaṇa. One day he saw a man and a fallen women embrace each other. With his lust aroused, he fell a prey to that woman. From then on he completely abandoned the path of virtue and led a sinful life. Hence we shall take him to lord Yama who will award him the punishment necessary for his purification.

Book Six Chapter 2

The Messengers of Viṣṇu said: Alas, the messengers of the deity presiding over righteousness punish the innocent. To whom then will the innocent turn for redress? And, if they whose duty it is to administer justice swerve from their duty, what will the masses do—for they follow the example of the leaders? The common people (having like animals abandoned their own reasoning) rest in the lap of Yama, depending on his judgement of right and wrong. How, therefore, can he indulge in wrong-doing? Would he not thus bring about untold calamity on these trusting folk? Messengers of Yama! This man has more than sufficiently atoned for all his sins in as much as he uttered the Lord's name, Nārāyaṇa, while calling his son. There is no greater purifier and redeemer in this world than the Lord's name which instantly cleanses one of all sins, however terrible; moreover by generating devotion for the Lord it destroys the very roots of sin. The name destroys all sins, whether it is taken while addressing someone or in jest or as an interjection or out of apparent disrespect. Should a man utter the word Hari even unwittingly when he falls or slips, or on breaking a limb or being bitten, scalded or beaten, then he does not deserve punishment. Other forms of expiation prescribed by the scriptures for great and small sins do counteract the effects of those sins, but do not touch the root, viz., the sinful tendency. But any name of the Lord taken even without grasping its meaning and efficacy brings about a subtle change in one's consciousness. For, the calling out of the Lord's name makes the Lord turn towards the devotee! Even as a potent medicine will do its healing work whether the patient is aware of it or not, the Lord's name, when it is uttered will do its work of transmutation. Hence, leave this man, Ajāmila, alone; he does not deserve to be taken to the abode of Yama.

Sage Śuka continued: Released by the messengers of death, Ajāmila beheld the four messengers of the Lord and wanted to speak to them, but they vanished. Recollecting the strange incident, Ajāmila (who had recovered his consciousness and strength) repented of his evil conduct and went away to Haridvāra or Gaṅgādvāra. There he practised intense austerities and yoga meditation. When the time came for him to drop his body, the same messengers of the Lord took him to the Lord's abode. He, too, obtained the body and status of a messenger of the Lord. Thus Ajāmila, who took the Lord's name unwittingly at the point of death while addressing his son, ascended to the Lord's abode; what doubt is there that a similar blessing awaits him who takes the name with faith.

He who recites or hears this auspicious story never goes to hell, nor will the messengers of Yama so much as look at him.

Book Six Chapter 3

Sage Śuka continued: The messengers of lord Yama returned to their master and questioned him: "How many rulers of beings are there in this universe, sir? For, today your authority was superceded by four shining beings who were able to cut the noose and liberate the sinner Ajāmila, merely because Ajāmila had uttered the name 'Nārāyaṇa', before we could bring him to you in strict accordance with your command."

Yama contemplated the lotus feet of the Lord and replied: "There is only one Lord, one ruler of the whole universe—not me. He pervades all. By him are we all bound together to do our duties allotted by him. No one, not even the gods like Brahmā, Śiva, etc., nor myself, nor the celestials can fathom his intentions and his will, enveloped as we are by his illusory power (māyā) and though we are of a sātvika (pure) nature. They whom you encountered are the charming divine messengers of the Lord, who protect his devotees.

"No one—not even gods and sages—knows the Bhāgavata Dharma (the path expounded by and leading to the Lord himself) except the creator, Nārada, lord Śiva, sanatkumārā, Kapila, Svayaṁbhu manu, Prahrāda, Janaka, Bhīṣma, Bali, Śuka and myself (Yama). According to this, the cultivation of supreme devotion to the lotus feet of the Lord is one's foremost duty. His attendants protect mortals who are devoted to him, in all ways—even from me (death). You have seen the power of the saving grace of the mere utterance of the divine name. It is a great pity, therefore, that vain pandits indulge in all sorts of futile actions. The wise, on the contrary, resort to his name; and even if they happen involuntarily to commit a sin, the name wipes out that sin.

'Do not approach such people as have taken refuge in the Lord's name. We have no authority over them. But, bring those vile creatures who do not taste the sweet nectarine name of the Lord. Bring to me those wicked people whose tongues do not recount the names and the glories of the Lord, whose hearts do not dwell at the lotus feet of the Lord, whose heads do not bow to śrī Kṛṣṇa even once, and who have not rendered service even once to lord Viṣṇu.

"I humbly pray that the offence that I have committed through my messengers, who entered into a vain disputation with the messengers of lord Nārāyaṇa, may be forgiven."

Such is the glory of the divine name, O king Parīkṣit. And such is this soul-uplifting story that I heard from the lips of sage Agastya.

Dakṣa and Nārada
Book Six Chapter 4

Sage Śuka continued: I told you earlier that the pracetā, when they emerged from the lake, began to destroy the forest. Soma intervened with the wise admonition: "It is not right to destroy these poor trees, especially for one whose duty it is to protect the people. They, too, have been created by the Lord to serve as nourishment for the people. The immobile creation is food for the mobile and similarly the footless for the footed ones, the handless for the handed and the quadruped for the bipeds. Desist from this foolish destruction and follow the example of your father: for parents are the true friends of children; eyelashes, of the eye; a husband, of a woman; a king, of the people; a householder, of mendicants; and the wise, of the ignorant. Restrain your anger, and you shall transcend the play of the qualities of nature and earn the grace of the Lord, whose body is comprised of animate and inanimate creation." Having said this, Soma gave to the pracetā the girl Māriṣa, who in course of time gave birth to Dakṣa Prācetasa.

At first Dakṣa Prācetasa created the many species of beings by sheer will. But, they did not multiply. Hence, he began to perform tapas and contemplate the Lord with the prayer: "Salutations to the supreme being whose nature the jīva does not know (even as an object is unaware of the power of the perceiving faculty) but who is revealed in a pure mind when it is completely free of all modifications called thoughts. He is not that which is uttered by word, proved by the intellect, perceived by the eyes or with the mind; these are only qualities and not the nature of reality itself, which is only inferred from the creation and dissolution of the universe. Whatever is done or caused to be done by whomsoever to whomsoever, for whatever purpose and whenever—all that is one Brahman alone. Salutations to that which is common to diverse systems of philosophy, some affirming and some denying. May that supreme being grant my prayer."

The lord appeared in his radiant form in front of Dakṣa as he was, praying thus. Overwhelmed by this, Dakṣa fell prostrate at his feet and remained silent. The Lord said: "It is my wish that the created beings should multiply. Before creation I alone existed. Through my māyā the infinite potencies that were hidden in me became manifest. Brahmā, the gods and you are all my own manifestations; you were created, but not through the womb. The time has now come when creation should multiply through the sexual intercourse of man and woman. Hence, accept the hand of Asiknī (the daughter of Pañcajana) and procreate other beings through her." Having said this the Lord vanished from Dakṣa's sight.

Book Six Chapter 5

Sage Śuka continued: Dakṣa begot by Asiknī ten thousand sons known as haryaśvā. Commanded by their father to multiply the race, they proceeded to the lake called Nārāyaṇasara to perform tapas. One day sage Nārada approached them and said: "Without fully knowing the extent of the world, how can you beget progeny? In the same way, you should know the place inhabited by one person, a hole without an outlet, the woman with many forms, the husband of the harlot, the river running in opposite directions simultaneously, the house built of twenty-five materials and the swan." The haryaśvā meditated upon this riddle and knew that it referred to oneself—of which the world is the subtle body, the Lord is the sole ruler, the intellect is the woman with many forms, identification with the intellect is the husband of the harlot, māyā is the river running in opposite directions, self-realisation (which is the path of no return) is the hole without an outlet, the human personality is the house built on twenty-five categories, and wisdom is the swan. They reflected over the significance of the sage's teaching. Without direct self-realisation and direct experience of all these factors, they queried, what is the use of worldly activities? They at once took to the path of renunciation.

Dakṣa heard of this and, though grief-stricken, he begot by his wife a thousand more sons, called śabalāśvā. At the command of their father, they too went to the same Nārāyaṇasara to do penance, mentally praying to the Lord: "Salutations to lord Nārāyaṇa, the supreme puruṣa of the purest satva!" Shortly thereafter, the sage Nārada approached them and exhorted them to follow the footsteps of their elder brothers. Inspired by his words, these sons of Dakṣa also took to the path of renunciation.

Dakṣa was greatly annoyed when he came to know of this. When he met sage Nārada, he angrily said: "Appearing in the garb of a holy man you have done us a great disservice, in as much as you have prevented my sons from discharging their threefold obligation to the sages, the manes and the gods. They had no opportunity to ponder over the worthlessness of worldly activities. Dispassion for the world and its pleasures cannot be gained by listening to what others say. A man does not immediately know the falsity of sense-objects except through direct experience; only through such experience can he develop a distaste for them—not by hearing the testimony of others. You have therefore, unnecessarily and prematurely, unsettled the minds of these young people, and thus interfered with the process of creation. You shall, therefore, have no settled existence; you will wander forever." The sage smilingly accepted the curse: such is the conduct of the great ones—even if they are capable of retaliation they are forbearing and forgiving.

Book Six Chapter 6

Sage Śuka continued: Thereafter unto Dakṣa and Asiknī were born sixty daughters, of whom ten married Dharma, thirteen the sage Kaśyapa, twenty-seven the moon, two each married Bhūta, Angirā and Kṛśāśva and the rest married Tārkṣya. By their descendants is the whole universe populated.

Bhānu, Lambā, Kakubh, Jāmi, Viśvā, Sādhyā, Marutvatī, Vasu, Muhūrta and Saṅkalpā were Dharma's wives. Bhānu's grandson was Indrasena. Lambā's son Vidyota gave birth to clouds. Kakubh's son Saṅkaṭa begot Kīkaṭa from whom the fortresses emerged. Jāmi's son was Svarga, of whom Nandi was born. Viśvedevā were born of Viśvā, Sādhyā of Sādhyā, and Arthasiddhi of Sādhya. Marutvān and

Jayanta (a part manifestation of the Lord) were born of Marutvatī. Muhūrta gave birth to the division of the day into periods of forty-eight minutes. Saṅkalpā gave birth to Saṅkalpa (thought), and Kāma (desire) was born of the latter. The eight vasū (Droṇa, Prāṇa, Dhruva, Arka, Agni, Doṣa, Vasu and Vibhāvasu) were born of Vasu. Their progeny are the emotional states, the qualities of the life-force, the cities and towns and so on.

Of Bhūta and Sarūpā were the eleven rudrā born (Raivata, Aja, Bhava, Bhīma, Vāma, Ugra, Vṛṣākapi, Ajaikapāt, Ahirbudhnya, Bahurūpa, and Mahān). Rudra's attendants were born of another wife of Bhūta. Angirā and Svadhā adopted the manes as their sons. Vinatā, Kadru, Pataṅgi and Yāmiṅī were the wives of Tārkṣya. Vinatā bore the Lord's vehicle Garuḍa, and the dawn. Kadru begot the serpents. Kṛśāśva begot Dhūmrakeśa by his first wife Arci, and Vedaśirā, Devala, Vayuna and Manu by Dhiṣaṇā.

Soma (moon) married the twenty-seven constellations. Dakṣa had cursed Soma because he preferred one of them (Rohinī) but when propitiated by Soma, modified the curse—hence the waning and waxing of the moon. Aditi, Diti, Danu, Kāṣṭhā, Ariṣṭā, Surasā, Ilā, Muni, Krodhavaśā, Tāmrā, Surabhi, Saramā and Timi were the wives of Kaśyapa, who gave birth to all the living beings on earth. Of Timi were born the aquatic creatures. Samarā gave birth to wild animals. Buffaloes, etc., were born of Surabhi. Of Tāmrā were the wild birds born. Muni gave birth to nymphs and Krodhavaśā to reptiles. Vegetables were born of Ilā. Surasā gave birth to demons. Ariṣṭā is the mother of celestial musicians. Kāṣṭhā gave birth to animals with uncloven hooves. Of Danu were born the dānavā, the great warriors. One of them, Vipracitti, gave birth to a hundred and one sons, of whom Rāhu became an immortal, while the rest remain Ketū (comets). Vivasvān, Aryamā, Pūṣa, Tvaṣṭā, Savitā, Bhaga, Dhātā, Vidhātā, Varuṇa, Mitra, Śakra and Vāmaṇa are the twelve sons of Aditi (Ādityā), the gods. Vivasvān begot by Samjñā, Śrāddhadeva, Yama and Yamī; and through Chāyā, Śanaiścara and Sāvarṇi. Aryamā begot by Matṛkā sons known as carṣaṇī, full of wisdom. Through them the creator evolved the human race.

Indra and Vṛtra
Book Six Chapter 7

Sage Śuka continued: One day, Indra, the king of gods, was seated on his throne in heaven surrounded by all the gods and celestial beings, while heavenly bards were singing his glory. The preceptor of the gods—Bṛhaspati— entered the court; but Indra did not even rise from his seat to greet him. Bṛhaspati could have punished Indra for this misdemeanour, but he did not do so. He did not wish to encourage the royal haughtiness. He quietly left.

Indra immediately realised his blunder, and repented at heart. Power and position corrupt all, and Indra was no exception. "Who will covet the wealth, power and position even of the king of heaven? On account of such wealth, power and position I, the king of gods, have fallen to the level of the demons in conduct." Indra sought the presence of Bṛhaspati, but the latter had become invisible!

The guru-less, guideless Indra became like a rudderless ship. His enemies (the demons) who came to know of the incident invaded his kingdom and inflicted an ignominious defeat upon the gods. The gods went to the creator and bemoaned their fate.

The creator, Brahmā, said: "It was because you misbehaved towards your preceptor that you suffered defeat at the hands of your enemies, who are strong because they follow their preceptor and honour him. With the strength that this devotion to the preceptor bestows upon them, they may even occupy my abode! He who is devoted to the holy men, the Lord and cows, does not encounter misfortune. Therefore, go to Viśvarūpa, who is a holy man of great austerity, and beg him to guide you, though he is sympathetic towards your enemies. Bear with his weakness, for this is the only way open to you."

The gods, thereupon, went to Viśvarūpa and prayed: "We have come to you as your unexpected guests, O holy one. Kindly listen to our prayer. For, the teacher is the image of the supreme being; father of the creator; brother of Indra; mother of earth; sister of compassion; an unexpected guest of virtue; a guest of fire; and all beings of oneself. We have been defeated in battle by the demons, because we are without a preceptor.

Viśvarūpa said: "The profession of a priest (who squanders or sells sacred knowledge) is indeed ignominious. We should remain poor and live on what chance brings us, not serve you as your priest. However, how can I disregard a request from nobles like you? I shall, therefore, accede to your wish, at the expense of my own interests and life itself."

Book Six Chapter 8

Sage Śuka continued: As the preceptor (priest) of Indra, Viśvarūpa taught him the famous Nārāyaṇa kavacaṁ (a powerful prayer for protection).

Viśvarūpa said: "When confronted by danger a devotee should bathe, sit facing the north and recite the prayer sacred to Nārāyaṇa. By the mystic process known as nyāsa he should transmute his body into the holy name of the Lord. Contemplating the self as the supreme being endowed with power, knowledge, austerity and resplendence, he should pray:

"'May śrī Hari protect me in all ways. May the divine fish protect me in water; the divine dwarf on land; the Lord of colossal form in the air; lord Narasiṁha in the forest and in battle; the divine boar on the road; lord Rāma on mountain peaks and other places. May Nārāyaṇa protect me from violent actions; Nara, from pride; Datta, from neglect of yoga; Kapila, from the bondage of karma; sanatkumāra, from passion; Hayagrīva, from deriding the deity; Nārada, from sins against devotion; the divine tortoise, from hell; Dhanvantari, from ill-health; Ṛṣabha, from fear caused by duality; yajña, from ill-fame; Balarāma, from mobs; Śeṣa, from serpents; Vyāsa, from ignorance; Buddha, from heresy; Kalki, from the sins of the kali age.

"'May Keśava protect me with his mace early in the morning; Govinda, with his flute, at sunrise; Nārāyaṇa, in the forenoon; Viṣṇu, with his discus, at midday; Madhusūdana, with his bow, in the afternoon; Mādhava, at dusk; Hṛṣīkeśa, in the first part of the night; Padmanābha, during the second part and at midnight; may the Lord bearing the Śrīvatsa protect me during the fourth part; Janārdana, with the sword, during the last part of the night; Damodara, during twilight; Viśveśvara, at dawn.

"'O discus, wielded by the Lord, burn my enemies. O mace, crush my enemies. O conch, with your powerful sound, drive away all evil spirits. O sword of the Lord, cut down my enemies and blind them. May all our enemies and all our sins from which fear arises, be destroyed by the divine name of the Lord.'

"O Indra, this prayer affords protection and will enable you to disarm your enemies. He who wears this kavacaṁ (shield or armour) releases from fear whomever he looks at or touches with the foot. He has no fear from the kings, robbers, evil spirits, planets, wild animals or other enemies." It was with the help of this prayer that Indra was able to overcome his enemies.

Sage Śuka continued: The brāhmaṇa Viśvarūpa had three heads and mouths: one drank soma like the gods, the other ate food like humans and the third drank liquor like the demons. While he appeared to perform religious rites to propitiate gods, he secretly directed part of the offerings to the demons. When Indra discovered this hypocrisy he angrily cut off Viśvarūpa's heads. It was a sin, since Viśvarūpa was a brāhmaṇa. Indra humbly accepted the sin and suffered for a year, after which he shared it among earth, water, trees and woman. While transferring a quarter of the sin to each of them, he also conferred upon them a compensatory boon. The earth's share is seen in barrenness: and the boon ensures that a pit dug in the earth soon gets re-filled. Water's share is seen as foam and bubbles: and its boon is revealed in the inexhaustible supply of springs, etc. The trees' sin is seen in the gum they exude: and the boon enables chopped off branches to grow again. The woman's share of the sin makes her menstruate: and the boon sustains her constant sexual urge.

Viśvarūpa's father, Tvaṣṭā, heard of Indra's crime. Enraged, he performed a special religious rite with the intent of creating an enemy for Indra. As a result a great demon, whose darkness or shadow seemed to envelop the three worlds and who was, therefore, known as Vṛtra, was born. He grew rapidly to gigantic proportions. Tormented by him, all beings ran in confusion. The gods rushed towards him and hurled their most powerful weapons at him with all their strength. But that demon swallowed them all without the least difficulty. Thus outwitted by him, the gods ran to lord Nārāyaṇa again and prayed:

"All beings are afraid of death. Death is afraid of the Lord. May that Lord protect us. He who, appearing as fish protected the earth, will protect us against this demon Vṛtra. May he by whose grace Brahmā the creator did not fall into the waters of the deluge, but went on to create the universe, protect us. May he by whose grace alone, we, the gods, are able to create the universe already created by him, protect us. May he who is ever-existent and who, by resorting to his own māyā, manifests himself in every age as gods, sages, animals and men, protect us, treating us as his own self."

The Lord appeared before the gods, along with his radiant attendants. The gods, overwhelmed with devotion, fell down on their faces and prayed again, in the following words.

The Gods prayed: Salutations to the spirit of sacrifice! No created being here knows your true greatness. Salutations to the Lord of infinite glory. You reveal yourself as supreme bliss when, through the practice of devotion, the ignorance which veils you within is destroyed. Unaided and unaffected, you create, sustain and dissolve the entire universe, which is difficult for us to understand. In truth, we do not quite know whether you also have the emotional experiences associated with the creation, sustenance and dissolution of the universe, as we do, or whether you are their silent and unaffected witness. Maybe both these contradictory states blend in you, since you transcend our understanding which asserts that these contradictions preclude each other. Nothing can be attributed to you, since you are transcendent; at the same time, everything may be attributed to you since you are the sole reality.

Almighty Lord! Even these diabolical beings (known as daityā and dānavā) are in reality your own manifestations. Yet, when they indulge in their destructive activities at other then their allotted time, you yourself incarnate (by means of your own māyā) as gods, human beings, beasts or aquatic creatures, seemingly to punish them and thus to restore dharma. Therefore, we pray to thee, O Lord; get rid of this demon Vṛtra, if you think fit, and thus free us from the fear that torments us. You are the indweller of all beings and hence you do not need to be reminded or informed of the wishes and the prayers in the hearts of all beings: it therefore behoves you to fulfil this noble wish of ours and get rid of this demon Vṛtra who is tormenting the three worlds. Salutations to lord Hari who, as the very self, dwells in the hearts of all as the witness. Salutations to Kṛṣṇa, the embodiment of bliss and the wealth of the good, who is both the path and the goal of all.

The Lord said: I am pleased, O best among divinities, with your devout prayer; the prayer which you have now offered to me will confer awareness of the self and also devotion to me, upon one who recites it. Everything becomes possible when I am pleased, and hence my devotee does not seek anything other than my pleasure. Therefore, a wise man does not point out the path of worldly activity to others, but leads all along the path of devotion. O Indra, go to the sage Dadhīci, who has become exceptionally strong through austerity and prayer. He taught the supreme Nārāyaṇa kavacaṁ to Tvaṣṭā, who passed it on to his son from whom you learnt it. Beg of him to give you his bones with the help of which you will be able to overcome Vṛtra.

Book Six Chapter 10

Sage Śuka continued: When the gods approached the sage Dadhīci, he said in jest: "Life indeed is most dear to all human beings, O gods; how can one ever agree to part with it?" The gods answered: "O sage, for a magnanimous soul like you, what is difficult to give up? What you have hinted at is true: selfish people do not consider the problem of the person from whom they ask for a gift. But, one who is capable of giving it will never say no."

Dadhīci then replied: "I was only jesting in order to elicit your teaching concerning dharma. Here and now I shall relinquish my body, so that you may have the bone you need. The body is indeed perishable; even trees and mountains pity the man who does not use that body while it lasts, to earn dharma or fame. This indeed is the noble quality of the devotee: he rejoices and grieves in sympathy with all beings. It is regrettable that man does not serve others with his possessions, which are his only temporarily and which really belong to others."

Thereupon the sage fixed his mind on the absolute and did not even know when the body ceased to live. The architect of the gods, Viśvakarma, then fashioned a weapon known as vajra with the bone of the sage. Armed with this, Indra marched against Vṛtra. A fierce battle took place between Indra and Vṛtra and their two armies. The demons in Vṛtra's army were dazzled by the very look of the vajra. The demoniacal hosts attacked the divine forces with various weapons. The gods intercepted these missiles and tore them to pieces. The demons, when their ammunition had been exhausted, began to hurl rocks and trees; and the gods intercepted these too, and ground them to powder. None of these even touched the gods, just as insults and injuries do not touch an exalted soul.

Seeing this, Vṛtra's followers began to flee. To them thus fleeing out of cowardice, Vṛtra spoke as follows: "Friends, listen to me. Death is natural and inevitable to all that have taken birth. If one can win heaven or fame at the cost of one's life, isn't that the most welcome end? There are two modes of dying which are praiseworthy: either practise yoga and, with your whole inner being absorbed in the infinite, drop the body: or embrace death heroically on the battlefield, without showing your back to the enemy."

Book Six Chapter 11

Sage Śuka continued: The demons paid no heed to what Vṛtra said to them, but continued to retreat. Enraged, Vṛtra now addressed the gods: "Why do you, O gods, take such vain delight in harassing these bodies of demons, which are no more valuable than the excretions of their mothers' bodies? Is it valour to pursue terror-stricken enemies? If you are really brave, why don't you fight me?" Vṛtra then rushed upon the divine ranks and trampled the gods mercilessly. Mace in hand Indra rushed at Vṛtra, intending to kill him. But Vṛtra playfully caught the mace with his left hand! In turn he hit, with that very mace, the elephant-vehicle of Indra. Stunned, the elephant retreated. Soothed by the touch of Indra's hand, it advanced. But Vṛtra did not strike again. Instead, he spoke to Indra as follows:

"I am glad, O vile slayer of a brāhmaṇa, that you are standing in front of me. I shall discharge my debt to my brother whom you unrighteously murdered. He was a brāhmaṇa, your preceptor, a man who was free from sin and who had attained self-realisation, and he was actually engaged in performing a religious rite on your behalf. If, on the other hand, I should die, I shall be happy to let the birds and beasts prey upon my flesh. Then, free from karma, I shall take refuge in the dust of the feet of the holy ones.

"O Indra, why don't you use your thunderbolt? It will not fail in its aim as your mace did, because it has been strengthened by the power of the Lord himself and by the asceticism of Dadhīci. Victory, prosperity and virtue abide where the Lord is. When you kill me with that thunderbolt, I shall meditate upon the Lord and reach the abode of the sages. O Indra, the Lord does not bestow on the devotee the pleasures of the three worlds, which only promote hatred, fear, vanity and suffering. On the contrary, our Lord obstructs his devotees' worldly and heavenly ambitions so that they may be single-mindedly devoted to him. By such obstructions one should infer the Lord's grace.

"I pray to the Lord: Lord, at death, may I be born as a humble servant of your devotees. May my mind contemplate you, my speech glorify you constantly and my body be engaged in your service. I crave only for you and not for the abode of Dhruva nor that of Brahmā. Nor do I crave for yogic power nor even for liberation. My mind longs to behold you, even as a fledgling longs to see its mother, or a calf the cow's udder, or a beloved wife longs for her husband."

Book Six Chapter 12

Sage Śuka continued: In fact, Vṛtra preferred death to victory! Yet, realising the duty of a warrior on the field of battle and the will of the Lord, he rushed at Indra, holding aloft his trident. He hurled it at Indra, who, while intercepting the weapon, cut off Vṛtra's arm with his thunderbolt. Vṛtra wielded his mace with the other hand and hit Indra in such a way that the thunderbold dropped from Indra's hand. At this, Indra was ashamed of himself. But Vṛtra calmly asked Indra to take up the thunderbolt and fight on. He said to Indra:

"O Indra, kill your enemy with the thunderbolt. Do not feel despondent now. Victory or defeat does not depend upon military strength, but upon the Lord's will. All these worlds with their guardian deities are under his control, functioning as time, and carry on their work helplessly like a caged bird. Not knowing him (who functions as energy, strength, life-force, death and immortality) people think they are responsible for their actions and their results. Without his will, the individual soul and nature are totally powerless to create, sustain or dissolve the universe. The Lord himself brings living beings into this world, using other beings (the parents) as an excuse; and he himself takes their life away, using other beings as an excuse. Life, prosperity, fame and such other blessings that a man enjoys, seek him at the appropriate time, even as their opposites seek him at other appropriate times. Therefore one should remain even-minded in fame and infamy, victory and failure, pleasure and pain, life and death. Look at me, O Indra. Though you have cut off my arm and destroyed my weapon and though defeat stares me in my face, I am fighting hard! Warfare is a gamble; no one knows who will win. And it is not our concern either."

Indra was full of admiration for Vṛtra's wisdom. "You have surely overcome your demoniacal disposition, O Vṛtra, and attained the status of an exalted soul of great wisdom. This indeed is a great wonder." Thus discussing the highest aspect of dharma, they continued to fight. Indra cut off Vṛtra's other arm and it fell with the mace. Vṛtra collapsed. Lying on the battlefield he opened his mouth wide and swallowed Indra! Yet Indra did not die, but emerged tearing the demon's abdomen, wielding the divine thunderbolt. At last, Indra cut off Vṛtra's head with the thunderbolt. From the body emerged an effulgent form, the very soul of Vṛtra, which entered into the Lord.

Book Six Chapter 13

Sage Śuka continued: In fact, Indra was afraid to kill Vṛtra, though the gods demanded it. He remembered that he had already killed one holy man (brāhmaṇa), but luckily for him this sin had been taken over by earth, water, tree and woman. Vṛtra, too, was a brāhmaṇa;

and to kill him was sin, too. He wondered how he could get rid of it.

But the sages reassured him, telling him that they would help him absolve himself of that sin by conducting a horse-ritual, which is reputed to propitiate the Lord, whose pleasure dispels all sins in a moment. Yet after killing Vṛtra, even on this assurance from the sages, Indra was not at all happy. No doubt all the gods and the sages were happy that their tormentor had been killed.

Indra suffered from a guilty conscience. This guilty conscience robbed Indra of his peace of mind and burned his whole being, as it were. One who commits sins, ignoring his conscience, is deserted even by his good qualities. Indra actually saw this sin pursuing him in the form of an ugly woman suffering from consumption. Fleeing from her, Indra entered the Mānasa lake and hid in a lotus stalk. There he remained, constantly contemplating the Lord in his heart.

During this period, Nahuṣa, a mortal king, ruled as Indra. However, Nahuṣa provoked the anger of Indra's wife Śacī, who cursed him for his vanity; and he was quickly thrown into the mortal world.

In the meantime, Indra's penitence and his contemplation of the Lord had purified his heart; and so the sages prayed to Indra to resume his duties. They then performed the famous horse-ritual which is capable of wiping out all sins. Thus was Indra rid of his sins.

This all-purifying story concerning Vṛtra (the great devotee of the Lord) and the victory of Indra, is full of the Lord's glory. It should, therefore, be recited or heard on all auspicious occasions. It will bestow on its narrators and listeners, wealth, fame and long life, will free them from sinful tendencies and will enable them to conquer internal and external enemies.

Citraketu
Book Six Chapter 14

King Parīkṣit said: Living beings are countless; among them only some rare ones seek their ultimate good. Only a few among them aspire for liberation. Among those aspirants, one in thousands reaches perfection. It is extremely rare to find, even among those perfected ones, one who is exclusively devoted to lord Nārāyaṇa. Such being the case, how was it possible for a sinful person like Vṛtra to cultivate such marvellous devotion to the Lord?

Sage Śuka replied: In that connection sage Vedavyāsa, as well as Nārada and Devala, narrated to me the following history:

Once upon a time there was a king called Citraketu, who ruled over Sūrasena country. He had many wives, but no issue. In spite of all his wealth and pleasures, this king knew neither peace nor happiness. One day sage Angirā visited him and enquired about his welfare. Citraketu replied: "O sage, you know everything, because your heart has been purified through asceticism and therefore your vision is clear. The illimitable wealth and the kingdom that I possess do not give me happiness, as I am without a son. I pray, save me."

The sage thereupon performed the necessary ritual, and, handing the remnants of the ritual to the king, he said: "By merely eating these remnants your queen will beget a son who will be the cause of both great joy and great sorrow to you." Soon after this blessing the queen gave birth to a lovely boy. He was the apple of all eyes, especially of the king and the boy's own mother. This particular lady grew in the king's esteem too, and he began to neglect the other wives who had failed to give him a son.

Jealousy entered the hearts of the other wives of the king, who in desperation poisoned the prince. Finding the baby sleeping too long, the queen asked the nurse to pick him up and bring him to her. The nurse found the child dead: she fainted. The women of the household fainted too. The king became unconscious. The queen (mother of the child) beat her breasts and lamented aloud: "O creator, how can you be so foolish as to destroy your own creation so prematurely? You are our enemy. There is in fact no order in this world: the aged survive the young sometimes. You engender affection in our hearts in order to carry on your work; and yet you cut asunder that affection, without mercy."

As they were mourning the death of the child, sage Angirā appeared before them.

Book Six Chapter 15

Sage Śuka continued: To the king thus grieving, the sages Angirā and Nārada said: "O king, for whom are you grieving? Do you know what this child was before he was born, and how he was related to you in your past birth and what your relation will be to him in the next incarnation? Just as particles of sand come together and part from each other in a stream, people come together and part in the stream called time. We, you, they—all these mobile and immobile creatures—neither were these such before they were born nor will they be such after death; and, therefore, they are not so even now. The Lord creates beings with beings who are incapable of creating themselves, though he has no desire to be fulfilled by doing so. All these speculations about the body and the embodied being have been created by ignorance. They are not real."

Thus instructed, the king regained his sense and enquired about the identity of the sages. Sage Angirā replied: "I am Angirā who performed the religious rite for you to have a son. Knowing that you are despondent, this sage Nārada and I have come to you. For, grief is incompatible with such a devotee of the Lord and holy man as you are. In fact, even in the first instance I could have imparted wisdom to you and cautioned you to desist from this desire for progeny. But, you craved for a son and hence I conferred upon you that boon. That has enabled you to experience immediately and directly the misery of having a son. Even so, all worldly objects and relationships are fraught with sorrow. All relationships are merely conceptual. They appear and disappear like a palace in the cloud. On account of hidden tendencies of past incarnations, man thinks of these objects and relations as real, and indulges in further action.

"The one direct cause for man's sorrow is his ignorant feeling that his body is the self. Correct and diligent investigation into the nature of the self is the only sure cure for this malady."

The king had by then completely regained his balance of mind. Nārada taught him a sacred prayer and said: "O king, perform the last rites to the dead child. Repeat this most holy prayer and you will be able to behold the Lord after seven days. Even the gods are freed from delusion only when they resort to his lotus feet."

Book Six Chapter 16

Sage Śuka continued: Nārada then showed Citraketu the soul of his departed son ascending to the other world. Addressing that soul, Nārada said: "Look at your parents and relations grieving here. Come down and occupy the body again and live a happy life."

That soul, however, replied: "I am everlasting and I am free from the changes that affect the body. In which incarnation, therefore, were these people my parents and kinsmen? Everyone is related to everyone else in one or the other of their numerous incarnations. All these relationships are transitory; and the feeling of mine-ness exists only so long as the physical relationship exists. The soul is neither friendly nor hostile to anyone. The self is the silent witness of all, neither involved in friends or foes nor in the chain of cause and effect."

Hearing this, the wonderstruck mourners shed their grief. They performed the last rites to the dead child. The women responsible for the child's death performed the prescribed penance. The devout Citraketu learnt the following prayer from Nārada:

"Salutations to lord Vāsudeva, Pradyumna, Aniruddha and Saṅkarṣaṇa. Salutations to consciousness and supreme bliss, which delights in the self and is peaceful and free from perception of duality. Salutations to Hṛṣīkeśa, the cosmic being, who is free from māyā, who is beyond speech and thought, who is nameless and formless and transcendental. Salutations to Brahman who is omnipresent, in whom the universe exists and dissolves, who is untouched by mind, intellect, etc., and who is the subject by whose grace the mind, senses, etc., function. Salutations to the supreme being whose feet are pressed by the great devotees."

Book Six Chapter 16

Sage Śuka continued: After thus initiating the king into the holy prayer, the sages returned to their hermitages. Citraketu devoutly repeated the prayer for seven days, as instructed by Nārada. At the end of that period Citraketu became the chief of the celestials known as vidyādhara. A few days later he sought the abode of Śeṣa, where he saw the Lord himself in all his radiance and glory. Citraketu, who was greatly overwhelmed with devotion, bathed the Lord's feet with his tears of love. After some time he began to extol the Lord:

"Lord, you are invincible. Yet you are conquered by those who are even-minded and holy; and they in their turn are conquered by you, too. You give yourself out of pure compassion to those who worship you unselfishly. You were before the atoms were formed; you will be after the universe is dissolved; you and you alone exist even now. This universe is but an atom in your infinite being. Only the ignorant adore the gods and neglect to adore you, the infinite being. Adoration of the gods through rituals, fraught as they are with the infliction of pain upon oneself and upon others, is tainted by sin. Even the best of them can only take one to heaven; whereas he who adores you with even a selfish motive has his heart gradually purified. They who are exclusively devoted to you are not haunted by feelings of 'I' and 'mine', as is the case of those pursuing other paths which involve violence to oneself or other beings. Self-mortification inflicts pain on you, the indweller, and violence done to other creatures is sinful. All our sins are wiped out by your vision. Salutations, salutations to thee, O Lord who are the life of our life, by whose grace and power alone the senses and the gods function in the universe."

The Lord, who was highly pleased with this hymn, said to Citraketu: "Blessed are you, O Citraketu, for you have achieved the goal of your life, which is to see me. Verily, I am the self of all beings. I am their creator. Both the logos and the supreme being are my bodies. In the dream state a man sees many beings within himself, and in the waking state he sees himself as a single individual (he himself being the substratum for both these). Similarly, a man should regard all the beings in the universe and himself as identical with me. I am the consciousness that is the unity in diversity; when one forgets me he is entangled in diversity and worldly activity. Such activity is the cause of sorrow, whereas non-volitional activity is wisdom. Such wisdom gives birth to devotion to me. Cultivate this wisdom and you will soon attain perfection." Having said this the Lord disappeared.

Book Six Chapter 17

Sage Śuka continued: For a long time thereafter Citraketu lived in the valleys of mount Sumeru, having the glories of lord Vāsudeva sung by celestial women. One day as he was flying in the air he noticed that Śiva was sitting on mount Kailāsa surrounded by sages and celestials. His consort Pārvati was on his lap. Looking at this Citraketu laughed aloud and remarked: "How unbecoming it is for a god like lord Śiva to embrace a woman in an open assembly! Yet, he is expounding the path of righteousness to sages, and he has the external appearance of an anchorite!"

Hearing this, lord Śiva and the sages smiled but did not reply. However, Śiva's consort Pārvati was annoyed and cursed Citraketu.

Pārvati said: "Who is this celestial to teach us what is righteousness? Is he wiser than the creator Brahmā and the sages, that he comes forward to teach us the righteousness that they do not know? He must be punished for his impudence, for such an arrogant person is not fit to worship the feet of lord Viṣṇu. O Citraketu, you will be reborn as a demon. Having worked out the evil propensities there, my son, you will never again be impudent."

Citraketu knew that the curse was for his own good and so he welcomed it. He spoke to Pārvati: "Mother, I welcome your curse, as it is uttered to purify your child. In fact, no one (neither oneself nor another) is responsible for one's sorrow: it does not exist! In this material universe distinctions between joy and sorrow, heaven and hell, are arbitrary and ignorant. Hence, I do not pray that the curse be withdrawn; but I do pray that you may forgive my rashness." He flew on, with an unruffled mind.

Pārvati was astounded at this! Lord Siva explained to her: "My dear, they who are devoted to lord Nārāyaṇa have no fear anywhere—in heaven, in hell or in liberation they see no difference. Curses and blessings are seen to be different only by the ignorant and deluded souls who long for pleasure and are averse to pain. They who are devoted to lord Vāsuseva do not crave for anything. Hence, though Citraketu was capable of uttering a counter-curse, he did not do so, and is flying away in peace."

This Citraketu was later born as Vṛtra, O Parīkṣit. He who recites this holy story in the morning, is freed from bondage.

Book Six Chapter 18

Sage Śuka continued: I have already narrated to you how Kaśyapa's wife Diti gave birth to Hiraṇyākṣa and Hiraṇyakaśipu. Both of them were killed by lord Viṣṇu, the friend of Indra. Diti was therefore very angry with Indra. She thought: "How foolish of Indra to consider the body as immortal and therefore destroy those who are inimical to it! Does that man know his ultimate good who harms others for the sake of the body, which is nothing but worms, faeces or ashes? I must give birth to a son who will kill this wretched Indra."

Having thus resolved, she strove to win her husband Kaśyapa's pleasure. The sage, deluded by affection, granted her a boon of her choice. This was not surprising, though Kaśyapa was a sage: for the creator, when he saw that his first-born sons were not interested in progeny, turned half of his own body into a female, which robbed men of their wisdom. On that occasion, Kaśyapa extolled her devotion to her husband, and explained that to a woman her husband is the Lord himself. Diti revealed her heart's desire: to bear a son who would kill Indra. Kaśyapa was shocked by this unrighteous desire and was sorely distressed at heart. He reflected: "A woman's face is charming and her speech sweet, but her heart is as sharp as a razor. No one is dear to a woman. To fulfil her ambition she would even kill or bring about the death of her husband, son or brother." Yet, so as not to break his promise, and at the same time to save Indra, the sage blessed her conditionally: "Such a son will be born to you if you observe the vow known as pumsavana for a period of one year. If the vow is not thus observed, your progeny will become Indra's friend." The vow involved observance of perfect purity with regard to her person, her clothes and her surrounding, her food and drink, as also her eating and sleeping habits. After eating she should thoroughly wash her mouth so that no particle of food remained in any part of the mouth. She should not sleep at sunrise or sunset, or with her head to the north or west. She should daily worship the cow, the brāhmaṇā, goddess Lakṣmī, lord Viṣṇu, and also women whose husbands were alive. Diti made the vow as suggested and put it into practise immediately.

Indra came to know of this. Worried, he became her servant in disguise, watching for an opportunity to obstruct her vow. One day, towards the end of the year, due to non-vigilance, Diti slept at dusk with a few particles of food in her mouth. Quickly Indra entered her body and with his thunderbolt cut the foetus into forty-nine pieces, all the time asking them: "Don't cry" (mā-ruda). But, by the grace of the Lord they were still alive. This was the fruit of Diti's worship of the Lord for almost a year.

On waking up she noticed Indra and the forty-nine babies. The vow observed in honour of the Lord had taken her hate away. On her enquiry, Indra confided to her what he had done in self-defence, and begged her pardon. He then went to heaven surrounded by the forty-nine maruts (wind-gods), who were so called because Indra had asked them 'mā-ruda'.

Book Six Chapter 19

At Parīkṣit's request for the details of the pumsavanam rite, sage Śuka continued: The wife should commence the vow on the first day of the bright fortnight of Mārgaśīrṣa month. She should offer the following prayer to the Lord: "Salutations to the Lord who is totally desireless, richly endowed with qualities like compassion, prosperity and strength. Salutations to the consort of lord Viṣṇu. May you be pleased with me." Repeating the text: "Salutations to the Lord of infinite potencies, whom I adore," she should perform worship in the prescribed manner with invocation, bath, dress, etc. After this, with the remnants of the food offered to the Lord, twelve oblations should be poured into the sacred fire, with the mantra: "Oṁ namo bhagavate mahāpuruṣāya mahā vibhūti pataye svāhā." The above prayer should be repeated ten times, and then the following hymn recited:

yuvām tu viśvasya vibhū jagataḥ kāraṇaṁ paraṁ
iyaṁ hi prakṛtiḥ sūkṣmā māyā śaktir duratyayā (11)
tasya adhīśvaraḥ sākṣāt tvam eva puruṣaḥ paraḥ
tvam sarva yajña ijye yaṁ kriye yam phalabhug bhavān (12)
guṇa vyaktir iyaṁ devī vyañjako guṇabhug bhavān
tvam hi sarva śarīry ātmā śrīḥ śarīre 'ndriyā śayā

nāma rupe bhagavatī pratyayas tvam apāśrayaḥ (13)
yathā yuvāṁ trilokasya varadau parameṣṭhinau
tathā ma uttama śloka santu satyā mahā'śiṣaḥ (14)

"O lord Viṣṇu! O goddess Lakṣmī! You are the soul and the body of the universe. You bestow all boons upon your devotees. May my noble wishes come true." The woman should also serve her husband, seeing the Lord in him. Even if either observes this vow, both are benefited. Thus observing the vow for a year, the wife should fast on the last day. The husband should pour into the sacred fire twelve oblations of rice boiled in milk and mixed with clarified butter. Then he should eat, and feed his wife, too.

Observing this vow a man obtains his desired object. It is of particular value to a woman, who will obtain longevity for her husband also.

Book Seven

Hiraṇyakaśipu and Prahrāda
Book Seven Chapter 1

King Parīkṣit asked: You mentioned that the Lord killed the demons for the sake of Indra. How can this be reconciled with the Lord's impartiality?

Sage Śuka replied: The Lord is indeed impartial. The guṇā (qualities) of prakṛti (nature) constitute the universe, which is subject to time. They function in his light and hence he presides over them. With the passage of time one or the other of the guṇā gains supremacy. In accordance with that, and in conformity with the time, the Lord promotes the cause of gods and sages when satva is in ascendency, that of the demons when rajas is in ascendency, and that of the lower spirits when tamas is ascendent. The Lord is in fact the unaffected witness. Yudhiṣṭhira asked a similar question of Nārada. Listen to Nārada's answer.

Yudhiṣṭhira said: O sage! When the wicked Śiśupāla, who hated and therefore insulted lord Kṛṣṇa, was eventually killed by the Lord, we saw that his soul entered into the Lord, though we hear that the tongue of one who blasphemes against God will develop white leprosy. I cannot understand this mystery. Graciously explain it to me.

Nārada replied: The body of all beings is the product of the elements. And, through ignorance the false notions of 'I' and 'mine' are born. Then there arise feelings of pain and pleasure, honour and dishonour, praise and censure, etc. All these are absent in the Lord. Hence he who fixes his mind on the Lord, whatever may be his intention, earns his grace. Many have become one with him by fixing their mind upon him through love, hate, fear, friendship and devotion. For instance, the gopī attained him through love, Kamsa through fear, Śiśupāla etc., through hate, and Vṛṣṇī by being related to him, you by friendship and we by devotion to him. Moreover, Śiśupāla and Dantavakra were the Lord's own attendants in his abode. One day the sages sanatkumārā arrived at his abode and sought to enter. The Lord's attendants, Jaya and Vijaya, taking them to be mere boys, prevented them from doing so. The sages thereupon pronounced a curse upon Jaya and Vijaya: "You have lost your discrimination! Hence you are unfit to be here serving the Lord's lotus feet. Descend as demons." Later they mitigated the curse by granting: "You will return to your abode after three incarnations." Hence they were born as Hiraṇyākṣa and Hiraṇyakaśipu, Rāvana and Kuṁbhakarṇa, Śiśupāla and Dantavakra. Purified by their whole-hearted devotion to the Lord through enmity, they have returned to the Lord's abode as his attendants.

Book Seven Chapter 2

Nārada said: When the Lord in the guise of a divine boar had killed Hiraṇyākṣa, his brother Hiraṇyakaśipu was terribly angry. He said: "The mean gods had my brother killed by Viṣṇu who, though impartial, had been won over by them through service. I shall myself kill that Viṣṇu and avenge my brother's death." He ordered his demoniacal hosts: "Viṣṇu depends for his existence on rituals and righteousness, of which the holy ones are the custodians. By destroying them, therefore, Viṣṇu is destroyed." The demons fell to their task. Hiraṇyakaśipu performed the last rites of his dead brother and spoke thus to the grieving mother and other relations:

"Grieve not. For to a hero, death facing the enemy is a source of glory. The soul is eternal. Birth and death, meeting and parting from loved ones or enemies, are all related to the body, and are assumed when the self ignorantly identifies itself with the body. I have heard the following story to illustrate this:

"Once upon a time there was a king called Suyajña who had been killed in battle. His wives and other relations wept and wailed, sitting around the dead body. The wives were ready to ascend the funeral pyre. In the meantime the sun set and death appeared on the scene in the guise of a child and spoke to them:

"'How foolish adults can be in this world! They wail for the dead, not knowing that their own death is knocking at the door.

Blessed are we children, for we have no such fear. He who protects us in the womb of the mother is the only real protector in this world. We are all pawns in the hands of providence. A thing dropped on the road is safe if providence decrees so; that which is protected in the house disappears if providence decrees so. The destitute in a forest lives protected by providence; he who is well concealed in the house dies if providence wills it so.

"'Karma brings the body into being. But the self is independent of the body. Fire, air and space appear to have a shape when associated with certain forms; but they are truly independent and formless. You do not see now the person who spoke through the body of this kind; but, even before he died, you did not see the person who spoke through his body! To think of these as real is ignorance, which is the cause of death. Two birds were flying one day. A hunter caught the female bird. The male ignorantly stood there wailing and the hunter killed it too. Not seeing your own death knocking at the door, you wail for the dead man!'

"Hearing the words of the child, the king's relations were freed from grief. Even so, you should not grieve for my brother."

Hearing the words of Hiraṇyakaśipu, the widow fixed her mind on the highest truth and became peaceful.

Book Seven Chapter 3

Sage Nārada continued: In order to make himself invincible, Hiraṇyakaśipu undertook awe-inspiring penance. In the valley of mount Mandara he stood on his big toe with arms uplifted and eyes turned towards the sky for thousands of years, without even drinking water. The power of this penance began to torment the gods, who had returned to their own abodes when he retired to the forest. The gods approached Brahmā and submitted: "Lord, Hiraṇyakaśipu is engaged in unprecedented penance in order to become another Brahmā. By penance he hopes to change the world order from righteousness to unrighteousness. We beg of you to do what is needful."

Brahmā the creator, thereupon went to where Hiraṇyakaśipu was and said to him: "No one has so far performed such penance, and no one will in the future, either. By such effort and endeavour I have been conquered by you. Arise, and ask of me any boon you like and I shall grant it to you." Brahmā sprinkled Hiraṇyakaśipu with a few drops of water from his water-pot. The demon had been reduced to a skeleton, his body had been eaten by worms and he had been completely covered by ant-hills. He came out of the ant-hills and shone as radiantly as before. With folded palms, he prayed to Brahmā:

"Salutations to the first cause, the ruler of the three worlds! You are time itself, which reduces people's lives with every passing moment. This world of matter, Lord, is your own body through which you enjoy the objects of the senses, though at the same time you remain a silent witness, unaffected by them. If you would like to grant me a boon of my choice, I pray: May I not die at the hands of anyone created by you; may I not die within a house or outside it, during the day or at night, through any kind of weapons, either on the earth or in the sky, either at the hands of men or animals, gods, demons or serpents. May I have undisputed lordship over all embodied beings. May I be endowed with glory like yours."

Book Seven Chapter 4

Sage Nārada continued: In answer to his prayer, Brahmā the creator conferred upon the demon the boons he sought, though they were most difficult to gain. Thus assured of invincibility the demon Hiraṇyakaśipu quickly brought under his control gods, celestials, human and other beings. In pursuance of his original resolve, he forbade all religious activities enjoined by the scriptures. He had established himself on the throne of Indra and exacted homage from the gods and sages. Such was the power he had gained by his penance that the earth and the heaven obeyed his commands and yielded up their treasures. The only things he had not controlled were his own mind and senses. Hence, he was not happy and contented.

The guardians of the universe resorted to the lotus feet of lord Viṣṇu and submitted their woes. Unseen, the Lord's voice rumbled thunderlike, the assurance: "We know it already. When the demon oppresses the holy ones, the dumb creatures and dharma, and when he ill-treats his own high-souled son Prahrāda, we shall kill him. Bear with him till then."

In the meantime, Hiraṇyakaśipu begot four sons, the eldest of whom was the noble Prahrāda. Though born of a demon he had none of the demoniacal qualities. He revered the elders as he would revere God himself. He treated all his equals as his brothers. He had a balanced mind and fully controlled senses. Even the gods admired and emulated his divine nature.

Though still a child he had forsaken childish play: his heart had been powerfully attracted by śrī Kṛṣṇa. He did not perceive the world as others did. Whatever he was doing (sitting, walking, eating, lying down, drinking, talking) he was conscious only of Kṛṣṇa and not of his actions. Thinking of the Lord and contemplating his glories he sometimes cried and sometimes laughed. Sometimes he shouted and sometimes he danced without inhibition. Sometimes with his own individuality completely lost, he behaved as if he himself was the Lord. Such devotion to the Lord earned for him the association of the Lord's devotees.

Book Seven Chapter 5

Sage Nārada continued: King Hiraṇyakaśipu entrusted Prahrāda to the sons of the preceptor Śukrācārya. After a while, when the boy came to visit the father, the latter asked him: "Tell me: what do you regard as good?" The boy instantly responded: "One should leave his home, which is the root of all delusion as it fosters false notions of 'I' and 'mine', and take refuge in the lotus feet of lord Viṣṇu." The king sent him back to school warning the teachers that they should not expose his son to such 'heretical' doctrines. The teachers wished to know where the boy acquired them. He replied: "Freedom from ignorance and from the delusion of diversity is the fruit of the Lord's grace alone. It is by his grace that my mind, of its own accord, dwells at the Lord's feet." The masters, however, punished him for his impudence and they continued their atheistic and irreligious instruction.

Once again the boy returned to the palace, where the father fondly enquired about the lesson that he had learnt at school. Instant was Prahrāda's response: "The highest form of learning, father, is devotion to lord Viṣṇu, which is cultivated by these nine practices—hearing, singing, remembering his glories; service of the Lord, his worship, prostrations, servitude, friendship with him and total self-surrender." The enraged king threw the boy down and demanded to know who had taught him this doctrine. Prahrāda himself replied: "Of course, the teachers are not to blame. The minds of those attached to the world, worldly relationships and objects are not drawn to the feet of the Lord. Only when they are purified by bathing themselves in the dust of the feet of holy men does devotion arise in their hearts."

Recognising in the boy his own death, the king threw him down and ordered him to be killed immediately. He said to his servants: "Turning his back on his own kith and kin, he is devoted to the killer of his uncle." For though the son was part of his own body as it were, he threatened the life of the whole and it was wiser to sacrifice the part than to lose the whole. The servants of the king struck the boy with various weapons and tried other methods (throwing him down a mountainside, goading an elephant to trample him, employing wind, fire, flood and even poisons and rocks to kill him) but all to no avail. As the king showed signs of dejection, the sons of Śukrācārya consoled him: "Do not take the boy seriously. As he grows up he will surely give up these childish beliefs. Or, let our father the sage Śukrācārya come back, and in his company the boy will give up his heretical beliefs." The boy was sent back to school. Though the schoolmasters continued to impart to him instructions concerning the three aims of life—duty, economics and pleasure (aesthetics)—Prahrāda showed no interest in these. His only interest was love of God.

Book Seven Chapter 6

One day when the teacher was away and he had been invited by his schoolmates to join them in play, Prahrāda said to them: Friends, this human life is extremely precious. Therefore one should cultivate devotion to God and the virtues that are conducive to God-realisation, even from childhood. In fact, man has no other duty in this world. Just as we get unhappiness without our striving for it, we shall also get happiness in this world without effort, by the force of our past karma. One should not therefore waste one's energies in seeking happiness, which in any case does not lead to the supreme security of the Lord's lotus feet. One should, while the body is still vigorous, strive to reach the Lord's feet.

How fleeting life is here! Even if a man lives for a hundred years, half of it is spent in bed. Of the remaining fifty, twenty is wasted in childish play and adolescent diversions. Yet another twenty is occupied by senility. The short span that remains after all this is wasted by ignorant man in useless pursuits of pleasure, which only create greater anxiety and a sense of insecurity.

Yet, friends, the problems of the ignorant man are insurmountable! Since his senses are not controlled he is unable to turn away from the objects of pleasure which he considers indispensable to him, from his wife and children who appear to him to be his only security and hope, and from his possessions to which he ignorantly clings. He has come to regard sex and the palate as the sources of pleasure; how can he understand their real nature? Even when pains, failures and frustrations stare him in the face he does not awaken to their true origin—lust for pleasure—which he therefore does not easily give up. On the contrary he endeavours to amass more wealth, often by robbing others of theirs, although he knows it to be sin.

One who is caught in the snare of diversity (I, you, he) who therefore differentiates between his possessions and others', and who constantly endeavours to increase his at the expense of others, cannot attain self-realisation, though he be learned. The company of such people should be avoided by all means. On the other hand, God-realisation does not demand much exertion because God is omnipresent! It demands association with the holy ones and compassion and friendliness for all. It is from them that we learn the truth which opens our eyes and which enables us to realise that the universe is an appearance and the Lord alone is real. In fact, it was on account of my association with Nārada that I attained this wisdom.

Book Seven Chapter 7

Questioned by the boys as to how he happened to come into contact with the sage Nārada, Prahrāda said: When our father had retired to the forest, Indra invaded our realm and routed the demons, who fled. The gods looted the palace and Indra siezed my mother, the queen. Nārada, however, intervened and Indra allowed him to look after her and the baby she was expecting: Nārada reassured Indra that that child was the Lord's devotee. In order to console my mother the sage used to impart the highest wisdom to her. She herself has forgotten it now, but by Nārada's grace, I remember it.

Only the body is subject to birth, existence, growth, maturity, decay and death, which are symptoms of the passage of time; not the spirit. The self is eternal, free from decay, pure, one without a second, pure awareness (subject), the support of all, changeless, self-seeing (aware of self, but not as object) cause (not effect), all-pervading, unattached and without any veil. By means of these twelve characteristics a wise man should recognise the self. By the subtle process of enquiry (using the formula 'not this') the wise seeker should, even while living in this body, arrive at the truth concerning the self. He should realise that the states of the mind and the consequent actions and their reactions, which keep the wheel of birth and death revolving, are all the play of the guṇā (qualities) of nature, and that they do not affect the self in the least.

This alone ought to be done by you: burn the very seeds of

karma (which is of the nature of the three guṇā) by going beyond the function of the intellect. This is yoga. Of the thousands of yoga practices the following has been declared, by the Lord himself, to be that practice by which one develops supreme love for the Lord: worshipful service of one's guru, fellowship of devotees, worship of God, singing his glories, adoring his images, etc., and by lovingly serving the Lord seated in the hearts of all creatures.

When this love reaches the highest intensity one attains the Lord. The following are some symptoms that indicate such love: on hearing of the Lord, the devotee sings loudly, he is delighted, he is absorbed in contemplation, he becomes totally desireless and heaving a sigh he laughs and weeps. This is the bliss of Brahma-Nirvāṇa. Anyone can attain to this state. The Lord does not take into account one's caste, genes, character, scholarship or proficiency in rituals; but only one's devotion. Without devotion all else is empty show. Therefore, by every means develop this exclusive love for the Lord.

Book Seven Chapter 8

Sage Nārada continued: Thus instructed by Prahrāda, his schoolmates also turned away from their demoniacal traditions and became the Lord's devotees. Hearing of this the king became infuriated. Angrily, he demanded of Prahrāda: "Spurning my authority, which governs the conduct of even the gods, on whose strength do you dare to violate our hallowed traditions?" Prahrāda, the purest embodiment of the highest culture, replied with his mind unruffled, in unfaltering words which sprang from an unclouded understanding of the truth: "The Lord, O father, is my strength, and he is your strength too. He is the inner controller of all beings. Please abandon the false notion that he is your enemy. He is our protector. Indeed, one has no enemies at all outside oneself: the uncontrolled, impure mind alone is one's enemy. And that enemy can be conquered only by cultivating love for the Lord."

Hiraṇyakaśipu's anger burst its bounds. Catching hold of the young boy, he shouted: "I am the Lord, there is none other. I shall soon sever your head, you fool. I shall see who comes to save you. If your Lord is everywhere, why is he not in this pillar?" Saying so, he knocked a pillar with his powerful fist. The pillar broke and a terrible sound shook the earth. It was as though the cosmic deluge was about to overtake the whole universe. The power that broke that pillar broke the cosmic egg, as it were, and released the divine manifestation.

Anxious to substantiate the words of his devotee (viz., that he is present in all) the Lord manifested himself in that pillar in the form of a man-lion, neither human nor animal. The demon was puzzled, He had never before encountered such a being. It had terrifying and brilliant eyes. Its mouth was fearful to look at; the tongue was a sharp as a sword. The crown of its head touched the sky. It seemed to have countless arms. The deadly claws of its hands were its weapons! The demon, who sought to prevent death from all known creatures in the world, was confronted with this manifestation which was unlike any being in the world. He knew that the divine intelligence cannot be cheated. Yet, he rushed at the being. As the demon neared the Lord, he seemed to be swallowed up by lord Narasiṁha even as shadow disappears in light. Yet, he hit the Lord with his mace. The Lord playfully caught the demon but the demon slipped through his hand. Again the Lord caught him and threw him down on his lap (neither on earth nor in the sky). While he was sitting on the threshold (neither inside nor outside) the Lord tore the demon's body with his fingernails (no weapons). Thus he fulfilled his mission without falsifying the boon granted by Brahmā.

The gods, celestials and sages had by this time arrived upon the scene. Brahmā, Rudra, Indra and the other groups of gods and demi-gods paid their homage to lord Narasiṁha.

Book Seven Chapter 9

After the frightened gods and other celestials had extolled the Lord from a distance, Prahrāda alone approached the Lord and uttered the following prayer: O Lord, hosts of gods and celestials constantly sing your glories. But you do not look to their wealth, ancestry, austerity, appearance, learning, energy, brilliance, glory, strength, valour, intelligence or yoga. You are pleased only with devotion. Moreover, you are not in need of glorification. He who glorifies you attains glory. When the true face is adorned with ornaments, the face in the mirror looks more beautiful too. Lord, abandon your anger, its purpose accomplished. People extol you in order to get rid of fear. I am not afraid of you, O Lord, as these gods and celestials are; but I am terribly afraid of this ever-revolving wheel of birth and death—O, when will you take me to your lotus feet, which is final liberation? Enough of this wandering in this maze of transmigration, O Lord: grant me that wisdom which will enable me to resort to the company of the holy ones, where I could hear and then sing your glories. There is no protector, no saviour, no healing agency in this world except your grace. Whatever is done by whoever, however and whenever, it is all done by you.

Māyā is your own power that makes the world appear to be real, veiling the reality. Hence only you can protect us from māyā. Even the gods trembled before the anger of my father, and he has been slain by you. I do not covet the status of the gods or Brahmā. Give me shelter at thy feet. The universe is your own energy. From it sprang the creator, who propitiated you and brought the universe into being. Since then you have protected the universe again and again, assuming various forms—human, subhuman and divine.

The impure mind does not delight in your stories and glories. Such a mind is distracted in various ways: by the sense of taste in one direction, by the generative organ in another, and even so by the sense of touch and the stomach, etc. Preyed upon by these many have fallen into the limbus: I pray to thee, O Lord, save them by your grace. Only you can do so effortlessly. Without grace, disciplines like the vow of silence, austerity, meditation and samādhi only prove to be a means of livelihood or of vanity (in the case of hypocrites). Therefore the wise cultivate the yoga of devotion.

Sage Nārada said: The Lord placed his hand on the head of Prahrāda, a blessing not enjoyed even by Brahmā and Lakṣmī, and said: "I am pleased with you. Ask for any boon." But Prahrāda, the greatest of his devotees, remained silent.

Conquest of Three Cities
Book Seven Chapter 10

Sage Nārada continued: The wise Prahrāda prayed to the Lord: "My heart does not seek any object in the three worlds, O Lord. Moreover, he who prays for blessings is not your devotee, but a trader. If you wish to grant me a boon O Lord, grant that no desire whatsoever may arise in my heart. Desire eclipses all that is good and noble in one's heart and desirelessness is the gateway to liberation. I salute the Lord again and again." Highly pleased with this, the Lord blessed him. He decreed that Prahrāda would rule the world for a long time, exhausting his past merits by enjoyment and his past demerit by present meritorious actions, and eventually attain union with him.

Prahrāda then sought the Lord's forgiveness for his father's sin, to which the Lord graciously replied: "Not only he, but twenty-one generations have been purified by the birth of a devotee like you in their family. And wherever such a devotee dwells, it becomes a hallowed place." The Lord warned Brahmā not to confer boons on wicked people, and then he disappeared.

I have thus narrated to you, O king Yudhiṣṭhira, the story of the redemption of Hiraṇyakaśipu, brother of Hiraṇyākṣa, both of whom were the Lord's own attendants; and how they, on their release from the demoniacal form, attained to his likeness. You are all even more fortunate than Prahrāda, in that the same lord Kṛṣṇa was your own maternal uncle's son and friend. And he it was who obtained for lord Rudra the title of 'Destroyer of the Three Cities'! Listen, I shall narrate to you that sacred story, too.

Defeated by the gods, who had the Lord as their support, the demons approached the magician Maya, who built for them three flying cities (satellites) made of gold, silver and steel. The demons moved so fast that they were almost invisible, and invincible, and destructive. The gods approached lord Śiva, who hit the cities and killed its inhabitants. The demons however had a well of nectar in which they bathed the dead heroes, who came to life! Lord Viṣṇu came to the gods' rescue: he assumed the form of a cow with the creator as the calf, and drank away the well of nectar. Then the Lord provided lord Śiva with the armour necessary to fight and destroy the three formidable cities. Thus was the gods' task achieved. Even so there are innumerable exploits of the Lord.

Sanātana Dharma
Book Seven Chapter 11

Yudhiṣṭhira then requested the sage to expound the sanātana dharma (eternal religion).

Sage Nārada said: Bowing down to the Lord by whom dharma is upheld, I shall narrate to you sanātana dharma, as revealed to me by Nārāyaṇa. The sources of this dharma are: (1) Lord Nārāyaṇa himself, (2) the teachings of those who know it and (3) the conduct by which one's innermost self attains to ineffable peace. Thirty characteristics have been laid down for the emulation of one who would love to live this dharma: truthfulness, compassion, austerity, purity, endurance, self-control, sense-control, non-violence, continence, renunciation, scriptural study, straight-forwardness, contentment, service of those endowed with equal vision, gradual withdrawal from worldly activity, perception of paradoxes in life, silence, self-enquiry, distribution of food etc., among human and other beings (looking upon them as one's self); hearing and singing the glories of, remembering, serving, worshipping and bowing to the Lord, who is the goal of the great ones; regarding oneself as the servant or the friend of the Lord and surrendering oneself to him. This is man's highest dharma by which all are pleased.

He is twice-born, in whose family the sacred rites have been performed without interruption. The twice-born should perform the rites, study the scriptures, perform charity and observe the fourfold division of one's life (the celibate student, householder, recluse and monk). Study etc., are the duties of a brāhmaṇa. Security of the subjects is the duty of the king. Business is the duty of a vaiśya (trader). Service of all the others is the duty of a śūdra. Diverse occupations, receiving gifts, begging, collecting left-over grains—are the brāhmaṇa's livelihood. One should not usurp the duties of his superior, except in extreme distress. One should in no circumstances degrade himself by indulging in base occupations.

Self-control, sense-control, austerity, purity, contentment, forgiveness, straight-forwardness, wisdom, compassion, realisation of the Lord and truthfulness—are the brāhmaṇa's characteristics. Bravery, strength, firmness, resplendence, renunciation, self-control, forgiveness, splendour of Brahman, peace and protection—are the royal characteristics. Devotion to God, guru, and the Lord, nourishment of the three classes of beings, faith, industry and dexterity—are the characteristics of the trader. Service, purity, humility, performance of simple rites, non-stealing, truthfulness, protection of the holy ones and cows—are the characteristics of a śūdra. The duty of a woman is to serve her husband, regarding him as the Lord himself. Everyone who is devoted to the duty determined by one's own nature will soon transcend the qualities of nature. One's nature alone determines to which caste he belongs.

Book Seven Chapter 12

Sage Nārada continued: The young student should live in the house of his teacher. At dawn and dusk he should worship his guru, the sacred fire, the sun and the Lord, in the appropriate manner. He should also repeat the gāyatrī mantra during both dawn and twilight. He should learn his lessons (the vedā, etc.,) from his teacher, for whom he should have great reverence. He should beg for his food from the village, offer it to the guru, and eat only when the latter permits. He should preserve the moral excellence of his character and should avoid the least unnecessary dealing with women. Woman is to man what fire is to butter: and this holds good till one attains self-realisation, when the sense of duality is totally consumed.

All this moral restraint applies to the householder as well, though he is permitted to have sexual relations with his wife at the appointed time. The student, after learning the vedā thoroughly and after giving the teacher suitable presents, may either enter the life of a householder or retire to the woods should he so wish, or even live with his teacher as a lifelong celibate. He should recognise the presence of the Lord in the sacred fire, in the guru, in himself and in all the elements, though in truth the Lord is not confined to any of them. One who follows sincerely the rules of conduct laid down for the stages of life shall attain God-realisation, whether he be a celibate student, householder, recluse or monk.

The recluse who has retired to the forest should unreservedly expose himself to the inclemencies of the weather, and resort to a hut only for the purpose of worshipping the holy fire. He should not eat cooked food or raw vegetables, but only sun-ripened fruits. He should pay no attention at all to grooming his body, nor cut his hair, pare his nails or be obsessed by ideas of cleanliness. He should thus live for a period of twelve, eight, four, two years or one year, but should beware lest this hardship pervert his intellect.

Then two courses are open to him: if he can, he should become a wandering monk. If he cannot, he should resort to fasting. He should offer the sacred fire into himself, give up all feelings of 'I' and 'mine' and merge the various sense-faculties and functions into their causes, which are the subtle cosmic elements. He should then merge the mind in the moon, the buddhi in Brahmā, the self-consciousness in Rudra, the citta in lord Vāsudeva and the jīva in the absolute. Thereafter he should merge earth in water, water in fire, fire in air, air in space, space in the principle of egoity, egoity in mahat, that in the unmanifest, and the unmanifest in the absolute. Thus he should realise the self as absolute consciousness and rest in peace, like fire without fuel.

Book Seven Chapter 13

Sage Nārada continued: If he is capable he should enter the life of a wandering mendicant. Clad in nothing but a loin cloth, with no possession other than his body, he should wander the whole world, alone, not staying at any place for more than a night. Homeless, he should live on alms, be friendly towards all, his heart constantly delighting in the Lord, his inner vision introverted so that he perceives all beings in the self. He should discover the true nature of the self at the junctions between sleep and wakefulness. Neither longing for the inevitable death, nor wishing to prolong evanescent life, he should bide his time. He should avoid all manner of earning his livelihood, attaching disciples to himself or indulging in secular activities. He should keep himself away from all disputes and never take sides in controversies. He should not indulge in vain discourses, nor commence any kind of work. The stage of life of a wandering mendicant is not associated with the preservation or otherwise of dharma; in fact, he is not even bound to preserve any mark of identification. Being wise, he might wander like a madman or an aimless child. Listen to a dialogue in this connection between Prahrāda and a holy brāhmaṇa.

Once Prahrāda went on a pilgrimage in search of holy ones. On the way he saw a brāhmaṇa lying on the ground, covered with dust. Recognising his greatness, Prahrāda asked him: "Holy one! Your body is robust and strong as if you are very rich and leading a life of luxury. But to all outward appearances you are a mendicant. Able-bodied people in the world are actively engaged in various occupations. How is it that you are lying idle here?"

The brāhmaṇa replied: "After countless lives in other species I have luckily gained this human birth, which is conducive to enlightenment. I have also seen here the miserable life that householders lead when they are given to acquisition of wealth and indulgence of the senses. They surely seek happiness—but, alas, in the wrong quarter. Bliss is in the self, not in objects where men look for it—even as a thirsty man might look for water in a mirage, ignoring a pond covered with lilies. Wealth only brings fear: the bee collects the honey, someone else kills the bee and takes away the honey. But the python is carefree, it eats what comes unsought. Hence I have adopted the lifestyle of the python. I do not condemn or commend the examples of these worldly men, but I pray that they too might become one with the Lord. Look within, and the notion of diversity will dissolve in its own creator—the mind. The reality will shine of its own accord." Hearing this, Prahrāda was enlightened.

Book Seven Chapter 14

On Yudhiṣṭhira enquiring about the duties of a householder, sage Nārada replied: The householder should perform all his duties solely for the sake of the Lord. He should cultivate the fellowship of holy men and at the same time allow his affection for his relations to drop away.

Free from personal ambitions, he should allow the other members of the family to conduct the family affairs. He should contentedly enjoy the wealth and the comforts that providence brings him unsought. Only that much is one's own, which is enough to fill one's stomach: he who owns more than this is a thief who deserves to be punished. He should regard as his own children even the animals, birds and reptiles in the neighbourhood: what indeed is the difference between them and his children?

Even a householder should not exert himself too much for dharma, acquisition of wealth or enjoyment. He should share whatever he has with all—including animals. Thus he overcomes the notion of mine-ness. He should overcome mine-ness even towards his wife. All these are related to the perishable body!

Daily he should perform the five great sacrifices: to the animals, to human beings, to the ancestors, to the sages and to God. Indeed, the Lord is greatly pleased when a householder feeds a holy brāhmaṇa. He should perform the appropriate rites to propitiate the ancestors during the appointed periods of the year. Such periods have been declared by the knowers of truth to be auspicious for the performance of japa, meditation, rituals, charity, etc.

There are many places specially holy and sacred to the Lord to which the householder should go on pilgrimages. In brief, that place is holy where a holy man dwells or has dwelt, where the images of the Lord are worshipped and where holy rivers flow. Spiritual practices in these holy places yield thousand-fold benefits.

Sages and seers have unanimously declared that lord Hari alone is worthy of our worship. No wonder, therefore, that even during the rājasūya rite they elected lord Kṛṣṇa to receive the highest honour. The entire universe and all beings are rooted in the Lord; and therefore to please him is to please all. The divine is present even in sub-human bodies; but since the human being is capable of self-realisation, he is regarded as the foremost abode of the Lord and therefore fit to be worshipped. However, since human beings are subject to love and hate, worship of God's images has been prescribed. But such worship does not yield any fruit if the worshipped despises anyone. The holy ones are most adorable—they sanctify the world by their very presence!

Book Seven Chapter 15

Sage Nārada continued: People of different temperaments pursue different paths. Some are devoted to the rituals prescribed by the vedā, while others devote themselves to the study and the recitation of the vedā. There are those who resort to the path of knowledge, and others take to the path of devotion.

He who is treading the path of rituals and who wishes to propitiate the gods or the ancestors by means of those rituals, should make the offerings to them through the holy ones, or in the absence of holy ones through other people, looking upon them as the very embodiments of the Lord himself. He should avoid feeding large numbers, as this would lead to the sacrifice of quality at the altar of quantity. Such offerings should be pure and should not involve the least harm to any living being. One aspiring for holiness should refrain from violence in thought, word and deed: there is no higher dharma than this. Self-control is the best sacrifice.

The aspirant to holiness should avoid the five forms of unrighteousness: (1) vidharma, or conduct which obstructs dharma; (2) paradharma, or conduct prescribed for others; (3) upadharma, which is imitative conduct and therefore hypocritical and showy; (4) chala, or conduct which is deceitful; (5) ābhāsa, or conduct motivated by selfish desire and generated by one's own whim.

One should develop contentment by all means. One should never strive to acquire and to hoard wealth. To a contented man there is happiness in all directions, just as the shod foot is safe even while walking on stones and thorns. It is only when one seeks the pleasures of sex and of the palate that man resorts to the life of a dog. A greedy man loses his fame, his learning and his wisdom. Lust is quelled by fasting; anger ceases when its consequence manifests itself; but there is no cessation of greed, even if a man becomes the lord of the earth. Even learned men, who can dispel the doubts of others and preside over assemblies, fall on account of discontent.

One should conquer desire, by non-gratification; anger, by desirelessness; greed, by seeing the evil of wealth; fear, by grasping the truth; grief and delusion, by wisdom; pride, by service of saints; obstacles to yoga, by silence; violence, by self-restraint. One should overcome pain caused by others, by means of compassion; pain due to destiny, by equanimity; pain caused in oneself, by the practice of yoga; and sleep, by increasing satva. All these, however, can be had through service to the guru (preceptor) without which none of the above practices will be fruitful. They will be fruitless if the aspirant regards the preceptor as just another mortal like himself. The preceptor is the Lord.

Sage Nārada continued: Whatever teaching is found in the scriptures is aimed at enabling man to control his senses and his mind. Any teaching that does not fulfil this purpose is useless, and any practice that does not lead to God-realisation is wasted labour. One who is really keen on attaining this control should become a recluse, live in a secluded place without attachment to anything or anybody, lead an extremely simple life and live on alms.

There in that secluded place he should have a seat made of grass, deerskin and cloth, seated on which he should practise meditation. Repeating Oṁ, he should fix his gaze at the root of his nose and control his prāṇa by means of regulation of inhalation and exhalation, till the mind abandons desires; when, like fire without fuel, it attains to a state of total quiescence. If the recluse returns to any form of worldly activity he is to be pitied, for it is as if he eats vomited substance—having known that the body is an unreal phenomenon, he again invests it with importance. Similarly, the householder neglecting his duties, the student violating the vow of celibacy and the recluse neglecting self-restraint, are all a disgrace to their order of life, and should be ignored by a wise man.

To whichever order of life he belongs, he who has realised the oneness of his self with the supreme being will be free from every type of craving. The pairs of opposite—like attachment and aversion—and evils like lust, anger, greed, grief, vanity, etc., are all born of rajas and tamas. These, and even some satvic qualities (like misdirected compassion), are our enemies. With the help of his association with holy ones, and the grace of the Lord, a wise man should slay these enemies with the sword of wisdom, or else they will throw him into this stream of transmigration.

Two types of actions are described in the vedā: pravṛtti, which causes the soul's return to mortal existence, and nivṛtti, which leads him to immortality. Scripturally ordained duties (known as iṣṭā) and social service (known as pūrta) are generally selfish, and bring in their train mental unrest and rebirth, the soul taking the dark path. They who walk the path of renunciation (nivṛtti) merge duties in the senses, senses in the mind and so on, till the jīva is merged in the supreme: they ascend through the bright path and do not return to mortal existence. He who knows these two paths is never deluded.

Sage Nārada continued: The ignorant assume the world to be real, even as the child believes a mirror-reflection to be real. This thing which is shadow and not substance and is comprised of the five elements, is not a product of their combination nor modification. Material substances are said to be compounded of the subtle elements; if intuition informs us that these substances are unreal, who can assert the reality of the subtle elements? We believe in the individuality of beings only so long as we ignorantly believe that there is diversity in the supreme being! Even scriptural injunctions and prohibitions apply only to the relative plane, which is enveloped by delusion.

Hence, the wise man should live the unity of thought, action and substance, and attain self-realisation. To realise the unity of cause and effect—their difference being non-existent—is unity of thought (bhāva advaita); to offer unto the supreme being all actions (mental, verbal or physical) is unity of action (kriyā advaita). To realise the unity of oneself with wife, son, etc., and all embodied beings, and thus to merge self-interest with common interest, is unity of substance (dravyā advaita).

By all means one should adhere to one's own duty, which should be discharged for the sake of the Lord, with intense devotion to him. One living in this manner, earning his livelihood, can attain to the realm of lord Kṛṣṇa, if he is devoted to the Lord. O king, all of you have been able to overcome many troubles and difficulties with the help of lord Kṛṣṇa; even so you will attain final liberation too, through his grace. For he is the supreme being himself, though he dwells amongst you as a human being.

In a previous incarnation I was a celestial bard, very fond of wine and women. One day the gods peformed a religious rite to which I went, surrounded by women. I was drunk and singing profane songs, even on the way. This offended the gods, who cursed me to be reborn as a śūdra. Immediately I was born as a maidservant's son. In that birth I resorted to the company of the holy ones and was devoted to the Lord, with the result that I am now a mind-born son of the creator himself. Such is the glory of devotion to the Lord.

Sage Śuka concluded: Taking leave of Kṛṣṇa and Yudhiṣṭhira, sage Nārada left their presence.

Book Eight

Book Eight Chapter 1

Sage Śuka said: Sated with worldly life, Svayaṁbhu manu retired to the forest. Standing on one foot he meditated upon the Lord for a hundred years, reciting the following prayer:

"The universe is made sentient by him, but the universe does not know him. He is awake when the world sleeps! This does not know him; but he knows it. Whatever exists is the self. Having renounced the world one should delight in the self, and never yield to greed. Take refuge in him who sees all but is not seen by any. That is the reality which has neither beginning, middle nor end, neither friend nor foe, neither inside nor outside, yet which is the universe. His body is the universe. He is self-luminous, ancient and unborn. The universe emerges from and resolves into him. The sages, too, remain active here because they see his creative and redeeming activities. He who performs his duties unattached, is liberated. He acts, but is not bound. One who follows this example never suffers. I take refuge in the Lord who is righteousness, who lays down the law and who himself observes the law."

The demons, preceiving manu thus engaged in austerities, sought to devour him. However the Lord, manifesting as yajña, destroyed them and ruled as Indra. Even so in the Svārociṣa, Uttama and Tāmasa Manvantarā, the Lord incarnated and, with the assistance of different Indrā and gods, upheld dharma. In Svārociṣa he was known as Vibhu, who practised lifelong celibacy. In Uttama he was known as Satyasena. And in the Tāmasa Manvantarā he was known as Hari, who protected the great elephant-devotee from the grip of an alligator.

Gajendra
Book Eight Chapter 2

Sage Śuka continued: In days of yore there was a mighty mountain called Trikūṭa. It was laden with noble metals and precious gems. Its caves were visited by celestials and sages. Lions, other wild beasts and many varieties of birds lived in the valleys of this mountain, which were enriched by rivers and lakes.

In one valley there was a wonderful garden which belonged to Varuṇa. The garden was known as Ṛtumān. Celestial women often sported there. Terrestrial and celestial trees abounded in this garden, which enjoyed eternal spring. In the centre there was a lake of extraordinary charm. Even the lotus flowers in that lake were golden. A number of varieties of ducks sported on the surface of the lake, enhancing its beauty.

One day a huge elephant entered that garden, followed by its retinue of female elephants and young ones. The leader was so mighty that the whole mountain and the forest shook with its footfall. It was so powerful that even lions and other wild animals fled from its path, whereas the weaker animals roamed freely without fear of being attacked by the elephant. All the elephants were thirsty. The leader smelt the presence of the lake and therefore they went there to slake their thirst. Getting into the lake, the leader drank and playfully sprinkled water with its trunk on the females and the young ones, ignorant of the fact that a calamity was about to befall them.

In that lake dwelt an alligator, which seized the foot of the leader of the elephant herd and began to drag it into deep waters. There ensued a terrible tussle between the two. The females could only trumpet. The males in the herd, too, found themselves helpless. Both being equally powerful, neither could succeed. Thus a long time passed. The elephant was growing weak; and the alligator was growing strong. Faced with imminent death it dawned upon that elephant: "These, my earthly relations, are unable to help me and relieve me from the jaws of the alligator. So, let me take refuge in the supreme being. Let me seek the refuge of that Lord who runs to the rescue of one who, tormented by the serpent called death, surrenders to him. He is death unto death itself."

Sage Śuka continued: The elephant, Gajendra, then remembered an excellent prayer it had learnt in the previous birth and recited it.

Gajendra said: I salute the supreme being, the uncaused cause of all creation, by whom this universe was created, in whom it rests and into whom it will disappear; and whose creative energy is this universe, both when it is manifest and when it is unmanifest. Even when this manifestation has been withdrawn, his light continues to shine. May that Lord whose truth even gods cannot realise protect me. Salutations to that Lord who is without form, yet dwells in all forms, and who himself manifests as all forms through the mysterious illusory potency, māyā. He is free from merit and demerit and yet seems to have these on account of the same mysterious māyā. Salutations to the Lord who is totally free and unattached to anything, who is incapable of being realised by one who is attached to the body or the world. Salutations to the Lord who is the goal of those noble ones who are ever unattached! Salutations to the Lord for whose vision sages retire to the forest in order to contemplate on him uninterruptedly. He is the witness of all the senses and the mind. He is ever free; and he can free from bondage to ignorance, those who take refuge in him. I salute that first Person who is infinite, full, extremely subtle and beyond the reach of the senses, he whom the great souls who are totally desireless, desire to realise. I salute the Lord who is ever free and who alone can confer freedom upon all beings fallen into ignorance, as I am.

By a small part of his being the universe with its infinite names and forms has been created. He is neither male nor female, neither human, subhuman nor superhuman. He is neither a cause nor an effect. He is beyond all description. He is that which remains after all descriptions have been negated by the process of 'not this', 'not this'. May he reveal himself to me.

Lord, I do not pray that I may be relieved from my present calamity; but I do pray that the veil of ignorance that prevents your realisation may be lifted.

When Gajendra uttered the above words, the creator and the other gods did not respond as the elephant had offered its prayer to the supreme being. Immediately, lord Hari manifested himself on the spot. Seeing him, the elephant offered him a flower with its uplifted trunk, and said: "I salute the lord Nārāyaṇa, the guru of all." The Lord instantly severed the head of the alligator and relieved the elephant.

Book Eight Chapter 4

Sage Śuka continued: The soul of the alligator immediately assumed the form of a celestial who, for the sin of pulling the sage Devala's leg while he was bathing in the same lake as himself, had been cursed to be reborn as an alligator. Released from that curse by the Lord's discus the celestial resumed his original form, bowed to the Lord and ascended to his abode.

In his previous birth the elephant had been a pāṇḍya king, by name Indradyumna, who ruled the drāviḍa country. At one stage in his life the king had become an ascetic and had taken a vow of silence. One day after his morning ablutions he was about to worship the Lord. Just then the sage Agastya arrived there with his retinue of disciples. The royal ascetic, who was observing the vow of silence and who was about to worship lord Viṣṇu, did not pay any attention to the sage, the living embodiment of the Lord himself (since the sages were the foremost among his devotees). Seeing that the royal ascetic had succumbed to the vanity of asceticism and to the ignorant assumption that the ritualistic worship was superior to the adoration of the sage, the latter uttered a redeeming curse: "May you be reborn as an ignorant animal, an elephant."

Indradyumna did not resent the curse, but accepted it as his own destiny. He took birth in the elephant species. However, on account of the merit earned through the worship of the Lord he regained his memory (of the sacred hymn) at the right moment. By the grace of the Lord the bondage of ignorance that bound Indradyumna to the world was cut asunder. His heart thoroughly purified by the vision of the Lord, the devotee was instantly transformed into a divine attendant of the Lord with a body and dress similar to his. Seated on Garuḍa along with the Lord, Indradyumna, too, ascended to the Lord's abode. Highly pleased with the devotee the Lord ordained: "He who remembers me, you and this episode is freed from all sin. He who sings the hymn sung by you every day during brāhma-muhūrta (two and a half hours before sunrise) will enjoy unclouded memory at the hour of his death."

The inspiring episode of the Lord's redemption of Gajendra has the power to ward off all evil, particularly of bad dreams, etc., if it is recited or heard with faith and devotion.

Churning of the Ocean and Mohinī
Book Eight Chapter 5

Sage Śuka continued: The fifth manvantara (world cycle) was presided over by Raivata. During this cycle the Lord manifested as Vaikuṇṭha. In the sixth manvantara presided over by Cākṣuṣa, (the son of Cakṣu) the Lord became partially manifest as Ajita (the son of Vairāja and Sambhūti) who, taking the form of a tortoise, supported mount Mandara when the ocean was churned.

O king, before the creation of nectar which made the gods immortal, whenever there arose a battle between the gods and the demons the latter used to massacre the gods. Therefore righteousness began to wane.

Troubled by this state of affairs, Indra, Varuna and other gods approached the creator Brahmā. Brahmā contemplated the supreme being for a moment and said: "The entire universe has been evolved out of a small part of that supreme being. He is the supreme Lord. Let us therefore pray to him for succour. He has neither friend nor enemy. Periodically, embracing the qualities of satva, rajas and tamas, one after the other, he promotes the welfare of all embodied beings in his own mysterious ways. At the present time he is united with satva, the principle of preservation; and therefore, it is an auspicious period for us to resort to his protection." Thereupon they went to the realm of lord Ajita and prayed to him:

"We resort to the Lord who is an unwinking witness of our senses and our mind. He it is who dwells close to the jīva as its best friend, and whom the jīva realises through the practice of yoga. No created being—not even we who are evolved by his satva—can comprehend the truth of his being. May that Lord of immense glory protect us—he whose feet are the earth, whose generative fluid is water, whose mind is the moon, whose mouth is fire, whose eye is the sun, whose life-breath is the air and whose sense of hearing is space. From his strength Indra was evolved, from his grace the gods, from his anger Śiva, from his intellect Brahmā, from his sexual organ the progenitor, from his bosom Lakṣmī (the goddess of wealth), from his chest dharma, from his shadow the manes, from his back adharma, from his mouth brāhmaṇa, from his arms the warrior, from his thighs the farmer, from his feet the servant, from his lower lip greed, from his upper lip love, and from his eyebrows Yama (the god of death) were evolved. His body represents these and other categories.

"O Lord, be gracious to us so that we may behold thee. You alone assume various forms, O Lord, and perform actions which are beyond our capacity. Hence we deem that action to be the best action which is dedicated to you."

Book Eight Chapter 6

Sage Śuka continued: In answer to their prayer, lord Hari appeared before them. His presence, which was dazzling like a thousand suns rising together, blinded the gods. Only Brahmā and Śiva beheld him, dark green in complexion with ruddy eyes, clad in a golden yellow garment—a divine body unsurpassed in beauty. The gods (including Brahmā the creator, and Śiva the redeemer) bowed to the Lord and sang his glories again:

"Salutations to that transcendental being which is beyond birth, manifestation and death. In this divine form we perceive the three worlds and ourselves. This cosmic form is therefore fit to be worshipped by all. The universe is in you, but you are unaffected by it. We are immersed in bliss at your very sight. We pray, guide us on the best way to achieve the object we have at heart."

The Lord then addressed them: "Go and make peace with your enemies, the demons, who have time in their favour. When there is a great task ahead one should befriend even enemies. Once the task is accomplished, then you can suitably deal with these wicked ones. Deal with them amicably. One's object is more easily achieved by kindness than by anger. Throw into the ocean of milk the best of all herbs. Install mount Mandara as the churning rod. Tie the serpent king Vāsuki around this rod. The demons and all of you should then churn the ocean. I will be on your side. The demons will only toil and get fatigued; you will receive the fruit of this churning. In the initial stages poison may emerge: you should not be frightened. Then all manner of desirable objects may come up; do not cast your greedy eyes on them. Even if the demons lose their temper, you guard yours well. Your purpose will surely be achieved."

The Lord instantly vanished from their sight. The gods then went to the demon king Bali. Indra spoke to him in affectionate tones, and revealed the Lord's plan for the churning of the ocean of milk. Bali was highly pleased with the proposal and decided to cooperate. All of them together uprooted mount Mandara and tried to transport it to the ocean. On the way they dropped it, out of exhaustion. As it fell it crushed many gods and demons. The Lord himself came to their rescue and playfully lifted the mountain with one hand and deposited it on the seashore.

Book Eight Chapter 7

Sage Śuka continued: The gods and the demons solicited the help of

Vāsuki (the serpent) assuring him of a share in the fruits of the labour; and entwining him around the mountain, they began to churn the ocean. The Lord, who is the master of strategy, took hold of the head of the serpent along with the gods; but the demons objected to this, feeling that the tail was an inferior part to hold! The gods readily yielded, holding the less dangerous tail of the serpent.

The mountain began to sink in the ocean on account of its weight. The Lord, however, came to the rescue; assuming the form of a tortoise he bore the mountain on his back. He himself animated the demons, assuming the demoniacal aspect; and he animated the gods through his sātvika aspect. He and he alone entered Vāsuki and produced suspended animation in him. He, too, sat on the mountain top pressing it down. Thus, everyone concerned was charged with the energy of the Lord; and they churned the ocean with great enthusiasm. In fact, when there was no sign of the nectar, the Lord himself began to churn the ocean vigorously!

All of a sudden there issued from the ocean the most terrible poison— Hālāhala. Tormented by this terrible poison all beings fled to lord Sadāśiva and prayed for protection. "Lord, we take refuge in you; pray save us from this poison which is burning the three worlds. For you are the supreme being whose limbs form the universe. Again and again you have graciously protected living beings by destroying their enemies. Therefore, we take refuge in your lotus feet."

His heart moved by this prayer, the Lord said to his spouse Pārvatī: "Look at this terrible calamity that has befallen creation. Surely I must do something immediately to counteract this poison. When one is ready to sacrifice oneself for the welfare of other beings it is indeed the sign of a noble heart. The Lord is supremely pleased with such a devotee. Hence I shall instantly swallow this poison." The divine spouse gladly assented to this noble intention on the part of her lord. Lord Siva then cupped his palms, collected the poison and swallowed it. So terrible was its force that it turned his throat black. A few drops that fell through his fingers are borne even now by snakes, scorpions and other poisonous creatures and herbs. Thus did Śiva save the creation. They indeed are good who share the agonies of the afflicted: that indeed is the best form of worship of the omnipresent Lord.

Book Eight Chapter 8

Sage Śuka continued: When a calamity had thus been averted, the gods and the demons carried on with the churning with greater vigour and enthusiasm. From that ocean there first emerged the cow, which the sages took, for it facilitated the performance of vaidika rites. Then came the horse Ucchaiḥśravā: the demon king Bali took it. Next there appeared the elephant Airāvata. Indra refrained from claiming it, in obedience to the Lord's admonition. This was followed by a rare gem, Kaustubha, which was worn by lord Hari on his chest. After this there appeared the celestial tree Pārijāta, which fulfils everyone's desires. Then came the Apsarā, celestial nymphs. They were followed by goddess Lakṣmī, who captivated the hearts of all. All the gods paid her homage. Holding a garland in her hand she looked around for a suitable bridegroom. She mused: "He who has austerity has not overcome anger; he who has wisdom has not overcome attachment; he who is great has not overcome desire; he who depends upon another, how can he be the lord? He who is righteous is not friendly towards all beings; one who has renounced everything does not make it the means to liberation; he who has strength is still subject to time; he who is free from attachment is unfit for companionship; he who has long life has not praiseworthy conduct; he who is of exemplary conduct has an uncertain span of life; where both these exist, there is inauspiciousness; he who is endowed with auspiciousness does not desire me!"

Having thus deliberated the goddess eventually chose lord Hari, who enshrined her in his own bosom. The gods celebrated this auspicious wedding. The goddess gazed upon them and they were fortunate. The demons looked on with envy.

Then from the ocean there issued Vāruṇī, the intoxicating drink, which the demons immediately grabbed. Finally there appeared a wonderful person known as Dhanvantari, the founder of the science of medicine, who was a part manifestation of the Lord himself. He had a pot of nectar in his hand. The demons quickly snatched the pot of nectar from his hand and began to run away. The bewildered gods approached lord Hari, who assured them of his succour. By his deluding potency he caused dissension among the demons. The weak ones even argued that it was unfair to take the whole pot away, depriving the gods of their share. "The gods also worked hard to produce this nectar. They should have their share in it. This is the eternal law," they argued. While they were thus quarrelling among themselves there appeared on the scene the most beautiful damsel, who was none other than the Lord's own deluding potency.

Sage Śuka continued: The demons were running away with the pot of nectar, quarrelling among themselves as to how it should be shared. They saw the bewitching damsel looking tantalisingly at them, and completely lost their hearts to her. They froze to a standstill, forgetful of their mission and their intention of running away with the pot of nectar. They openly expressed their admiration of her, repeatedly plied her with questions: "Oh you beautiful damsel, who are you, who are your parents, why have you come here?" With their hearts and minds completely possessed by her, they said to her: "Here is the pot of nectar. We, the sons of Kaśyapa, are all brothers. All of us exerted equally to obtain this nectar. We cannot make up our minds how it should be distributed. Pray, you do it for us. We shall gladly accept whatever you do as perfectly just." The Lord (in the disguise of the beautiful Mohini) took the pot of nectar from them, and after extracting a promise from them that they would abide by her decision, 'right or wrong', she agreed to distribute it.

All the gods and the demons then had their ritual bath and worship of the sacred fire; they celebrated the auspicious occasion by doing charity to the brāhmaṇā, etc. They then decked themselves gorgeously and seated themselves ready to quaff the nectar and become immortal!

Mohini had the gods and the demons seated in separated rows, and then appeared amongst them with the pot of nectar on her hand. Bewitching all with her amorous smiles and glances, she walked into their midst; while the demons were gazing at her spell-bound she distributed the nectar among the gods. She decided that it was unwise to give the nectar to the aggressive demons. They too, honoured their promise to her and kept quiet! One demon, however, was clever enough to sit with the gods, between the sun and the moon. Mohini had given him a share of the nectar, which he had quickly swallowed before the error was pointed out by the sun and the moon; whereupon Mohini (lord Viṣṇu) at once decapitated him. The nectar had touched and immortalised his head, but the body perished. He became Rāhu (who causes eclipses). When the distribution of nectar among the gods was completed Mohini resumed the original form of lord Viṣṇu.

Though their action, their motive, and so on were the same, the gods obtained nectar, and not the demons; the gods had taken refuge in the Lord's feet. That action is unfruitful which is directed towards one's own body, relations, etc., and the same action becomes fruitful when the perception of diversity is abandoned and the action is directed to the Lord, who is the self of all.

Book Eight Chapter 10

Sage Śuka continued: Both the gods and the demons worked together to produce the nectar; only the gods got it and the demons had to be deprived of it, as the latter had turned away from lord Vāsudeva. After fulfilling his mission the Lord returned to his abode.

The frustrated demons waged a terrible war against the gods. In their earlier encounters the demons could crush the gods in no time, but this battle was different. The gods had been strengthened by the nectar and the grace of the Lord. They were able to reply suitably.

The two armies closing in on each other looked like two oceans colliding, with their respective aquatic monsters waging fierce battle. The gods and the demons had their own mounts, insignia and other paraphernalia. Surrounded by the gods, Indra, mounted on the white elephant Airāvata, shone like the sun. He was attacked by Bali. Similarly, other demons were fighting other gods. They used all kinds of weapons in the battle. Elephants and horses, the heads and the limbs of dead warriors covered the battleground. Here and there headless bodies were seen to be running around with uplifted arms holding weapons; and there were also severed heads looking at the warriors.

Bali shot at Indra with ten missiles, the elephant with three, the four guards of the elephants with one each, and the driver with one. But Indra cut them all down with his own weapons. Bali took up a more deadly fire-arm; but Indra knocked it from Bali's hand before he could fire it. Bali then used his magical powers; he created a mountain which appeared over the gods. From that illusory mountain fell burning trees, serpents, lions and tigers and also evil spirits, which seemed to harass the gods. The gods were unable to deal with this diabolical magic. Instantly, the Lord himself appeared on the battlefield. At that very moment the illusions created by the demons vanished; for the very remembrance of the Lord is the surest way to overcome all trials and tribulations. The demon Kālanemi hurled a lion at the Lord, who instantly killed both the demon and his lion. Similarly, several other demons like Mālī, Sumālī and Mālyavān were struck down by the Lord himself.

Book Eight Chapter 11

Sage Śuka continued: With the illusion created by the demons dispelled by the arrival of the Lord, the gods regained their composure and their strength. Indra then went forward to attack Bali, challenging him and his followers to do their worst, and boasting that the gods would secure the victory in battle. With great wisdom Bali replied: "To those engaged in battle, fame, victory, defeat and death follow one another, as ordained by time. The enlightened ones therefore do not give vent to exultation or to grief: but, you are not enlightened since you believe that you can bring about victory and defeat!"

In the ensuing battle Indra struck Bali down with his thunderbolt. The valiant Jambha then rose to give battle. Wielding a terrible mace Jambha crippled the elephant of Indra. Indra's charioteer Mātali quickly brought a chariot. With his thunderbolt, Indra decapitated Jambha. At once three great warriors Bala, Pāka and Namuci came to fight Indra. Pāka struck both Mātali and the chariot simultaneously with a hundred missiles. Then he hit Indra with fifteen missiles. Indra was completely hidden within the shower of these missiles. Emerging from this he wielded his thunderbolt and slew Bala and Pāka.

Namuci thereupon fought Indra with his lance. Indra cut the lance into a thousand pieces and hit back with the thunderbolt, but for the first time it proved to be powerless. Indra was puzzled and distressed. At the same time he heard a celestial voice: "Namuci cannot be killed by either dry or wet weapons on account of a boon granted to him. Choose another." Reflecting over this warning Indra took a piece of foam floating on the sea (which was both wet and dry) and with it beheaded the demon. All the gods rejoiced.

But the creator did not rejoice. He deputed the sage Nārada to pacify Indra and the gods. Nārada counselled them to abandon this wanton destruction. The gods accepted the advice. The sage Uśanā then revived the lifeless Bali, the ruler of the nether world. On thus being revived the demon king did not feel sorry for the outcome of the battle with the gods, for he had realised the truth. The sage also brought back to life fallen demons whose limbs were intact.

Book Eight Chapter 12

Sage Śuka continued: Hearing of the Lord's exploits as Mohini, lord Śiva mounted his vehicle along with his consort Umā, and, surrounded by his retinue, went to the abode of the Lord. The Lord received Śiva with love and reverence. Śiva then extolled the Lord:

"You, O Lord, are the all in all. Only ignorant people perceive diversity in you. You are the one, you are the many—and you transcend all. Some sages who are exclusively devoted to your lotus feet, completely freed from attachment to the here and the hereafter, realise that you are the absolute being; others know you are the law that governs creation; others say that you are the reality that transcends both spirit and matter; yet others look upon you as being endowed with nine divine powers (vimalā, utkarṣiṇī, jñāna, kriyā, yoga, prahvī, satyā, īśānā and anugrahā); yet others meditate upon you as the eternal puruṣa. But no one can truly know your reality. Your incarnations in this universe are delightful to contemplate. I have come here to perceive the form in which you deluded the demons and distributed the nectar to the gods."

The Lord replied that that form would excite passion, and he promised to reveal it to lord Śiva. Instantly the Lord disappeared. Śiva was bewildered and began to look around. At a little distance he saw an extremely beautiful young girl playing with a ball in the middle of a garden, now and then casting a seductive eye on lord Śiva. At one stage, as she ran after the ball, the wind blew her clothes away. Completely overpowered by passion, lord Śiva began to pursue her. She pretended to elude his grasp, and to wriggle out of his embrace. As he ran after her, his seed escaped; and where it fell it turned into mines of silver and gold. Immediately Śiva regained his composure, understood the Lord's deluding power and bowed to him. The Lord blessed Śiva, saying: "My māyā will not overpower you any more." Śiva again bowed to the Lord. Śiva said to his consort Umā (Pārvatī): "Did you see this mysterious māyā of the Lord which could overpower even me, though I am a ray of the Lord? What wonder, then, that others are easily deceived by the power of the Lord's illusion."

I salute the Lord whom the unrighteous cannot realise, whom the devout can reach and who, assuming the disguise of a charming girl, deluded the demons and distributed the nectar to the gods who had taken shelter at his feet.

Book Eight Chapter 13

Sage Śuka continued: I shall now describe to you the progeny of the seventh manu, who is the Lord of the present world-cycle. He is known as Śrāddha Deva, the son of Vivasvān, the sun. His ten sons are: Ikṣvāku, Nabhaga, Dhṛṣṭa, Saryāti, Nariṣyanta, Nābhāga, Diṣṭa, Karūṣa, Pṛṣadhra and Vasumān. The twelve aspects of the sun, the eight vasū, the eleven rudrā, the ten viśvedevā, the forty-nine marut, the two aśvin and the three ṛbhū are the gods. Purandara is the Indra. Kaśyapa, Atri, Vasiṣṭha, Viśvāmitra, Gautama, Jamadagni and Bharadvāja are the sages. In this world-cycle the Lord's incarnation is that of Vāmana, the divine dwarf.

The eighth manvantara will be presided over by Sāvarṇi, the son of the sun-god Vivasvān and Chāyā. Nirmoka, Virajaska and others will be his sons. Sutapā, Virajā and Amṛtaprabhā will be the gods. The demon king Bali will be Indra, by the grace of God. Gālava, Dīptimān, Rāma, Aśvatthāmā, Kṛpācārya, Ṛṣyaśṛnga, and Vyāsa will be the sages. The Lord's incarnation will be that of Sārvabhauma.

The ninth manu will be Dakṣasāvarṇi, the son of Varuṇa. Bhūtaketu, Dīptaketu and others will be his sons. The Pārā, the Marīcigarbhā, etc., will be the gods. Adbhuta will be Indra. Dyutimān and others will be the sages. Ṛṣabha will be the Lord's incarnation.

The tenth manu will be Brahmasāvarṇi. Bhūriṣeṇa and others will be his sons. The Suvāsanā and the Viruddhā will be gods. Haviṣmān, Sukṛti, Satya, Jaya and Mūrti will be the sages. Śambhu will be the Indra. Viṣvaksena will be the Lord's incarnation.

The eleventh manu will be Dharmasāvarṇi. Satyadharmā and others will be his sons. Vihaṅgamā, Kāmagamā and Nirvāṇarucī will be the gods. Vaidhṛta will be Indra. Dharmasetu will be the Lord's incarnation.

The twelfth manu will be Rudrasāvarṇi. Devavān and others will be his sons; Haritā, etc., will be the gods with Ṛtadhāmā as Indra. Tapomūrti, etc., will be the sages; and Svadhāmā will be the Lord's manifestation.

The thirteenth manu will be Devasāvarṇi, with Citrasena, etc., as sons, Sukārmā and Sutrāmā as gods, Divaspati as Indra, Nirmoka, etc., as sages; and Yogeśvara the Lord's incarnation.

The last and fourteenth manu will be Indrasāvarṇi, with Uru, etc., as sons, Pavitrā and Cākṣuṣā as gods, Śuci as Indra, Agnibāhu, etc., as the sages, and Bṛhadbhānu will be the Lord's incarnation.

Thus has a kalpa been described to you, O Parīkṣit.

Book Eight Chapter 14

Sage Śuka, in reply to a question from Parīkṣit, said: The manu and their sons, the gods and their king Indra, and also the sages, are all under the control of the Lord himself. During each world-cycle the Lord incarnates himself by at least a part of himself. Guided by him the manu lays down the law and promotes the fourfold dharma—asceticism, purity, compassion and truth. The rulers of the people safeguard religion and religious practices. The gods enjoy the ritual offerings and promote the prosperity of the people.

The Lord himself, through the great sages, who are but embodiments of the rays of the Lord, imparts wisdom to the people in every age. Through other sages, who are also part-manifestations of the Lord, he himself formulates the rules governing the performance of rituals. Yet again, assuming the form of masters of yoga, the Lord himself teaches yoga (or the way to God-realisation).

He plays the role of the lords of created beings and promotes creation. He himself is the ruler who chastises the wicked. He is time who destroys everything.

Though he is diversely glorified by means of his diverse names and forms, the Lord is not perceived by the people, who are all deluded by māyā.

Bali
Book Eight Chapter 15

Sage Śuka continued: Bali had been defeated by Indra in battle, even killed by him. Later he was revived by his guru Śukra (or Uśanā) and he returned to his own realm, where he applied himself heart and soul to the service of his guru. Śukra and other sages were highly pleased with Bali. They organised a grand ritual called Viśvajit (or the conquest of the universe) for him to perform. An important part of this ritual consisted in giving away all one's possessions. By this Bali propitiated the Lord and won his grace.

From the sacred fire there arose a divine chariot with divine armaments. Bali received these. He was also blessed by his own grandfather, Prahrāda, and his guru, Śukra. Thus suitably equipped, and after taking the guru's blessings, Bali invaded the capital of heaven along with a mighty army. The capital of the celestial realm was beautiful, prosperous and grand. Its pleasure gardens, where there was eternal spring, were inhabited by lovely birds and beasts. The holy river Ākāśa-Gaṅgā itself provided the moat, and the walls of the fortress were made of pure gold. Conceived and constructed by the divine architect Viśvakarma, the city was well laid out—with roads and pavements, etc., paved with gems and precious stones.

Nymphs of unsurpassed beauty and unfading youth looked even more beautiful as they walked along the roads through the yellowish glow of molten gold. Celestial music could be heard everywhere. The unrighteous have no admission here; only the righteous can enter.

When this city was besieged by Bali its inhabitants grew panic-stricken, and Indra approached his guru Bṛhaspati to ascertain how Bali had grown so strong so soon. Bṛhaspati replied: "We know how Bali has become so powerful; it is through the blessings of the holy ones, sage Bhṛgu and other sages of self-realisation. Their spiritual energy has been transmitted to Bali. It is unwise to fight Bali. Therefore, leave heaven for a while. The power Bali earned by the sages' blessings he will soon lose when he insults them. You will then regain your throne." Indra obeyed the commands of his guru and Bali occupied the throne vacated by Indra.

Book Eight Chapter 16

Sage Śuka continued: Indra's defeat depressed Aditi, his mother. In the meantime her husband, the sage Kaśyapa, returned home after a long absence during which he was immersed in deep samādhi. Seeing the cheerless face of his wife and the lustreless state of the house, he questioned her: "Have any of our duties been neglected in my absence? Has the sacred fire not been worshipped by you daily? Has any stranger calling at our door been turned away, without being offered even water? Such a house is not a home but a jackals' den. And, are your children well?" In reply Aditi assured the sage that all religious activities had been carried out without the least negligence, but informed him of the triumph of the demons over her children. "Pray, devise some means by which the demons can be defeated."

Kaśyapa marvelled at the illusory power of the Lord (māyā) which, clouding people's vision of the reality, led to their attachment to illusory relationships to husband, children, etc. All of these spring from the false identification of the eternal infinite self with the transient and finite body. However, he said: "Your desire will be fulfilled by the Lord. I shall relate to you the sacred observance known as payovrata, which is highly pleasing to the Lord, who grants all our noble desires.

"This should be observed in the month of Phālguna, commencing from the new moon day. One should bathe thrice a day, after applying earth to his body with the appropriate prayer. He should then recite a hymn in praise of the glorious Lord in his various aspects. After this he should offer due worship to the Lord with invocation, bathing, food-offering, etc. With that food he should feed some devotees. He should feed two holy brāhmaṇā with rice boiled in milk and sugar. Then he should feed his beloved ones and relations.

"This should be done for twelve days. During this period he should observe the vow of celibacy strictly. He should sleep on the ground. He should not indulge in useless conversations at all. He should live on milk alone.

"On the thirteenth day he should perform the regular worship as described above and then worship the fire. He should bestow liberal gifts on the holy ones. He should feed all without any distinction—especially the destitute, the sick and the unhappy people—knowing that through them he is gratifying the Lord himself. He shall then break his fast.

"This is a great universal vow, which bestows on one who observes it all the boons that he or she desires. Therefore O dear one, observe this payovrata for the fulfilment of your wish."

Book Eight Chapter 17

Sage Śuka continued: Aditi observed the payovrata scrupulously for the prescribed twelve days, with a heart devoted to and mind concentrated on the Lord. On completion of the vow the Lord himself appeared before her in all his divine majesty. She prostrated herself before him, and then rising, she endeavoured to glorify him with a voice choked with love, tears streaming down her face:

"You are the worshipful one, and you invariably manifest yourself in order to relieve the distress of the oppressed. When you are pleased you grant to your devotee long life, a strong and beautiful body, all one's desires, unequalled prosperity, heaven, earth and the netherworld, all divine qualities, the three goals of human life and wisdom itself—and also things like victory over enemies!"

The omniscient Lord blessed her, saying: "We know the wish of your heart, O mother of gods. You wish that the demoniacal usurpers of Indra's throne should be driven away by me, and your son re-installed as Indra. It shall be done: for my worship shall never go in vain. Yet, we know that the demons enjoy the blessings of the holy ones on account of the demons' devotion to them. Hence, time is on their side. They cannot, therefore, be conquered by force. Some other way has to be found. I shall be born as your son, with a ray of my being, and shall then do what is necessary. Keep this a secret: then shall your object be surely achieved."

The sage Kaśyapa intuitively realised that the Lord had entered his mind with a ray of his being. Intensely contemplating upon the Lord he transferred this ray, along with his seed (which had been preserved over a long period of time whilst he was in samādhi, and thus made powerful), into the womb of Aditi. Seeing that she was radiant with the Lord himself in her womb, the creator Brahmā paid his homage to the Lord: "Lord, you hold the three worlds within yourself and also transcend it. The entire universe floats in you even as a piece of straw floats in a river. You yourself have created all beings in this universe and entered them as their inner controller. May you always triumph."

Book Eight Chapter 18

Sage Śuka continued: On the most auspicious day known as Vijayā-Dvādaśī, the twelfth day of the bright half of the month Bhādrapada, when the moon was in the lunar mansion of Śravaṇa, and during the period known as Abhijit which is conducive to victory, the Lord manifested himself in the house of the sage Kaśyapa, as the son of Aditi. All the celestials rejoiced, sang and danced. The Lord's earthly parents (the sage Kaśyapa and his noble wife Aditi) were filled with delight, and repeatedly exclaimed: "Victory, victory to the Lord." The Lord, who at the very moment of his manifestation had four hands and other divine insignia and was clad in yellow, quickly assumed the size of a young boy of short stature, a dwarf.

Soon, they decided to invest him with the sacred thread. At this ceremony the gods themselves paid him homage. Savitā taught him the Gāyatrī. Bṛhaspati gave him the sacred thread. Kaśyapa gave him the grass-girdle. Mother earth gave him the deer-skin. Soma gave him the staff. Aditi gave him clothes. Dyauḥ (god of space) gave him an umbrella. Brahmā gave him the water-pot. Sarasvatī gave him a rosary. Kubera gave him the begging bowl. Umā gave him alms.

Learning that Bali was performing the horse-rite in order to propitiate the Lord, the divine dwarf (Vāmana) went there. As he entered the place of worship his radiance outshone even the sun and the splendour of the assembled sages. They all rose to welcome this dwarfish brāhmaṇa boy endowed with extraordinary radiance. Bali also worshipped him in the appropriate manner and sprinkled on his own head the water in which Vāmana's feet had been bathed. Then, Bali said to Vāmana:

"Welcome, O holy one! I salute you. Today is indeed the most blessed day of our life. Our ancestors are blessed. Today the sacred fires assume a special sanctity, and I consider that they have been kindled properly. By sprinkling the water sanctified by contact with your feet, this land and myself have been purified of all sin. I humbly beg of you to receive from me whatever you may want."

Book Eight Chapter 19

Sage Śuka continued: The Lord was highly pleased with the words of king Bali and replied as follows:

"Well said, O king! You are worthy indeed of your preceptors and of your grandfather, the devotee Prahrāda. No one who has taken birth in your family has turned a mendicant away or shied away from battle. Though Viṣṇu killed Hiraṇyākṣa after great difficulty, he (Viṣṇu) sang the glories of his enemy long after his death. Hearing of his brother's death, Hiraṇyakaśipu actually went to Viṣṇu's abode to take revenge. Viṣṇu did not want to face him! He therefore made himself very small, and entering Hiraṇyakaśipu's nostrils, placed himself in the demon's heart. Hiraṇyakaśipu searched for Viṣṇu everywhere and could not find him, as he was only looking outside. He thereupon abandoned the search, presuming that Viṣṇu was no more. Enmity in this world lasts only till the grave. In your family, again, Virocana gave away his own life to the gods. Knowing that you are a worthy descendant of these great ones, I ask of you just for that much of earth which could be covered by my three paces."

Bali was pleased to hear the glories of his ancestors, but he pleaded that Vāmana should ask for more: "One who returns from my abode shall not beg again". To which the Lord replied: "All the objects in the three worlds cannot satisfy even one man without control of mind and senses. The more he gets, the more will he want. Discontentment and greed lead to transmigration of souls; contentment is an aid to liberation. Therefore I shall be content with three paces; I am content with such wealth as is necessary." Laughing at what he considered Vāmana's immaturity, Bali got ready to give away the land Vāmana asked for. His guru Śukra, however, intervened: "Beware, O king, this dwarfish brāhmaṇa is lord Viṣṇu himself. He has assumed this form in order to deprive you of your dominion. He will instantly resume his cosmic form and measure the universe with two paces. How will you honour your promise to grant him three paces of earth? I do not approve of this promise. A householder should utilise his earnings for (1) religious merit, (2) honour, (3) accumulation of wealth, (4) pleasure and (5) the use of himself and relations. You should not give away your own livelihood. One who responds 'yes' (Oṁ) to the mendicants loses all his wealth and lives an unhappy and discontented life. If one says 'No' (I do not have anything to give) he loses his honour and is dead while living. However, it is better to break a promise, which is allowed (1) towards women, (2) in jest, (3) for a wedding, (4) to preserve life, (5) in great danger, (6) to protect cows and holy ones, (7) where otherwise violence might result. Falsehood then preserves life, and life is the tree of which truth is the fruit!"

Book Eight Chapter 20

Sage Śuka continued: Bali kept silent for a moment and then, with a mind deeply concentrated and introverted, he replied: "Worshipful and holy one! I fully appreciate your statement of the duties of a householder. But, I recall mother earth's proclamation that she could endure any sin but falsehood. Wealth abandons a person at his death: why should he not abandon it earlier? Noble ones like Dadhīci and Śibi even gave up their lives so that others might live. The world has long since forgotten the pleasure and possessions won and enjoyed by our mighty ancestors; only their honour is remembered. Great heroes are not difficult to find, but it is not easy to find one who gives away his fortune to another person. Be it lord Viṣṇu himself or my worst enemy, I shall honour my promise and shall give the land to this dwarf. Even if he binds me, I shall not hurt him or go back on my word." Śukrācārya was annoyed by this irreverent impertinence and cursed his disciple Bali: "You have arrogantly disregarded your guru's words; you shall fall from your position." This curse, too, was ordained by the divine will, and unperturbed by it, Bali proceeded to solemnise the gift. The celestials celebrated this event by singing: "This noble soul has performed a difficult task: he has given away the three worlds to his enemy, fully aware of the consequences."

At the same time the Lord grew in stature till his cosmic form enveloped the whole universe. Bali beheld the glorious cosmic form; the nether regions at his soles, the earth at his feet, mountains in his shanks, the sky in his knees, the marut in his thighs, twilight in his loincloth, the demons in his anus, the sage-progenitors of creation in his genitals, the firmament in his navel, the seven oceans at his sides, the stars on his chest, dharma in his heart, Ṛta and Satya in his breasts, the moon in his mind, goddess Śrī in his bosom, sound in his throat, the gods in his arms, the four directions in his ears, heaven in his crown, clouds in his hair, air in his nostrils, sun in his eyes, fire in his mouth, the vedā in his organ of speech, the god of water in his palate, injunctions and prohibitions in his brows, day and night in his eyelashes, anger on his forehead, greed in his lips, love in his sense of touch, water in his semen, adharma in his back, death in his shadow, māyā in his laughter, plants and herbs in his hair, rivers in his arteries, rocks in his nails, the creator in his intellect, gods and sages in his senses. Seeing this cosmic form with the divine potencies as weapons, the demons became frightened.

The Lord covered the earth with a single stride. Space was covered by his body and the directions by his arms. The second pace covered the heavens; there was no place for the third.

Book Eight Chapter 21

Sage Śuka continued: The creator Brahmā and other celestials, gods and sages adored the foot of the Lord which had reached the highest abode of the gods. As part of the worship Brahmā poured water on that foot and that water flowed down as the holy river Gaṅgā. Then the Lord resumed his dwarfish form. The demons were greatly enraged at the way in which lord Viṣṇu had deprived their leader of his dominion, especially when, on account of his ritualistic vow, he could not indulge in violence. They felt that it was their duty to stand up and fight for their master Bali. As they rose, the servants of the Lord rose in response. The latter were powerful and began to slay the demons.

Bali then spoke to his followers: "Desist from this vain attempt, O demons. The same Lord who promoted our welfare and success some time ago and who caused the defeat of the gods, is now causing the reverse to happen. One cannot defeat time by strength, wise counsel, intelligence, fortresses, mantrā, drugs or the four methods by which victory is attained (viz., conciliation, gift, confusion and punishment). Retreat for the present and restrain yourselves till time becomes favourable for us." The demons laid down their arms.

Garuḍa, the servant of lord Viṣṇu, then bound Bali with the cords of Varuṇa, and took him prisoner. At this all the inhabitants of the earth and the heaven wailed aloud. Lord Vāmana then said to

Bali: "You had given me three paces of land. By one I measured the entire earth-plane. By the other 'foot' I covered the heaven. How are you going to redeem your promise and find room for my third 'foot'? If you cannot, then you are guilty of violating your pledge. The only just punishment for such conduct is life in the infernal regions for some time; such has been the decision of your guru also. He who fails to honour his promise of a gift has no place on this earth—let alone a place in heaven— and descends into the nether world."

Book Eight Chapter 22

Bali replied: Lord, place the third 'foot' on my head, which is dearer to a man than all his possessions. To be punished by the noble and the divine is indeed a blessing. In the disguise of an enemy you are my greatest benefactor, for you have enabled us to realise directly, intimately and immediately the evils of occupying a position of power, and the ever-present possibility of falling from such a position. In fact, my grandfather Prahrāda took refuge at your feet, realising that no good can be achieved by being devoted to a body that abandons oneself, to kinsmen who are in fact robbers waiting to take away one's wealth, to a wife whose infatuation is the cause of transmigration, and to a house and so on which only intensify his bondage to worldly life. I consider it my good fortune that I have been brought to your presence.

At that very moment the divine Prahrāda arrived and said: Lord, it was you who bestowed upon Bali this dominion, this position as Indra and this power; and today you are taking back what is your own, thus relieving him of the possible cause for arrogance and delusion.

Bali's wife Vindhyāvali, said: The entire universe is your own creation, O Lord. Only ignorant people claim sovereignty over regions of this universe. When everything is already yours, what can anyone offer you?

Brahmā prayed: Having worshipped you, how can Bali come to grief? Therefore, O Lord, release him from his bondage.

The Lord said: When I want to bless someone I first take away his good fortune and wealth, which cause him to ridicule other people and even me. Of course, in the case of one who is not thus swayed by wealth and in whom (noble) birth, (praiseworthy) action, age (youth), form (beauty), knowledge, power, wealth and so on do not generate pride and arrogance, such good fortune is my grace. Bali has already overcome my māyā; hence he remains unshaken by calamity, by being forsaken by his own kinsmen and by being cursed even by his own preceptor. He deserves a place in my realm. However, since he has a desire to be Indra for some time, he shall be Indra in the next world-cycle. In the meantime he shall rule the netherworld, a position worthy of being sought even by the gods. My own discus will protect him in every way even against any manifestation of demoniacal tendencies. Mace in hand, I shall myself guard Bali's subterranean territory.

Book Eight Chapter 23

Freed by the Lord from his bondage, Bali said: Indescribably great is the glory of devotion to your lotus feet, O Lord, for bowing to them once with sincerity even a vile demon like me has earned blessings which the celestials find hard to obtain.

Prahrāda added: O Lord, your ways are indeed mysterious. You, who are the Lord of the universe, has volunteered to be ever present in the netherworld to protect it! It is indeed a great wonder that you have thus chosen us, demons, on whom to shower your blessings, which are eagerly sought by celestials and sages. You have created the universe playfully by your own māyā. You are the self of all. Yet, you condescend to shower abundant grace upon your devotees in preference to others; this indeed is a great wonder. Such indeed is the nature of the wish-yielding tree (that it fulfils one's wishes without examining credentials).

The Lord replied: Prahrāda, to go the netherworld along with your grandson Bali. You will always behold me there, mace in hand: ignorance shall not approach one who thus sees me always in front of him.

Sage Śuka continued: In obedience to the Lord's command, Prahrāda and Bali went to the netherworld, after once again bowing to the Lord. The Lord himself commanded the sage Śukrācārya to conclude the ritual which Bali had undertaken, and which had been interrupted by the foregoing episode. Śukra humbly replied: "By your very presence that ritual has attained total fulfilment. In fact, by the very utterance of your name all defects attending rituals (whether due to the improper utterance of mantra or otherwise) are removed. Yet, since it is your command, I shall conclude this ritual." This was done.

The Lord then installed Indra on the throne of heaven and himself ruled the universe as Indra's younger brother, for the gods with Brahmā at their head had elected lord Vāmana as the Lord of the entire universe. The gods, sages and celestials then returned to their respective abodes.

Such is the glory of the Lord, O Parīkṣit. No one can adequately describe his glory; this is only a glimpse that I have given you. This wonderful story of the Lord's incarnation as Vāmana should be recited on all religious occasions. It is capable of leading its votary to the highest state of blessedness.

Divine Fish
Book Eight Chapter 24

In response to Parīkṣit's prayer, sage Śuka related the story of the Lord's incarnation as the divine dolphin: The Lord assumes a body from time to time for the protection of the holy, noble and enlightened ones, and of righteousness in general. Such manifestation does not affect him in the least, since he is free from the play of the guṇā, irrespective of whether the body assumed is human, super-human or sub-human.

At the end of the previous world-cycle, the creator had retired from his work; the cosmic deluge flooded the universe and a demon called Hayagrīva carried away the vedā. Even before this happened, one day when king Satyavrata was offering libations to his ancestors on the bank of the river Kṛtamālā the Lord appeared in the water as a small fish. It prayed to the king for protection, so he put it in his water-pot; but soon it grew too big for the pot. The king gransferred it successively to a pond, a small lake and a big lake, as it grew bigger and bigger. Eventually he took it to the ocean; there he realised that the dolphin was the Lord himself. The dolphin spoke to him, saying: "On the seventh day from now the world will be submerged by the deluge. However, you will notice a large boat on the ocean. Board it along with the sages, herbs and animals. I shall appear there as a horned dolphin. Tie the boat to my horn. I shall protect you all."

Even so, the rain and deluge arrived; and with it the boat. The king boarded it, as instructed by the Lord. The divine dolphin arrived; and the king tied the boat to the horn of the dolphin. Secure in his protection, the king praised the Lord: "O Lord, fools blinded by ignorance engage themselves in varied actions, hoping to attain happiness, but they find that happiness recedes further away. Ignorant man chooses another ignorant man as guru and is misled; for the ignorant guru offers only unwise counsel. Hence we resort to you who are the foremost guru of unfailing wisdom. Pray, show us how to cut asunder the knots of ignorance by which our hearts are bound."

The divine dolphin then revealed to them (the king, the sages, etc.,) the highest knowledge of the sāṅkhya, yoga and purāṇa. When Brahmā rose from his sleep the Lord restored the vedā to him (having wrested them from the demon Hayagrīva). Satyavrata became Vaivasvata manu. We bow to the lord Matsya (dolphin) who thus protected the vedā and taught the highest wisdom to the king Satyavrata and the sages.

Book Nine

Book Nine Chapter 1

Sage Śuka said: Pray listen to the following brief narration of the generation of the descendants of manu (mankind): to describe it fully, even a hundred years are insufficient.

Śrāddhadeva, the son of Vivasvān and Saṁjñā, became the manu of the present cycle, vaivasvata manvantara. He had no issue. Therefore the sage Vasiṣṭha decided to conduct a ritual in honour of Mitra and Varuṇa in order that the manu might be blessed with a son. Śraddhā, manu's wife, privately approached one of the officiating priests and prayed that a daughter might be born to her. This priest therefore made a slight distortion in the mantra, as a result of which a daughter was born. Sorely disappointed the king complained to Vasiṣṭha, who clearly saw the priest's mistake. Thereupon Vasiṣṭha prayed to lord Viṣṇu himself; and the lord empowered the sage Vasiṣṭha with the ability to change the sex of the child. Thus manu's daughter, Ilā, became a son called Sudyumna.

One day prince Sudyumna, accompanied by his retinue, went to the forest to hunt. They went to the foot of mount Meru where lord Śiva was alone with his consort, Pārvatī. As soon as they entered the forest the prince, his horse and all his followers became females. There is a reason for this.

Long, long ago a sage entered the very same forest and came to that very spot when lord Śiva and his consort Pārvatī were alone. At the appearance of the sage, Pārvatī became terribly embarrassed and shaken. The sage turned and went away. However, seeing the embarrassment caused to his consort, lord Śiva pronounced the curse: "Anyone venturing into this forest will be turned into a woman". Since then no male had dared to go there.

Sudyumna, now a woman, wandered in that forest for some time. On seeing her the god Budha (the planet Mercury) fell in love with her. Budha married her and begot through her a son called Purūravā. While thus playing the role of a woman Sudyumna thought of the sage Vasiṣṭha, who instantly appeared before him. Vasiṣṭha then prayed to lord Śiva on behalf of Sudyumna. Lord Śiva graciously ordained that Sudyumna would regain his manhood, but that every alternate month he would be a woman—thereby preserving the substance of his original decree, and at the same time obliging the sage. Thus, partially relieved, Sudyumna returned to his kingdom. Thereafter, he begot three sons, Utkala, Gaya and Vimala, who later became rulers of southern Bhārata. After a few years Sudyumna retired to the forest, having crowned his son Purūravā king.

Book Nine Chapter 2

Sage Śuka continued: When Sudyumna thus renounced the world and retired to the forest, Vaivasvata manu felt sorry; for he desired to have a son. He worshipped the Lord for the fulfilment of this desire, as a result of which he begot ten sons, the eldest of whom was Ikṣvāku.

One of these sons, Pṛṣadhra, had been appointed by his guru to tend a herd of cows. One night while Pṛṣadhra was vigilantly guarding them it became totally dark on account of clouds; under cover of this darkness a tiger stole into the herd and caught hold of a cow, which cried aloud in agony. Pṛṣadhra was there instantly. He drew his sword and, mistaking the brown head of the cow for that of the tiger, killed it, at the same time injuring the tiger which ran away. In the morning he realised the grievous error. Guru Vasiṣṭha, however, cursed him that he had forfeited his princehood on account of this sin and he should wander as a śūdra (servant-caste). Gladly receiving this curse Pṛṣadhra undertook a lifelong vow of celibacy and developed exclusive devotion to the Lord. Free from all attachment, tranquil, with his senses controlled, free from greed and living by what chance brought him, with his self delighting in the self, he roamed the earth like one who was blind, deaf and stupid. One day he was consumed by a forest fire and he attained the absolute.

Kavi, the youngest son of manu, also retired to the forest while still young and attained self-realisation. From his son, Karūṣa, the ruling class known as the Kārūṣā descended and they ruled the northern regions. From another son Dhṛṣṭa descended the ruling class called Dhārṣṭā who became brāhmaṇā.

Marutta, descendant of Diṣṭa (another son) became an emperor and performed an unparalleled and spectacular ritual in which all the utensils were of gold. All the gods were pleased with the rich offerings, and the brāhmaṇa received rich gifts also. It is said that the wind-gods themselves waited upon the guests in this rite. Another great descendant of Marutta was king Tṛṇabindu, who was an abode of divine virtues. He married Alambuṣā, a celestial nymph, and had a number of sons and a daughter by her. Further on in the same line was born Viśāla (who built the city of Vaiśālī) and Somadatta (who became devotee of the Lord and attained god-realisation). Janamejaya was the grandson of Somadatta.

The other sons of manu had their own descendants.

Chyavana
Book Nine Chapter 3

Sage Śuka continued: King Śaryāti was another son of Vaivasvata manu. He had a beautiful daughter named Sukanyā. One day the king went to the forest and tarried for awhile at the hermitage of the sage Chyavana. There the girl noticed an ant-hill which had two holes on one side, through which she saw two shining objects. In childish playfulness she took a thorn and pricked them. Immediately blood spurted from the hole; and simutaneously the members of the royal entourage found that they could not pass faeces and urine. King Śaryāti, who had attained self-realisation, questioned: "Has anyone in my entourage harmed the sage Chyavana in any manner?" His own daughter confessed her playful mischief. The king then went to the ant-hill and begged for the sage's pardon.

The aged sage hinted that he would like to marry the princess, to which the king readily agreed. After giving his daughter away to the sage in marriage the king returned to his palace. Sukanyā served the sage with all her heart and soul. The sage had a terrrible temper; but she divined his every wish and gave him no cause at all for displeasure.

One day the two celestial physicians, the aśvinīkumārā, called on the sage who asked them to rejuvenate him and make him youthful, in return for which he promised to give them a drink of soma to which they were not entitled. They took him to the pool of the siddhā and asked him to plunge into it. The sage did this. There emerged from the pool three identical and radiant divine youths! Bewildered, Sukanyā prayed to the aśvinīkumārā to point her husband out to her. Pleased with her loyalty, they did so.

Soon after, king Śaryāti paid a visit to the hermitage. Finding his daughter living with a young man he severely admonished her infidelity to the aged sage. But on discovering the truth, he was highly pleased.

With the assistance of the king the sage performed the soma rite and gave some of the juice to the aśvinīkumārā. At this Indra was enraged and raised his thunderbolt to hit the sage, who however, paralysed that hand! From then, the aśvinīkumārā received soma.

Uttānabarhi, Ānarta and Bhūriṣeṇa were born of Śaryāti. Ānarta begot Revata, who had a hundred sons. One of them Kakudmī, had a daughter Revatī. Once he took his daughter Revatī to the creator's realm to consult the latter about a suitable match for her. Kakudmī had to wait for a short while as a music recital was in progress there. On its conclusion, when he approached the creator, the latter said: "Whoever you had in mind when you came here, his sons and grandsons have all died. Ages have passed on earth during the few moments you spent here. Return and give her in marriage to Balarama, the elder brother of Kṛṣṇa." The king did so, and retired to Badarikāśrama.

Ambarīṣa
Book Nine Chapter 4

Sage Śuka continued: Nābhāga was the son of Nabhaga. The boy spent an unusually long period of time in the house of his preceptor and then returned to his father's palace. When the time came for the brothers to divide the ancestral property among themselves, Nābhāga was given the aged father himself as his share! The aged father, however, said to his son: "Do not take this injustice to heart, my son. Some holy ones who are engaged in performing a religious rite repeatedly, are confused by the ritual. Teach them a couple of prayers. They will surely bless you with wealth." The son did so, and as the holy ones were ascending to heaven they left behind them much wealth for Nābhāga. However, at the same time an awesome being descended upon that very spot where the rite had been performed and claimed the remnants of the ritual (the wealth) as his share. This being was lord Rudra. Both of them then went to the aged Nabhaga for arbitration and Nabhaga declared that the remnants of the rite belonged to Rudra. Lord Rudra was highly pleased with both father and son and admired their justice and truth. He bestowed self-realisation upon the son and gave him all the wealth that the holy ones had left behind.

Nābhāga's son was Ambarīṣa. In course of time he inherited the vast dominion and its great wealth. But Ambarīṣa had no use for them. He regarded life as a long dream and wealth and so on as dream-objects with no intrinsic worth. He was devoted to the Lord with all his heart. His mind was absorbed in lord Kṛṣṇa's feet. His speech constantly glorified him. His hands were ever busy in his service—sweeping the temple, etc. His ears were filled with his stories. His eyes constantly beheld the Lord's images and temples. His body rejoiced in touching the limbs of God's devotees. His nose smelt only the holy basil sanctified by God's worship. His feet circumambulated holy places. His head bowed to the Lord's feet. His sole desire was for God's service and his love was directed towards God's devotees. He ruled the kingdom in accordance with the wise counsel of the holy ones, regarding all his actions as the Lord's worship. However he also performed a number of scriptually-ordained sacrifices in which he bestowed lavish gifts on all the participants, including the gods. With the development of devotion to the Lord, dispassion for all worldly objects and enjoyments also grew in him. The Lord, too, had commanded his own discus (sudarśana) to protect the devotee in every way.

Book Nine Chapter 4

Sage Śuka continued: Ambarīṣa undertook the vow known as the dvādaśī vow to propitiate the Lord. On one occasion he had fasted the previous day and on the dvādaśī day had concluded an elaborate worship of the lord with intense love and devotion. He worshipped the holy ones too, and made extravagant gifts to them. Just as he was about to break his fast the great sage Durvāsā, who was renowned for his terrible temper, appeared. Ambarīṣa humbly greeted the sage and invited him to accept his hospitality. Readily consenting to this request, Durvāsā went to the river to bathe.

On the dvādaśī day, one who observes the vow should eat within a certain period. There was just about one quarter of an hour left for this period to elapse. Anxious to observe the vow and also not to show disrespect to Durvāsā, Ambarīṣa, on the advice of the holy ones, sipped a little water. After a short while Durvāsā returned; and on coming to know that the king had sipped water before the sage had been duly honoured, he became furious. He tore a matted lock from his head and hurled it at Ambarīṣa. This lock became terrible demoness which came to swallow Ambarīṣa.

The Lord's discus, which was ever present near Ambarīṣa, quickly destroyed the evil spirit and rushed towards Durvāsā. The thoroughly frightened sage began to run for his life. The discus pursued him. Finding no refuge in the three worlds, the sage went to Brahmā the creator for protection, but Brahmā pleaded inability to help. Then he went to lord Rudra who also could not help him, beyond directing him to lord Vāsudeva (Viṣṇu). Durvāsā fell at the feet of the Lord, confessed his sin in having offended the Lord's devotee, and craved forgiveness.

The Lord, however, replied: "O holy one, I am under the control of my devotees and, so to speak, I am not independent. My devotees have abandoned their wives, children, houses, wealth and even their lives for my sake; how then can I forsake them? Good and noble people are my heart; and I am their heart. They do not know any reality other than me; nor do I know anything but them. I shall therefore suggest that you should beg of Ambarīṣa himself to forgive you. That is the only way to avert the calamity that threatens you. Penance and worship yield desirable results only to holy ones who are humble; if they are practised by vain and arrogant people they yield undesirable results—as in your case. Hasten therefore to Ambarīṣa and ask for his forgiveness."

Book Nine Chapter 5

Sage Śuka continued: Durvāsā came back to Ambarīṣa and clasped his feet, craving forgiveness. Ambarīṣa was greatly embarrassed when the sage touched his feet. Ambarīṣa then offered a prayer to the Lord's discus:

"You, O Sudarśana, are fire, the sun, the moon and the elements; you destroy all missiles. Be pleased with this sage. You are the protector of the universe. You are the effulgence of the Lord. You are the dispeller of the darkness of ignorance. At the command of the Lord you destroy all wickedness in the universe. If we have discharged our duties properly, let the holy sage Durvāsā be spared and protected by you: by this you would be conferring a great boon upon us, too."

Instantly the discus, which till then had been scorching the sage Durvāsā, became cool. Highly gratified with this turn of events the sage said: "Today I have seen the glory of the Lord's devotees: they do good even to those who have harmed them. For the devotees of the Lord there is nothing difficult or impossible to do and there is nothing that they find difficult to give up, because they are established in love of him. Hearing his name is itself sufficient to destroy one's sins."

A great calamity thus averted, Ambarīṣa then begged of the sage to have his meal; after thus serving him and obtaining his permission, Ambarīṣa broke his fast. While leaving the palace Durvāsā pronounced a blessing: "O king, this edifying story of yours will be sung by people for all time to come, as long as this earth lasts."

Thus the king Ambarīṣa ruled the earth over a long period of time, whole-heartedly devoted to the Lord. Ultimately he entrusted the kingdom to his sons, who were equally devoted to the Lord, and retired to the forest as a recluse.

Whoever recites or reflects upon this auspicious story of the royal sage, Ambarīṣa, will grow in devotion to the Lord.

Book Nine Chapter 6

Sage Śuka continued: Ambarīṣa had three sons: Virūpa, Ketumān and Śambhu. Virūpa's son was Pṛṣadaśva, whose son was Rathītara. Rathītara had no issue. In answer to his prayer, the sage Angirā begot through his wife a number of sons. They were considered brāhmaṇā endowed with martial spirit. From the nostrils of Vaivasvata manu, as he sneezed, was born Ikśvāku. He had a hundred sons, of whom Vikukṣi was the eldest. Some of them became rulers of the north, some of the south, etc. On one occasion, during a ritual, the king Ikśvāku asked his son Vikukṣi to bring suitable meat for offering to the manes. Vikukṣi went hunting, but as he was hungry he unwittingly ate part of the offering. This made the offering impure. On the advice of the priests the king banished his son for this fault. The king received the highest teaching from the sages and attained the supreme after he cast off his body. Vikukṣi returned home and was duly enthroned.

Vikukṣi's son, Purañjaya, became famous and earned many titles. When he waged a successful war against the demons, Indra himself assumed the form of a bull and carried Purañjaya, who was hence called Indravāha and Kakutstha. Six generations later in the same family was born Śābasta, by whom the city known as Śābastī was built. Into the same family Yuvanāśva was born. He had a hundred wives but no issue, and therefore retired to the forest. The compassionate sages there organised a rite in order that the king might have an issue. That night the king felt very thirsty and, while the priests were asleep, drank the consecrated water which was reserved for his wives. In consequence he himself became pregnant, and in due time a son split the abdomen of the father and emerged. The child cried. Indra came forward to suckle the baby with his index finger dripping with nectar. Since Indra had said: "The baby will suck me (mām dhātā)" he was known as Māndhātā. By divine grace Yuvanāśva did not die, but after living in the hermitage for some time attained liberation.

Māndhātā had three sons and fifty daughters. At that time there was a holy man named Saubhari who was doing penance in water. There he witnessed the mating of fish, which awakened sexual desire in him. He asked Māndhātā for a girl. Māndhātā replied: "You can marry whoever desires to marry you." The sage understood the veiled refusal and challenge: 'Which girl will marry such a senile man?' He transformed himself into a charming youth whom all the fifty girls desired and married. He lived with them for a long time in supernatural luxury. One day he reflected thus: "I was an ascetic, but because I witnessed the mating of fish I have fallen into the sense-trap. One desirous of liberation should never associate with the sensuous. He should be alone and totally devoted to the Lord." He once again abandoned his home.

Hariścandra
Book Nine Chapter 7

Sage Śuka continued: Māndhātā's son Purukutsa went to the subterranean region called Rasātala, where he killed the gandharvā (who were enemies of naga or serpent-demons), as recompense for which the nāgā promised that he who recalled this incident would not suffer snake-bites.

In his family was born Triśaṅku who, because of his father's curse, became a cāṇḍāla (untouchable), and tried to ascend bodily to heaven using the ascetic power of Viśvāmitra. When he was rejected in heaven he gained an abode for himself in space by the power of Viśvāmitra (and is seen even today as a star).

Triśaṅku's son was Hariścandra. Hariścandra had no issue. On sage Nārada's advice he propitiated lord Varuṇa and promised that if he was blessed with a son he would sacrifice him to Varuṇa. A son was duly born. Lord Varuṇa demanded the sacrifice. Deterred by intense love and attachment for the child, and in an attempt to postpone the tragedy, king Hariścandra agreed to fulfil his promise ten days after the birth, then when the baby cut his teeth and so on, till he promised to offer his son as a sacrifice when the boy was able to put on his armour.

At that stage the son Rohita heard of the father's promise to lord Varuṇa. Rohita went away to the forest to save himself. In the meantime Hariścandra developed dropsy. Hearing of this, Rohita was about to return to the palace. He was met on the way by Indra who warned him that he would surely be sacrificed to Varuṇa if he returned to the palace, and advised him to go on a long pilgrimage. After six years Rohita bought from Ajīgarta his middle issue, by name Śunaḥśepa, and returned with him to the palace.

Hariścandra offered Śunaḥśepa as the sacrifice and was instantly relieved of his dropsy. Sages like Viśvāmitra, Vasiṣṭha and others officiated in this rite. Highly pleased with this, Indra gave the king a golden chariot. Viśvāmitra, pleased with the honesty and truthfulness of Hariścandra, instructed him in the highest knowledge. The king thereupon withdrew his consciousness from the elements and through the yoga of sublimation attained the supreme being.

Sagara
Book Nine Chapter 8

Sage Śuka continued: Into Rohita's family was born king Bharuka, who retired to the forest. When he died one of his wives wished to follow her husband but was prevented by the sage Aurva, as she was expecting a baby. Her co-wives poisoned her but she did not die. She gave birth to Sagara, so-called because he was 'born with poison'.

Sagara became an emperor, having won a victory over several kings. To celebrate his sovereignty he set out to perform the aśvamedha rite. He therefore released a horse in preparation for this rite. The horse was stolen by Indra who left it near the hermitage of lord Kapila. Sagara's sixty thousand sons went in search of the horse, discovered it in the hermitage of lord Kapila, and, concluding that he was the thief pretending to meditate, they rushed at him with intent to kill him. The lord opened his eyes and they were reduced to ashes. It is of course not right to say that these princes were burnt by the anger of lord Kapila. How can such a dark quality as anger manifest in one whose very presence is purifying? How can perception of duality exist in one who manifested himself on earth to launch the vessel of the highest wisdom (sāṅkhya)? The sons of Sagara were burnt by their own wickedness.

Sagara had another son, Asamañjasa. He was called 'not a good man', because his actions appeared to be not good: for instance he would playfully throw babies into the river. When he was scolded for this he would (by his yogic power) bring the babies back and go away. Aṁśumān was the son of Asamañjasa. Aṁśumān went in search of the horse, along the path taken by his uncles. He too reached the hermitage of lord Kapila. There he bowed to lord Kapila, recognising him as lord Viṣṇu himself, and prayed: "Even the gods do not know you in truth. No one knows your essential nature, though you are the indweller of all beings. How can an ignorant being like me hope to analyse and judge who you are? I bow to you; and by the very sight of you the bondage of ignorance has dropped away." Lord Kapila said: "You can take the horse away. As for your uncles, they will be revived by the waters of the Gaṅgā." Taking the horse with him, Aṁśumān returned. Sagara concluded the rite and eventually attained the supreme being.

Bhagīratha
Book Nine Chapter 9

Sage Śuka continued: Aṁśumān practised austerities in order to bring Gaṅgā down, but died before succeeding in his attempt. His son Dilīpa, lost his life in the attempt. Dilīpa's son, Bhagīratha, obtained a vision of the celestial river Gaṅgā after intense austerities. She said: "I am ready to come down to the earth. But someone must be found who is powerful enough to arrest my force as I descend on earth. Moreover, sinners will wash away their sins by bathing in me. How can I be purified?" Bhagīratha offered two solutions: "Lord Rudra will bear the force of the descent of Gaṅgā. Holy men who purify the whole world will purify the holy river Gaṅgā when they bathe in her waters: for in them the all-purifying Lord is ever present in all his glory." Bhagīratha then prayed to lord Śiva, who agreed to break the force of the descent of Gaṅgā. He cautiously bore the waters, that had touched the hallowed feet of lord Hari, on his own head. Bhagīratha then led Gaṅgā to where the ashes of his great-granduncles lay. When the waters of the Gaṅgā touched the ashes the uncles ascended to heaven. This is no wonder, for Gaṅgā derives her purity from the touch of the Lord's feet.

Into Bhagīratha's family was born Saudāsa, who had also earned the nicknames of Mitrasaha and Kalmāṣapāda. Once, while hunting, he killed a demon but released the demon's brother, who thereafter entertained a terrible grudge against him. He disguised himself as a cook and got himself employed in the king's kitchen. One day, the sage Vasiṣṭha visited the king and the mischievous cook served human flesh to the sage! Enraged, the sage cursed the king, saying: "For this sin you will be turned into an evil spirit." Learning that it was the mischief of the cook, the sage reduced the sentence to twelve years. The king was about to counter-curse the sage, and with this intent took water in his hand: but on the counsel of his wife he restrained himself and poured the cursed water on his own feet so that it might not harm any living creature, and thus he became known as Mitrasaha (friend) and also Kalmāṣapāda (as the cursed water had polluted his own foot). The king roamed as an evil spirit. One day he saw a brāhmaṇa couple engaged in love-play. Mercilessly he swallowed the husband. The wife, who knew intuitively the royal identity of the ogre, pleaded with him not to kill her husband who was a noble ascetic and learned brāhmaṇa. But finding that her plea did not make any impression on the ogre she cursed him: "If you touch your wife in sex-play, you will die." She then consigned her husband's skeleton to the funeral pyre and followed him to the other world. Therefore, the king, even after resuming his former form, had no son. At the king's suggestion, Vasiṣṭha begot a son through the queen. The foetus remained in the mother's womb for seven years and was delivered only when Vasiṣṭha hit her abdomen with a stone.

Into the same family was born Khaṭvāṅga, a great ruler, who knew of his impending death just an hour before. Immediately he mentally renounced the three worlds, seeing that they were completely hollow and essenceless, and surrendered himself to the Lord. Immediately Khaṭvāṅga attained realisation of the absolute (or the realisation of the omnipresence of lord Vāsudeva).

Rāma
Book Nine Chapter 10

Sage Śuka continued: Khaṭvāṅga's grandson was Raghu and his grandson was Daśaratha. In response to the gods' prayer the Lord himself incarnated as Rāma, Daśaratha's son. He abandoned the kingdom to honour the promise of his father and roamed the forest, served by his brother and Hanumān. He lost his beloved wife, built a bridge and exterminated the host of wicked demons—may that Rāma protect us!

During a rite performed by the sage Viśvāmitra, Rāma chastised several demons who disturbed it. Playfully he strung the bow of lord Śiva and won Sītā's hand as the prize. He then humbled Paraśurāma who had relentlessly routed the warrior-class. In obedience to the command of Daśaratha he renounced his kingdom, relations, friends and home and went to the forest along with Sītā and Lakṣmaṇa. There he punished the wicked Śūrpaṇakhā and other demons. Śūrpaṇakhā's brother Rāvaṇa had conceived a passion for Sītā and had therefore sent Mārīca, disguised as a golden deer, to help him kidnap Sītā. Mārīca himself was killed by Rāma. As if to illustrate the fate of those attached to women, Rāma became grief-stricken at his separation from Sītā. He bestowed liberation on the blessed devotee Jaṭāyu.

Gaining the friendship of Sugrīva, Rāma discovered the whereabouts of Sītā and marched towards Laṅkā. The ocean gave way to him. He had a bridge built of mountain peaks, and having marched across, he invaded Laṅkā. Surrounded by the vānara army, Rāma gave battle to the host of demons and eventually killed Rāvaṇa, whose merit had been expended by the abduction of Rāma's wife, Sītā. The demonesses surrounding Rāvaṇa's dead body wailed aloud in sorrow for the demon whose passion had brought untimely death upon himself.

Rāma installed Vibhīṣaṇa on the throne of Laṅkā; then, accompanied by Sītā, Lakṣmaṇa, Sugrīva and Hanumān, he flew back to his native Ayodhyā, his 'exile' period having come to an end. He was greeted by his younger brother Bharata, who had 'ruled' the kingdom as vice-regent of Rāma's sandals, which he had installed on the throne. All his relations and the people of Ayodhyā rejoiced to see Rāma back in their midst. Rāma was duly installed on the throne of Ayodhyā. During his reign there was no sickness (physical or mental) and no crime. Righteousness and prosperity prevailed in the land. By their own conduct Rāma and Sītā had illustrated the highest ideals of family life.

Book Nine Chapter 11-12

Sage Śuka continued: Lord Rāma performed a sacred rite to propitiate his ownself, viz., lord Viṣṇu. It was wonderful that during the rite he gave away everything he had: he gave away his entire kingdom and all his wealth to the holy ones whom alone he considered fit to govern a kingdom. He had only the clothes he wore to call his own. Sītā, his consort, had also followed Rāma's example and given everything away. Highly acclaiming this noble action, the holy ones however returned the kingdom to Rāma for him to rule. They prayed: "We salute the Lord who, entering our hearts, wipes out our ignorance. We salute lord Rāma of unobstructed wisdom, of great renown and at whose feet bow those who are devoted to non-violence."

Rāma used to wander the capital incognito in order to ascertain the wishes and the will of the people. One night he heard a man rejecting his wife with the words: "You have lived in the house of another—even as Sītā has done. Rāma may be too fond of his wife to find fault in such conduct; but not I. I will not accept you back." Bowing to public opinion (although it was hard to accept) Rāma sent his consort, Sītā, away to the forest, though she was just then expecting a child. Soon after, she gave birth to twin sons, Kuśa and Lava. Sītā entrusted them to the care of the sage Vālmīki and then entered the earth. News of this tragedy filled Rāma with further grief: they enacted this divine drama merely to show that infatuation between men and women always leads to grief and suffering, even in the case of the gods.

After this, Rāma ruled the country for a period of thirteen thousand years. Then he ascended to his own divine realm. Extermination of the demons and the wicked people by lord Rāma need cause no wonder: even the fact that in his battle with Rāvaṇa and his hosts, Rāma was assisted by 'monkeys' (vānarā may mean 'tribesmen'), need not cause any wonder. For Rāma was the Lord himself, and his glory is immeasurable. Everyone who came into contact with the Lord during his incarnation as Rāma attained to the supreme abode.

He who repeatedly hears the auspicious story of Rāma is freed from the bonds of karma.

After Kuśa, in the solar dynasty, among others, came Hiraṇyanābha, who was a yogi and disciple of sage Jaimini who imparted self-knowledge to Yājñavalkya. The last member of this clan so far has been Bṛhadbala, who was killed by your father Abhimanyu. This clan will continue till the end of the kali age, with Sumitra as the last member. After this, Maru, the perfected yogi who lives in Kalāpagrāma, will revive the solar dynasty.

Book Nine Chapter 13

Sage Śuka continued: King Nimi was the son of Ikṣvāku. After commencing a religious rite Nimi requested Vasiṣṭha to participate in it. Vasiṣṭha replied that he had already accepted another invitation from Indra, and that he would return to Nimi's ritual after completing

Indra's. However, Nimi continued the ritual with the help of other priests. He did not regard the ritual as all-important since everything in this world is passing. Vasiṣṭha returned in due course and was greatly annoyed by what he regarded as an insult to him. He therefore cursed king Nimi: "You think you know everything but you will fall." The king also counter-cursed him in similar words. Vasiṣṭha had therefore to take birth as the son of Urvaśī and the gods Mitra-Varuṇa.

The holy men officiating at the rite embalmed the body of Nimi and prayed to the gods participating in the ritual: "May Nimi come back to life!" The gods granted this prayer. However, Nimi, who had not yet been fully resuscitated, spoke: "I do not wish to be revived. I consider this body to be a prison. No wise man longs to live in a body, on account of the ever-present fear of its passing away (death); every wise man longs to worship the lotus feet of the Lord. I do not wish to be embodied, for the body is the abode of suffering, grief and fear." The gods thereupon granted: "Without a body, reside in the eyes of all beings." (The opening and the closing of the eyelids are performed by him.)

Later the priests officiating at the ceremony churned the body of Nimi and extracted a living cell from it, capable of growing into another living human being. Thus was a son born of Nimi. This son was called Janaka, the father of a new line of kings. Since he was the son of a disembodied person he was also known as Vaideha, son of Videha. He was also known as Mithila because he was born of churning. The city Mithilā was founded by him.

There have been many descendants of this royal line, O Parīkṣit. All of them were royal sages of the highest wisdom on account of their association with great yogī like the sage Yājñavalkya. They were all freed from the dual forces like pleasure and pain, though they continued to live a householder's life.

Book Nine Chapter 14

Sage Śuka continued: Atri was a son of Brahmā the creator. Of his tears of joy was born the moon-god Soma, full of nectar. The creator appointed him to preside over the protection of the holy ones, medicinal plants and herbs, and to be the foremost among the stars. Once Soma seduced Tārā, the wife of the celestial preceptor, Bṛhaspati (Jupiter). Tārā gave birth to Budha (Mercury). Purūravā was the son of Budha. He was exceedingly beautiful and of good nature, on account of which the celestial nymph Urvaśī fell in love with him.

Urvaśī approached him with love, and placing before him two rams said: "I shall live with you so long as you protect them. There is just one more condition: I should not see your naked body except during our sexual union." Purūravā readily agreed and they lived happily together.

Urvaśī was missed in the court of Indra, the king of gods. He despatched a few celestials to search for her and bring her back. They went to Purūravā's palace and stole away the rams at night. Hearing their cry, Urvaśī was terribly upset and upbraided Purūravā for not rushing to their aid. The king at once left the bed and rushed out in haste, without putting on any clothes. The celestials left the rams nearby and disappeared, after momentarily illumining the whole place with their own light. In that light Urvaśī saw Purūravā's naked body and, in accordance with her own resolve, left him.

The king went after her, entreating her to return. The nymph, however, pointed out to him that relationship between man and woman is often fraught with selfishness, grief and sorrow. She said: "Immortal women inspire confidence in ignorant men and then abandon all friendly feelings towards them; and they seek newer and newer conquests." She promised however, to be with him for a day after one year. She fulfilled this promise but the king was not satisfied. He then offered a prayer to the celestials, who gave him a vessel with fire in it, suggesting that he should worship the Lord through it and earn Urvaśī as the prize. But the passionate king took the vessel itself for Urvaśī and roamed about with it. When he discovered the truth he left it in a forest. When the tretā age dawned he recalled the rules of fire-worship and went back to the forest. Since he did not find the fire he kindled the ritual fire with the help of wood, and performed the rite to attain Urvaśī. He contemplated the lower piece of wood as Urvaśī, the upper one to be himself, and that between as their progeny. This gave rise to three fire rituals. After thus contemplating and generating the fire, Purūravā attained the celestial realm.

Before the tretā age, there was but one vedā or the Oṁ, there was but one God, Nārāyaṇa, one fire rite and one caste. It was Purūravā who made them into three.

Paraśurāma
Book Nine Chapter 15

Sage Śuka continued: One of the descendants of Purūravā was Gādhi, the son of Kuśāmbu. Gādhi had a daughter, Satyavatī, whom the sage Ṛcīka desired to marry. Doubtful of his worthiness, Gādhi demanded a thousand horses of Ṛcīka. Ṛcīka quickly got them from the god Varuṇa, and thus won the hand of Satyavatī. Both Satyavatī and her mother were desirous of an offspring, so sage Ṛcīka prepared caru (a rice preparation) and uttered holy mantrā over it. The intention was that the portion that Satyavatī would eat would bless her with a holy brāhmaṇa boy and her mother would beget a warrior. The mother, who imagined that Ṛcīka would naturally favour his wife more than the mother-in-law, consumed her daughter's share! Satyavatī was distressed when Ṛcīka told her what the consequence would be, and obtained from him the boon that not her son but her grandson would be a cruel fighter. This grandson was Paraśurāma.

At that time there was a great king known as Arjuna, who on one occasion playfully caught hold of the mighty demon, Rāvaṇa, and imprisoned him. This Arjuna was one day roaming the forest and happened to come to the hermitage of Jamadagni (father of Paraśurāma). The king was treated to a royal feast, with the help of the cow of plenty, Kāmadhenu. The king Arjuna was envious of the ascetic's possession of the cow which yielded inexhaustible riches, and so had her taken away by force. When the sage's son Paraśurāma heard of this atrocity, he took his axe and pursued the king.

Arjuna saw the radiant but fearful form of the brāhmaṇa Paraśurāma pursuing him and ordered his mighty army to challenge him. Paraśurāma soon disposed of the army and Arjuna faced this powerful adversary alone. He showered missiles upon him but Paraśurāma destroyed them by his counter-missiles, and then cut off the many arms of Arjuna and finally chopped off his head. He returned to the father's hermitage with the cow. But, his father was not pleased! The sage Jamadagni said: "Son, we are holy brāhmaṇā who attained to our position of respectability on account of our patience and forgiveness, which enabled Brahmā the creator to gain his status too! By forgiveness the spiritual wealth of the brāhmaṇa shines and with forgiveness is the Lord pleased. Killing a king is more heinous a crime than killing a brāhmaṇa. Therefore go on a pilgrimage to the holy places dedicated to the Lord, in order to remove this sin."

Book Nine Chapter 16

Sage Śuka continued: Paraśurāma went on a year's pilgrimage and then returned to the father's hermitage. One day while his mother Reṇukā was bathing in the river she saw a celestial sporting with nymphs. Her heart was slightly disturbed at seeing such a charming celestial. However, soon she returned to the hermitage. The sage knew what had happened and commanded his sons to behead the sinner. Only Paraśurāma obeyed. Highly pleased with him, Jamadagni asked him to choose a boon: Paraśurāma at once asked that his mother be brought back to life and that she should forget the assassination! The boon was granted.

The sons of Arjuna were waiting for an opportunity to avenge the death of their father who had been killed by Paraśurāma. One day they went to the hermitage when Paraśurāma was absent and assassinated the sage Jamadagni. Reṇukā wailed aloud. Hearing this, Paraśurāma hastened home to witness the tragedy. Picking up his deadly axe he rushed to Māhiṣmatī (the capital of Arjuna) and in the centre of the city he created a mountain of the heads of the warriors he killed, and a river with their blood. Still, his anger was not appeased. Making the killing of his father an excuse and coming to the conclusion that therefore all kings and warriors were wicked, he took upon himself the duty of exterminating the warrior community twenty-one times.

Paraśurāma then re-united his father's head with the trunk and placed it near the sacred fire with which he propitiated the Lord. At the end of this ritual he gave away all that he had to the officiating priests. Thus, he purified himself of the sin of killing the kings, and the sage Jamadagni was freed from the undesirable consequence of being killed. With the wholeness of his body restored and spiritualised he became one of the seven sages who protect the universe. Paraśurāma dwells in mount Mahendra even now: he will be a sage in the next cycle.

Gādhi had a son known as Viśvāmitra, who had one hundred and one sons (collectively known as madhucchandā). He also adopted Ajīgarta's son Śunaḥśepa and appointed him to be the eldest. One day Śunaḥśepa was about to be sacrificed by Hariścandra, but by propitiating the gods (as advised by Viśvāmitra) he was saved. Fifty of Viśvāmitra's sons refused to accept Śunaḥśepa as their elder brother. The sage cursed them to be born as barbarians. The other fifty-one accepted to do the bidding of the father and the sage blessed them that they would be fathers of heroes. Thus was the clan of Viśvāmitra ramified.

Yayāti
Book Nine Chapter 17-18

Sage Śuka continued: Purūravā's son Āyu had five sons—Nahuṣa, Kṣatravṛddha, Raji, Rambha and Anenā. Nahuṣa had six sons—Yati, Yayāti, Saṁyāti, Āyati, Viyati and Kṛti. Yati had no interest in the worldly life, so in course of time Yayāti became king and made his four other brothers governors of the four quarters of the kingdom.

The demon-chief Vṛṣaparvā had a daughter Śarmiṣṭhā, and the preceptor of the demons, Śukra, had a daughter Devayānī. They were once bathing with friends in a small lake when they saw lord Śiva pass by. All of them hurried out of the lake and put on their clothes. By mistake Śarmiṣṭhā put on Devayānī's clothes. Enraged, Devayānī spoke insultingly of the royal clan which she considered inferior to the priest class: "We brāhmaṇā represent the mouth of the Lord: how dare the daughter of the demon-chief put on our garments?" Strong willed Śarmiṣṭhā returned the compliment by insulting the priest class: "You are but a beggar-maid who waits at our door like a crow!" and crowned it by disrobing Devayānī and throwing her into a well.

Yayāti happened to come to the well soon after and he gave Devayānī his own upper garment and held out his hand to lift her out of the well. Devayānī demanded that since he had held her hand he should wed her, though she was of the priest class and he a king. He too agreed, recognising it as the will of God. Devayānī returned to her father and informed him of Śarmiṣṭhā's misdemeanour. Touched to the quick, sage Śukra decided to leave the city. The king Vṛṣaparvā pleaded with the sage to change his mind. The sage looked to his daughter to ascertain her wish. Devayānī stipulated the condition: "Śarmiṣṭhā should serve as my servant." This was agreed upon.

Śukra gave Devayānī in marriage to Yayāti, but warned the king not to seduce Śarmiṣṭhā. Devayānī later gave birth to a son. Śarmiṣṭhā longed for a son and approached Yayāti, who fulfilled her desire. Angered at this, Devayānī returned to her father's house. Śukra cursed Yayāti in anger: "You will lose your youth and instantly become old." Yayāti pleaded that he had not had enough of worldly pleasures. Śukra granted that Yayāti could transfer his old age to any young man. Yayāti approached his own sons, of whom the first three firmly refused, while Pūru agreed to receive his father's old age, saying: "This is my foremost duty. The son who divines his father's intentions and fulfils them is the best; the middling son does what he is told; the worst son carries out his father's behest reluctantly. He who refuses to obey his father is the father's refuse." Thus Yayāti regained his youth and enjoyed the pleasures of the world with Devayānī, and also fulfilled his religious duties.

Book Nine Chapter 19

Sage Śuka continued: Soon Yayāti woke up to his spiritual degradation. One day he told his wife a story which was autobiographical: "Once, my dear, a she-goat had fallen into a well. A male goat which happened to pass by managed to rescue the she-goat, which fell in love with the male and married it. They enjoyed life, till the male was sought by another female goat. The first she-goat became jealous and returned to its owner, followed by the male goat. The owner castrated the male goat, but yielded to its bleating prayer and restored its virility. Once again the male and the she-goat continued to enjoy sensual pleasures."

Yayāti went on: "Even so, I am caught in the net of the pleasures of the senses. Know this for certain, my dear: not all the food, wealth and women of the world can appease the lust of a single man of uncontrolled senses. Craving for sense-pleasures is not removed but aggravated by indulgence even as ghee poured into fire increases it. He who has given up all notions of diversity and looks upon all as the one self, experiences delight in all directions. One who aspires for peace and happiness should instantly renounce craving and seek that which neither grows old, nor ceases even when the body ages. Therefore one should not remain alone with one's own mother, sister or daughter, for the senses are powerful and lead astray even a wise man. For a thousand years I have enjoyed the pleasures of the senses, but the craving has not diminished. I am therefore renouncing this worldly life, desirous as I am of realising the absolute."

He returned youth to Pūru and received old age in return. He entrusted the kingdom to his sons and retired to the forest where, by constant meditation on the supreme, he was soon absorbed into it. Hearing Yayāti's conclusions Devayānī also conceived dispassion for worldly enjoyments and attained to the lotus feet of lord Vāsudeva.

Duṣyanta
Book Nine Chapter 20

Sage Śuka continued: Pūru's descendant was Duṣyanta, son of Raibhya. One day this royal sage had gone to the forest hunting. Near the hermitage of the sage Kaṇva he saw a beautiful young girl, with whom he fell in love at first sight. "You must be of royal blood," he said, "otherwise my pure heart would not long for you." "Yes," she replied, "I am Śakuntalā, the daughter of the royal sage Viśvāmitra, born of Menakā." They married each other in accordance with the gāndharva rite (i.e. by personal choice). Soon the king returned to his palace. Some months later Śakuntalā gave birth to Bharata.

After a while Śakuntalā went to her husband's palace along with Bharata. The emperor however did not recognise her! At that time, a celestial voice resounded: "The mother is but a vessel in which the father begets a child. Accept this (Bharasva), your child, and do not slight Śakuntalā. The son who begets children leads his father out of the abode of Yama. You are the father of this child; Śakuntalā speaks the truth."

In course of time Bharata, who was a part manifestation of the Lord, became the emperor. He performed an astonishing number of horse rites—fifty-five along the banks of the holy Gaṅgā, and seventy-eight along the banks of the holy Yamunā. The officiating priests received lavish presents through these rituals. The grace of the Lord earned as a result of these rituals freed Bharata from the effects of the Lord's māyā. He also performed the maṣṇāra rite on an unprecendented scale. He conquered all the neighbouring territories. He rescued from the nether-world the wives of gods who had been kidnapped by demons and imprisoned there. Heaven and earth yielded all their wealth to him and to his subjects, without much effort.

Bharata had three wives and through them three sons. However, these wives abandoned the boys as they did not resemble the father. To prevent the extinction of the clan the marut (wind-gods) gave to Bharata the child born of the sage Bṛhaspati and his brother's wife Mamatā, who had been abandoned by the parents for fear of calumny. That child was Bharadvāja.

Rantideva
Book Nine Chapter 21

Sage Śuka continued: A descendant of Bharadvāja was the great Rantideva, whose glory is sung both in this world and in the other. Rantideva was a king, but lived the life of a mendicant on what he obtained without effort. Yet, the unhappiness of others was of greater concern to him than his own and so he gave away whatever he had to others. As a result, he and his family often had to go without food. Once he had to starve thus for forty-eight days.

On the morning of the forty-ninth day he got some food, milk and water. As he was about to eat it, along with his family, a brāhmaṇa came to him. Seeing the Lord himself in that holy man,

Rantideva gave him part of the food. The brāhmaṇa ate and went away. As Rantideva once again prepared to eat, a man of the servant-class (śūdra) appeared. Rantideva again divided what was left and gave him a share. Soon after this śūdra guest departed another man came, surrounded by dogs. All of them were hungry. Seeing them Rantideva gave away whatever food remained. There was only water left for him now. But before he could drink it an untouchable appeared and asked for water. Rantideva was moved by compassion and he said: "I do not desire to be endowed with wealth or psychic powers, not do I desire final liberation. May I enter the hearts of all embodied beings so that I may take on their sorrows and they may be freed from sorrow. My hunger and thirst, fatigue and suffering all disappear when your thirst is quenched." Then and there the holy trinity (Brahmā the creator, Viṣṇu the protector and Śiva the redeemer) appeared before Rantideva and revealed that it was they who had earlier come in the guise of the brāhmaṇa, the śūdra and the untouchable. Rantideva did not crave for any boons. He had risen above māyā and the qualities of nature.

In Bharadvāja's family were also born Hastī (who built the city named Hastināpura), the pañcālā, the maudgalyā (who were brāhmaṇā), Ahalyā (the wife of sage Gautama) and also Śaradvān. Śaradvān one day saw the celestial Urvaśī at a distance; and his seed escaped him and fell on reeds. It however assumed the form of a pair of children—a boy and a girl. King Śāntanu took the twins and brought them up. The boy was Kṛpa, the teacher of the kauravā; and the girl was Kṛpī, the wife of the teacher Droṇācārya.

Book Nine Chapter 22

Sage Śuka continued: Ahalyā's father Bharmyāśva had a son named Divodāsa. In his line many heroes were born, including Kuru the lord of Kurukṣetra, (whose mother was the daughter of the sun-god), Bṛhadratha whose wife gave birth to two halves of one body (which were joined together by a female spirit named Jarā and became Jarāsandha) and Pratīpa who had three sons—Devāpi, Śantanu and Bāhlīka. Devāpi retired to the forest and Śantanu became king. Śantanu had such a healing hand that whoever he touched became healthy and youthful. During his reign there was no rain, because Śantanu ruled while his brother was alive and eligible for the throne. Śantanu sent messengers to beg of Devāpi to return to the throne; but Śantanu's minister had sent his agents to destroy Devāpi's faith in the vedā and dharma. When Devāpi turned heretic, rain fell, for he had forfeited his claim to the throne. Later, disillusioned Devāpi took to the practice of yoga.

Śantanu begot through Gaṅgā the noble Bhīṣma; and through Satyavatī, two sons called Citraṅgada and Vicitravīrya. Satyavatī had previously borne the sage Vyāsa who taught me this *Bhāgavataṁ* because I was of a tranquil disposition. Citrāṅgada was killed, and Vicitravīrya died of phthisis. Vyāsa begot through the wives of Vicitravīrya, two sons Dhṛtarāṣṭra and Pāṇḍu, and through a servant-maid, Vidura. Dhṛtarāṣṭra begot a hundred sons. Pāṇḍu was under a curse which prohibited sexual intercourse with his wives, who therefore bore five sons through the agency of the gods. They were the pāṇḍavā. The pāṇḍavā had a son each through their common wife Draupadī, and other children through other wives. Of Arjuna and Subhadrā (the sister of lord Kṛṣṇa) your father Abhimanyu was born. All the kurū had perished during the great war but you were miraculously saved by lord Kṛṣṇa when Aśvatthāmā tried to destroy you before your birth.

When you meet your death after being bitten by the serpent Takṣaka, your son Janamejaya will set out to destroy the serpent species. He will rule the whole world. His son Śatānīka will be learned in the vedā, in the science of rituals (which he will acquire from the sage Yājñavalkya) and also in the knowledge of the self (which he will obtain from the sage Śaunaka). Śatānīka's great-great-grandson Nemicakra will rule from Kauśāmbī when Hastināpura will be washed away by the river Gaṅgā. Thus this line will continue up to the end of the kali yuga.

Book Nine Chapter 23

Sage Śuka continued: Anu was another of Yayāti's sons and in his line was born Bali, who was issueless. Through his wife the sage Dīrghatamā begot six sons—Aṅga, Vaṅga, Kaliṅga, Suhma, Puṇḍra and Andhra, each of whom founded a kingdom. Aṅga's descendant was Romapāda who had no issue. King Daśaratha gave him a daughter, Śāntā, in adoption, and the sage Ṛṣyaśṛnga married her. Once when there was a drought this sage was induced to enter into the kingdom, which broke the drought. The sage later performed a religious rite, as a result of which Romapāda was blessed with children. He also performed a similar rite as a result of which king Daśaratha begot the divine sons, lord Rāma and his brothers.

I shall now describe to you the line of Yadu: even by hearing of this dynasty a man is freed from all sins, because the Lord himself took birth in this dynasty, assuming the form of a human being. Sahasrajit, Kroṣṭā, Nala and Ripu were the sons of Yadu, the other son of Yayāti. In that line was born of Kṛtavīrya, the famous king Arjuna (hence known as Kārtavīrya-Arjuna). He had obtained the knowledge of the self from lord Dattātreya (a part manifestation of the Lord) and also possessed many psychic powers. No other king could compare with him in glory and magnificence. He lived and ruled for eighty-five thousand years. Madhu was a descendant of this Arjuna, and Vṛṣṇi was Madhu's son. The yādava dynasty owes its existence to Yadu, Madhu and Vṛṣṇi. Another member of this famous dynasty was Śaśabindu, who was a great yogi and possessed all the excellent qualities one could think of.

Then came Jyāmagha whose wife Śaibyā was issueless. But the king was so afraid of his wife that he did not marry again. He had once invaded the kingdom of the bhojā and having won the war, he returned with a princess of the bhojā as a prize. It greatly annoyed Śaibyā to see another woman in the royal chariot. But the quick-witted king pacified her by saying: "She is your daughter-in-law". He was trembling as he spoke, so the gods and the manes took pity on the king and blessed them that Śaibyā should bear a son. This son Vidarbha later married that bhoja princess, Bhojyā.

Book Nine Chapter 24

Sage Śuka continued: Among the descendants of Vidarbha and Sātvata, Devāvṛdha and Babhru—the latter two attained great eminence. Mahābhoja was the seventh son of Satvāta. He was pious and noble, and his descendants were the bhojā. Among Sātvata's descendants were Devaka and Ugrasena, who were born of Āhuka. Devaka had many sons and daughters, among whom was Devakī. Vasudeva married all the sisters. Ugrasena, too, had many sons and daughters, among whom was Kamsa. Of another descendant, Śūrasena, were born ten sons, including Vasudeva. When Vasudeva was born, the celestial kettle-drums sounded and hence he earned the nickname Ānaka-dundubhi. Kuntī and four other girls were also born of Śūrasena. This Kuntī served the sage Durvāsā, from whom she learned a magic formula. Curiosity prompted her to use it even while a virgin. The sun-god appeared before her and blessed her with a son. She hid him in a box and consigned it to a river, afraid as she was of public opinion. Kuntī's sister Śrutadevā begot Dantavaktra, of demoniacal disposition, through Vṛddhaśarmā. Another sister, Śrutaśravā, begot through the king of Cedi, Damaghoṣa and Śiśupāla—also of demoniacal disposition.

Vasudeva had several wives—Devakī and her sisters. Through Rohiṇī he begot Bala and others. Through Devakī he begot several sons, including lord Saṅkarṣaṇa and lord Kṛṣṇa who was the eighth child, and also your grandmother Subhadrā.

Whenever there is decline of righteousness here and an increase of sin, then the lord manifests himself. The whole universe has been created, is protected and dissolved by the Lord's illusory power or māyā. But the Lord's grace leads one to the ultimate goal of all evolution, self-realisation. When the earth was ruled by demons disguised as kings and rulers, the Lord incarnated himself as lord Kṛṣṇa, along with lord Saṅkarṣaṇa, and performed many wonderful deeds. Even listening to his glory once, a man is freed from the bonds of karma. Through every one of his thoughts, words and deeds, sweet smiles and delightful pastimes, the Lord brought great joy to the people who were fortunate enough to be his contemporaries. They (especially the womenfolk) who drank the celestial beauty of his richly adorned face were never sated, and were annoyed with Nimi (who presides over the eyelids making them close for an instant now and them) for interrupting their vision of the Lord.

Book Ten

Kaṁsa Imprisons Vasudeva and Devakī
Book Ten Chapter 1

Sage Śuka continued: Demons were ruling the earth which, unable to bear their burden, sought redress by petitioning Brahmā the creator. He, with lord Śiva, sought the grace of the Lord. The gods heard the divine voice: "The Lord knows the unfortunate condition of mother earth. He will soon descend upon the earth in human form. You too, should take birth as human beings to serve him as his companions." Highly pleased with this divine assurance, the gods returned to their abode.

On earth, Ugrasena was the ruler of Mathurā—and Kaṁsa was his son. His cousin, Devakī, had been married to Vasudeva, and Kaṁsa did Devakī a great honour by himself driving the chariot. A celestial voice was heard: "Fool, the eighth child of the very lady you are thus honouring will bring about your death." Seized with fear and anger Kaṁsa was about to kill Devakī but Vasudeva intervened and pleaded:

"You are a glorious prince; and this girl is your cousin-sister, a woman, and she is just married. Is it proper for you to kill her on this auspicious occasion? Death is born with every embodied being—now or in a hundred years, everyone has to die. Just as a caterpillar leaves one blade of grass after it has found another, the soul leaves one body when it has found another. Knowing this, one should desist from harming others; only he who harms another for his own good is afraid of others. Hence do not kill this cousin of yours."

But Kaṁsa was in no mood to listen. Vasudeva further reflected: "As long as one is able one should avoid and prevent death. Let me try another method. I shall offer to hand my children over to Kaṁsa, if any are born, and if Kaṁsa lives till then! Moreover, one cannot divine the divine plan." Vasudeva said to Kaṁsa: "O noble one: you have nothing to fear from Devakī, but only from her son. I shall hand her children over to you to do as you please with them." Kaṁsa believed Vasudeva's words and spared Devakī's life. Vasudeva took his first son to Kaṁsa. Pleased with his honesty, Kaṁsa told him to take the child back, saying: "There is no danger to me from this one, for the celestial voice mentioned only the eighth child."

The sage Nārada, however, warned Kaṁsa: "The people of Vraja—the vṛṣṇī led by Vasudeva and the yadāvā led by Devakī—are all gods, of whom you should beware." He also hinted at the divine plan which was unfolding itself. The wicked Kaṁsa at once imprisoned Vasudeva and Devakī and killed every one of their babies, deposed Ugrasena and usurped the throne.

Devakī's Conception
Book Ten Chapter 2

Sage Śuka continued: Kaṁsa began to take vigorous steps to persecute the yadāvā and the vṛṣṇī. He gathered around him a number of demoniacal beings and wicked kings and he began to harass the yādavā, who fled the kingdom. Those who remained behind swore allegiance to him. In the meantime, six children were born of Vasudeva and Devakī, all of whom were faithfully handed to Kaṁsa by Vasudeva, and all of whom were immediately put to death by the wicked Kaṁsa. The Lord's own ray (or part) known as Ananta entered Devakī as the seventh issue.

At the same time, the Lord in his abode commanded his own power, māyā: "O goddess, transfer the foetus from the womb of Devakī to that of Rohiṇī (another wife of Vasudeva). Then I shall enter Devakī's womb as her eighth child. You should at the same time incarnate as Yaśodā's daughter: you will thus earn a place of glory in the heart of humanity. People will erect temples for you and worship you in your various aspects as Durgā, Bhadrakālī, Vijayā, Vaiṣṇavī, Kumudā, Caṇḍikā, Kṛṣṇā, Mādhavī, Kanyakā, Māyā, Nārāyaṇī, Īśānī, Śāradā and Ambikā." Māyā did as directed by the Lord. People who heard of what happened felt sorry thinking that Devakī had had a miscarriage.

Soon after, the Lord entered into the heart of Vasudeva, as a result of which this great devotee shone with extraordinary brilliance. Then Devakī conceived the Lord in her own heart, transferred there by the noble Vasudeva. Seeing Devakī shine with the divine effulgence enclosed within her body, Kaṁsa surmised that the Lord himself was about to manifest on earth in order to exterminate the wicked. He considered the possible courses he could adopt to safeguard his position. The most straight-forward solution was to kill Devakī herself. This solution, however, was distasteful even to the wicked Kaṁsa. He thought: "He who lives by practising intense cruelty upon others is dead while living: people hate him, and after leaving this earth he goes to hell." Yet he could not ignore the danger. Hence, he was constantly thinking of the Lord while sitting, lying down, standing, eating, walking—he saw the Lord alone everywhere.

Book Ten Chapter 2

Sage Śuka continued: The gods and the sages headed by lord Śiva went to the prison cell where Devakī and Vasudeva had been incarcerated, and offered their prayer to the unborn Lord:

"Lord, you ever fulfil your resolve; you hold truth alone as the supreme; you are the truth in the past, present and future. You are the source of the subtle elements, and you dwell in them, being the very reality of these elements. Your eyes are truth and order, and you are the very self of truth— we take refuge in you. The ancient tree known by the title of creation has but one ground (divine nature), two fruits (good and evil and other such pairs of opposites), three roots (the trinity or the three guṇā), four essences (the four human pursuits—dharma, wealth, pleasure and liberation), five divisions (the five organs of perception, etc.), either the six states of the self (birth, existence, growth, maturity, old age and death), or the six afflictions (hunger, thirst, sorrow, infatuation, old age and death), the seven components (chyle, blood, flesh, fat, bone, marrow and vital fluid), eight boughs (the five elements, mind, buddhi and the ego), the nine openings (eyes, ears, nostrils, the mouth and the two organs of excretion), two birds (the individual consciousness and the indwelling omnipresence), and ten leaves (the five principal prāṇā and the five subsidiary prāṇā—prāṇa, apāna, vyāna, udāna, samāna, nāga, kūrma, kṛkala, devadatta and dhanañjaya). You are the source of this tree, which you preserve and protect, though you are forever an uninvolved witness. They who are devoted to you cross the ocean of birth and death as if it were no bigger than the footprint of a calf;

and they leave their example behind which enables others to cross this ocean, too! They do not ever stray from the path to God-realisation; they boldly step on the very obstacles themselves and ascend to their goal. Your devotee who hears, narrates and remembers your names and glories is not born again.

"Lord, you have again and again incarnated in this universe to re-establish dharma. You incarnated as the dolphin, horse, tortoise, man-lion, boar, swan, prince, a brāhmaṇa, and in other forms. You always protect us. Now, too, O Lord, relieve this earth of the burden of evil."

Having offered this prayer, the gods returned to heaven.

Birth of Kṛṣṇa
Book Ten Chapter 3

Sage Śuka continued: The most auspicious hour of the Lord's birth drew near. The entire nature rejoiced as if to welcome the divine babe. Divine music and prayerfulness filled the air. At midnight the Lord was born of Devakī who shone in all her radiance as a goddess, just as the moon shines when it rises over the horizon. Vasudeva feasted his eyes on the divine baby endowed with four arms and with the other insignia of lord Viṣṇu. Because he was in a prison he celebrated the occasion by mentally giving away great gifts to the holy ones. He sang the praises of the Lord: "You are indeed the supreme person who appears to be the indweller of all though you have not actually entered anyone on account of your omnipresence (and therefore you cannot enter anyone!), and who assumes the role of the creator, preserver and redeemer. Even so, your present birth as our son is a divine mystery. You will surely put an end to evil on earth; but for the present I am anxious lest Kaṁsa, who killed your elder brothers for fear of you, might harm you too." Devakī too, sang his praises in similar terms: "A person, afraid of death, is unable to find refuge anywhere in the world; but when he resorts to your feet, he is rid of all fear. We are afraid of Kaṁsa; and you alone can save us from that fear."

The compassionate Lord said to Vasudeva and Devakī: "In your previous incarnation as Pṛśni and Sutapā, you had no issue and both of you performed unprecedented penance. When I appeared before you and offered to bestow a boon upon you, you asked for a son like me. Since none can be like me, I myself was born as your son, with the name Pṛśnigarbha. In your next incarnation as Aditi and Kaśyapa, I was born as Upendra, also known as Vāmana. Once again for a third time I am born as your son. My word is ever true. People can recognise me only when I assume a human form. In this incarnation, by loving me both of you will attain the highest state of liberation."

Immediately after this he became an ordinary baby. Prompted from within by the Lord, Vasudeva took the divine child in a basket and stepped out of his prison cell. The prison guards were fast asleep. The heavy prison doors, secured with locks and chains, opened of their own accord as soon as Vasudeva neared them with the divine baby. There was a light drizzle, but the divine serpent Śeṣa shielded the baby with his hoods. The river Yamunā was in flood; but she yielded a passage to Vasudeva and the Lord. All this was brought about by the Lord's own power—māyā. Vasudeva went to Vraja. All the cowherds there were asleep. Yaśodā had just given birth to a girl who was the lord's own māyā who had incarnated at the same time. She had immediately fallen asleep, not knowing whether it was a boy or girl. When she awoke, Yaśodā found a baby boy next to her, for Vasudeva had placed his own son there, and taking Yaśodā's daughter had returned to the prison cell.

Book Ten Chapter 4

Sage Śuka continued: As soon as Vasudeva re-entered the prison cell with the girl in his arms, the doors closed of their own accord. Hearing the cry of the baby the guards sprang to their feet and informed Kaṁsa, who hurried to the prison, afraid as he was of the eighth child. Ignoring Devakī's plea, he grabbed the girl and hurled her on a stone. However, the baby flew up, and there Kaṁsa beheld the graceful form of the divine mother of the universe, Mahāmāyā, with her eight arms holding various divine weapons. She laughed at his foolishness and said: "What is the use of trying to kill me, O fool! Your death has taken birth somewhere else. Therefore, do not harm the innocent." The divine mother since then has come to be worshipped in many places under different names.

Kaṁsa was thoroughly shaken by this turn of events. Immediately he released Vasudeva and Devakī from their shackles, and clasping their feet, begged their pardon: "Forgive me, a sinner, for killing so many of your innocent children. But do not grieve: for they only reaped the fruits of their own past karma. Moreover, changes like birth and death only relate to the body, not to the self. Only they who mistake the self for the body and vice versa, assume that they kill or that they are killed. You are pious souls full of wisdom. Forgive my wicked actions." Devakī and Vasudeva appreciated Kaṁsa's wise words. Vasudeva said: "It is only the differentiation 'This is mine and that is not mine' that is born of ignorance, which causes sorrow in this world. One who rises above this differentiation goes beyond sorrow."

Kaṁsa convened his council of advisors and narrated to them what had happened and what Mahāmāyā had said. They, the demons, eagerly assured Kaṁsa that they were ready to help him in every way possible. "We shall kill all babies who are about ten days of age. Who can stop us?" asked they. "For the gods are cowards and are terribly afraid of you. Even the trinity cannot stand before you. Viṣṇu abides alone, in the secret chambers of his devotees' hearts. Śiva dwells in a forest. Brahmā is doing penance. But, we should not procrastinate. For if an adversary gains power it is difficult to deal with him, even as a neglected ailment or the senses that have not been disciplined in time before a bad habit is formed, are difficult to bring under control once they have taken deeper root. Viṣṇu, who is the main support for the gods, abides where sanatana dharma (the eternal religion) prevails, whose mainstay are the holy ones. Hence, we should destroy them too." Thus they resolved to harm the holy ones, for thus would their merit come to an end.

Book Ten Chapter 5

Sage Śuka continued: Nanda rejoiced to know that he had been blessed with a son. With the help of the priests he performed the post-natal ceremonies, during which he distributed lavish gifts to the honoured and holy ones. Material substances are purified by time, bath (washing), purification, religious rites, austerity and rituals, as also by gifts and contentment; but the self is purified only through self-knowledge.

The whole countryside rejoiced. Every house wore a festive appearance. Cowherds and cowherdesses dressed and adorned themselves and in every way manifested the delight that radiated from their hearts. It was as if every house, every family, every man, woman and child had suddenly been granted their greatest wish. Everyone told everyone else of the good news. All of them then made a pilgrimage to the palace of the chieftain Nanda and offered individual and collective prayers to the Lord to protect the child in every way. While the women were doing all this, the men abandoned themselves to merry-making, smearing one another with curds and butter and tripping one another in fun. Rohiṇī the other wife of Vasudeva, moved about, highly honoured by Nanda. The goddess of fortune had come to dwell in Vraja, now that the Lord himself had taken his abode there.

Nanda had to go to Mathurā to pay his taxes to Kaṁsa. Anxious as he was for the safety of his son, he cautioned the cowherds to protect the state and the people with great care, and went to Mathurā with a heavy heart. Vasudeva heard of Nanda's visit to Mathurā and called on him after the latter had completed his official duties. They fondly embraced each other and then Vasudeva spoke to Nanda: "I am delighted that after all you have been blessed with a son. I hope that the people in Gokula are happy and prosperous. And I hope too that the cattle are in good health and have plenty to eat and drink. Is my son well in your house, living as your son and loved by you all? The wise ones insist that dharma, prosperity and pleasure are to be cherised only when they are shared with one's loved ones, not if they are in distress. Hence the joy and welfare of one's kith and kin are of great importance." Nanda, for his part responded: "We know that many of your children were put to death by Kaṁsa and that your only daughter has been taken away from you also. Yet, all this is the unseen fruit of one's own past action. He who sees thus does not grieve."

Vasudeva then urged Nanda to return to Gokula quickly, for he had a premonition of calamities in Gokula. Nanda left at once from Mathurā and proceeded swiftly to Gokula.

Pūtanā
Book Ten Chapter 6

Sage Śuka continued: In the meantime, a demoness called Pūtanā had gone to Vraja, on the orders of Kaṁsa. Such demonesses and evil spirits have access only to those places where the Lord's stories and glories are not narrated and heard, even if the household duties are properly discharged. Pūtanā had cleverly disguised herself as a charming young woman, rivalling Lakṣmī herself in beauty. She was a member of Kaṁsa's party sworn to carry out his programme of infanticide. By and by she entered Nanda's house and beheld the infant Kṛṣṇa. While Yaśodā and Rohiṇī were looking helplessly on, bewitched by her physical beauty, Pūtanā took the divine infant and placed him on her lap, apparently out of love, and began to suckle him. Her breasts, however, had been smeared with the most deadly poison.

The divine infant sucked hungrily at her breast, and sucking the poisoned milk (which did not affect him at all) he drew away her very vital airs. Yelling in mortal agony she tried to extricate herself, but she could not. Her mortal convulsions lifted her body up into the sky, and her form had returned to that of a demoness. She fell, crushing trees under that huge body which was ugly and fearful to look at.

The cowherdesses of Vraja were frightened but happy. They considered it a stroke of the greatest good fortune that the little infant was saved from such a terrible calamity. And, they busied themselves with occult rites to ward off evil spirits that caused such phenomena. Uttering the names of the Lord, they touched the different parts of Kṛṣṇa's body so that the evil spirits might have no access to that divine body. Mother Yaśodā suckled Kṛṣṇa and put him to bed. In the meantime, Nanda had returned to Vraja and marvelled that Vasudeva had foreseen the calamity, surely through his supernatural vision! He lovingly embraced Kṛṣṇa.

The citizens of Vraja cremated the body of Pūtanā which wafted a celestial aroma while it burned, for she had been purged of all sin when the Lord himself sucked her breast. She had therefore attained the status of the Lord's mother. This demoness, the killer of infants, reached the highest abode because she suckled the baby Kṛṣṇa, though with evil intent. How indescribably great would the devotee's reward be if he loved the Lord with the purest devotion in his heart!

One who listens to this story of Pūtanā's redemption will cultivate supreme devotion to the Lord.

Tṛṇāvarta; Yaśodā's Vision
Book Ten Chapter 7

Sage Śuka continued: The beloved baby turned on his abdomen, and this event was celebrated in Vraja with great joy. The baby had been adopted by every family in Vraja and every event in his life therefore became a joyous occasion in the life of every household. During the festivities the mother had left the baby underneath a cart laden with pots of milk etc., and was talking to other women. The mother did not hear the baby cry. Seemingly indignant, he kicked the heavy-laden cart with his tiny feet. The cart overturned and crashed, spilling its contents all over the place. The mother and others rushed to the spot and thanked the stars that the baby was safe. The cowherd boys told the elders that the cart had been overturned by baby Kṛṣṇa kicking it, but the elders were reluctant to believe this story. They had special prayers said by the brāhmaṇā for the welfare of the divine child, for they had great faith in such prayer. It is said that an evil spirit had entered the cart and had attained release from its disembodied state by the touch of the Lord's feet.

On another occasion Yaśodā was fondling the baby on her lap. Suddenly she felt that he had grown as heavy as a mountain peak. She marvelled at it but could not find a proper explanation for this phenomenon and only prayed that it might not portend evil.

One day the whole countryside was in the grip of a sandstorm. People could not even see their own bodies! Yaśodā was gripped with fear, for she could not find the divine baby. She fainted. A demoniacal lieutenant of Kaṁsa had assumed the form of the whirlwind and had carried the baby away. Soon the baby became so heavy that the demon could not carry him any more. Nor could he drop the baby, since Kṛṣṇa held him by the throat. Assuming his own form the demon dropped down dead, with the baby Kṛṣṇa playing upon his chest. The sandstorm subsided and the people of Vraja saw the hideous form of the demon, with the baby Kṛṣṇa playing upon it. They rejoiced that the baby had been miraculously saved.

On another day Yaśodā was suckling the baby. As she was caressing the little mouth, Kṛṣṇa yawned; she saw in it the entire universe—the sky, the stars, the sun, the moon, and all beings. She marvelled at the sight; but was also afraid and apprehensive.

Book Ten Chapter 8

Sage Śuka continued: The time for naming the child arrived. Nanda begged of the famed astrologer Garga to name the children of Yaśodā and Rohiṇī. Garga expressed apprehension: "If Kaṁsa comes to know he might suspect that Yaśodā's child was born of Devakī, and might seek to harm him." They therefore decided to have the boys named in the utmost secrecy in the cow-pen. Garga revealed: "This boy has had many incarnations. Previously he has had white, red and yellow forms, and this time he has a dark form. He has had many names and forms, suited to the occasion. In this incarnation he will be known as Kṛṣṇa, the dark-complexioned, and since he is Vasudeva's son they will call him Vāsudeva. He is equal to Nārāyaṇa himself. Enemies cannot harm those who are devoted to him and who love him. Therefore look after him well. The other boy will be known as Bala and Rāma."

The two boys were growing up rapidly. They moved about on

all fours making sweet sounds with little bells tied round their ankles. Their bodies were often covered with dust and mud, which enhanced their charm. They were the delight of the women of Vraja. They were so restless and mischievous that their mothers were in constant worry and anxiety concerning their welfare. Soon they began to walk.

Once the cowherdesses complained to the mother Yaśodā: "Sometimes your boy untethers the calves before milking time; he steals butter and milk from our houses, and he gives it to monkeys, too; and if they won't eat, he smashes the pots. If he gets nothing to eat in a house, he leaves the house after making the infants in it cry. Nothing can be hidden from him, for he illumines the room by his own radiance and knows the contents of every pot without looking into it. After doing all this, he comes to you quietly as though he is completely innocent." On another occasion they complained to Yaśodā: "Your son has swallowed some mud." When Yaśodā chided him, he pleaded: "I have not eaten mud; see!" In his mouth Yaśodā saw the entire universe, including Vraja and herself! Thoroughly shaken, she began to ask herself: "Is this hallucination or real?" and mused: "Only God knows what is truth. I take refuge in him. It is through his illusory power that I consider myself Yaśodā, wife of Nanda, and that this is my son." Kṛṣṇa quickly cast the veil of illusion over her and she once again regarded Kṛṣṇa as her beloved, mischievous son.

O Parīkṣit! When Brahmā commanded the gods to incarnate in Vraja, Droṇa and his wife Dharā had prayed that they might develop the greatest devotion to the Lord during such an incarnation. Hence Droṇa was born as Nanda and Dharā as Yaśodā, with the supreme privilege of adoring the Lord himself as their son.

Book Ten Chapter 9

Sage Śuka continued: One day Yaśodā, the mother, was busy churning curds to make butter. Milk was boiling on the stove. With her mind completely absorbed in the contemplation of the wonderful doings of the divine child Kṛṣṇa, she was churning the curds. Kṛṣṇa went up to her, demanding to be fed. While she was suckling him the milk boiled over, so she laid him on the floor and rushed to save the milk. Pretending great annoyance, Kṛṣṇa broke the pot of curds and left the room.

Yaśodā soon returned and found that the pot of curds had been broken. But she could not find Kṛṣṇa there. He was in another room where fresh butter was stored. He had overturned a wooden mortar and, standing on it, was taking the butter out of the pots and feeding a monkey standing near him. When she approached him with a rod in her hand he feigned extreme fear, jumped down from the mortar and ran away with the mother pursuing him.

Unimaginably beautiful was the spectacle when Yaśodā caught hold of this lovely child Kṛṣṇa, whom even yogī fail to comprehend through one-pointed concentration. As if afraid of punishment he was weeping aloud and rubbing his eyes with the free hand, smearing the tear-diluted collyrium over his cheeks. Yaśodā threw the rod away. She wanted to tie the child to the wooden mortar. She took a piece of string, wound it round the mortar at one end and tried winding it around Kṛṣṇa's waist at the other. It was just a little short, so she fetched more string. More and more and more: but all the time it was just a little short for the purpose. She stood bewildered, amazed, puzzled and fatigued.

When Kṛṣṇa saw this, he quickly allowed himself to be bound. Thus did he demonstrate that he who is omnipresent and infinite and therefore inaccessible to the mind and senses, can be bound by the cords of love. Such grace is not enjoyed even by the gods. The Lord is not easily attained by embodied beings (or, they who consider 'I am the body'), or by men of great erudition. He is attained by those who love him with all their being.

Redemption of Kubera's Sons
Book Ten Chapter 10

Sage Śuka continued: Dragging the mortar behind him, Kṛṣṇa liberated the two sons of Kubera who had been transformed into trees by Nārada's curse. Once upon a time, these two celestials were bathing in a celestial river with nymphs, naked. Nārada happened to come that way. Seeing him the nymphs quickly covered themselves, but the intoxicated sons of Kubera did not, proud as they were of their position.

Nārada reflected thus: "Pride of wealth and of ancestry causes confusion of intelligence; and such pride is always accompanied by women, gambling and liquor. The proud man kills animals, assuming his own body to be immune to old age and death. Is there any greater foolishness than to entertain such pride? Poverty indeed is a blessing for those blinded by pride, for the poor man looks upon others as his own self and understands their troubles and sorrows. And the poor man's own suffering serves as penance to destroy the effects of past karma. Resorting to the company of holy ones, the poor man will develop devotion to the Lord and reach his lotus feet." Thus resolved and intent on saving the sons of Kubera from their own pride, Nārada cursed them that they would be transformed into two trees, as they stood like trees with their bodies uncovered. He blessed them that even in that state they would remember their action and that when the Lord would come near them they would be freed from the curse.

Lord Kṛṣṇa knew this and, in order to fulfil the devout Nārada's prophecy, he went between the two trees with the wooden mortar behind him. The mortar was caught between the trees and when Kṛṣṇa pulled it as he moved on, the force caused the trees to break and fall. Out of them two shining beings arose. They prayed: "O Kṛṣṇa, you are the supreme being, puruṣa, prakṛti and all. You have taken this fullest incarnation on earth this time in order to bless mankind with prosperity and salvation. Only through the grace of Nārada have we been able to behold you. We pray that our speech may be devoted to singing your glories, our ears to listening to such glories, our minds to your feet, our limbs to your service, our heads to bowing to your seat in all, and our sight to seeing the holy ones who are your own manifestations." Receiving the Lord's blessings and bowing to him again, the celestials vanished.

Vatsāsura and Bakāsura
Book Ten Chapter 11

Sage Śuka continued: Hearing the noise of the trees falling, the people rushed to the spot. Kṛṣṇa's young friends described what had taken place. Some believed, others did not, but all of them were apprehensive and worried by the succession of mishaps. Yet the baby Kṛṣṇa continued to play the role of a human baby, playing with friends and doing odd jobs at home. Nanda was worried and he decided to move away from what he considered haunted Gokula: Kṛṣṇa had miraculously escaped from Pūtanā, Tṛṇāvarta, the overturned cart and the falling trees, but they could not afford to take any more chances. All the villagers were unanimously behind Nanda in his decision so they moved to a small forest known as Vṛndāvana. Kṛṣṇa was delighted to see Vṛndāvana, the Govardhana hill and the sandy bank of the river Yamunā.

Kṛṣṇa and his elder brother Balarāma had grown up now into young boys, and so delighted to tend the cows. They would lead the cattle to the pastures, let them graze the whole day and then bring them back to the village. One day while the cows were grazing, Kṛṣṇa saw a strange calf and recognised it as a demon, Vatsāsura by name. Calmly going behind it he caught hold of its hind legs, whirled it in the air and hurled it against a tree. The demon fell down in his own hideous form, his disguise having departed with his life. The other cowherds applauded Kṛṣṇa's heroism.

On another occasion, these protectors of the universe (Kṛṣṇa and Balarāma), while performing their assumed duties of protecting the cattle, were standing near a pond while the cattle slaked their thirst. Kṛṣṇa noticed a heron standing at a distance, eyeing him suspiciously. He know that it was another demon, Bakāsura, a friend of Kaṁsa, deputed to destroy him. This demon pounced upon Kṛṣṇa and swallowed him. At this the cowboys were shocked and speechless. But, in a few moments, the demon disgorged Kṛṣṇa, for the Lord had burnt the throat of the demon! The demon then attacked Kṛṣṇa with his bill. Kṛṣṇa caught hold of the bill, parted it, and tore the neck of the demon disguised as a heron. The boys looked on as if it was wonderful sport. On their return to the village they announced the thrilling encounters in which Kṛṣṇa came out victorious. The villagers marvelled at how many times this divine child had been attacked and how every time he came out victorious!

Thus recounting the supernatural doings of Kṛṣṇa and Balarāma, Nanda and the other villagers spent their days totally unaffected by the miseries of worldly existence.

Aghāsura
Book Ten Chapter 12

Sage Śuka continued: One day Kṛṣṇa left the village early, along with the other boys. He had planned to have a picnic in the forest. Reaching the forest, the boys engaged themselves in play while the cows were grazing. How supremely blessed they were that they could thus play with the supreme being himself, who is the object of yogī's meditation! Great indeed is the good fortune of the people of Vraja. He, the dust of whose feet is hard to gain even by great yogī, was present with them in person. This was surely the fruit of their own accumulated merit.

To that spot came a demon by name Aghāsura, deputed by Kaṁsa. Agha was the brother of both Pūtanā and Bakāsura, whose deaths at the hands of Kṛṣṇa he wanted to avenge. Aghāsura lay on the road, disguised as a huge python with its mouth wide open, the lower lip on the ground and the upper lip touching the clouds. He wanted to swallow the whole crowd, including the cattle, and waited for them to walk in.

The playful cowherd boys were walking along the road towards Agha. They mistook its mouth for a cave, its upper jaw for the clouds, its tongue for a road, its breath for fierce hot wind, etc. When someone among them suspected it to be some ferocious living being, the others reassured him. Even if that were so, Kṛṣṇa would surely deal with it as he had dealt with the demon Bakāsura.

Kṛṣṇa noticed the python and wished to halt his friends. But they had already begun walking into its mouth. The demon waited for Kṛṣṇa to enter. In order to protect his own friends and the cattle, Kṛṣṇa decided to enter, too! As the Lord entered the mouth, the demon-python closed his mouth. In his throat the Lord grew to gigantic proportions, thus choking him. Out of breath and asphyxiated, the python's eyes popped out and he died. Kṛṣṇa revived the cowherds and the cattle by a mere glance from his eyes. The demon's life-force had broken the skull and through that hole Kṛṣṇa and the others emerged. As Kṛṣṇa stood looking at the demon an ethereal light from the python entered into the heart of Kṛṣṇa. The demon had attained salvation. No wonder: for the Lord himself had entered the body of this demon, and what would the Lord not bestow on such a one! He bestows salvation on those who enthrone him but once in their heart.

The redemption of Aghāsura took place in Kṛṣṇa's fifth year; but the boys narrated it to the villagers in his sixth year as if it had just occurred.

Discomfiture of Brahmā
Book Ten Chapter 13

Questioned by king Parīkṣit as to how this lapse of a year took place, sage Śuka continued: When they had all thus emerged from the body of the python-demon, Kṛṣṇa led them to the sandy bank of the river for the picnic. The calves were allowed to graze freely and the boys sat down with Kṛṣṇa in the centre, ready to eat. They had all brought food with them; and they used leaves and the bark of trees for plates. They were in high spirits and ate the food, laughing and joking and talking. In their midst, Kṛṣṇa was seated with his flute stuck in the folds between his abdomen and his cloth, the horn and the stick under his armpit, rice mixed with butter on his left palm and condiments held between the fingers, making his friends rejoice and laugh. The celestials looked on at this divine spectacle of the Lord of the universe playing the role of a child.

In the meantime the calves had strayed away from the scene, and the cowherd boys were worried. Kṛṣṇa reassured them and left the place in search of the cattle, leaving his friends on the bank of the river. While Kṛṣṇa was searching for the cattle, Brahmā the creator (who was watching the playful pastimes of Kṛṣṇa), kidnapped both the calves and the cowherd boys and hid them away—and himself, too. Not finding the calves, Kṛṣṇa returned to the river only to find that the cowherds were missing too! In a moment, he understood that it was the work of Brahmā.

The Lord demonstrated the scriptural declaration: "All this is indeed Viṣṇu", by himself becoming the calves and their adornments, and the cowherds with all their belongings. A complete replica of the calves and the cowherds kidnapped by Brahmā had been brought into being, with the same size and colour, the same age and characteristics, the same name and mentality. Kṛṣṇa himself had become all these. That evening Kṛṣṇa entered the village, driving the cattle, which were his own self, and surrounded by the cowherds, who were his own self, too. Once in the village the cowherds drove the calves (all of whom were Kṛṣṇa himself) into the respective houses, and dwelt there.

Book Ten Chapter 13

Sage Śuka continued: From that day all the cowherds and cowherdesses in the village had the greatest good fortune of treating Kṛṣṇa himself as their own son, and tending to Kṛṣṇa himself who stood as the calves in their yard. The cowherdesses discovered that their sons had overnight become extremely dear to them. The cows became ever increasingly restless to caress and feed their calves. The cowherds could never become angry with their boys, whatever be the provocation. Balarāma, the Lord's elder brother, was puzzled and curious: "What is the reason for this sudden outpouring of love in our village for the boys and the calves?" Intuitively he saw that these boys and these calves were not the sages and gods that they were before, but the Lord himself. At his request, Kṛṣṇa revealed the secret to him.

After one full human year, Brahmā returned to Vraja and there saw Kṛṣṇa playing with the boys and the calves as before, in the woods. He had tried to delude Kṛṣṇa; but now he himself stood amazed by the enchanting power of Kṛṣṇa. The calves and the boys he had kidnapped were still under the spell of Brahmā's illusory power: and yet here were these calves and boys playing with Kṛṣṇa. He could not tell one from the other, for both were identical. As he thus stood in amazement his illusory power was overwhelmed by Kṛṣṇa's illusory power, even as the darkness of night, as it sets in, assimilates the darkness caused earlier by fog: and he beheld there all the cowherd boys and the calves transfigured into many Kṛṣṇā; and then, only the Lord, attended by divinities. He realised that they were all identical with the absolute, infinite being.

As Brahmā the creator stood bewildered by the Lord's own illusory power, Kṛṣṇa withdrew that power so that Brahmā might regain his composure and perceive the truth. Brahmā at once saw the holy Vṛndāvana where all beings lived in peace, love and harmony, shedding even what may be regarded as natural enmity because of the presence of the Lord himself in their midst. In that Vṛndāvana, Brahmā saw the supreme being himself playing the role of a cowherd boy, searching for the calves and the cowherds, holding partly eaten food in his left hand—everything was as it had been before Brahmā kidnapped the calves and the boys. Brahmā the creator fell at the feet of Kṛṣṇa and offered his apologetic prayer.

Book Ten Chapter 14

Brahmā said: I salute you, O Lord who appears as the son of a cowherd, with tender feet, holding the cane, flute, etc., and a ball of rice in one hand. In truth, even I cannot fully comprehend your glory; only they who are exclusively devoted to you know you in essence. People who neglect devotion, which confers manifold blessings, and resort to other spiritual practices, are wasting their efforts and are pounding husk. To your devotee you reveal your transcendental nature without attributes, name and form. Unasked, final liberation seeks him.

Except through devotion this ego is difficult to overcome. How foolish I was to cast a spell over you! Where am I, endowed with a body composed of the elements, presiding over this egg of an earth-plane, and where are you, Lord, through every pore of whose body countless such eggs pass as if they are no larger than minute atoms. You are Nārāyaṇa, the very self of all beings ('nara' means 'collection of living beings', 'ayanam' the soul). You are their inner controller ('ayanam' also means 'prompter'). You are their witness ('ayate' means 'knows'). You are Nārāyaṇa because you abide in the products of Nara (God or man). But even that is not the truth; it is your māyā, or sport. I myself could not perceive your form as Nārāyaṇa except when you revealed it to me; but you revealed it to your mother Yaśodā when you allowed her to perceive the cosmos in your abdomen. Originally, even here, you alone existed, and when I kidnapped the calves and boys you alone existed as all of them, and again now you alone exist. Even so you alone exist at all times, whether the universe is manifest or unmanifest. Through your māyā you alone exist as all the gods, you incarnate in divine, human and sub-human species. Even this illusory universe appears to be real only because it is based upon you and its manifestation takes place in you. Bondage and liberation are mere words, even as day and night are in relation to the sun.

Therefore, Lord, grant me devotion to your feet now and in my future births. May I be reborn in any form in this Gokula, where I can bathe myself in the dust sanctified by your feet. Let them who think they know you say so: I know that you are beyond the reach of mind (thought) and speech (expression).

Taking leave of Kṛṣṇa, Brahmā returned to his abode. Kṛṣṇa returned to the bank of the river where the cowherds, just then released from their hypnotic state, were waiting to conclude the picnic. When that evening they returned to the village, they announced that Kṛṣṇa had killed a big snake that very day.

Dhenuka
Book Ten Chapter 15

Sage Śuka continued: The two divine boys were now grown-up and they became cowherds and took the cows out to graze. Kṛṣṇa enjoyed the beauty of nature: the songs of the birds, the hum of the bees and the sounds made by the beasts delighted him. He watched how grass and other little plants embraced the feet of Balarāma and eulogised him: "Lord, look how blessed these little plants are in that they kiss your feet so that the state of ignorance, which was responsible for their birth as trees, might cease. Surely, they were holy men in their past lives." Sometimes overcome by fatigue, they rested. Balarāma would rest his head on the lap of another cowherd and Kṛṣṇa would gently press his elder brother's feet. When Kṛṣṇa lay down, others served him. Kṛṣṇa thus effectively veiled his own divinity by his illusory power and lived the life of a common cowherd.

One day a cowherd, Śrīdāmā, said to Kṛṣṇa and Balarāma: "Yonder is a forest of fruit trees, which is jealously guarded by a demon Dhenuka, who has the form of a donkey and is a man-eater.

Hence people are afraid to go there and therefore no one has tasted the fruits whose fragrance, which can be perceived from here, is so tantalising. If you wish, you can make the fruits available to us." Kṛṣṇa and Balarāma laughed heartily, and they all proceeded towards the forest. Balarāma shook the trees and the fruits fell in great numbers, to the delight of the cowherds.

Very soon, however, the demon Dhenuka came charging at Balarāma and kicked him with his hind-legs. Balarāma caught hold of the legs of the demon, whirled him overhead and dashed him over the trunk of a tree. He died even while being whirled around. The impact of the body hitting the tree was so great that quite a few trees fell down, scattering the fruit all over the place. The enraged relations of the demon—other donkeys—rushed towards Kṛṣṇa and Balarāma; but Kṛṣṇa and Balarāma playfully disposed of them.

Rid of the fear of the demons, the people of the village ate the fruits of the forest.

As Kṛṣṇa re-entered the village the villagers feasted their eyes on the countenance of Kṛṣṇa. His hair soiled by dust raised by the hooves of the cows, only enhanced his natural charm. When the bees (eyes) thus drank the nectar (beauty of Kṛṣṇa's face) the anguish in their hearts caused by his absence during the day-time disappeared, and delight filled their hearts.

Kāliya
Book Ten Chapter 16

Sage Śuka continued: A section of the river Yamunā known as Kālindī had been so heavily polluted by a poisonous creature called Kāliya, that living beings approaching the bank of the river died. Kṛṣṇa, the Lord who had incarnated to protect all and to eliminate evil, went to the river, climbed a tree and jumped into the polluted waters in which he playfully sported. The serpent which was the cause of this pollution immediately encircled the Lord and tried to crush him. The Lord remained motionless. Seeing this the cowherds who had accompanied him to the river fell into a swoon and the cows lowed piteously. Seeing evil omens and afraid that their darling Kṛṣṇa was in danger, the women of the village scrambled out of their houses and followed Kṛṣṇa's footprints to the river. Nanda and others were about to jump into the poisoned river to rescue Kṛṣṇa, but were restrained by Balarāma.

Kṛṣṇa was moved by the distress of his companions and cows. Miraculously his body began to expand; the serpent therefore left him but reared up to strike him. Kṛṣṇa began to dance around the snake, like lightning; the snake following his movements was soon exhausted. Lowering its heads with his hand, Kṛṣṇa jumped on them and began to dance, to the accompaniment of celestial music and drum. With his hoods crushed under the dancing feet of Kṛṣṇa, Kāliya contemplated lord Nārāyaṇa, and fell into a swoon. Seeing this, his wives came up and prayed to Kṛṣṇa: "It is but meet that you should punish this serpent. Nay, it is not punishment but a blessing, for it purifies him; your anger is a blessing, for it has destroyed the sin for which our husband was born as a snake. He is indeed blessed to have received your footprints on his heads. They who have received the dust of your feet on their head do not desire any earthly or heavenly rewards nor even liberation: for that itself is the greatest attainment. We salute you again and again. All beings—peaceful, violent and ignorant—proceed from you alone. At present, however, you have resolved to protect the gentle ones. Pray forgive this, your servant." Kāliya also prayed: "We serpents, Lord, are by nature violent and poisonous. It is difficult for living creatures to overcome their natural disposition by their own strength and effort. Only you can enable us to overcome your māyā."

Thereupon Kṛṣṇa commanded the serpent to quit that river in order that human beings and cattle might not perish, and to reside in the ocean. Kāliya did so. The river was free from pollution and people and cattle were happy.

Kāliya; Forest Fire
Book Ten Chapter 17

Sage Śuka continued: There was a reason for Kāliya living in the Kālindī river. On every new moon day the nāgā (serpents) made an offering to Garuḍa (the divine eagle) to ensure their own protection. Kāliya however failed to offer his homage to Garuḍa, proud as he was of his own power. A terrible fight ensued between Garuḍa and Kāliya. Hit violently by Garuḍa, Kāliya slipped into the Kālindī river. This river was out of Garuḍa's bounds, for earlier he had caught a fish in that pool and thus earned sage Saubhari's curse: "If you catch any aquatic creature in this pool again, you will die at once." Only Kāliya knew of this curse, and hence he had taken refuge in it. But now, although he had to leave the security of the pool, he had found greater security in the boon granted by Kṛṣṇa: "Garuḍa will not trouble you, since your hoods are adorned with my foot-print."

When Kṛṣṇa emerged from the polluted river everyone rejoiced.

They who were as good as dead came back to life. Balarāma laughed heartily for he knew Kṛṣṇa's true identity and he was neither afraid nor affected by Kṛṣṇa's encounter with Kāliya. Brāhmaṇā came to Nanda and advised him: "Your son Kṛṣṇa has been saved by providence from a terrible calamity. In thanksgiving, you should give rich gifts to the brāhmaṇā and earn their blessings." So Nanda gave away cows and gold to the brāhmaṇā.

The entire crowd decided to spend the night on the bank of the river, tired as they were on account of the day's happenings. In the middle of the night they saw a wild-fire all around them. Scorched by this encircling fire, they prayed to Kṛṣṇa: "Kṛṣṇa, our Lord, Rāma of unequalled strength; this fierce fire is burning us. Lord, protect us from this terrible fire; we are your own and we cannot abandon your feet, the source of our fearlessness."

Seeing the pitiable plight of the people, Kṛṣṇa swallowed the forest fire.

Pralamba
Book Ten Chapter 18-19

Sage Śuka continued: It was summer. But in Vṛndāvana, it was forever springtime. The blazing sun shone pleasantly over Vṛndāvana, bringing warmth but not heat. The air was constantly cooled by the numerous ponds and was laden with the fragrance and the pollen of flowers. The earth was thickly carpeted with many-hued flowers for the Lord to sport on; and the birds and beasts entertained him with their sweet notes. He loved them. He was love.

The cowherds loved him, too. They were all gods disguised as cowherds. Even so Kṛṣṇa and Balarāma were incarnate divinities, playing the role of cowherds. All of them were one day playing various games. They looked charming in their side-curls as they ran, turned around holding each other's hands, long-jumped, threw weights, tugged at one another and wrestled. When the other boys danced Kṛṣṇa and Balarāma sang and played on musical instruments, shouting "Good, very good."

In the meantime a demon by name Pralamba slipped into the ranks of the cowherds, himself disguised as a cowherd. Kṛṣṇa recognised him, and hence admitted him! Kṛṣṇa then suggested that they could all divide themselves into two groups, one headed by himself and the other by Balarāma. They would play various games, and each member of the defeated party would carry a member of the victorious one. Thus is went on for some time; now one party and now the other being victorious. At one stage Kṛṣṇa's party was defeated. So the demon Pralamba, who was on the Kṛṣṇa's side, had to carry one member of Balarāma's party. He carried Balarāma.

As he was running away from the playground, Pralamba discovered that Balarāma had suddenly become unbearably heavy. Crushed by his weight, Pralamba abandoned his disguise and appeared as a demon of gigantic size. Balarāma was dazed for a moment; but quickly he remembered his divine nature and hit the demon with his fist, with the power of a thunderbolt. The demon fell dead.

The cowherd boys rejoiced and congratulated Balarāma on his feat and offered prayers for him.

On another occasion, while the whole party was enveloped by a wild-fire, Kṛṣṇa asked all of them to close their eyes and he swallowed the fire. The people recognised him to be an immortal.

Book Ten Chapter 20

Sage Śuka continued: Vṛndāvana was bathed in the rains during the monsoon season. The sun, who had taken up moisture from the earth in the form of vapour during the summer, now released it in the form of rain, even as a wise ruler who collects taxes from the people spends the money in social services for the welfare of all. The rain laden clouds tossed by the winds and cut by lightning hurriedly emptied and sacrificed themselves so that the starved earth might receive nourishment, even as a compassionate man might rush to the aid of a destitute. The earth, which was denuded and scorched till then, burst into life, even as an ascetic whose body grew emaciated during austerities grows stout and strong on completion of those austerities. Fireflies and not the stars shone at night, even as in kali yuga false doctrines and not the vedā are popular. The ocean, which was already turbulent, became even more so with the waters of the rivers rushing into it; even as the mind of an immature yogi, already distrubed by desire, becomes greatly agitated in the presence of a sense-object. The moon made the clouds shine in her light but was veiled by them; even as the jīva in whose light the ego-sense shines (functions) is veiled by it. The earth now presented a panorama of variegated colours—with green plants, red insects and mushrooms—and looked like a formidable army in formation. But, the mountains stood unaffected by the pouring rain, even as one whose heart is fixed on the Lord remains unaffected by the worst calamities. The Lord continued to lead the cows out for grazing. When it rained heavily he entered a cave or a thicket and enjoyed eating fruits and roots. It pleased him to see the cattle fully satisfied with their grazing, resting on the grass.

This was followed by the autumn. The waters of the lakes and the river which were muddy during the monsoon became crystal clear once again, even as the mind of a yogi who had strayed from the path and whose heart had therefore been sullied regains his purity and clarity on returning to the path. The clouds that had given up their waters during the monsoon now shone white and bright, even as men of renunciation shine in their spiritual lustre after giving up all desires for the pleasures of the three worlds. Farmers desirous of carefully conserving the water resources, vigilantly controlled the water flowing out of their fields and reservoirs, even as a diligent yogi controls the expenditure of his vital force through the channels of the mind and the senses. As the moon is surrounded by stars, so Kṛṣṇa, surrounded by his friends, brought delight to the hearts of all. The temperate climate brought relief to the hearts of all except the women of Vṛndāvana whose hearts had been stolen by Kṛṣṇa.

Book Ten Chapter 21

Sage Śuka continued: While Kṛṣṇa and Balarāma took the cows out of the village for grazing and when they re-entered the village in the evening the young women of the village could not take their eyes off the divine brothers, especially Kṛṣṇa. He wore garlands of different flowers and he loved to wear a peacock feather on his head. He wore a loincloth of yellow silk. He loved his flute and frequently played on it. To the gopī (cowherdesses) the music of the flute thenceforth meant Kṛṣṇa; it reminded them of Kṛṣṇa.

The Gopī said to one another: The only blessing and fruit for one possessing eyes is to behold the radiant countenances of lord Kṛṣṇa and Balarāma as they drive the cattle of the village away to pasture. Beautifully adorned and elegantly dressed, these two boys appear like consummate actors. What merit has this flute acquired, that it drinks the nectar that flows from the lips of Kṛṣṇa though it rightfully belongs to us gopī; the rivers and the bamboos (the parents of the flute) rejoice that their offspring enjoys this rare privilege.

Blessed is Vṛndāvana, for it enhances the glory of the whole earth; for Vṛndāvana is hallowed by the dust of the Lord's feet. Not only are we captivated by the music of Kṛṣṇa: look at these deer, look at these celestial women in the sky, look at these cows and their calves—all of them stand entranced when Kṛṣṇa plays on his flute. And, look at the birds living in the trees in the forest: they are not interested in the fruits because they are absorbed in the celestial nectarine music of Kṛṣṇa. Surely, they are sages in disguise. Even the river swells and embraces with its waves the feet of Kṛṣṇa, enchanted by his flute. Lo, look at the mountain: can't you see that, hearing the music of the flute, its hairs (the grass and the shrubs) stand on end. Blessed is the mountain that it is able to offer to the Lord food, water and shelter.

Stealing of Gopī's Clothes
Book Ten Chapter 22

Sage Śuka continued: Some young virgins of Vraja had lost their hearts to Kṛṣṇa. During the month of Mārgaśīrṣa (December-January) they worshipped the goddess Kātyāyanī with the mantra 'kātyāyani mahāmāye mahā yogin-yadhīśvari, nanda gopa sutaṁ devi patim me kuru te namaḥ' (O goddess Kātyāyani, make Kṛṣṇa my husband). They rose very early and bathed in the river every day before they performed this worship.

On the last day they had gone to the river for their bath as usual. They had disrobed themselves and, leaving their clothes on the bank of the river, they were bathing naked. Having come to know of this, Kṛṣṇa arrived there. Quickly gathering up the clothes, he climbed up a tree. From there he said to them: "If you want your clothes, come out of the water and receive them from me." All their pleadings to make him do otherwise having failed, the girls came up. Highly pleased with their devotion to him, the Lord said to them: "Bathing naked in a river is unethical. You were observing a religious vow; and this offence might make the vow ineffectual. Hence, hold both your arms up in salutation and come, and I shall give you your clothes." The penitent girls thereupon bowed to Kṛṣṇa and received their clothes from him; they were not angry with him at all, for they loved him and realised the justice of the punishment he meted out to them.

Kṛṣṇa said to them: "I know your heart's desire, O chaste girls, and it shall be fulfilled. Desire directed towards me is no desire at all, even as seed roasted in fire is no seed. You will soon realise the fruit of your worship of the goddess." The girls then returned to the village.

Kṛṣṇa went along with a few friends through a grove; and pointing to the trees, he said to the friends: "Blessed is the life of a tree, friends. They afford food and shelter to all beings, and they never turn anyone away without sharing what they have. By their fruits, leaves, flowers, roots, bark and stem (firewood) and by their shade, they serve all. This indeed is the greatest dharma—that one serves another and works out one's salvation with the life, wealth, intelligence and speech that one has.

Grace on Brāhmaṇa Women
Book Ten Chapter 23

Sage Śuka said: While thus wandering in the forest, the cowherds said to Kṛṣṇa: "We are oppressed by hunger; pray, give us something to eat." Kṛṣṇa then said to some of his companions: "Over there some brāhmaṇā (men of the priest class) are performing a sacred rite. Please go to them and, in the names of Balarāma and myself, ask them to give us all some food to eat." The cowherds went to those brāhmaṇā and said to them: "O holy ones, we are the servants and companions of Kṛṣṇa and of Balarāma, who are seated close by. We have all come far from home and we are hungry. Hence the Lord sent us to you to request that you provide us with food. Surely, you will fulfil the Lord's wish?"

There was no scriptural prohibition against the brāhmaṇā giving food away. Yet, they merely looked at the cowherds without saying 'Yes' or 'No'. Here was the Lord himself, as Kṛṣṇa, who was the very soul of the religious rite—being himself the time and the place, the different articles used, the sacred texts, the priests and the fire, the deity propitiated, the very soul of the worshipper and the rite itself—but the brāhmaṇā did not recognise him as the supreme being, the Lord himself. On account of their perverted intelligence, they saw him as a mere mortal. The cowherds returned empty-handed.

Kṛṣṇa laughed heartily and sent them back again, but this time to the wives of those brāhmaṇā. The cowherds went to the place and approached the womenfolk and said to them: "Kṛṣṇa, who is seated with his brother and friends yonder, sent us to you: we are all hungry, please give us some food." These words entered their ears as nectar. They had heard of Kṛṣṇa and they were very eager to feast their eyes upon him. Hurriedly they filled several vessels with all kinds of foods and delicacies and went to where Kṛṣṇa was seated.

The brāhmaṇā women saw the Lord moving about in the grove. His dark coloured body was covered by a yellow silk cloth. He was tastefully adorned in flowers and peacock feathers. One had rested on the shoulders of a companion and the other twirled a lotus. Receiving him through their eyes into their heart, these noble women embraced him in their very soul, and thus assuaged the pains of mortal existence.

Book Ten Chapter 23

Sage Śuka continued: Lord Kṛṣṇa welcomed the ladies: "Since I am your very self it is no wonder that you are so greatly devoted to me that you were not deterred by the risks involved in coming here. Now you can all go back to where your husbands are awaiting you, to carry on with the religious rite." The ladies, however, reminded Kṛṣṇa: "The scriptures declare that one who has reached your lotus feet does not return to mundane existence. And we have no attachment at all to our parents, husbands, children, etc., but we are attached to the holy basil leaves that have touched your feet. Moreover, our husbands would surely disown us for having come here without their consent." Kṛṣṇa, for his part, assured them that when they returned to their camp their husbands would not be annoyed with them for going away, and said: "Physical contact or proximity does not promote devotion in this world; the vital factor is to fix the mind on me." Kṛṣṇa and the cowherds then had their meal.

The ladies returned to their camp and the holy men duly concluded their rite. One of the women who had been prevented by her husband from going over with the party to see Kṛṣṇa, had entered into deep inward communion with the Lord and had been released from the body in that state.

Seeing all this the brāhmaṇā cursed themselves: "Fie upon our birth, fie on all the religious vows, fie on the accumulation of knowledge, fie on our ancestry, fie on our efficiency in the performance of the rituals—for all these have turned us away from the Lord. Surely, the Lord's māyā is so powerful that it can delude even yogī. We who profess to be the gurū of people were deluded by selfishness! On the other hand these womenfolk were not educated in the scriptures or rituals, they have not undergone any religious training nor have they performed austerity, yet in their hearts arose this deep and abiding devotion to Kṛṣṇa. Surely, we are blessed to have had these ladies as our partners in life, for through them we also develop devotion. Kṛṣṇa, the Lord of the three worlds, the Lord of Lakṣmī who protects the entire universe, did not stand in need of alms from our hands; he pretended to be hungry in order spiritually to awaken us. Yet, we neglected that opportunity. May the Lord forgive us." Though they were eager to behold Kṛṣṇa and Balarāma, they were restrained by fear—they knew that Kaṁsa was inimical to the divine brothers, and Kaṁsa was king!

Govardhana Hill
Book Ten Chapter 24

Sage Śuka continued: Kṛṣṇa noticed elaborate preparations being made by the villagers for the performance of a religious rite. He went up to his father and questioned him: "People engage themselves in actions, sometimes knowing their nature and sometimes without knowing their nature. In the case of the latter, the consequences are disagreeable and hence lead to failure. I see that elaborate preparations are going on for a rite. Kindly tell me what it is all about, to propitiate whom and why."

Nanda said: "We are about to perform a religious rite in honour of Indra. Indra, my child, is the god presiding over rain, and it is through timely and sufficient rain that we and our cows get our food. We therefore make offerings of the fruits of his gifts to him and thus earn his favour, which enables us to lead a happy and fruitful life."

Kṛṣṇa replied: "On account of karma (action) is one born, and on account of karma he dies. The actions he performed in the past bring him happiness and unhappiness, success or failure. What has Indra to do with all this? People are subject to their own nature and they act in accordance with their own nature; men, gods and demons are all guided by their own nature. On account of karma is a soul embodied or disembodied. Karma brings friends and foes and neutral beings. Karma alone is one's guru and even God. Hence rooted in one's nature one should be devoted to action, and do one's duty. That action which ensures one's true happiness in this world—that alone is divine. The cows, the brāhmaṇā and this hill are the sources of our happiness and prosperity; so let us worship these. Let us use the materials that have been gathered for the worship of Indra and worship the cows, the brāhmaṇā and the Govardhana hill. Let us distribute food to all creatures without any distinction of caste or social status, and all animals. Let us also feed the cows properly. Let us offer all foodstuff to the mountain."

Even so, it was done. Kṛṣṇa himself, as the indweller of the mountain, actually consumed the offerings placed before it. Kṛṣṇa himself, as the son of Nanda, made the offering, joyously exclaiming: "See how the god dwelling in this hill partakes of our offering." After the worship the cowherds returned to the village.

Book Ten Chapter 25-26

Sage Śuka continued: Angered by the denial of his privilege Indra commanded the special clouds, whose function is the dissolution of the universe, to destroy everything in the village of the cowherds. His mind clouded by pricked vanity, he forgot the divinity of Kṛṣṇa whom he considered a mere mortal. Thus impelled by the god of rain, the clouds burst over Vraja hurling rain with destructive force. Terror-stricken cowherds and cowherdesses sought the protection of Kṛṣṇa. Kṛṣṇa instantly saw that it was the work of Indra. He assured the people: "I shall at once use my divine powers and quell Indra's pride. The gods are endowed with purity but should not therefore consider themselves rulers of the world; destruction of their pride by me is conducive to their peace. I shall protect those who have sought refuge in me."

Saying so, the Lord playfully lifted up the Govardhana hill with one hand. Holding it up like a vast umbrella, the Lord asked the people of Vraja to take shelter under it. "Fear not that it will slip from my hand. Beneath it you will have no fear from the rain and the storm." The entire village—the people and the cattle—took shelter under the mountain, which was thus held by Kṛṣṇa for a whole week. Thus defeated in his purpose and thoroughly humiliated by Kṛṣṇa, Indra finally withdrew the clouds. Kṛṣṇa permitted the people to return to their abodes when the flood had subsided. Kṛṣṇa laid his mountainous burden down. Everyone admired and congratulated him.

They all then went to Nanda and expressed their wonder: "Who is this Kṛṣṇa? Even as a baby he killed the demoness Pūtanā and then successively so many other demons, and he conquered the terrible serpent Kāliya. Moreover, we are consumed by our love for him and he loves us too. And now, a boy of only seven years of age, he lifts this hill! We wonder what he is!" Nanda then revealed to them what the sage Garga had told him during the naming of Kṛṣṇa, and concluded: "I am certain now that Kṛṣṇa is a part manifestation of lord Nārāyaṇa." The villagers were convinced.

May Kṛṣṇa, who held up the Govardhana hill with one hand in

order to protect the people tormented by the torrential rains sent by Indra whose worship had been interrupted, be gracious to us.

Book Ten Chapter 27

Sage Śuka continued: The cow of heaven (Surabhi) and the lord of heaven (Indra) sought the presence of lord Kṛṣṇa. Bowing his head low in utter shame, Indra begged the Lord's forgiveness in the following terms:

Though you appear in the human garb, you are beyond all phenomena. You have no desire at all, yet you chastise the wicked for their own good. You are the father, the guru, the Lord of the world. You are time, and you assumed this embodiment for the good of the embodied beings, and to curb the pride of the haughty ones. Your supreme calmness in great crises shames the proud and awakens in them devotion to you. Your actions themselves admonish the wicked. Forgive my wickedness, Lord, and grant that such evil thoughts may never again arise in my mind.

Salutations to you, lord Vāsudeva, Kṛṣṇa and the chief of the sātvatā. Salutations to the Lord who has of his own will assumed a form suited to the prayer of his devotees, but who in truth is the all, the seed of all and the indweller of all. With my pride gone and my efforts turned to naught, I take refuge in the Lord, the guru and the self that thou art.

The Lord said to Indra: "It was in order to redeem you from your pride that I interrupted your worship. When I wish to bless someone, I rob him of the wealth of power and position. Abandon your pride. Rule the heavens as before."

The heavenly cow Surabhi hailed the Lord and desired that he should be crowned king (Indra) of the cows. Surabhi prayed: "O Kṛṣṇa! You are supreme yogi, the self of the universe and its source. You are the protector of the universe and we, too, have our saviour in you." She herself bathed the Lord with her own milk. Indra bathed him in the waters of the celestial Gaṅgā. He then crowned Kṛṣṇa king of the cows and called him 'Govinda'. The celestials sang and danced in ecstasy. The cows of the whole world rejoiced. And then, Indra returned to heaven.

Kṛṣṇa and Varuṇa
Book Ten Chapter 28

Sage Śuka continued: On one occasion, after having observed complete fast on the ekādaśi day (eleventh day of the lunar fortnight), Nanda rose early the next morning and went to the Kālindī for a bath in order to break the fast within the time allotted. He did not know that that period of the day was regarded as one favourable to the forces of darkness. Hence when he got into the water, messengers of Varuṇa, the god of water, grabbed him and took him away to the abode of Varuṇa.

The people of Vraja concluded that Nanda had been drowned, and wailed aloud. Hearing this, Kṛṣṇa went in search of his father, right down to the abode of Varuṇa. When Varuṇa beheld the Lord himself at his doorstep he welcomed him with great reverence and love. He said: "Today is indeed the most blessed day of my life for I have found the greatest treasure of the universe—the presence of the Lord. I salute you, the supreme being, who is beyond the realm of māyā. Here is your father. Forgive us, your humble servants, for having unwittingly offended you and for having brought your father here."

Kṛṣṇa and Nanda soon returned to Vraja. Nanda had seen the immense wealth of the abode of Varuṇa and had witnessed the high esteem in which his darling son Kṛṣṇa was held by the king of that abode. He narrated all this to his people. They marvelled, and wished that the Lord might transport them all to his divine realm! The Lord who is the indweller knew this and reflected thus: "People grope about in this world, now taking the upward path and now the downward path, all the time subject to ignorance, craving and selfish action, for they do not know the path to the self." Out of pure and supreme compassion Kṛṣṇa then revealed to the cowherds his own supreme abode—which is described as truth, consciousness and infinity, that Brahman which is beyond darkness and which is experienced by sages who have transcended the play of the three qualities of nature and where Kṛṣṇa was hymned by the vedā themselves. Having seen this to their great astonishment, they once again saw Kṛṣṇa in their midst.

Rāsa Līlā
Book Ten Chapter 29

Sage Śuka continued: It was autumn and in the clear blue sky the lovely full moon rose. The setting was ideal, thought Kṛṣṇa, for enacting a divine drama. Kṛṣṇa was seated in the forest and, wishing to shower his grace upon the cowherdesses, he played a few notes on his flute. The music fanned the flame of love for Kṛṣṇa, that constantly burned in the hearts of these women.

Spell-bound, they began to arrive at the spot where Kṛṣṇa was seated. Some were milking the cows, some were boiling the milk, some were cooking food, some were serving their husbands, some were nursing their babies, some were eating, some were dressing and decking themselves with ornaments. They dropped whatever they were doing at the moment they heard the flute of Kṛṣṇa and turned their steps towards him. No one could restrain them. It did not matter if they were not properly dressed and adorned. At the first sound of the music of the flute, their heart, their soul, their very life had already reached the feet of Kṛṣṇa; the body followed without volition.

Some, however, found that all the exits from the house had been bolted and locked. Contemplating on Kṛṣṇa in their hearts they sat there with their eyes closed. Intense longing for Kṛṣṇa burned in their hearts—and it burned the residue of past evil karma in them. In deep meditation they embraced Kṛṣṇa, and the bliss thus enjoyed worked out the residue of past good karma in them. Thus rid of both good and bad karma, and resorting to Kṛṣṇa, though as a lover, they attained the supreme abode and abandoned their physical bodies. This is truly so: one who loves or hates, fears or befriends the Lord is united with him. In fact, that was the very purpose of his incarnation: to make himself easily accessible to incarnate beings.

When they had all come to him, Kṛṣṇa spoke to them: "Welcome, blessed ladies! What shall we do? But, why have you come away from your homes at night? You parents and husbands will be worried. It may be that you are attached to me, for I am the self of all in which everyone finds delight. But it is the duty of a married woman to be devoted to her husband, regarding him as god, even if he is wicked, unlucky, aged, sick or poor. It is not necessary that my devotee should be physically close to me, but should hear and sing my glories and meditate upon me. Hence, return to your homes soon!"

Book Ten Chapter 29

The Gopī said: Do not thus spurn us, Lord. We have completely renounced all the objects of this world and have resorted to your feet. Kindly accept us as your servants. For even so does the Lord of the universe treat the seekers after liberation. You have taught us that service of our husbands is our foremost duty. Let that be so. But are you not the very self of all beings— hence the very self of our husbands? So, by serving you we are serving them. Even they who perform their duties and scriptural rituals are only worshipping you. When we have you with us, what merit need we seek to acquire through the members of our families?

In spite of ourselves, our hands refuse to do the work they were engaged in before; and our feet refuse to lead us away from you. What shall we do if we force ourselves to return to our houses in this state? By your smiles and glances you have kindled the fire of love in our hearts. Quench that fire with the nectar that flows from your lips, or else that fire will soon consume our entire beings.

Since we touched your lotus feet, our hearts do not wish to hold anyone else as dear. The goddess of wealth vies with the sacred basil leaf for the dust of your lotus feet. All the world seeks the blessings of that goddess; but we seek the dust of your feet. Listening to the music of your flute even birds and beasts are entranced, so how could concern for respectability restrain us from being magnetically drawn to you by that music? You have taken birth to save us from all fears and sufferings; hence, we beseech you, place your divine hands on our breasts and on our heads.

Sage Śuka continued: Smilingly approving of their prayerful decision the Lord sported with them. All of them began to sing and run about in the garden. He led them all to the bank of the river Yamunā, there to sport with them in diverse ways. Thus enjoying his loving attention, the gopī began to consider themselves the chosen ones, superior to all other women in the world. The Lord who is the indweller of all, knew this; and in order to destroy the pride of his devotees, he disappeared from their midst.

Book Ten Chapter 30

Sage Śuka continued: The gopī were stricken with grief when Kṛṣṇa thus disappeared. They were completely possessed by grief at their separation from him; their hearts were completely filled with love for him. The gopī remembered his form, his smiles, his gait and his actions, and re-enacted them in their own persons, totally oblivious as they were of their own bodies and the surroundings. In response to the longing of one gopī for Kṛṣṇa, another blissfully responded "I am Kṛṣṇa". When this attitude again yielded to the awareness of his absence from their midst, the wailing gopī searched the forest for their beloved.

In the loneliness and silence of the forest they could ask no human being about Kṛṣṇa's whereabouts, but they asked the flowers, shrubs and creepers. "Did our darling Kṛṣṇa pass this way; did you touch his tender lotus feet; did he inhale your fragrance; which way did he go?" they asked of the trees and creepers. "Let us ask the creeper," they said, "for, though embracing the tree, this creeper has surely touched the person of Kṛṣṇa, for lo and behold, there is evidence of ecstatic joy in the form of fresh sprouts." When the intensity of this agony of separation (viraha) once again lifted their consciousness out of the awareness of their own individuality, once again they were absorbed in Kṛṣṇa consciousness and re-enacted Kṛṣṇa's actions.

One gopī became Pūtanā and another who was Kṛṣṇa fed at her breast. One was the demon Tṛṇāvarta and another acted as Kṛṣṇa who killed that demon. One of them suddenly became Kṛṣṇa the cowherd and sweetly called out to the cows. Another produced the music of the flute. Another gopī lifted up a scarf and exclaimed: "Do not be afraid of Indra or the clouds of dissolution; look, I am holding up the hill for your protection." One gopī jumped on the head of another, treating the latter as the serpent Kāliya and admonished him to get away. Another gopī commanded the cowherds to close their eyes while she (Kṛṣṇa) drank the forest-fire. Thus they lived in Kṛṣṇa as Kṛṣṇa himself.

Book Ten Chapter 30

Sage Śuka continued: While they were thus roaming they suddenly saw Kṛṣṇa's footprints, which sent thrills of ecstasy through their bodies. Soon they saw other footprints which they recognised as the footprints of a lady. "Whose are these footprints? Who is that blessed lady who has earned Kṛṣṇa's special favour? Surely, she must have worshipped the Lord with such intensity of devotion that he, leaving us behind, has taken her away. The very look of those footprints of the lady who enjoys the love of Kṛṣṇa, which belongs to all of us, is painful. Lo and behold, the lady's footprinits are not visible here. Surely, Kṛṣṇa must have shown even greater favour to her by lifting her up on to his own shoulders. There is no doubt about that, for here Kṛṣṇa's own footprints are heavier. And on this spot the Lord must have set her down and braided her hair and decked her with flowers, some of which are still strewn about this place." Thus they traced the path which Kṛṣṇa had taken after disappearing from their midst.

Their surmise was true. The lady whom Kṛṣṇa had singled out for his attention had at one time felt highly elated that she enjoyed a place of pre-eminence in the heart of Kṛṣṇa. Yielding to pride and arrogance, she demanded that Kṛṣṇa should carry her. "All right, then, jump on my shoulders!" Kṛṣṇa, said, and when she had done so, he disappeared mysteriously. She wailed aloud: "My Lord, the beloved of my soul, where are you? Dearest friend! I am your humble servant. Let me behold you." The lady was inconsolably miserable. That is the state in which the other gopī found her during their search for Kṛṣṇa. That lady (Rādhikā?), too, was full of anguish over the loss of Kṛṣṇa's company, and remorse at having been responsible for it.

Now, all of them continued the search. Their minds were saturated with thoughts of Kṛṣṇa. With their whole beings absorbed in him, they were talking of him, imitating his behaviour and singing his glories alone: they had no thought of themselves or their homes. Soon there was total darkness and they returned to the sandy bank of the river where they began to sing the glory of Kṛṣṇa.

Book Ten Chapter 31

The Gopī sang: Because you were born there, Vraja is even more prosperous. Indeed, the goddess of wealth dwells there permanently now. Beloved, see how your devotees are wandering about in search of you. By the shafts of your love-laden eyes you have robbed us of our very lives. Yet you have indeed saved us, the people of Vraja, time and again from diverse calamities. We know that you are not the playmate of the gopī, and that you are the indwelling witness of all beings. You have taken birth among the sātvatā at the specific prayer of the creator.

Lord, bless us by placing your hand on our heads—the hand that grants freedom from fear to those who take refuge in you. Accept us as your humble servants and reveal your face to us. Place on our bosom your lotus feet, which destroy the sins of those who bow to you, which walk behind the cows and calves, which are the abode of prosperity and which danced over the hoods of Kāliya. Beloved, revive the depressed spirits of us all with the nectar that flows from your lips. Even the nectar of your glorious stories revives the spirits of the afflicted. They are sung by the wise and they destroy evil, bestow auspiciousness and are tranquillising. Blessed are they that listen to them.

We are unhappy to think that your tender feet are pricked by thorns and shrubs. We are unhappy when you go away every day to pasture the cows. We are only happy when you return to the village. We gaze at your beautiful countenance with the curly locks laden with the dust raised by the cows walking in front of you. We curse the deity that fixed eyd-lids over our eyes that prevent us from continuously gazing at you and drinking the divinity of your face.

Beloved Lord, grant us the nectar of your lips which the blessed flute enjoys and thus acquires the power to enchant people. Abandoning all attachment to husband, children and other relations we have sought your feet: pray, do not abandon us. Your birth in Vraja has removed the sorrow of its people; do not now torment us by your separation.

Book Ten Chapter 32

Sage Śuka continued: Thus the gopī, filled with an eagerness to behold the Lord, sang, talked like one insane, and wept. In their midst appeared Kṛṣṇa, wearing a sweet smile on his countenance and a yellow silk garment on his body, looking like the enchanter of cupid himself. All the gopī were beside themselves with joy, and they expressed it in no uncertain terms. One squeezed his palms, another placed his arm on her shoulders, one pressed his feet upon her bosom, one looked at his face with unwinking eyes and another looked similarly at his feet. Another took him into her through her eyes which she closed at once, and with hair standing on end in ecstasy, she embraced him in her own heart, seated like a yogi. Their agony had been completely removed.

Kṛṣṇa led them all to the bank of the river where they found a sandy beach which was illumined by a flood of moonlight. There they prepared a seat for him with their own scarves. Kṛṣṇa seated there, surrounded by the beautiful gopī, presented a heavenly spectacle. Sitting close to him the gopī questioned him: "Some love those who love them, others love even those who do not love them, and yet others do not love even those who love them! Can you tell us why?"

Kṛṣṇa said: Friends love one another actuated by selfish interests; there is no true friendliness there, but only self-interest. Others love even those who do not love them—this is like paternal affection; here the love is actuated by dharma and friendliness, and it is blameless. Yet others do not love even those that love them: they are either sages who delight in their own self, they whose desires have all been fulfilled, ungrateful people or they who hate their own benefactors and elders. As for me, I do not love even those who love me, so that they may never forget me nor take me for granted, but remain forever immersed in quest of me—like a poor man who found a pearl which he lost and is, therefore, for ever looking for it. It is on this account that I disappeared from your midst for a while. But, I tell you, even if I am born again and again for many millennia, I will not be able to repay the debt I owe you nor to recompense your pure love for me.

Book 10 Chapter 33

Sage Śuka continued: Enthralled by the loving words of Kṛṣṇa, the gopī formed a circle around him, and Kṛṣṇa commenced the rāsa dance. By his own divine powers Kṛṣṇa appeared between every two gopī. The dance commenced. Celestials crowded the heavens to witness this rare scene. Kṛṣṇa and the gopī thus danced, their bodies swaying, rocking, whirling, and their dresses and tresses flying around. The gopī joined with Kṛṣṇa in singing; one gopī excelled the other and everyone applauded everyone else's effort. A gopī, overcome by fatigue, caught Kṛṣṇa's shoulder; another gopī fondly kissed the arm of Kṛṣṇa which was resting on her shoulder and experienced a blissful state of ecstasy. Another gopī, who was also slightly tired, pressed Kṛṣṇa's hands to her bosom. Thus they sported with the Lord, with his arms around their necks. Embracing them, touching them, looking at them, smiling at them and so forth, the Lord sported with them even as a child would play with its own reflections. It is said that the celestial bodies—the moon and the planets and the constellations—stood still, witnessing this wondrous play of the Lord who was in truth revelling in his own self all the time.

Then, surrounded by the gopī, the Lord entered the waters of the river. There again he played with the gopī who sprinkled him with water as the celestials watched and rejoiced. Afterwards Kṛṣṇa roamed the groves and gardens on the bank of the river, even there surrounded by the gopī.

Parīkṣit asked: How was it that the Lord, who incarnated as Kṛṣṇa to establish righteousness, thus sported with others' wives?

Sage Śuka replied: What appears to be transgression of dharma is noticed in the conduct of the great, but it does not taint them. A wise man would accept their precepts as authoritative and emulate only those actions of theirs which are in accord with their precepts, not others. Non-volitional, spontaneous actions of those who have transcended ego are totally unselfish and are beyond the realm of virtue and vice. How could there be sin in relation to actions of the Lord, the dust of whose feet purifies the worst sinner?

Kṛṣṇa is the indweller of all—of the gopī (with whom he sported) and of their husbands (who, therefore, were not annoyed with him at all). In the early hours of the morning, the gopī reluctantly returned to their homes.

He who devoutly listens to this great episode in the life of Kṛṣṇa will easily develop self-control and will be blessed with supreme devotion to Kṛṣṇa.

Sudarśana and Saṅkhacūḍa
Book Ten Chapter 34

Sage Śuka continued: On another occasion all the people of Vraja went to Ambikā Vana. There they bathed in the river Sarasvatī and then worshipped lord Śiva and Pārvatī. Observing complete fast, they spent the night on the bank of the river. A huge python came upon that spot and, tormented by hunger, it began to swallow Nanda. He began to cry out in distress: "Kṛṣṇa, Kṛṣṇa, this huge snake is swallowing me; I have taken refuge in you, kindly save me." All the cowherds rushed to his help, with lighted torches. Even when these were applied to it the python did not let Nanda go. Then Kṛṣṇa came, and merely touched it with his foot. Immediately, out of the body of that python a shining celestial person emerged. He bowed to Kṛṣṇa, who asked him: "Who are you?"

The celestial told his story "I am a celestial named Sudarśana. Once I was extremely handsome and I used to fly around in aerial vehicles. One day I saw some deformed sages and laughed at them. They cursed me to be born as a python. That curse, too, has proved to be a great blessing for it has earned for me the touch of your lotus feet. One who utters your name is purified of all sins; it is no wonder therefore, that he who is touched by your feet is thoroughly purified. Grant me leave to go."

Nanda escaped from death and the cowherds marvelled at the glory of Kṛṣṇa.

One day Kṛṣṇa and Balarāma, together with the womenfolk of Vraja, were singing and dancing in the forest. When the women heard the melodious songs of the two brothers, they swooned with delight. In the meantime Śaṅkhacūḍa, an attendant of Kubera, the god of wealth, arrived there. He forced all the womenfolk aboard a vehicle and drove away with them whilst they cried to Kṛṣṇa for help. The brothers ran after the wicked demi-god and soon overtook him. Realising his mistake, Śaṅkhacūḍa abandoned the women and ran for his life. Kṛṣṇa pursued him while Balarāma stood guard over the women. Kṛṣṇa caught up with him, beheaded him, and presented to Balarāma the jewel which had adorned the head of Śaṅkhacūḍa.

Book Ten Chapter 35

Sage Śuka continued: During the daytime, when lord Kṛṣṇa went out to graze the cows, the gopī or cowherdesses keenly felt his separation and hence sang about him:

"When the consummate flautist Kṛṣṇa gently presses the flute to his lips and delicately lets his fingers dance on it, even celestial women are entranced by the love it kindles in their hearts.

"Nay, Kṛṣṇa's music captivates the hearts even of deer and cows, so they forget to chew the grass hanging from the corners of their mouths!

"When Kṛṣṇa calls out to the cows, the rivers become agitated! They lift up their arms (the waves), to catch grains of dust hallowed by his feet; but hearing his voice they are stilled and their motion arrested.

"When they hear Kṛṣṇa, trees and creepers are thrilled and they let honey flow, and bees, cranes, swans and other birds hover around him.

"When Kṛṣṇa sings, the cloud rumbles keeping perfect time, and shielding him as an umbrella, showers flowers over him.

"Even Indra and Brahmā, when they hear his music, are unable to fathom its subtle charm; no wonder that we, the women of Vraja, lose all consciousness of our bodies and the world when we behold his face.

"When Kṛṣṇa plays with his companions on the bank of the Yamunā a gentle breeze fans him, and the celestials sing his praises.

"Here comes Kṛṣṇa who is the protector of Vraja and the cows, with elders bowing to his feet and with the cattle returning from pasture at the close of the day. He appears fatigued, but even so he is beautiful and delightful to look at, with his garland covered with the dust of the hooves of the cows—his dear ones. As he strolls in, like a little elephant, he removes the distress in our hearts caused by our separation from him during the daytime."

Thus did the gopī sing of him. They had lost their hearts to him in total love and self-surrender.

Ariṣṭa
Book Ten Chapter 36

Sage Śuka continued: Then there came to Vraja another demon by name Ariṣṭa, disguised as a bull. At his approach the people of Vraja were frightened, cattle began to run away, and it is said that when he bellowed, cows and women were delivered of their babies. The cowherds and their wives ran to Kṛṣṇa for protection. Kṛṣṇa rolled up his sleeves, and slapping his arms in the manner of wrestlers, he faced the demon: "You fool! I am here only to destroy wicked beings like you!" The bull charged at him, but Kṛṣṇa playfully stopped it and pushed it back. He pulled out its horns and killed it with them.

With the latest news of Kṛṣṇa's valourous deed, sage Nārada came to Kaṁsa's court. He revealed to the demon-king all the secrets concerning Kṛṣṇa's birth, how Vasudeva had exchanged his son for Nanda's daughter, and how Kṛṣṇa had playfully destroyed all the demon-agents of Kaṁsa. Kaṁsa in his mad fury almost killed Vasudeva, but the sage restrained him and then went away. Kaṁsa imprisoned Vasudeva and Devakī.

Kaṁsa took counsel with his demon-ministers and gave orders: "Keśī must go to Vraja and kill Kṛṣṇa and Balarāma. Failing this, they must be brought here and killed by the foremost among wrestlers, Muṣṭika and Cāṇūra. Failing this, they should be killed by the most powerful among elephants, Kuvalayāpīḍa. As an excuse for inviting the brothers, I command that a sacrificial rite be commenced to propitiate lord Śiva with animal sacrifice."

At the same time, Kaṁsa called Akrūra and told him in a friendly tone: "I rely upon you alone at this crucial juncture of my life. I have come to know that Kṛṣṇa is destined to kill me. I want you to go to Vraja and invite Kṛṣṇa and Balarāma, on my behalf, to witness the sacrificial rite that I have decided to perform. However, before they reach the palace, either the wrestlers or the elephant will kill them. Once they have been killed I shall myself ensure that all the people that are opposed to me are exterminated, including my father who is hoping to ascend the throne. When all the thorns in my side are thus removed, I shall rule as the undisputed ruler of the whole world. The entire plan depends upon you now."

Akrūra replied: "Your plan to save yourself has indeed been very well thought out. But having planned, one should remain unaffected by success or failure, for that is in the hands of the gods. People entertain high hopes, though the divine will is contrary to them! Yet, I shall do as you say."

After this dialogue, Kaṁsa returned to the women's apartments and Akrūra to his house.

Keśī and Vyoma
Book Ten Chapter 37

Sage Śuka continued: In obedience to the command of Kaṁsa, the demon Keśī hastened to Vraja in the disguise of a terrible horse. When it entered the village all the people were frightened by its fiery neighing and by the way it seemed to run amok. Soon Kṛṣṇa challenged it; and it appeared to invite him to a duel! Roaring as if it was a lion the horse rushed at him and, turning around, it hit at Kṛṣṇa with its hind legs. Before its legs could touch him, Kṛṣṇa caught hold of them, whirled the horse over his head and playfully threw it quite a distance. It took the horse a few minutes to recover from the fall. Then it rushed towards Kṛṣṇa once again, with its wide open mouth emitting fire, as it were. Lo and behold, Kṛṣṇa deliberately thrust his hand into its mouth. The animal could not harm him; for the Lord's hand soon swelled, choking it. Unable to breathe the demon assumed his own form and inhaled his last breath. Kṛṣṇa then drew his arm out and walked away as if nothing had happened.

Nārada, the celestial sage, then approached him and spoke to him in secret: "Kṛṣṇa! You are the infinite Lord. With the help of māyā, your own mysterious power, you create, sustain and dissolve the universe. You have descended into this mortal world in this human form in order to destroy evil and to promote righteousness. No wonder therefore, that this demon, who was the terror of even the gods, was so easily killed by you." Nārada also revealed to Kṛṣṇa that the Lord (Kṛṣṇa) would soon destroy all the demons, including Kaṁsa, that the Lord would rule from Dvārakā, and that he would preside over the destruction of millions of people in the Mahābhārata war. Bowing to the Lord, the sage returned to his abode in heaven.

On another occasion, when the Lord was engaged in play (of

thieves and watchmen) with his companions, the demon Vyoma mingled with them in the disguise of a cowherd boy. During the play, posing as a 'thief' in the game, Vyoma carried away many of the Lord's companions and hid them in a cave. Kṛṣṇa soon discovered this and caught him red-handed. The demon resumed his original form and tried in vain to extricate himself from Kṛṣṇa's grip. Kṛṣṇa dashed him to the ground; and that was his end. Then he went to the cave, forced it open and released his companions, who were exceedingly happy to be freed.

Akrūra
Book Ten Chapter 38

Sage Śuka continued: Requested by Kaṁsa to invite Kṛṣṇa and Balarāma to come to Mathurā, Akrūra was in ecstasy in anticipation of his meeting the divine beings. "What have I done to merit this supreme blessing?" he thought. "I am a worldly-minded man, how is it possible that I shall see the supreme being? No, I should not think thus. For, while being borne down by this stream called Time, someone crosses it at some time! Today I shall behold the Lord: and naturally I consider that today all my sins have been destroyed and my birth has reached its goal. Even the wicked Kaṁsa has done me a great service by thus sending me to Kṛṣṇa. Today I shall behold Kṛṣṇa's feet which are adorned by the creator himself, but which now tread the forest trails behind the cows and are affectionately pressed by the cowherdesses to their bosom. He who is beyond all cause-and-effect relationship and beyond the pale of ignorance, is today seen in the gardens of Vraja playing with mere mortals as if he were one among them. Today I shall behold the Lord who is the goal of the great ones, who is the supreme guru of all and who is a delight to behold: for the omens are all auspicious." Akrūra then mentally rehearsed his meeting with the Lord, and was already in a state of bliss. He was sure that the Lord, being the indweller of all, would not regard him (Akrūra) as an enemy sent by Kaṁsa, but as a humble devotee.

Akrūra's chariot entered Vraja towards the evening. On the road he beheld the footprints of Kṛṣṇa. He instantly jumped down from his chariot and rolled in the dust hallowed by the touch of Kṛṣṇa's feet, exclaiming with tear-filled eyes: "These are indeed Kṛṣṇa's footprints."

Soon he was in the divine presence of Kṛṣṇa and Balarāma. He saw them as none other than the supreme being himself. He fell at their feet. They embraced him warmly and let him into their house. Balarāma then washed Akrūra's feet and Kṛṣṇa brought him food and garlands. Nanda enquired of him: "Are you well, O Akrūra? But, then, living at the mercy of the most wicked Kaṁsa, what peace or security can one hope to have?" Thus attended to by the divine family and with Kṛṣṇa himself pressing his feet lovingly, Akrūra forgot the fatigue of his journey from Mathurā.

Book Ten Chapter 39

Sage Śuka continued: While enquiring about the welfare of kinsmen in Mathurā, lord Kṛṣṇa said: "Alas, on my account my parents have been subjected to great suffering; on my account several children have been put to death. We are both happy to see you here. Kindly tell us what we may do for you." In response to the Lord's enquiry Akrūra narrated all that had happened in Mathurā: Nārada's revelations and Kaṁsa's plot. At this, Kṛṣṇa and Balarāma laughed aloud and then informed their father, Nanda, of the king's invitation. Nanda at once ordered all the villagers to collect curds, butter and other dairy products which he and his retinue would offer to the king. All the men were busy preparing for the visit to the capital.

But the womenfolk were profoundly disturbed and distressed. They gathered together and began to weep and wail aloud: "How cruel you are, O ruler of the world, in that you bring people together, and even before they have achieved their end you draw them apart! Who gave this man the name Akrūra which means 'one who is not cruel'? He is indeed most cruel in that he is taking our very life away from us. Ah, look at our darling Kṛṣṇa! He does not even look at us now; he is indifferent, having neither a friend nor an enemy here. He is above all; but maybe he will become enamoured of the ladies of the city and forget us! Surely, it will be a great day for them when they behold the radiant face of our Lord." When the chariot was ready to leave they openly wept aloud "Govinda, Dāmodara, Mādhava" for they were completely devoted to Kṛṣṇa and could not bear the pangs of separation from him. They ran after the chariot, and some fell in a swoon. Seeing their pitiable plight Kṛṣṇa sent them a message: "I shall come." Forever afterwards these women were continually talking to one another about Kṛṣṇa, thinking of him constantly.

Akrūra stopped the chariot on the bank of Kālindī to say the mid-day prayers, while Kṛṣṇa and Balarāma remained seated in the chariot. Akrūra went into the water. When he immersed himself in it he saw Kṛṣṇa and Balarāma seated in the water, in all their radiance. He raised his head from the water and assured himself that they were still seated in the chariot. Yes. It was no hallucination. Once again he immersed himself in the water. This time he beheld a most glorious spectacle. He saw the Lord resting on his serpent-couch on the ocean of milk, surrounded by the gods and celestials. He saw the Lord's radiant body in all its detail. He saw the Lord's divine powers waiting upon him—śrī (wealth of every sort), puṣṭi (mourishment), sarasvatī (knowledge and wisdom), kānti (splendour), kīrti (fame), tuṣṭi (satisfaction), ilā (earth), ūrjā (omnipotence), vidyā (enlightened intelligence), avidyā (ignorance), śaktī (power) and māyā (illusion).

Book Ten Chapter 40

Akrūra prayed thus: Salutations to you, O Nārāyaṇa, the cause of all causes, the uncaused cause, from whom all the elements and even their causes have originated. None of the evolutes can possibly know you. Yet, some yogī meditate upon you as the indweller of all bodies and some holy men worship you by means of scripturally-ordained rituals. Others having renounced the doership of all actions and with their inner self tranquil adore you, who art pure consciousness itself, by means of jñāna yajña (worship in which knowledge or wisdom itself is the article and the ritual used). Yet others worship you in your diverse or single aspect. Some worship you as Śiva in the manner prescribed by several teachers. Yet all of them worship you alone, for you are all these aspects or divinities. Just as rivers having their source in the mountain flow down to the plains and merge in the unity of the ocean, even so all beings worship you alone in diverse ways.

The three qualities of nature give birth to all beings, including the gods. Nature is your nature. Hence eventually all beings return to you. You are the cosmic being. The whole of nature represents various parts of your being. You are totally free and unattached, since you are all and therefore the witness of all minds. You yourself incarnate in this world from time to time. I salute your past incarnations—as the divine fish, the horse-headed Hayagrīva, the divine tortoise, the boar, the man-lion, the dwarf, Paraśurāma and Rāma. I salute you, Kṛṣṇa and Balarāma, the Lord incarnate. Salutations to your glorious incarnations as Buddha and Kalki.

All beings in the universe are overpowered by your deluding

agency māyā. Hence we mistake the body for the self, we mistake appearance for truth, shadow for substance, sorrow for bliss. On account of ignorance we have turned away from you in pursuit of pleasure, even as a fool runs after water in a mirage, leaving behind a pond covered with its own produce (moss). I take refuge at your feet, Lord. Pray protect me.

Book Ten Chapter 41

Sage Śuka continued: Even as Akrūra was thus offering his prayer, the vision was withdrawn. Akrūra completed his prayers and returned to the chariot. Looking at his dazed countenance, Kṛṣṇa asked him: "Did you see something wonderful in the heavens or on the earth or in the river?" To which Akrūra devoutly replied: "I have seen you, and I am seeing you right in front of me. What can be more wonderful than this?"

They now reached the outskirts of Mathurā, the capital of the kingdom. Kṛṣṇa said to Akrūra: "Uncle, you had better go into the city first; I shall follow you later on." Akrūra could not contemplate the idea of parting from the Lord. With tearful eyes and heavy heart, he pleaded: "Do not forsake me, Lord, who am your humble servant. Please sanctify our house with the dust of your feet, for thus are the ancestors and the celestials pleased. Worshipping them the king Bali attained to the supreme state, attainable only by the greatest among devotees. The water sanctified by the touch of your blessed feet purifies the three worlds, and by that water were the sons of Sagara revived. I salute you, the Lord of lords!"

Kṛṣṇa replied that he would visit Akrūra's house after accomplishing his mission in Mathurā. Akrūra then went ahead. Kṛṣṇa and the party settled down in the outskirts of Mathurā, and then they walked into the city. Kṛṣṇa took a keen interest in the magnificent fortifications that confronted him. He admired the architecture and the sheer affluence that met his eyes everywhere. For their part, the women of the city feasted their eyes on the two divine persons.

Kṛṣṇa saw a washerman with nice clothes and said to him: "Give my brother Balarāma and me good clothes to wear and you will attain blessedness." But the arrogant washerman, who was devoted to Kaṁsa, contemptuously refused, so Kṛṣṇa picked his head off his shoulders with his little fingers, and then both the brothers helped themselves to the clothes. A little while later they met a weaver who offered them lovely brocades and garments; Kṛṣṇa showered his choicest blessings upon him. Again, they came upon a florist named

Sudāmā who literally worshipped Kṛṣṇa and decked them with the most colourful garlands. Highly pleased with him, the Lord conferred upon him all the boons of his choice. He, as also the weaver, sought only one boon; that of uninterrupted devotion to the lotus feet of the Lord.

Kubjā
Book Ten Chapter 42

Sage Śuka continued: Wandering further into the city Kṛṣṇa saw a hunchbacked, but otherwise good-looking, young woman carrying sandal-paste. Kṛṣṇa demanded some sandal-paste. Thereupon the woman revealed that it was for Kaṁsa, who was very fond of the sandal-paste prepared by her. "But, who is more worthy of it than you?" she said, and gave it to them with affection and eagerness. When Kṛṣṇa and Balarāma applied that sandal-paste to their torsos, they shone even more beautifully. Highly pleased with this offering of the hunchback, Kṛṣṇa pressed her feet with his own and with two of his fingers lifted her chin up, and her body, which till then had had three curves, became straight. Such is the glory of seeing the Lord and serving him. By virtue of the very touch of his hands, the hunchback became a very beautiful woman. She too was charmed by the very appearance of the divine boy and, overcome by passionate love for him, invited him to her house. Kṛṣṇa lovingly promised to visit her after accomplishing his mission in Mathurā.

Kṛṣṇa enquired about the place where the bow of Śiva had been placed. He went there and wanted to lift it up. Those who stood guard tried to prevent him, but he grabbed it. He lifted the bow with his left hand and broke it into two. The sound made by the bow as it broke was heard even by Kaṁsa. Kaṁsa's men rushed towards Kṛṣṇa. But, Kṛṣṇa and Balarāma, each armed with half that broken bow, drove all the warriors away. Soon the sun set; the two brothers and their retinue returned to the outskirts of the city and to their caravan, where they spent the night.

Kaṁsa had heard of the way in which Kṛṣṇa and Balarāma had driven away his warriors, and was really worried. He spent a restless night unable to sleep. When he tried to sleep, he dreamt dreams which foreboded evil.

The next day dawned and the followers of Kaṁsa were preparing the arena for the wrestling match. When it was ready the people of the city assembled in the galleries. Kaṁsa himself took his seat in the royal box. Renowned wrestlers were getting ready for a fight.

Nanda and the cowherds who had been specially invited by Kaṁsa took up their seats in a place reserved for them.

Kuvalayāpīḍa; Cāṇūra
Book Ten Chapter 43

Sage Śuka continued: Kṛṣṇa, Balarāma and their companions and relations greeted the next and (as it proved to be) most eventful morning, with prayers. The Lord heard the din of the kettledrums and the shouts of the wrestlers and went to the arena out of curiosity. Just outside the arena stood the mighty elephant Kuvalayāpīḍa. Kṛṣṇa asked the rider of the elephant to move away, but instead, goaded by the rider, the elephant charged! The elephant caught Kṛṣṇa in his trunk; but the Lord slipped away and stood under the belly of the elephant. Then he went behind the animal and, holding it by its tail, dragged it along for quite some distance and wheeled it round and round. At one stage in this spectacular duel Kṛṣṇa feigned a fall. The angry elephant plunged its tusks into the ground; but Kṛṣṇa had moved away. Maddened with frustration, the elephant charged again. Kṛṣṇa caught hold of its trunk and playfully tilted it; it fell down. Kṛṣṇa pulled out its tusks and with them despatched the animal and its keepers to the abode of death.

Kṛṣṇa and Balarāma then entered the arena, tusks in hand, their beautiful faces beaded with perspiration. They presented an extraordinary spectacle. To the wrestlers Kṛṣṇa appeared to be a thunderbolt; to men, a superman; to the women, the very embodiment of cupid; to the cowherds, a kinsman; to the immortal kings, a chastiser; to the parents, a child; to Kaṁsa, death itself; to the ignorant, a little boy; to the yogī, the supreme truth; and to the vṛṣṇī, a great divinity. He entered the arena with his brother. The people assembled in the arena received Kṛṣṇa into their hearts with all their senses, minds and intellects. And they began talking to one another about Kṛṣṇa, about his birth as the son of Vasudeva, about his transference to Vraja and about his childhood exploits, etc.

At the same time the wrestler, Cāṇūra, invited Kṛṣṇa to a duel: "This is the king's pleasure, young man: and people attain all their desires and prosperity by doing what pleases the king." Kṛṣṇa replied: "No doubt we shall do what pleases the king, as we are also subjects of Kaṁsa. But in all duels the contestants should be of equal strength, otherwise the duel is unrighteous." Cāṇūra interrupted: "Sure enough. But, though you two appear to be young boys, you are obviously not so—look what you have done with the mighty elephant Kuvalayāpīḍa. You are fit to be challenged by me, and Balarāma by Muṣṭika."

Death of Kaṁsa
Book Ten Chapter 44

Sage Śuka continued: Immediately the two duels commenced: Cāṇūra with Kṛṣṇa, Muṣṭika with Balarāma. The wrestling was a wonderful spectacle. Kṛṣṇa and Balarāma wrestled with Cāṇūra and Muṣṭika with professional skill and extraordinary strength and vitality. Yet the spectators, especially the womenfolk, were indignant that such unequal contest should be allowed by the king and the elders. "It is unrighteous," they said to one another, "and we should leave the place where such injustice and unrighteousness prevails. Or else we become participants in the crime. Are these tender youths a match for these ruffians, Cāṇūra and Muṣṭika? How lovely and charming do these two young men look! Blessed indeed are the women of Vraja who are able to feast their eyes on them every day!"

Kṛṣṇa decided to dispose of Cāṇūra. The duel entered the final phase. Cāṇūra threw Kṛṣṇa down and hit him. Brushing this lightly aside, Kṛṣṇa caught Cāṇūra by his arm, whirled him overhead and dashed him on the ground—the demon was dead. At the same time Balarāma hit Muṣṭika, who fell dead, vomiting blood. Several of the followers of these two wrestlers rushed towards Kṛṣṇa and Balarāma and were quickly disposed of by them. The lesser wrestlers ran away.

Terribly angered by all this, Kaṁsa shouted: "Take these two insolent boys away and banish them from my kingdom. Execute Vasudeva, their father, and also my father Ugrasena." However, Kṛṣṇa sprang up to the royal box in the arena and caught hold of the arm of Kaṁsa even as he was trying to draw his sword. Kṛṣṇa threw Kaṁsa down and jumped on his chest. Kaṁsa was dead: but because night and day, while breathing, while eating, drinking, talking, walking and sleeping, Kaṁsa was constantly thinking of Kṛṣṇa, Kaṁsa attained a state of liberation which is extremely difficult to attain.

The eight brothers of Kaṁsa rushed towards Kṛṣṇa and Balarāma but the latter took care of them. There was a shower of flowers on Kṛṣṇa, and the heavenly bards sang the glories of the Lord. Everyone was happy, except of course the wives of the dead demons, who wailed aloud: "O lord of Bhoja, Kaṁsa, you know the code of right conduct, and yet you ruthlessly oppressed righteous men and brought untold harm to innocent people. Hence you have been reduced to this state. No one who oppresses and harms innocent people can hope to be happy in this world. We have seen that anyone who disrespects Kṛṣṇa, the Lord, the protector and preserver of the universe, cannot prosper."

Kṛṣṇa himself comforted them. He then released his parents, Vasudeva and Devakī, from the prison and bowed to them and touched their feet. They, on their part, were speechless, for they realised that incarnate divinities were themselves bowing to their feet.

Guru Sāndīpani
Book Ten Chapter 45

Sage Śuka continued: Out of supreme love for his parents Kṛṣṇa at once spread the veil of illusion over their minds and, fondly calling them 'Father' and 'Mother', begged of them to forgive him for not delighting them with his company during his childhood. "Great is the punishment that he, who neglects the service of his parents, receives in the abode of Yama and even here. Such a one is truly dead though alive who does not look after his aged parents," said Kṛṣṇa. Vasudeva and Devakī were delighted, and fondly embraced him.

Then Kṛṣṇa crowned Ugrasena (the father of Kaṁsa) king, in the presence of all the people, some of whom had returned from self-imposed exile, now that their tormentor Kaṁsa was dead. Kṛṣṇa now turned to Nanda, his foster parent, and addressed him in the most affectionate terms: "You have indeed been most loving and affectionate to us. Truly he is the father and she the mother who nourishes as one's own child, a child abandoned by the parents who gave it birth. Kindly return to Vraja, and I shall soon follow you there." The Lord loaded them with gifts and they reluctantly took leave of him.

Soon after this, Vasudeva invested Kṛṣṇa and Balarāma with the sacred thread and the two divine brothers entered the brahmacarya stage of life. They were indeed the lords of all arts and sciences, and they possessed perfect knowledge; yet concealing this, they went to the hermitage of Sāndīpani, desiring to live with a guru. They served the guru with the utmost devotion, thus exemplifying the ideal of devotion to one's preceptor. There they studied all the scriptures, all the arts and sciences. They had to hear a teaching only once and they were masters of that teaching. When they were ready to take leave of the guru, they requested him to choose what he wanted from them. Fully aware of their divine powers, Sāndīpani asked that his son, who had been drowned in the sea, be brought back.

At once Kṛṣṇa went to the ocean, whose presiding deity told him that it was a demon known as Pañcajana who had taken the life of the young man. Kṛṣṇa entered the ocean and killed the demon Pañcajana who had the form of a conch. But the young man was not found. Kṛṣṇa went to the abode of Yama and blew the conch. Hearing this, Yama came forth and readily restored the young man to Kṛṣṇa. The guru was pleased and blessed Kṛṣṇa: "He who has pupils like you— all this desires are instantly fulfilled. May your glory purify everyone. Kṛṣṇa and Balarāma then returned to Mathurā.

Book Ten Chapter 46

Sage Śuka continued: Uddhava was a beloved friend of Kṛṣṇa. One day Kṛṣṇa said to him: "Please go to Vraja, dear friend, and bring solace on my behalf to the gopī there. These simple women of Vraja are enduring the anguish caused by their separation from me only in the hope of seeing me again. Their minds are absorbed in me; I am their life; for my sake they have given up all worldly relationships and all worldy duties. I am their sole support."

Soon Uddhava was on his way to Vraja. He entered the village at about the same time as the cattle were returning from pasturing. He drove through the village with its houses where the sacred fire and the holy men were revered and worshipped. Uddhava alighted at the house of Nanda, who was delighted to meet him. Nanda enquired of the welfare of all their common friends, their kith and kin in Mathurā and particularly of the welfare of Kṛṣṇa and Balarāma. He recounted the boyhood exploits of Kṛṣṇa—the recitiation of which had become their best nourishment. He could not proceed very far, for he was overcome with emotion. Listening to the story of Kṛṣṇa, Yaśodā was enraptured, shedding profuse tears of love.

Moved by their love of Kṛṣṇa, Uddhava said: "Supremely blessed are you both, for you have such devotion to lord Kṛṣṇa. Balarāma and Kṛṣṇa whom you regard as your sons, are actually the material and the efficient cause of the whole creation. They are the pradhāna and the puruṣa. You are indeed most blessed to have had them as your sons. Yet Kṛṣṇa has no father, mother, son or relations, because he is not the physical body. Yet again, he incarnates here in different species of existence. Kṛṣṇa is not only your son; he is the lord Hari, the very self and the son of all; nay, he is everyone's father, mother and god. Indeed nothing that is seen or heard, stationary or moving, big or small in the three periods of time, exists independent of the Lord who alone is the All in truth." Thus they spent the whole night conversing about Kṛṣṇa.

When the sun rose the next day the gopī of Vraja saw the royal car standing in front of Nanda's house. They remembered that Akrūra had come in such a car and deprived them of their very lives, as it were, by taking Kṛṣṇa away. They wondered if Akrūra had come back—and what else he would do! At the same time, Uddhava returned to Nanda's house from the river, after concluding his morning prayers.

Book Ten Chapter 47

Sage Śuka continued: The gopī saw Uddhava, who had been clad in a manner similar to Kṛṣṇa and in whom they recognised a friend and a devotee of Kṛṣṇa. They approached him, bowed to him and enquired of him about Kṛṣṇa. "We know that you are the Lord's friend and messenger," said the gopī, "and obviously you have come to talk to his parents. What else is there in Vraja which he should remember? People, even ascetics, cherish memories of their kinsmen; but the friendship of others ceases when the object is achieved." But the gopī continued to recall and narrate the boyhood exploits of the Lord, with their hearts filled with love and eyes filled with tears.

One of the gopī saw a black bee hovering around her and addressing it, poured out the love of her heart for Kṛṣṇa, in such language that it could have applied to Uddhava, too! "Why have you come here, and what will you gain by singing the glories of Kṛṣṇa to us? Having stolen our hearts once, he has deserted us. Indeed, why should he value our friendship, he whose feet are adored by Lakṣmī, the goddess of wealth? For his sake we abandoned our homes and all our human relationships. For his sake many have fully controlled their inborn tendencies, their likes and dislikes, and are leading the life of mendicants. The very mention of his name fills us with distress and utter despair. Tell us, can you take us back to Kṛṣṇa?"

Understanding the import of this address to the bee, Uddhava said: Glorious devotees of Kṛṣṇa! You have with your own lives laid a unique path to god-realisation—that of supreme love. Hear now Kṛṣṇa's special message to you: "You can never be separated from me, for I am the life and the very self of all. I created, sustain and withdraw the universe, by myself within myself. The self is ever-pure, it is consciousness itself and should be sought in and through the three states of consciousness. At all times one should be in that state of mind in which he sees the world as an object seen in a dream. All the different spiritual practices are ultimately aimed at such control of the mind! For this purpose it is not necessary that you should all be physically near me. Often, when you are physically away from me you will be spiritually closer to me."

Book Ten Chapter 47

Sage Śuka continued: The gopī were delighted to hear Kṛṣṇa's message and asked Uddhava:

"Does Kṛṣṇa ever remember us who were so fond of him, even though he is surrounded by women of princely status now? Does he ever mention us in his conversatioins with you all, and does he recall the most blissful moments we spent with him during the rāsa-dance? Will he ever come back to us and quench the fire of torment that is scorching us on account of our separation from him? We know that to be hopeless is the only way to achieve happiness; yet we are unable to give up hope that one day we shall be re-united with Kṛṣṇa. Everything in Vraja—the cows, the music of the flute, the pastures—reminds us of Kṛṣṇa. Our minds constantly dwell in him. O Lord, Lord of the goddess of prosperity, Lord of Vraja, you alone relieve all suffering; please redeem Gokula from the ocean of suffering."

Overwhelmed by the supreme devotion that he saw embodied in the gopī, Uddhava spent several months in their company, constantly talking about Kṛṣṇa. He thought: "These simple cowherd women have fulfilled the purpose of human birth, whereas the priests and pundits are wasting theirs in the useless pursuits of rites and rituals. These gopī, appearing to be of sinful conduct, are yet more saintly and divine than the holy ones, on account of their supreme devotion to Kṛṣṇa. Let me be reborn as a plant or blade of grass in Vraja so that I may be bathed in the dust of their feet. I salute the dust of the feet of the gopī, who purify the three worlds by singing the glories of Kṛṣṇa."

Uddhava was about to take leave of Nanda and the people of Vraja. They prayed: "May our minds and all our thoughts rest forever in the lotus feet of Kṛṣṇa. May our speech always glorify him. May our bodies bow to him who is all-pervading, and may we ever serve him. Whatever be our destiny, may we ever be devoted to lord Kṛṣṇa."

Uddhava returned to Mathurā and narrated everything to Kṛṣṇa. He fell at Kṛṣṇa's feet and bathed them with the tears of supreme love.

Akrūra; Kubjā
Book Ten Chapter 48

Sage Śuka continued: Lord Kṛṣṇa remembered the promise he had made to Trivakrā, the hunchback whom he had restored to health and beauty. Accompanied by Uddhava, he called on her. She was beside herself with delight. She greeted them and gave them seats and then washed, clothed and decorated herself. Noticing that she was shy, Kṛṣṇa himself drew her to him and allowed her to press his feet to her eager bosom. She embraced him and thus rid herself of her suffering. At her request Kṛṣṇa stayed in her house for several days and then returned to his home, along with Uddhava. One who wins the grace of the Lord, which is most difficult to attain, and then seeks mere gratification of the mind and the senses, is indeed unfortunate.

Kṛṣṇa also remembered the promise he had made to Akrūra, and paid a visit to his house along with Balarāma and Uddhava. Adrūra was in ecstasy, for although Kṛṣṇa and Balarāma were younger than he was, Akrūra recognised their divinity and worshipped them. He prayed to them: "You indeed are the very incarnations of the Lord and his supreme power. You alone create and sustain this universe. You are the indweller of all beings. You are beyond the reach of ignorance. You are not bound by the body, which you apparently wear in sport. You are unborn, eternal and infinite. By your own will you assume a body made entirely of satva, for the preservation of dharma. No wise man should seek any refuge other than you, the friend of all and the giver of all (including yourself). It is our great good fortune that you have graced our house with the dust of your lotus feet; be pleased, O Lord, to snap the bonds of son, wife, wealth, friends, house, body, etc., which are the products of your own māyā."

For his part, Kṛṣṇa replied: "We are but your children; you are our elders. Wise men should worship people like you. Even the gods are selfish, but not so holy men like you. Of course holy rivers and images of god purify the devotee after a considerable period of devotion to them, but the holy ones purify one who beholds them but once. Kindly visit Hastināpura and ascertain what is going on there. The pāṇḍavā have returned from their exile. But, Dhṛtarāṣṭra, who is in the hands of his wicked sons, does not seem to be in a mood to do justice to his nephews. After you have acquired first-hand knowledge of the situation there we shall decide upon the appropriate course of action to protect our friends and devotees."

Book Ten Chapter 49

Sage Śuka continued: Akrūra went to Hastināpura. There he met the aged king Dhṛtarāṣṭra, his sons and counsellors, the great Bhīṣma, the sons of Pāndu and their mother Kuntī. All of them exchanged greetings with Akrūra. Kuntī and Vidura informed Akrūra of the unjust, harsh and partial treatment that the sons of Pāndu were receiving at the hands of the old king, who was completely in the vile grip of his vicious sons.

With tears in her eyes, Kuntī said to Akrūra: "Do my relations in Mathurā remember me at all? How is Kṛṣṇa, my divine nephew; does he have a thought for us, his own people, suffering injustice at the hands of my brother-in-law and his sons? Will he bring us solace and relief from our suffering?" Thinking of Kṛṣṇa, she burst out: "Kṛṣṇa, Kṛṣṇa, the supreme yogi, who is omnipresent, protect me who has taken refuge at your feet, grieving along with my children. I do not see any refuge other than your feet which alone can ensure our liberation. I take refuge in you, O Kṛṣṇa, and I salute you, the supreme being, the Lord of yoga." Akrūra tried to console her by reminding her that her children had been fathered by divine beings, which guaranteed their protection.

Before returning to Mathurā, Akrūra approached Dhṛtarāṣṭra and counselled him: "You have ascended the throne because your younger brother Pāndu passed away. This imposes a tremendous responsibility upon you. You will discharge it nobly and attain prosperity only if you are impartial towards your own sons and your nephews. After all, whatever may be our relationship with others, we do not live with them forever! One is born alone, and one dies alone; and one enjoys the fruits of his good deeds and suffers the fruits of his misdeeds, also alone! Hence, it is useless blaming others for one's own actions. All that one acquires in this world by means righteous or unrighteous, leaves one. Realise that this world is a long dream and be not deluded by attachment to your own, and thus act unjustly towards others."

Dhṛtarāṣṭra however pleaded his inability to adopt the wise counsel of Akrūra, though he appreciated the wisdom. He could not tear his heart away from his sons, though he knew that they were bent on evil. "Who can counter the will of the Lord who has taken birth among the yādavā for the extermination of earth's burden? I salute the Lord whose ways are indeed mysterious," he said.

Akrūra then returned to Mathurā and reported everything to Kṛṣṇa and Balarāma.

Jarāsandha
Book Ten Chapter 50

Sage Śuka continued: Jarāsandha was Kaṁsa's father-in-law. Learning from his daughters that Kṛṣṇa had killed Kaṁsa, Jarāsandha became wild with rage and marched towards Kṛṣṇa's Mathurā with a huge army. Seeing this, Kṛṣṇa reflected: "I should destroy this army of Jarāsandha; but I should not kill him now. If his life is spared he is sure to gather around him more and more wicked people to attack me, and he will thus save me the trouble of finding them! I am born in this world for this purpose alone—to reduce the burden of the wicked people on earth and for the protection of the good. Even so have I had several incarnations in the past in order to protect dharma." Having thus resolved, he approached his brother Balarāma and exhorted him to take immediate steps to protect the people of Mathurā.

At the same time two aerial cars descended near them, equipped with various shining missiles. Mounting them, Kṛṣṇa and Balarāma emerged from the city. Kṛṣṇa blew his conch (or siren) which created panic in the enemy army. Jarāsandha spoke derisively of Kṛṣṇa's youthful appearance and challenged Balarāma. Jarāsandha discharged such a profusion of ballistic missiles at the two divine brothers that they were completely obscured—to the consternation of the women spectators. Soon they emerged from this and returned the fire, which destroyed the entire army of Jarāsandha. In fact, the river that was flowing nearby was covered with the carcasses of animals, chariot wheels, shields, etc. This need not cause any wonder, as the Lord alone creates and sustains the entire universe!

Balarāma seized Jarāsandha and would have killed him but for the intervention of Kṛṣṇa. Jarāsandha was released and allowed to go; he went with his head bowed low with shame. Kṛṣṇa and Balarāma returned to Mathurā, where they presented king Ugrasena with the jewels and the wealth they had recovered from the battlefield.

Again and again Jarāsandha collected an equally large army of wicked soldiers, and invaded the city of Mathurā—seventeen times in all. Every time Kṛṣṇa and Balarāma destroyed the army, but spared Jarāsandha's life. That was Kṛṣṇa's intention. While he was planning the eighteenth invasion, Kālayavana, a chief of the yavanā, invaded Mathurā. Kālayavana had heard from Nārada that only the yādavā rivalled him in strength. Seeing this new development, Kṛṣṇa had an impregnable fortress built almost overnight by the architect of the gods. In this fortress the Lord had the entire population of Mathurā take shelter.

Mucukunda
Book Ten Chapter 51

Sage Śuka continued: As Kṛṣṇa emerged from the gates of the fortress, Kālayavana came forward to challenge him to a duel. As Kṛṣṇa was unarmed, Kālayavana also disarmed himself and pursued Kṛṣṇa on foot. Kṛṣṇa began to run, but all the time seeming to be within the reach of the yavana. Soon Kṛṣṇa entered a cave on the mountainside. Kālayavana followed him, hurling insults at Kṛṣṇa: "Why do you run away from your enemy?" In the cave the yavana found someone asleep and thought it was Kṛṣṇa. He kicked that person with his foot. The sleeping person awoke and, by a mere look at the man who had disturbed his sleep, reduced him to ashes.

It was Mucukunda, a son of Māndhātā, who was asleep in the cave. He had unwinkingly protected the gods over a long period of time. Later, when Guha (the second son of lord Śiva) assumed command of the celestial forces, the gods relieved Mucukunda of his onerous duty and asked him to choose a boon. Mucukunda wished to sleep undisturbed, and the gods granted him this privilege, declaring that anyone who distrubed his sleep would be reduced to ashes. Hence Kālayavana met with his end.

An instant later Kṛṣṇa appeared before Mucukunda. Mucukunda was thrilled to behold the Lord and intuitively knew that he was an incarnate divinity. He questioned the Lord: "By your radiance, which excels the light of the sun, the moon and the fire, I conclude you are an incarnation of Viṣṇu. Pray, tell me who you are, in what family or clan you were born, and what are your qualities and your noble deeds." He introduced himself to Kṛṣṇa and told him how he came to sleep in the cave and how Kālayavana got burnt.

The Lord said: My child, my incarnations and my deeds are countless, and they cannot be renounted even by me! Someone may even count the particles of dust in this world; but no one can count my incarnations, my divine qualities and my deeds. I shall, however, tell you of my present incarnation. In response to the prayer of Brahmā, the creator, I was born as the son of Vasudeva. I have destroyed many wicked people, including Kaṁsa. In fact, even this Kālayavana was burnt by me through your fiery eyes. I willed it so. And, I am here now because in days of yore you had devoutly sought me. Ask of me any boon of your choice.

Thus spoken to by the Lord, the great devotee Mucukunda offered the following prayer to him.

Book Ten Chapter 51

Mucukunda said: Lord, people who are deluded by your own māyā (illusory power) do not worship you, but cling to the house, etc., where they seek pleasure but get only endless pain instead. Having attained a human birth here, which is hard to get, people of wicked disposition do not worship you but fall into this blind well of worldliness. Look at me: I was a haughty ruler and had surrounded myself with powerful men, and mistaking this body as my self had become attached to wealth and worldly relationship. But you yourself as the Time-spirit creep into the life of man, unnoticed by him, and reduce him to naught! The very same body which was designated a king, surrounded by armies and animals, is consumed by time and is then called excrement, ashes or worms!

Lord, even the world-conqueror becomes a prey to lust and therefore a slave to the pleasures of the senses. Or, he performs good and charitable acts, thereby winning a holiday in heaven, even becoming its ruler. But, it is only when one's cycle of birth and death is about to halt that one meets with a holy man; such a meeting generates devotion to you, which puts an end to the transmigration of the soul.

You ask me to choose a boon but you have already conferred on me a great boon by relieving me of the pride of sovereignty. I do not seek any boon other than the constant worship of your feet: who would ever seek any other boon (which would surely bind one's soul) after one has obtained a sight of your divine feet? Hence, I reject all desire for worldly blessings which are within the realm of the three qualities of nature, and take refuge in your feet: you are the supreme person, of the nature of pure consciousness. Tormented by karma and the inner enemies of undivine nature, I have by your grace obtained your vision: protect me O Lord.

The Lord said: It is only to reveal the true nature of your devotion that I offered you a boon! Practise asceticism and get rid of the past sins of hunting etc., though they were incidental to your status as a king. In your next incarnation you will be born as a holy brāhmaṇa and will reach me, without doubt.

Rukminī
Book Ten Chapter 52

Sage Śuka continued: Mucukunda saluted the Lord again. He came out of the cave and noticed that men and animals were small in size: he had obviously been asleep for ages. He understood that kali yuga (the dark age) had set in and decided to go away to the Himālaya to adore lord Nārāyaṇa.

Kālayavana having been killed, his army was easily routed. While Kṛṣṇa was returning to his fort with the booty, Jarāsandha intercepted him. Still not intending to kill him, Kṛṣṇa and Balarāma dropped the wealth they were carrying and began to run, with Jarāsandha at their heels. They ascended a high mountain peak and disappeared in the mist. Unable to see them, Jārasandha set fire to the whole mountain and, thinking they were dead, returned to his city. Kṛṣṇa and Balarāma however leapt from the mountain peak to the plains below and returned to Dvārakā, their fortress.

Some time later the king of Ānartas, named Kakudmī, gave his daughter Revatī in marriage to Balarāma; and Kṛṣṇa married Rukmiṇī in accordance with the rākṣasa (demoniacal) tradition, after carrying her away to the discomfiture of Śiśupāla and others. I shall narrate this interesting story in detail.

Bhīṣmaka was the king of Vidarbha. He had five sons (Rukmī and others) and one daughter (Rukmiṇī). Rukmiṇī had heard of Kṛṣṇa and had fallen in love with him. Kṛṣṇa, too, had made up his mind to marry her. But Rukmī, who hated the Lord, wanted to give her away to his friend Śiśupala. When the date of the wedding had been fixed Rukmiṇī sent a pious brāhmaṇa as her messenger to Kṛṣṇa.

Kṛṣṇa duly welcomed this holy man and revealed: "A contented brāhmaṇa obtains the highest blessings, while a discontented ruler of heaven suffers endless anguish. I salute again and again the holy brāhmaṇa who is contented with what he gets, who is friendly to all and who is free from egoism. Tell me what brought you to us." The brāhmaṇa informed Kṛṣṇa of the developments in Vidarbha and conveyed Rukmiṇī's message to Kṛṣṇa.

Rukmiṇī had said: Lord, having heard of your divine form and of your glories which, entering the heart through the apertures of the ears, remove the distress of one's whole being, (and to behold which is the supreme blessing on earth) my heart has entered into you. I have chosen you as my husband; and it is proper therefore that you should not allow anyone else to touch me. You need not even shed anyone's blood in order to achieve this. On the eve of the wedding I shall go to the temple of goddess Pārvatī. Please be in the vicinity and rescue me from this peril. If you do not, I shall give up my life.

The brāhmaṇa concluded: "This is the message; and now, Kṛṣṇa, do what you consider appropriate."

Book Ten Chapter 53

Sage Śuka continued: The Lord smilingly assured the holy brāhmaṇa that he was deeply in love with Rukmiṇī and had decided to marry her. He then found out from the brāhmaṇa the exact hour of the wedding, and got ready to go. Mounting a fast vehicle he reached the capital of Vidarbha in the course of one night.

In the capital of Vidarbha, the king Bhīṣmaka had made elaborate arrangements for the wedding of his daughter Rukmiṇī. All the scriptural rituals were being performed by brāhmaṇā well versed in them, and the king himself gave away rich gifts in charity. The king of Cedi, for his part, had also made similar preparations to ensure the happiness of his son, the bridegroom Śiśupāla. Śiśupāla and his family drove to the capital of Vidarbha and were accommodated in specially constructed palaces. All the demoniacal friends of Śiśupāla were there, ready to fight in case Kṛṣṇa should cause trouble; they too had all been accommodated in palaces. When Balarāma heard that Kṛṣṇa had gone alone to Vidarbha, he set forth accompanied by an army.

When Bhīṣmaka heard of the arrival of Kṛṣṇa and Balarāma he received them with due honours and special devotion, and lodged them in a palace. Rukmiṇī, who had been impatiently waiting for the return of the brāhmaṇa messenger, was losing hope: "Perhaps Kṛṣṇa has himself decided against accepting my hand, on account of some fault in me." She restrained her tears as she set out for the temple of the goddess. But she was encouraged by auspicious omens she saw. At the same time she saw the brāhmaṇa from a distance; and they communicated with each other without exchanging too many words. Rukmiṇī got the message. She then worshipped goddess Ambikā and prayed that she would soon marry Kṛṣṇa. Those citizens who were watching the procession and knew that Kṛṣṇa was in the city feasted their eyes on Kṛṣṇa and said to one another: "Only Kṛṣṇa is fit to be Rukmiṇī's husband, and Rukmiṇī is meant for Kṛṣṇa."

After the worship Rukmiṇī took part of the offerings she had made to the goddess, as a token of the goddess's blessings. She then left the temple and was walking towards the waiting chariot. Rukmiṇī, who was of exquisite beauty though she had not yet attained puberty, looked for Kṛṣṇa among the assembled princes. These princes, who had been robbed of their senses by her great charm, had for the moment been paralysed, and stood gaping. As she was about to mount her chariot, Kṛṣṇa sprang forward, grapsed her hand and helped her to his own vehicle, while the princes still stood looking on helplessly. However, as Kṛṣṇa's vehicle moved towards Dvārakā, the princes, headed by Jarāsandha, began to say to one another: "What a disgrace: while we great warriors were watching, the cowherds snatched away a princess!"

Book Ten Chapter 54

Sage Śuka continued: The princely comrades of Śiśupāla gave chase to Kṛṣṇa and the yādava army, which soon halted and turned to face the hostile forces. The enemy showered the yādava with formidable missiles. Kṛṣṇa reassured Rukmiṇī, who was afraid, and directed the full force of his divine power on the enemy. The enemy army was soon reduced to nothing, and the princes retreated. They consoled Śiśupāla with the highest wisdom: "Despair not. For in this world pleasure and pain, success and failure, honour and dishonour are not eternal but transient. It is time that brings these in quick succession and he who knows this does not yield to despair or grief."

Rukmī, the elder brother of Rukmiṇī, was inconsolable. Alone among the princes, surrounded by a battalion, he pursued Kṛṣṇa. Hurling abuse at Kṛṣṇa he invited the latter for combat. Quickly Kṛṣṇa destroyed his chariot, horses and flag with his missiles. Whatever weapons Rukmī took up, Kṛṣṇa cut them down with his own missiles in the twinkling of an eye. As Rukmī rushed towards him, Kṛṣṇa caught hold of him and lifted a sword to kill him. But Rukmiṇī pleaded with Kṛṣṇa for the life of her brother. Yielding to her persuasion Kṛṣṇa cut off part of the moustache and locks of Rukmī, who stood there utterly humiliated.

Balarāma soon reached the spot and spoke to all concerned: "It is not worthy of you thus to have disfigured a relative, which is equal to killing him. Where is the need to kill one who is already dead by his own deeds! Indeed, the creator has ordained that a warrior can kill his own brother under certain circumstances: hence a warrior's profession involves great cruelty. And foolish people indulge in cruelty for the sake of worldly objects and objectives. There is no friend nor enemy in this world for anyone. It is only on account of the Lord's deluding power (māyā) that a man considers another as a friend, an enemy or a neutral. In truth, the self is one in all beings; only fools perceive diversity. From the point of view of the omnipresent self there is neither union nor separation—all these and birth, death etc., pertain only to the body. Diversity is perceived by the ignorant man who is spiritually asleep and dreaming. He who is spiritually awake shakes off this perception of diversity and the consequent sorrow and delusion."

Rukmiṇī was consoled. Rukmī who had vowed not to enter his capital city without having defeated Kṛṣṇa and rescued his sister, built another city called Bhojakata and lived there, thus honouring his vow. Kṛṣṇa returned to Dvārakā and in the presence of all his people duly married Rukmiṇī. The people of Dvārakā rejoiced greatly at this most auspicious event.

Birth of Pradyumna
Book Ten Chapter 55

Sage Śuka continued: In course of time Rukmiṇī gave birth to a son. This baby was none other than the god of love, Cupid, who had been burnt to ashes by lord Śiva. This son of Kṛṣṇa later came to be known as Pradyumna and was the very image of the Lord in charm.

The demon Śambara knew that Pradyumna was destined to kill him; and hence sought to destroy the baby. He kidnapped the baby while the mother and child were still in the lying-in chamber, and threw him into the sea. The baby was swallowed by a big fish. The fish was caught (along with others) by a fisherman, who presented it to Śambara. Śambara gave it to the cook who cut the fish open and discovered the baby in its stomach—alive and safe. He gave the baby to a maid-servant of Śambara, known as Māyāvatī, who was none other than Rati, the consort of the god of love. The sage Nārada revealed to her the identity of the baby.

The boy grew up into a young man in the fond and affectionate care of Rati (or Māyāvatī, the maid-servant of Śambara). However her amorous behaviour towards him worried the young man, who still regarded her as his mother. Māyāvatī, however, narrated the whole story concerning his birth, etc., as revealed to her by the sage Nārada, and encouraged him to get rid of the demon Śambara. She also imparted to him the knowledge of Mahāmāyā, the power of illusion, with the help of which he could overcome all manner of spells and charms.

Pradyumna challenged Śambara to a duel. During the fight Śambara used all manner of illusory powers, but Pradyumna remained unaffected by them. Finally, with a sharp sword, Pradyumna severed the head of the demon, to the satisfaction of the gods and good men. Māyāvatī then escorted her lord by air to Dvārakā. As they were descending right into the inner apartments of the palace of Kṛṣṇa, the women hid themselves, thinking that Kṛṣṇa himself had come. Rukmiṇī, too, saw the couple and wondered who they were. Kṛṣṇa came along too, but remained silent, though he knew the truth. The sage Nārada appeared upon the scene and introduced the young couple to all concerned by fully narrating Pradyumna's biography. Rukmiṇī, who had been sorely afflicted by the loss of her first-born son, greatly rejoiced at the happy reunion. In every way the equal of his father, lord Kṛṣṇa, Pradyumna too, won the hearts of all womenfolk.

The Syamantaka Gem
Book Ten Chapter 56

Sage Śuka continued: In Dvārakā there was a devotee of the sun-god, named Satrājit. One day the sun-god gave Satrājit an extraordinary gem known as Syamantaka, which was exceedingly brilliant and which had the power of bestowing unlimited wealth upon its owner. Wearing that gem, Satrājit entered Dvārakā. People mistook him for the sun-god himself! Kṛṣṇa suggested to Satrājit that the gem should be handed over to him—as such gems should be in the possession of the king, Ugrasena, and be used for the good of all. But Satrājit did not listen.

On one occasion Prasena, the brother of Satrājit, went into the forest wearing the gem. He was killed by a lion, which was obviously fascinated by the shining gem which it carried away towards a cave. The famous Jāmbavān lived in that cave and he killed the lion and used the gem as a sort of toy to entertain his son. In the meantime, rumour was rife in Dvārakā that Kṛṣṇa had murdered Prasena and robbed him of the gem. In order to extricate himself from this calumny, the Lord, along with some people, pursued the path taken by Prasena. He found Prasena's dead body and signs that he had been killed by a lion. Further on he discovered the carcass of the lion at the mouth of the cave. In search of the gem, Kṛṣṇa entered the cave alone. Sure enough, the gem hung over a cradle!

Seeing Kṛṣṇa, the child's nurse cried aloud. Hearing her cries Jāmbavān appeared upon the scene. There ensued a fierce battle between Jāmbavān and Kṛṣṇa. After several days of fighting, only Jāmbavān, the mighty, felt fatigued. Surprised at this, Jāmbavān addressed Kṛṣṇa: "You are no doubt the Lord himself, the very life of all beings. You are the ancient person. You are the progenitor of the creator himself. You are Time. You are the supreme self of all. You were indeed Lord Rāma in your previous incarnation." When thus recognised and adored by Jāmbavān, Kṛṣṇa revealed to him the mission that brought him there. Jāmbavān gladly gave the gem away to Kṛṣṇa; and along with it he gave his daughter Jāmbavatī, in marriage to the Lord.

Meanwhile, in Dvārakā the people who had returned from the expedition without Kṛṣṇa were sunk in grief. Kṛṣṇa had entered the cave but had not emerged from it for days on end. Kṛṣṇa's mother and also Rukmiṇī and the others observed a vow in honour of the goddess and prayed for Kṛṣṇa's safety. Hence, when Kṛṣṇa returned to Dvārakā along with Jāmbavāti and the gem, they were all exceedingly happy and thanked the goddess for protecting the Lord. Kṛṣṇa invited Satrājit to his court and handed the gem over to him. Satrājit was ashamed of his own mean-mindedness for blaming Kṛṣṇa for the loss of the gem and also for the death of his brother. To make amends he gave his daughter Satyabhāmā in marriage to Kṛṣṇa, and even offered to part with the gem. Kṛṣṇa however asked Satrājit to keep it, but to allow its benefits to be shared by the people of Dvārakā.

Book Ten Chapter 57

Sage Śuka continued: When it was rumoured that the pāṇḍavā had been burnt alive by their cousins the kauravā, Kṛṣṇa went over to Hastināpura. Taking advantage of his absence, Akrūra and Kṛtavarmā arranged for Śatadhanvā to kill Satrājit and take the gem away from him. Śatadhanvā thereupon killed Satrājit while he was asleep and took the gem. Satyabhāmā was grief-stricken at the death of her dear father and immediately drove to Hastināpura to inform Kṛṣṇa of the murder.

Kṛṣṇa immediately returned to Dvārakā, determined to punish the wicked. The frightened Śatadhanvā approached his instigators, Akrūra and Kṛtavarmā, for help. Kṛtavarmā declined to help. Akrūra said: "How can anyone dare to antagonize Kṛṣṇa and Balarāma? Can we oppose Kṛṣṇa who playfully creates, sustains and dissolves this whole universe, and whose divine powers and actions common people do not recognise, deluded as they are by his māyā? Can we oppose him who held up the hill for seven days with one hand? I salute that lord Kṛṣṇa whose actions are all superwonderful, and who is the innermost self of all." Śatadhanvā entrusted Akrūra with the gem and ran away from the city. Kṛṣṇa was soon in hot pursuit of the criminal. Very soon, Kṛṣṇa (who was running on foot even as Śatadhanvā was doing) caught up with the culprit and cut off his head. On examining the body, however, he did not find the gem, and felt sorry: "We have executed him in vain, for the gem is not in his possession." Balarāma suggested that Śatadhanvā must have left it with a friend of his. Balarāma then went to Mithilā to spend some time with king Janaka, and there Duryodhana learnt the art of wielding the mace from Balarāma.

Learning of this, Akrūra left Dvārakā with the gem. Akrūra's father had earned the pleasure of Indra, the god of rain. As a result, wherever he (or his son Akrūra) lived it rained. So it happened that when Akrūra left Dvārakā people noticed evil omens, though probably it was a mere coincidence or the imagination of people; for Dvārakā, where the Lord dwelt, could not be overtaken by evil. However, when he came to know of this, Kṛṣṇa requested Akrūra to return to Dvārakā and said to him: "Surely the gem has been entrusted to you by Śatadhanvā. It belongs to the deceased Satrājit and should therefore be inherited by his daughter's children, as he had no sons. However, you need not give it to Śatyabhāmā, but you may keep it with you as you are a thoroughly trustworthy and pious person. However, in order to dispel the doubts that the gem has created in everybody's hearts, please show it to the court." Akrūra did so. And the people absolved Kṛṣṇa of complicity in the crimes relating to the gem.

He who reads and contemplates this wonderful story will be free from sin and calumny, and will enjoy peace of mind.

Kṛṣṇa's Marriages
Book Ten Chapter 58

Sage Śuka continued: Once, Kṛṣṇa went to Indraprastha in order to see the pāṇḍavā. They and their mother, Kuntī, received the Lord with great affection and veneration. Kuntī said: "Even when you sent Akrūra to enquire about us, we felt that our fortune had turned for the better. You have no illusions concerning your own or other people, for you are the well-wisher and self of all; yet, dwelling in the hearts of those who think of you, you destroy their misery." Kṛṣṇa spent several months with them all.

One day during this period Kṛṣṇa and Arjuna had gone to the forest, where Arjuna saw a charming lady living alone. On enquiry he learnt that she was Kālindī, who had vowed that she would wed none but the Lord himself, and was engaged in severe austerities towards this goal. Arjuna conveyed this information to Kṛṣṇa, who brought her to the city. On another occasion, acting as the charioteer of Arjuna, Kṛṣṇa offered the Khāṇḍava forest to the god-of-fire, who, pleased with this, presented Arjuna with the fire-arm, Gāṇḍīva, and an excellent vehicle. At the same time, as a token of his gratitude for having been rescued from the fire, the demon Maya built Yudhiṣṭhira a palace which was full of optical illusions.

Returning to Dvārakā, Kṛṣṇa duly married Kālindī. A little later, knowing that Mitravindā (the sister of Vinda and Anuvinda, the rulers of Avanti), sought him for a husband, the Lord took her away by force and married her also.

Nagnajit was the king of Kosala and had a daughter Satyā. In an attempt to choose the best suitor for her, the king had stipulated that only he who subdued seven wild bulls could claim her. Many princes had vainly attempted this feat and had returned with their bones broken. One day Kṛṣṇa went to the city and was joyously welcomed by the king. Kṛṣṇa asked for the hand of the princess; and the king, who was exceedingly eager to accede to his request, informed Kṛṣṇa of the vow he had made. The king was aware that his daughter too had mentally chosen Kṛṣṇa as her husband. Kṛṣṇa, by his divine power, multiplied himself into seven, and playfully subdued the seven bulls. The delighted king gave his daughter in marriage to Kṛṣṇa, along with an enormous dowry. The princes who had failed to win the hand of the princess became jealous and tried to intercept Kṛṣṇa as he was returning to Dvārakā with the bride; but Arjuna drove all of them away.

Later Kṛṣṇa married Bhadrā, a daughter of his father's sister. He also carried away a princess known as Lakṣmaṇā, of the Madra kingdom. He rescued and married the princesses whom the wicked Narakāsura had imprisoned.

Sage Śuka continued: The demon Naraka, the son of mother earth, had robbed Indra of his umbrella, and Indra's mother of her ear-rings. Hearing of this Kṛṣṇa flew to Prāgjyotiṣapura, along with Satyabhāmā. The town was surrounded by many fortifications and missiles but Kṛṣṇa reduced these to naught by his gada. The walls of the fort crumbled when assailed by his gada (mace?). The ultrasonic sound of his conch (?) destroyed the missiles outside the fort. At this, the five-headed demon Mura emerged from his submarine abode and rushed at Kṛṣṇa with his trident poised. The demon was like a blazing fire and the sun together! His roaring shook the earth. With two missiles Kṛṣṇa split the trident into three, and later hit the demon in the mouth. Mura hurled his mace at Kṛṣṇa and Kṛṣṇa returned the compliment. The next instant Kṛṣṇa cut off the five heads of the demon, whose body fell into the ocean like a mountain.

Mura's seven sons then gave battle to Kṛṣṇa, but Kṛṣṇa pulverised the weapons wielded by the demons and killed them, too.

Naraka himself then attacked Kṛṣṇa. He was surrounded by seaborne elephants (warships?) Seeing Kṛṣṇa seated in a space vehicle with Satyabhāmā, Naraka hurled a dreadful missile at him. Kṛṣṇa replied with unusual missiles endowed with two wings, which destroyed the army of Naraka with unfailing precision. Flying on his vehicle Garuḍa, Kṛṣṇa inflicted destruction upon the demon's elephants (tanks?), which withdrew into the city. Then Naraka fought Kṛṣṇa single-handed. He hurled at Garuḍa the dreadful missile which he had earlier used successfully against Indra's thunderbolt. This was ineffective. As Naraka was about to hurl another missile at Kṛṣṇa, the latter struck the demon down with his discus (revolver). The demon's friends bemoaned the loss; the holy ones rejoiced.

The mother of the demon thereupon returned to Kṛṣṇa the pair of ear-rings, a garland known as Vaijayantī and the umbrella belonging to Varuṇa, and also the Maṇiparvata. She prayed to Kṛṣṇa: "Salutations to the Lord whose navel has a lotus, who is adorned by a garland of lotus, whose eyes resemble a lotus and whose hands are like lotus. Salutations to the supreme person. You are the creator and the Lord of all the elements. Kindly bless this boy, the son of Naraka."

Having blessed the boy, the Lord entered the palace of Naraka, where the demon had imprisoned sixteen thousand princesses. He freed them and they unanimously sought him as their husband. By his divine power Kṛṣṇa multiplied himself into as many persons, and creating as many mansions, he led the life of an ideal householder in the company of these consorts.

Book Ten Chapter 60

Sage Śuka continued: One day the Lord was resting, attended upon by the maids of the royal household. Rukmiṇī, who was extremely devoted to the Lord, took the fan from the hands of one of the maids, eager to render that service to the Lord herself. She was most glorious to behold; and she herself was absorbed in lovingly gazing at the Lord and serving him. With a charming smile playing upon his lips and countenance, Kṛṣṇa said to her:

"Beloved One! I wonder what made you choose me, in preference to all those great princes, great warriors and men of great wealth and power. You are a princess; and in no way am I your equal. As a matter of fact, afraid of the wicked kings I have taken refuge in the ocean in which Dvārakā stands. Moreover, to wed one whose occupation is not evident and whose ways are different from the rest of the people of the world, is to court suffering. We are destitute; and we are resorted to by the destitutes: therefore, generally speaking, the wealthy and proud do not seek my company. Marriage or friendship between unequals in the matter of wealth, birth, power and future prospects, has been considered undesirable. Sometimes I feel that you have made a wrong choice, perhaps by mistake, and chosen me whom only beggars glorify and who has no qualities at all. It is not too late even now to correct this error and to choose a worthy partner. Again, you know that all the kings, including your own brother, are hostile to me. It was only in order to subdue their pride that I carried you away. For I have no desires at all for women, children or wealth, since I rest contented in my own self, doing nothing—even as a lamp shines in the house."

These words were exceedingly painful to Rukmiṇī. With tear-bedimmed eyes, shuddering at heart and with her hands powerless even to hold the fan, Rukmiṇī fell down in a swoon. Kṛṣṇa, who was merely teasing her out of affection with words that could be interpreted in two ways, was upset to see that they had upset Rukmiṇī. Embracing her with great affection and soothing her back to normal consciousness, Kṛṣṇa reassured her that he did love her dearly and that he had merely said what he had in order to listen to her rejoinder. "This indeed is the greatest joy of householders," said Kṛṣṇa, "that they can thus spend a few minutes in the company of their partners."

Sage Śuka continued: Thus comforted, Rukmiṇī said to the Lord:

"Surely, I am totally unlike you, Lord. You are the supreme being, adored by the trinity, and I am material nature endowed with different qualities and resorted to by the ignorant. It is true, even as you said, that you rest in the ocean of the devotee's heart, as if afraid of the qualities of nature. True, too, it is that you are the enemy of the wicked senses, and also that even your servants discard as useless the dark evil known as sovereignty. You are truly akimcana (you belong to none and nothing belongs to you) inasmuch as there is nothing other than you. They who are blinded by their possessions do not comprehend your true nature.

"I chose you for my husband knowing full well that you are the Lord, whose glory is sung by the sages who have turned away from all injury and violence. You are the very self of the whole universe. You were obviously jesting when you remarked that you were afraid of the kings and warriors; for the mightiest being on earth trembles in fear on hearing the sound of your weapons. Above all, your lotus feet grant liberation to your devotee. Who will be foolish enough, having once touched them, to turn away and seek the company of someone else? You mentioned the names of a few great princes with strength and valour, but I know that they are the slaves of their own womenfolk, to whom these princes are no better than pet animals. You said you had no desire for womenfolk; nor does a wise woman seek the body of a man as a husband, knowing that the body contains only filth such as flesh, bones, worms, excreta, etc. On the contrary, I seek only the sweet honey that flows from your lotus feet."

Kṛṣṇa was highly pleased to hear this and applauded Rukmiṇī. "I only teased you. You have rightly understood and interpreted the inner meaning of my words. You have rightly resolved. They who have obtained my company, which bestows final liberation, and who yet pray for worldly pleasures are foolish indeed. The wise ones seek liberation alone."

In the same manner Kṛṣṇa sported with his other consorts, assuming numerous forms, though he is ever nameless and formless and immersed in the bliss of his own self, and stands in no need of any other enjoyment.

Sage Śuka continued: Seeing that Kṛṣṇa was always with each one of his numerous consorts, each one thought and felt that he loved her alone. These consorts of Kṛṣṇa were unaware of his true and divine nature. Each bore him ten sons and, though they were skilled in the art of love, they were incapable of distrubing the mind and the heart of Kṛṣṇa. They rejoiced exceedingly in his company and, though there were many servant-maids in each household, preferred to serve him themselves.

Pradyumna and others were born of Rukmiṇī. Bhānu and others were born of Satyabhāmā. Sāmba and others were the sons of Jāmbavatī. Vīra and others were the sons of Nāgnajitī. Śruta and others were born of Kālindī; Praghoṣa and others, of Lakṣmaṇā. Vṛka and others were the sons of Mitravindā, while Sangrāmajit and others were born of Bhadrā. Dīptimān and others were the sons of Rohiṇī (the principal one of the sixteen thousand princesses espoused by Kṛṣṇa).

Pradyumna married Rukmavatī, the daughter of Rukmī, and begot through her the reputed Aniruddha. Rukmavatī had chosen Pradyumna for her husband for he was incarnate cupid himself. And, at her request, Pradyumna carried her away despite the opposition of the other princes assembled as her suitors. Rukmī bore a terrible grudge against Kṛṣṇa; but he did not wish to displease his sister Rukmiṇī, Pradyumna's mother.

For similar considerations, Rukmī gave away his grand-daughter, Rocanā in marriage to Pradyumna's son Aniruddha. For that wedding, Kṛṣṇa, Balarāma and other distinguished princes had assembled at Bhojakaṭa. Rukmī's evil counsellors prodded him to invite Balarāma for a game of dice and to defeat him, thus dishonouring him in public. Balarāma was not an expert in the game, though he was found of it. Rukmī won successive games, and the stakes were increased for every game. When the stakes were very high, Balarāma won! They played the next game for even higher stakes. Balarāma won again. Rukmī resorted to foul-play and declared that he had won. An incorporeal voice declared Balarāma to be the victor. Rukmī ignored it and on top of it, began to insult Balarāma: "You are a cowherd; what do you know of the game of dice which is a royal pastime?" Angered by this, Balarāma took an iron rod and killed the wicked Rukmī and other rulers who challenged him. Kṛṣṇa watched all this silently, neither saying 'this is good' nor 'this is not good', in order that he might not offend either Balarāma or Rukmiṇī.

The party then returned to Dvārakā.

Book Ten Chapter 62

Sage Śuka continued: The Lord's grandson Aniruddha also married Ūṣā, the daughter of Bāṇa.

Bāṇa was the eldest of Bali's children and he was generous and noble like his father. He ruled the wonderful city named Śoṇitapura. Bāṇa was highly devoted to lord Śiva who, pleased with him, granted him a boon of his choice. Bāṇa asked that Śiva should guard his city all the time. Thenceforth, Śiva stood guard at the gate of Śoṇitapura.

One day Bāṇa, full of pride of power, went to Śiva and said: "I salute lord Mahādeva, the guru of the whole universe, who fulfills all the desires of the people. Lord, you have bestowed a thousand arms upon me, but I have no one to fight with; and my thousand arms itch for a fight. I consider you are the only one whom I can truly challenge." Laughing at his insolence, Śiva replied: "Wait O fool, on the day your flag falls, one who is my equal will quell your pride."

Bāṇa had a daughter named Ūṣā. This little girl one day dreamt that she was being embraced by a charming youth; she opened her eyes to see that she was alone. Distraught with love, she kept muttering: "Where are you, my beloved?" Her friend Citralekhā painted the portraits of many gods, celestials and earthly princes; and Ūṣā recognised Aniruddha as the one who had sought her in her dream. Citralekhā, who possessed supernatural powers, abducted Aniruddha from Dvārakā, while he was asleep.

In the heavily guarded inner apartments of Bāṇa's palace, Aniruddha and Ūṣā were living a happy life. The guards of the apartments did not fail to notice that Ūṣā was no longer a virgin. They reported the matter to the king, who stormed into the inner apartments and discovered the truth. The powerful Aniruddha knocked down several of Bāṇa's soldiers. While he was doing so, Bāṇa bound Aniruddha with fetters of snakes. Seeing her lover thus bound, Ūṣā wailed aloud.

Sage Śuka continued: In Dvārakā, Aniruddha's disappearance caused concern, till the sage Nārada informed them of the facts. With a big army, Kṛṣṇa and Balarāma invaded Bāṇa's capital. The guardian deity, Śiva, along with his dreadful followers, defended the city. The spectacular battle that ensued attracted even the celestials, who witnessed it with hairs standing on end. Bāṇa's every missile was effectively replied to by Kṛṣṇa: Brahmāstra was stopped by Brahmāstra, the wind-missile was neutralised by the hill-missile, the fire-missile by rain-missile, lord Śiva's own missile by the Nārāyaṇa-missile. Confusing lord Śiva with the missile that causes confusion, Kṛṣṇa routed Bāṇa's army. Even Skanda retreated from the field and several of the enemy army generals were killed.

Bāṇa came rushing towards Kṛṣṇa wielding a most terrible weapon with five hundred nozzles and two missiles fixed to each nozzle. Kṛṣṇa knocked it out of Bāṇa's hand. Finding that her son was in great danger, Bāṇa's mother stood naked on the battlefield. While Kṛṣṇa averted his eyes from her, Bāṇa retreated and escaped into the city. But the fight continued between the forces of Śiva and those of Kṛṣṇa. A three-headed and three-legged being called jvara (the spirit of fever) now rushed towards Kṛṣṇa, who released his own jvara to stop Śiva's jvara. Kṛṣṇa's jvara scorched Śiva's jvara which, thus defeated, bowed to Kṛṣṇa and prayed that he should withdraw his own jvara. Kṛṣṇa did so and also ordained: "He who remembers this encounter of ours will not be affected by you (fever)."

Bāṇa returned to the battlefield and fought with his thousand arms. Soon Kṛṣṇa cut off almost all of Bāṇa's arms. Seeing this, lord Śiva pleaded: "You are the supreme being whose body is the universe! Kindly spare the life of this devotee of mine, Bāṇa." Kṛṣṇa replied: "I cut off his arms to quell his pride. I shall not kill him, for it has been my promise to Prahrāda that I shall not kill anyone born in Prahrāda's family. Bāṇa still has four hands, and though a demon, he will live in peace and happiness."

Bāṇa thereupon presented Kṛṣṇa with Aniruddha and Ūṣā, and retired into his city. Kṛṣṇa, accompanied by his son and new daughter-in-law and others, returned to Dvārakā, whose citizens were extremely delighted to welcome them back.

Sage Śuka continued: One day some of Kṛṣṇa's sons and others were playing in a garden, when they felt thirsty. They went to a well and found in it the body of a huge chameleon. They reported this to Kṛṣṇa, who went to the place to investigate. At his touch, the chameleon was transfigured into a charming prince, who, upon being questioned by Kṛṣṇa, narrated his own story as follows:

"I was a king named Nṛga and I am the son of Ikṣvāku. I was highly reputed for my charity, which was unbounded. I must have given away in charity as many cows as there are particles of sand on earth, stars in the heaven and drops of rain fallen on earth. The recipients of this charity were brāhmaṇā who were devoted to truth, austerities and study of the vedā.

"On one occasion the cow belonging to a brāhmaṇa had strayed into the herd that I had got ready to give away in charity. While the brāhmaṇa who had received the herd was driving it away, the brāhmaṇa to whom that single cow belonged, claimed ownership. The dispute was brought to me and I tried to pacify them, but could not. In the meantime, my body dropped and I was taken to the abode of Yama who asked me: 'Would you like to reap the fruits of your evil deeds or those of your noble deeds, innumerable as the latter are?' I chose to suffer the consequences of my evil deeds first. Yama therefore ordained that I should descend into the earth-plane as as chameleon. Yet my noble deeds had vouched for me the memory of my past birth. I was devoted to you then, and hence I am overjoyed to behold you."

The king bowed to the Lord, took leave of him and ascended the space vehicle which had arrived in the meantime to transport him to heaven. Kṛṣṇa then said to the assembled people: "Beware of unjustly dealing with a brāhmaṇa or of misappropriating his property. The brāhamaṇa's property is like fire which will destroy one who deals unjustly with it. He who misappropriates a brāhmaṇa's property without the latter's permission destroys three generations. He who robs a brāhmaṇa by force destroys ten generations before and ten generations after himself. Kings who covet the property of brāhmaṇa fall into the most terrible hells. May the property of a brāhmaṇa never find its way into my treasury! I adore the brāhmaṇa; and I exhort you to do so too. King Nṛga's story is an illustration of the fate of one who misappropriates the property of a brāhmaṇa, whether knowingly or unknowingly."

All of them then returned to their palace.

Sage Śuka continued: Balarāma was eager to see his friends and relations in Vraja and so went there. He was fondly greeted by the cowherds and the cowherdesses of Vraja. They made enquiries of their relations and friends in Dvārakā. They spoke of Kṛṣṇa: "Does he ever think of us?" they asked. They recalled the glorious period of his life in their midst. The cowherdesses wondered if the women of Dvārakā reposed faith in the words of Kṛṣṇa and if so, how! For Kṛṣṇa, appearing to be extremely fond of the gopī of Vraja, was yet able to snap the bonds of affection in a moment. "No one can withstand the loving glances and smiles of Kṛṣṇa," said another gopī, "and so even the women of Dvārakā succumb to him." Yet another gopī suggested: "If he can live without us, we should also learn to live without him; let us therefore talk of something else." Yet, they were irresistibly drawn to him, to his stories and glories. Balarāma, too, participated in the conversation and thus brought great joy to the gopī. Thus he spent two months in their midst.

A gentle breeze was blowing on the banks of the Yamunā. It was the full moon day and Balarāma was sporting with the gopī on the banks of the Yamunā. An intoxicating beverage known as vāruṇī issued from one of the trees in the forest. Drawn by its fragrance, Balarāma went up to that tree and drank the beverage. He was slightly intoxicated and in that state he roamed the forest. He called out to Yamunā to change her course and flow towards where he was so that he could bathe and sport with the gopī. Dismissing his command as the chatter of an intoxicated person, Yamunā did not pay any heed. Enraged, Balarāma took his plough and threatened to split the river Yamunā into a hundred small streams! He actually began to drag her by the end of his plough—making a deep furrow with the plough through which the Yamunā had to flow.

Yamunā pleaded for the Lord's mercy. "For a moment I had forgotten that you are the Lord himself. I take refuge in you. Pray, let me flow in a single stream as before," Yamunā prayed. Balarāma granted that prayer. Then he entered the water of the river along with the gopī and sported therein.

O king Parīkṣit, even today the Yamunā flows along the altered course, as a tribute to the strength and power of Balarāma.

Sage Śuka continued: While Balarāma was in Vraja, Pauṇḍraka, who was the king of Karūṣa, sent a messenger to Kṛṣṇa in Dvārakā, with a stern warning that he (Kṛṣṇa) should not consider himself Vāsudeva, as Pauṇḍraka was Vāsudeva. "Surrender your weapons and yourself to me," said Pauṇḍraka. When this message was conveyed to him, Kṛṣṇa and the others laughed heartily. Kṛṣṇa conveyed to Pauṇḍraka through the same messenger an equally stern warning that he desist from impersonation. Quickly following upon this Kṛṣṇa invaded Kāśi, where the ruler of Karūṣa was at that time.

Seeing this, both the king of Kāśi and Pauṇḍraka, the king of Karūṣa, marched with their armies out of the city. Pauṇḍraka had dressed himself like Kṛṣṇa, had the same weapons, (sudarśana etc.), the same yellow robe, the same garland, crown and all—all of which betrayed their imitation and artificiality. Kṛṣṇa laughed at this imitation of himself.

Pauṇḍraka's forces began to attack Kṛṣṇa and Kṛṣṇa easily destroyed them. Kṛṣṇa then closed in on Pauṇḍraka himself, destroyed his vehicle and then cut off his head. Immediately after that he severed the head of the king of Kāśi and had it transported by his missile into the city, so that it fell at the entrance to the palace. Pauṇḍraka, who had impersonated Kṛṣṇa, looked like him and thought of him constantly, ascended to heaven wearing a body like Kṛṣṇa. Kṛṣṇa and his people returned to Dvārakā.

In Kāśi, when they discovered that their king had been killed there was great mourning. The king's son vowed to avenge his father's death. With the help of the family priest he worshipped Śaṅkara, who offered him the boon of his choice. The prince revealed his intention and lord Śiva advised him to perform a special ritual, which he did. Out of that fire emerged a terrible being like a column of fire, which rushed towards Dvārakā. The people of Dvārakā were frightened and they resorted to the lotus feet of lord Kṛṣṇa.

Kṛṣṇa, who was omniscient, knew what that pillar of fire was, and also that such malevolent forces were powerless towards people who were devoted to holy men. Kṛṣṇa halted that pillar of fire with the fire generated by his own discus. The latter pushed the pillar of fire away and it returned to its own sender and destroyed the prince and the priests who organised the ritual for him. Lord Śiva had warned the prince that the power engendered by the ritual would not work against one who was devoted to holy men, but the prince in his passion to kill his father's killer did not heed that part of the advice.

He who contemplates this holy story is freed from all sins.

Balarāma and Dvivida
Book Ten Chapter 67

Sage Śuka continued: In those days there lived a vānara (usually regarded as a monkey), Dvivida by name, who was a friend of Narakāsura whom Kṛṣṇa had killed. To avenge his friend's death this vānara caused havoc in the land, especially in the environs of Kṛṣṇa's territory. He was endowed with the strength of ten thousand elephants, so the story goes. He caused landslides which destroyed houses. He stirred up tidal waves which flooded the seaside dwellings. He even dared to disturb the peace of the hermitages and to desecrate their rituals. In sadistic play he imprisoned men and women and even violated the latter.

One day, he heard sweet music in the neighbouring Raivataka hill, and went there. He saw Balarāma sporting with a group of ladies. The mad vānara, whose day of reckoning had arrived, began to destroy the forest and even to tease the women. The women laughed aloud, seeing his monkey-tricks. Balarāma was angered and he hit the vānara with a stone. The vānara dodged it, but continued to tease the womenfolk.

There then ensued a fierce battle between Balarāma and Dvivida, during which they hurled trees and stones at each other. Even though hit and wounded by Balarāma's powerful pestle, the vānara continued to fight. With his clenched fists Dvivida hit Balarāma hard on his chest. Lord Balarāma put away his other weapons and hit the vānara with his fist; his collar-bone broken, the vānara fell dead, vomiting blood.

Gods and holy men were watching the battle from their aerial vehicles; and they showered flowers on lord Balarāma, uttering their blessings: "Victory, victory to you!" and "Salutations, prostrations!" and "Well done, well done!" Having destroyed Dvivida, who was destroying the world, Balarāma returned to his own city, glorified by the people.

Book Ten Chapter 68

Sage Śuka continued: Kṛṣṇa's son by Jāmbavatī, Sāmba, abducted

Duryodhana's daughter, Lakṣmaṇā, during a convention held for her to choose a suitable partner. The kauravā pursued Sāmba, hurling abuse at him. Six great warriors, including Duryodhana himself, caught up with Sāmba and began to assail him with missiles. Sāmba, the son of Kṛṣṇa, was greatly enraged when several warriors thus attacked him, contrary to rules of warfare. Single-handed he showered missiles at all six of them, hitting their horses, their vehicles and themselves all at the same time. However, they overpowered him on account of their superior number, bound him and returned to their capital Hastināpura.

The yādavā heard of this outrage to Kṛṣṇa's son through the lips of the sage Nārada. Commanded by the king Ugrasena they were getting ready to invade Hastināpura, but they were stopped by Balarāma who did not approve of a major war on such a minor issue. He volunteered instead to go to Hastināpura and free Sāmba from the hands of the kauravā.

Reaching the outskirts of Hastināpura, Balarāma sent Uddhava with a message to the kauravā. The kauravā were delighted to hear that Balarāma had come to their city, but were not so pleased when he asked them to release Sāmba. Their wisdom overpowered by haughtiness caused by the illusion of power and might, they spoke derisively of the yādavā: "They enjoy the rulership of a kingdom at our sweet will and pleasure; see how they who are but shoes, claim the privilege of adorning our heads! How strange that they should command us and tell us what to do!"

Balarāma's anger was roused, "I shall destroy all of them," he said, and with his divine weapon (the plough) he began to uproot the entire city of Hastināpura and to drag it towards the Gaṅgā. The whole city shook, and the hearts of its inhabitants shook, too. The kauravā surrendered; they took both Sāmba and Lakṣmaṇā to Balarāma, and prayed to him: "Lord forgive us, who had forgotten your real glory. You uphold the entire earth; and in the end, after the cosmic dissolution, you alone exist. Salutations to the self of all beings and the wielder of all powers. We take refuge in you." Duryodhana not only gave his daughter in marriage to Sāmba, but bestowed rich presents upon the couple. Balarāma thereupon returned to his city, Dvārakā, and narrated the events to the assembled chiefs. Even today Hastināpura inclines towards the river Gaṅgā.

Sage Śuka continued: The sage Nārada heard that Narakāsura had been killed and that lord Kṛṣṇa had married the sixteen thousand princesses whom he had liberated from bondage to Naraka. This greatly astonished him, and he wondered how Kṛṣṇa lived. In order to see the great wonder for himself, he went to Dvārakā.

Dvārakā was a wonderful city whose landscape was studded with parks and gardens inhabited by varieties of birds; and lakes, big and small, whose surfaces were adorned by lotuses and swans. The city had nine hundred thousand mansions whose walls were of crystal, gold, silver and precious stones. Its layout had been beautifully planned; its roads, squares, markets, temples, etc., left nothing to be desired. The architect of the gods, Viśvakarmā, himself had designed and built it.

Nārada entered one of the mansions. In it the Lord was seated on a couch with Rukmiṇī. Seeing the sage enter the house, the Lord immediately sprang forward, greeted him, bowed to him, washed his feet and sprinkled that holy water on his own head, and made him sit on the couch. The Lord, who is the preceptor of the whole world, thus revealed his devotion to holy men. Hence it is that he is known as brahmaṇya-deva. The Lord then said to Nārada: "Pray tell us in what manner we may serve you?" The sage only prayed that the Lord's feet might forever be enshrined in his heart.

To satisfy his curiosity further, Nārada went to another house—there again he saw Kṛṣṇa and his consort engaged in different household duties, and there again Kṛṣṇa greeted him and worshipped him. From house to house, Nārada went. In every house he saw Kṛṣṇa and his consort—in each house Kṛṣṇa was engaged in one or the other of the household or religious duties. In the last house Nārada expressed his admiration of the Lord's divine powers, to which the Lord replied: "Holy one, I am the propounder of dharma, I practise dharma, I approve of dharma. I instruct others in dharma by my own example."

Marvelling at the supernatural powers of Kṛṣṇa, Nārada took leave of him. Thus did the Lord live the ideal life of a householder with his numerous consorts. He who contemplates this great truth will develop intense devotion to the Lord.

Sage Śuka continued: Śrī Kṛṣṇa would wake up in brāhma-muhūrta (two and a half hours before sunrise) and wash himself. Then he would meditate on the self which is beyond darkness, the one self-effulgent, infinite, eternal and pure being, designated by the name Brahman, whose infinite potentialities are indicated by creation, preservation and destruction of the universe. He would then bathe, don pure clothes and perform the dawn-worship and recite the holy gāyatrī mantra. He offered worship to the sun, to the ṛsī of all times and to the manes—all of whom are parts of his own being. He then bowed to the cows, brāhmaṇā, elders and to all beings mentally, for they were all his own self. In the same spirit he gave away rich presents to all—to his wives, his friends and ministers—and bestowed countless blessings upon them.

While the day was still young śrī Kṛṣṇa would ascend his vehicle and drive to the court. When Kṛṣṇa and the others had taken their respective seats the court jesters, musicians, dancers and poets would entertain them, and holy men would chant the vedā. The administrative work would commence.

One day a messenger entered the court and submitted a petition to śrī Kṛṣṇa. He had come on behalf of many kings imprisoned by Jarāsandha. He informed Kṛṣṇa that Jarāsandha was getting more and more despotic by the day and pleaded that the Lord should speedily redress their grievances. The kings prayed: "You are the almighty Lord of the universe and you have incarnated here to protect the good and to destroy the wicked. They who have taken refuge at your feet are freed even from their own past karma. Please free us from prison."

A moment later, Nārada entered the court. Kṛṣṇa himself got up from the throne and bowed to the sage and welcomed him with the greatest reverence. He enquired of Nārada about the welfare of the worlds. Prefacing his reply with the words: "You are omniscient and you know everything," Nārada submitted that Yudhiṣṭhira intended to perform the rājasūya rite which would be attended by all sages and the gods, besides the kings, and that thereby Yudhiṣṭhira would offer worship to śrī Kṛṣṇa. Nārada prayed that śrī Kṛṣṇa should forthwith go to Indraprastha and preside over the rājasūya rite.

Some members of the court, who were eager to get rid of Jarāsandha, were not very happy about this new proposition. Kṛṣṇa turned to Uddhava and asked for his wise counsel: "You are my own eye and you know what is the right thing to do. I have complete faith in you. Tell me what should be done and I shall do accordingly."

Book Ten Chapter 71

Uddhava said: Lord, devarṣi Nārada's suggestion achieves both objects. If Yudhiṣṭhira has resolved to perform the rājasūya, the conquest of the despot Jarāsandha is implied by it. Which means, again, the liberation of the imprisoned kings. But I have a suggestion to make: and that is that Jarāsandha must be disposed of in a duel, and not in organised warfare. He is devoted to brāhmaṇā and always obeys them. I suggest, therefore, that Bhīma should disguise himself as a brāhmaṇa and trick Jarāsandha into a duel. With your grace, Bhīma should succeed. And people will celebrate this, too, as your glory.

Sage Śuka continued: The plan was perfect, and the counsel was wise. Everybody approved of it. Kṛṣṇa instructed all concerned to prepare for the journey to Indraprastha. He reassured the imprisoned kings, through their own messenger, that their freedom was at hand. The Lord, accompanied by the queens and their retinue, got ready to leave for Indraprastha. The sage Nārada was delighted to see this and left by air, with Kṛṣṇa's permission.

Crossing many states on the way, Kṛṣṇa reached Indraprastha. The entire city wore a festive appearance. King Yudhiṣṭhira, his brothers and friends, awaited Kṛṣṇa's arrival at the gates. Fondly embracing śrī Kṛṣṇa, the abode of Lakṣmī, the king's eyes shed tears of love, his whole being experienced a thrill of joy, and his mind had abandoned the delusion of world-consciousness and had risen above the realm of inauspiciousness. His brothers, too, embraced Kṛṣṇa, who then worshipped the holy ones. Escorted by them, Kṛṣṇa entered the city.

There were flags and festoons everywhere. Golden arches greeted the Lord. There were gold pots filled with water at the threshold of all houses, as a mark of the fullness of heart with which people welcomed him. People wore their best dresses and the fragrance of scents and scented water filled the air. Every housetop had a golden dome on a silver pedestal. Kṛṣṇa admired the beauty and the prosperity of the capital city. Women rushed out of their houses to greet Kṛṣṇa and they envied the good fortune of the queens who accompanied Kṛṣṇa.

Kṛṣṇa entered the palace. When Kuntī, the mother of the pāṇḍavā, saw him, she rose from her seat and embraced him, along with Draupadī, her daughter-in-law. The king, beside himself with joy, even forgot to worship Kṛṣṇa for a time. Then Draupadī offered worshipful welcome to Kṛṣṇa's consorts.

Thus delighting the pāṇḍavā, Kṛṣṇa spent several months in the palace.

Book Ten Chapter 72

Sage Śuka continued: One day king Yudhiṣṭhira said to lord Kṛṣṇa: "I have a longing to worship you and the gods by the performance of the rājasūya rite. I pray to thee, make this possible. For, Lord, they who worship your sandals are rid of all evil, and they who meditate upon them attain liberation and worldly prosperity if they desire it. You are the self of all, and you are impartial. People get the rewards of their service, though you love them all equally."

Kṛṣṇa applauded the king's idea. "You and your brothers are invincible," he said in reply. "You are all born of the gods; and you yourself in particular have won me by your virtue, impossible for those who are not self-controlled. My devotee can never be overpowered in this world."

The king thereupon despatched his four brothers in four directions and himself organised the preparations for the rite. The brothers soon returned with great riches, having conquered the earth. Jarāsandha alone had refused to acknowledge the sovereignty of the king. Seeing the king dejected on account of this, Kṛṣṇa revealed to him Uddhava's plan to overthrow Jarāsandha. Kṛṣṇa, Arjuna and Bhīma went to Jarāsandha in the disguise of brāhmaṇā, and addressed him thus: "O king, may all be well with you! We have a request, if you will grant it. But, what is unbearable to the forbearing, from what will the wicked desist, what will the generous man not give, and who is a stranger to the equal visioned? He who fails to earn eternal fame by using his perishable body is to be pitied. Hariścandra, Rantideva, Śibi, Bali, and the brāhmaṇa, Mudgala, the hunter and the pigeon, and many others had thus attained the eternal, by sacrificing the transient."

Jarāsandha, however, had discovered (through the marks left by the bow on their arms) that these were not brāhmaṇā! Yet, he promised to give them what they wanted. The three discarded their disguise and Kṛṣṇa said: "Let us have a duel!" Jarāsandha himself chose to fight with Bhīma and provided weapons for Bhīma, too. The duel continued for twenty-seven days. During the day the two fought ferociously, but at night they were friends. Bhīma's enthusiasm began to flag. Kṛṣṇa, who knew the secret of Jarāsandha's birth, suggested to Bhīma that only by tearing his body into two could Jarāsandha be killed. During the next duel Bhīma did just that, and Jarāsandha was killed.

The almighty lord Kṛṣṇa, whose lotus feet liberate all beings from the terrible tyranny of birth and death, thereupon freed the kings who had been imprisoned by Jarāsandha.

Book Ten Chapter 73

Sage Śuka continued: Twenty thousand and eight hundred princes had been imprisoned by Jarāsandha! They had not washed their bodies and their clothes were dirty. They were emaciated and their faces were lustreless. They had lost all hope of freedom and they were in abject despair. When they beheld the divine face of śrī Kṛṣṇa all their miseries vanished and it was as if they had gained a new lease of life.

The Princes prayed: Lord, protect us, we have taken refuge at your feet. We harbour no ill-feelings towards Jarāsandha; for we consider it your grace that imprisoned us, because we had foolishly regarded the world as a permanent reality. Even as immature children mistake mirage for water, they whose hearts have not attained at-one-ment with you regard the ever-changing phenomena as enduring reality. Formerly, we had lost our insight to pride born of wealth, and we fought for greater power over others. In this endeavour we ignorantly brought about the destruction of our own peoples and we refused to perceive you standing ever before us in the form of death. It was truly your grace that descended upon us in the shape of Jarāsandha and awakened us to the truth. We have had a glimpse of this truth! And, we shall no longer desire wealth and power. May we be devoted constantly to your feet, Lord, We salute you; kindly instruct us in our duties.

Lord Kṛṣṇa said: You have rightly resolved, O kings! I have seen how wealth and power turn the heads of gods, men and demons, Turn away from the perishable body and the objects associated with it. Worship me. Fulfil the obligations of a householder—beget children, etc.—without being ensnared by pleasure, and protect your subjects. Welcome all that comes to you—pleasure and pain, gain and loss—without reacting to them, but with your heart centred in me. You will be established in the purest love for me.

Sage Śuka continued: The Lord then had all of them given a bath, clean clothes, food, etc., and chariots and jewels appropriate to royalty; they returned to their own territories. Thereafter they devoutly adhered to the Lord's instructions. Kṛṣṇa, Bhīma and Arjuna returned to Indraprastha, where a joyous and fond welcome awaited all of them.

Śiśupāla
Book Ten Chapter 74

Sage Śuka continued: With Jarāsandha thus redeemed, Yudhiṣṭhira sought Kṛṣṇa's blessings to commence the rājasūya rite. He invited all the sages and holy men, and countless other spectators assembled to witness the holy rite. The implements and the vessels used in the rite were all made of gold. Among the spectators were the trinity and the other gods. The rite commenced with their blessings and approval. On a certain day the assembly had to choose a person who was worthy of being accorded the first and the greatest honour.

Sahadeva said: I consider that śrī Kṛṣṇa is the only one who deserves that honour. He is the self of all, the entire universe (nay, this very rite) and the fire, the oblations, the mantrā, knowledge and yoga all hold him to be their goal. He is the self of the whole universe—creating, preserving and dissolving the universe out of himself by himself. He who would wish his gift to be multiplied infinitely should therefore make that offering to śrī Kṛṣṇa. By honouring him, we shall have all beings, including our own self.

Sage Śuka continued: Everyone acclaimed this, except Śiśupāla. Yudhiṣṭhira offered due worship to Kṛṣṇa. Śiśupāla said: "Rightly has it been said that time alone is the Lord. Under the influence of time even wise men make wrong decisions, just as you have done now. When there are great men of learning, austerity, wisdom and valour in this assembly, how can this cowherd be chosen to receive the foremost honour? He does not conform to any social order and is outside all codes of conduct; he defies scriptural injunction and accepted tradition. How can he be given the first place of honour?" Śiśupāla's merits had been exhausted. Kṛṣṇa did not say a word in reply. In accordance with the dictum ('He descends to hell, who, on hearing the Lord and his devotees ridiculed, does not leave the place') several holy men walked out of the assembly, and others rose up against Śiśupāla. Kṛṣṇa pacified them, in an instant cutting off Śiśupāla's head with his discus. To the amazement of all a light emerged from Śiśupāla's body and entered Kṛṣṇa: had not Śiśupāla constantly meditated upon Kṛṣṇa, though out of hatred? And this was the third incarnation of lord Viṣṇu's gate-keepers Jaya and Vijaya. The rite concluded. Everyone was highly pleased, except Duryodhana.

After spending some more time with Yudhiṣṭhira and the others, śrī Kṛṣṇa returned to Dvārakā with his retinue.

He who studies the stories of the redemption of Jarāsandha and Śiśupāla is freed from all sins.

Duryodhana's Humiliation
Book Ten Chapter 75

King Parīkṣit asked: O Sage, you said that everyone was pleased with the rite except Duryodhana. Why was he not pleased?

Sage Śuka continued: At the commencement of the rājasūya rite, Yudhiṣṭhira had appointed his brothers and others to look after various departments of activities. Bhīma was in charge of the kitchen. Suyodhana (Duryodhana's real name!) was in charge of the treasury. Sahadeva was to welcome the guests. Nakula was in charge of the stores. Arjuna served the holy ones. Kṛṣṇa himself washed the feet of all the guests. Draupadī served food to all. Karṇa, the magnanimous, bestowed gifts on all. These and the others discharged their duties well, eager to please the king.

On conclusion of the rite, Yudhiṣṭhira went to the holy Gaṅgā to have his ritual bath. Everyone, including the celestials, rejoiced. Śrī Kṛṣṇa, too, engaged himself in water-sports along with his consorts and they sprayed water on one another. Their wet clothes clung to their beautiful bodies and revealed their shapeliness. This innocent sport, however, raised wicked feelings in the hearts of impure people.

After the emperor had concluded his ritual bath, all the people bathed in the holy Gaṅgā and thus washed away their sins. The emperor, who saw God and God alone in all, then bestowed gifts on all the people, as an act of worship of the omnipresent Lord. After this, while most of the invited guests had taken leave of the emperor, some remained behind at his special request.

All the material affluence and spiritual glory on the part of his rival generated jealousy in the heart of Duryodhana. His heart was afire with jealousy to see Draupadī (to whom he was still greatly attached) lovingly serve her husbands. Something else added fuel to the fire. One day he was entering the court while Yudhiṣṭhira was seated there with his brothers and friends, surrounded by men and women. The celestial architect, Maya, had introduced optical illusions in his construction of the palace, thus the floor appeared to be a pool of water, and vice versa. Duryodhana fell into this trap, lifted his clothes up at the former and fell into the pool at the latter.

Encouraged by a smile from śrī Kṛṣṇa, the ladies laughed, though Yudhiṣṭhira tried to restrain them. Duryodhana was deeply hurt; and he immediately left for Hastināpura. It was no one's fault: the divine will of Kṛṣṇa was inexorable.

Śālva
Book Ten Chapter 76

Sage Śuka continued: Śālva, who was a friend of Śiśupāla, witnessed the discomfiture of the latter during Rukmiṇī's abduction by Kṛṣṇa, and had at that time vowed to exterminate the yādavā community. In order to accomplish his aim he undertook a very hard penance. Living on a handful of dust per day, he worshipped lord Śiva, who is easily propitiated. When in response to his devotion lord Śiva granted him a boon, Śālva asked for an aircraft which he could take where he willed, which could not be destroyed by the gods, demons or men, and which would bring terror to the yādavā. Lord Śiva granted this request; and the celestial architect, Maya, fashioned such an aircraft, called Saubha. It was made of steel and looked like a mini-city. It was totally dark within. It was inaccessible to anyone. It would go wherever its owner wished to go.

Seated in it, Śālva laid siege to Dvārakā while his army began to destroy its suburbs. Deadly missiles were showered by Śālva from the aircraft, Saubha. Kṛṣṇa's son Pradyumna came to the rescue of the yādavā, who were in distress. With his own missiles Pradyumna pierced the magic spell with which Saubha was surrounded and began to harass the aircraft, Śālva and his army. Saubha had been so designed by Maya that it appeared as many and as one; it appeared and disappeared, and others could not know where it was. It appeared to be on the ground and then it instantly appeared in the sky, on hill-tops or on water, Its movements were like that of a firebrand, without stopping at any one place even for an instant. The yādavā army hit relentlessly at the aircraft and the army of Śālva until Śālva himself fainted.

Dyumān, who had received many hits from the missiles discharged by Pradyumna, suddenly sprang upon Pradyumna and hit him on the chest with his heavy mace. With his chest apparently broken, Pradyumna fell into a deep swoon. His charioteer, with great presence of mind, immediately drove the chariot away from the field and thus saved the hero. When Pradyumna regained consciousness, however, he rebuked the charioteer for taking him off the battlefield—which could be interpreted as a cowardly action. For his part, the charioteer humbly replied that it was his duty, when the master's life was in danger, to avert such a calamity.

Book Ten Chapter 77

Sage Śuka continued: Pradyumna ordered his charioteer to take him back to the battlefield, and challenged Dyumān. Pradyumna hit Dyumān's horses, charioteer and Dyumān himself. The yādavā warriors mowed down the warriors in the army of Śālva and thus the fierce battle continued.

Kṛṣṇa, who was returning to Dvārakā from Indraprastha, saw evil portents which signified calamities. Soon after his return to the capital he found out what was going on; he placed Balarāma in charge of the defence of the city and he himself rushed to where Śālva was. Śalvā aimed his lance at Kṛṣṇa, which the latter broke into several pieces. Kṛṣṇa then showered missiles at the aircraft of Śālva. At the same time Śālva discharged a missile which hit Kṛṣṇa's arm and knocked away the weapon. The spectators marvelled at this feat and, proud of this achievement, Śālva hurled insults at the Lord. Kṛṣṇa calmly replied: "Heroes do not brag, their action is louder than their words."

Kṛṣṇa hit Śālva on the collar-bone. Śālva vomited blood and suddenly disappeared. A little while later a stranger appeared there with a message from Devakī: "Śālva has abducted your father, Vasudeva." Kṛṣṇa seemed to be upset by this news. At the same time Śālva appeared there, and right in front of the Lord, beheaded Vasudeva. Seeing this Kṛṣṇa remained plunged in sorrow for some time. Parīkṣit, this is the version of some sages who, contradicting their own conviction, ascribe such delusion to Kṛṣṇa. Where is delusion and sorrow born of ignorance; and where is unimpeded wisdom and lordship! He, the dust of whose lotus feet removes primordial ignorance—how can he be subject to delusion? Kṛṣṇa saw the reality, and the illusion created by the magical powers of Śālva vanished and with it the illusory Vasudeva.

Thereupon śrī Kṛṣṇa hit the aircraft with unfailing missiles. The aircraft was shattered and fell into the ocean. Śālva jumped on to the ground and rushed towards Kṛṣṇa. Kṛṣṇa swiftly cut off the arm that held the mace and then took up the discus (revolver) and with it shot Śālva's head.

At this the gods rejoiced and the survivors of Śālva's forces wailed in sorrow. Another friend of Śiśupāla and Śālva, Dantavaktra, now advanced to fight with Kṛṣṇa.

Dantavaktra said to Kṛṣṇa: I am lucky today that you have come before me, for now I shall discharge the debt I owe to my friends, Śiśupāla and others, by killing you. Though you are related to me you are my enemy, even as disease is to one's body.

Sage Śuka continued: Dantavaktra rushed towards Kṛṣṇa on foot, with a mace in hand. Kṛṣṇa jumped down from his chariot and, mace in hand, closed in on him. With one blow on his chest Kṛṣṇa killed Dantavaktra: lo and behold, from the body of the slain demon a ray of light emanated and entered into Kṛṣṇa's body. Śiśupāla and Dantavaktra were Jaya and Vijaya, the gatekeepers to the abode of the Lord.

Now Vidūratha, brother of Dantavaktra, came forward to fight Kṛṣṇa. Without any delay Kṛṣṇa cut off his head with the discus (revolver). After this śrī Kṛṣṇa returned to Dvārakā, his glories and victories being sung by the celestial bards. Thus, the Lord of yoga, śrī Kṛṣṇa, is always victorious, though people with limited vision consider that he is sometimes victorious and at others not.

Balarāma saw that war between the pāṇḍavā and kauravā was inevitable. He desired to remain neutral, and so went away on a pilgrimage. He visited many holy places and came to Naimiṣāraṇya where a number of holy men had assembled and were listening to a discourse by Romaharṣaṇa, a sūta (one born of a brāhmaṇa-woman and a kṣatriya-man). Balarāma noticed that this sūta occupied a place higher than the holy men and, in addition, did not rise to receive him. Balarāma said: "Knowledge does not edify one who is undisciplined and arrogant. For this have I taken birth: to destroy the hypocrites who pretend to be righteous, who are worse than unrighteous men." Saying thus, he killed the sūta.

The holy men assembled there reproached Balarāma: "We had requested him to occupy the elevated seat. By killing him you have incurred the sin of killing a brāhmaṇa. We know you to be the Lord: it is meet therefore that you impose an expiation upon yourself in order to set an example, without in any way compromising the inevitability of death and the invincibility of the missile you have used to kill this sūta." After due consideration, Balarāma said: "The scriptures say that a man himself is born as his son: hence I shall confer upon Romaharṣaṇa's son long life, health and anything else you desire." The holy ones thereupon advised: "Kill the terrible demon Balvala who is harassing us, and then go on a year-long pilgrimage of the country— thereby will you be rid of the sin of killing the sūta."

Book Ten Chapter 79

Sage Śuka continued: On the following full-moon day the religious rites of the sages were obstructed by Balvala's mischief. All kinds of dirt and rubbish rained over the ritual altar and a gigantic demon appeared in the sky. Balarāma brought the flying demon down to the earth with his plough (hala), hit him with his pestle (musala), and thus killed the demon. The gods and the sages showered their blessings upon him.

Immediately Balarāma left on his expiatory pilgrimage. He went to Prayāga, to Pulaha's āśrama, he bathed in the Gomatī, Gaṇḍakī, Vipāśā and Śoṇa rivers, went to Gayā (and offered worship to the manes), then to the confluence of the Gaṅgā and the sea, then to Mahendra hill (where he met Paraśurāma), then bathed in the Godāvarī, Veṇā and Bhīmarathī rivers, and the Pampā lake. After worshipping Kārtikeya he went to Śrīśaila (the abode of Śiva), and then to the holiest mountain, Venkaṭa, in the Drāviḍa territory; then to Kāñcī, to Kāverī, and to Śrīraṅga where Hari dwells; then to Ṛṣabha mountain, and to Mathurā and Rāmeśvaram (one who goes there is purged of all sins); then after bathing in the Kṛtamālā and Tāmraparṇī rivers, he went to the Malaya mountain where he met the sage Agastya; and then to Kanyākumārī, and then to Phālguna Tīrtha and Pañcāpsarasa; after touring Kerala and Trigarta, Balarāma went to Gokarṇa and then to Śūrpāraka; he bathed in Tāptī, Payoṣṇī and Nirvindhyā rivers; he went through the Daṇḍaka forest and then bathed in the Narmadā, and in the Manutīrtha. Thereupon he returned to Prabhāsa where he heard of the terrible war between the pāṇḍavā and the kauravā.

On the day that the final battle between Bhīma and Duryodhana took place, Balarāma went to Kurukṣetra and advised them to desist from the foolish duel. But, remembering each other's insults and hostile acts, they did not listen to him. He felt that it was their destiny to fight and die and so left the place and returned to Dvārakā.

Balarāma then went back to Naimiṣāraṇya where the sages greeted him. He blessed them with self-knowledge, by which they were able to realise the unity of all existence. O Parīkṣit, Balarāma is indeed the supreme being himself. Indescribable is his glory. He who meditates upon the great and glorious deeds of Balarāma develops intense devotion to the Lord.

Kucaila
Book Ten Chapter 80

Sage Śuka continued: There was in those days a poor brāhmaṇa who was a great friend of śrī Kṛṣṇa. This wise man lived the life of a householder, but without craving for sense-pleasure and without attachment to the objects of this world. He did not even dress himself properly, and so was known as Kucaila. His wife never had enough to eat and so earned the nickname Kṣutkṣāmā (endurer of hunger). She often pleaded with him to visit Kṛṣṇa, who would surely help them with some wealth. After some resistance (because he did not like the idea of praying to the Lord for wealth) he agreed to go and see Kṛṣṇa. "What will you give me to take to him as a present?" he asked his wife, who, knowing that one should not go to a king empty-handed, begged a small quantity of parched rice from the neighbours and gave it to him.

With a bliss-filled heart, the brāhmaṇa entered the city of Dvārakā, and then the palace of śrī Kṛṣṇa himself. Forgetting for a moment the queen Rukmiṇī and others, Kṛṣṇa ran forward to greet and embrace the emaciated, ill-clad brāhmaṇa. Kṛṣṇa himself washed the brāhmaṇa's feet and made him sit on his couch. Kṛṣṇa worshipped the brāhmaṇa, whilst Rukmiṇī fanned him. The people of the palace wondered who this brāhmaṇa was, who gained precedence over everybody else in the palace.

Kṛṣṇa said to the brāhmaṇa: "After returning from the house of the preceptor, what have you been doing, O friend? Only few people in this world live like me, a life devoted to duty, devoid of desire for pleasure. What a wonderful time we had in the house of our guru! In this world one should be devoted to one's father and then the guru who is the bestower of wisdom, who is none other than me. Only they lead a fruitful life who, with the help of the words of the guru, cross the ocean of becoming. I am not as well pleased with rites and rituals, austerities and quietude as with service of the preceptor. Do you remember how one day we were out gathering firewood for our preceptor, how we got lost in a storm and how our guru who searched for and found us the next morning was highly pleased with our self-sacrificing service? He then reminded us that a true disciple should sacrifice his very life for the guru and that only thus could one repay the debt he owes to the guru."

Kucaila could only say: "Yes, I remember. But most of all it was my greatest good fortune that I was with you, the goal of all knowledge, in the house of the blessed preceptor."

Book Ten Chapter 81

Lord Kṛṣṇa said to Kucaila: My beloved friend! What have you brought for me from your house? I am not fond of expensive and pompous gifts; but I am delighted to receive from a true devotee, a leaf, a flower, a fruit or even a little water.

Sage Śuka continued: Seeing that Kucaila was too shy to offer the small quantity of parched rice he had brought, and wishing to bless the poor devotee with wealth and happiness, Kṛṣṇa himself caught hold of the little pouch that contained the parched rice. "Ah, this is what I like most," said he and began to eat it. "Not only me, but the whole world is pleased with this gift," he said. As he was about to put another handful into his mouth, Rukmiṇī stopped him! Kṛṣṇa had given away the wealth of the world in return for one handful of the gift.

After spending the night conversing with Kṛṣṇa and enjoying the supreme bliss of the Lord's comapny, Kucaila left in the morning. He recalled the Lord's great love, humility, devotion to the brāhmaṇā, his supreme friendship and easy accessibility. He suddenly remembered that the Lord had not given him wealth; but he said to himself: "Kṛṣṇa obviously did not give me wealth, knowing that the poor man, when he is blessed with wealth, might forget him."

The poor brāhmaṇa found an unbelievable transformation in his village. His house had been transformed into a palace, with pillars of gems, bedsteads of ivory and gold, sculptured lamp-posts holding dazzling jewels which radiated light, and walls of quartz. The womenfolk of the house were well-dressed and well-adorned. He realised it was Kṛṣṇa's blessing. "What wonder," he thought, "he did not even mention this to me! Yet, he made so much of the little parched rice I had taken as my offering to him! May I be devoted to him, as his friend and servant, birth after birth! The Lord can surely bestow the wealth of the world on his devotee; but, knowing that such a blessing would prove to be a curse, he withholds it from his devotee."

Thus resolved, the poor brāhmaṇa lived in a householder's life without any attachment to wealth and pleasure, and his devotion to the Lord increased day by day. He who listens to this account of the

Lord's love for the holy ones, grows in the love of the Lord and is rid of karma.

Book Ten Chapter 82

Sage Śuka continued: On the occasion of a total eclipse of the sun, people from all parts of the country assembled at Samantapañcakam. That is the place where Paraśurāma filled five lakes with the blood of the wicked princes whom he executed. The yādavā were there, with Kṛṣṇa and his sons and grandsons. They had their bath in the sacred waters and worshipped the Lord according to tradition. Hearing this, the gopā and gopī of Vṛndāvana also reached Samantapañcakam. The reunion of Nanda and Vasudeva was a touching and moving sight. The yādava women and the gopī were delighted to meet and greet one another. The whole atmosphere was surcharged with love. Everyone talked of śrī Kṛṣṇa.

The kings and rulers of many states praised the yādavā: "Of all the people on earth, you are the most blessed, inasmuch as the Lord, for whose vision great yogī aspire, is constantly with you. You even enjoy blood-relation with him. You see him, you eat with him, you touch his body; seeing him once puts an end to the sorrow of transmigration—and he is with you all the time."

Rohinī and Devakī expressed their admiration of and gratitude to Yaśodā: "For fear of Kaṁsa we had to entrust our sons to you. They had not even seen their parents for a long time; and you looked after them without making any distinction between yours and others!"

The gopī, who were swimming in the ocean of love for Kṛṣṇa, received him again through their eyes into their hearts and became one with him. Kṛṣṇa too, met them privately, embraced them and said to them: "It is the Lord that brings people together and separates them. You are indeed supremely blessed in that you have such intense love for me. For, loving me is the path to immortality. Luckily you have already cultivated such love. I am the self of all beings; I am their origin, their life and their destination. All beings have the spirit as their innermost reality, and are clothed with bodies made of matter: I am in fact beyond all these—and yet all these exist in me." Contemplating this supreme message of the Lord the gopī attained enlightenment and prayed to the Lord that they might continue to love him for all time to come.

Sage Śuka continued: The gopī, who regarded Kṛṣṇa as their guru and their goal, bowed to him, realising him to be the supreme being himself. Elsewhere, at the same time, yādava and kauravā women met one another and sang the glories of the Lord. Draupadī, the wife of the pāṇḍavā, requested the consorts of Kṛṣṇa to narrate the manner in which śrī Kṛṣṇa had espoused each one of them.

Rukmiṇī, Satyabhāmā, Jāmbavatī, Kālindī, Mitravindā, Satyā, and Bhadrā (whose maternal uncle's son was Kṛṣṇa, and whose father, realising his daughter's supreme love for Kṛṣṇa, gave her in marriage to the Lord with great delight), narrated their respective stories.

Then, Lakṣmaṇā said: "I had also heard of the glories of the Lord from the lips of the celestial sage Nārada. I therefore resolved that I would marry no one else. Draupadī! Just as in your case your father had set up the revolving fish as a trial of merit for choosing the right partner for you, so my father had stipulated that only he was fit to marry me who could hit and bring down a revolving fish which was entirely hidden from view, but whose reflection could be seen in water. Many were the nobles who tried to win my hand. Some could not lift the bow, some could not string it. Even those who could do this could not locate the fish! Arjuna did all this, but failed to hit the fish. Kṛṣṇa came along, playfully strung the bow and easily brought the fish down. I was, of course, delighted. Kṛṣṇa seated me on the chariot with him and, while the other nobles were preparing to fight with the Lord, drove the chariot away to Dvārakā. Those who dared to fight had to flee or die. During our wedding my father gave rich presents to the Lord, who is full and infinite and lacks nothing. All of us indeed are supremely fortunate that we have Kṛṣṇa as our husband."

Rohinī, on behalf of the sixteen thousand consorts, then said: "You know how the Lord killed Narakāsura, how he rescued and married us. Blessed one, we do not long for sovereignty of the earth or heaven, nor even for salvation. Our sole desire is that we may adorn our heads with the dust of Kṛṣṇa's feet. We crave for the touch of the feet of the Lord, for which the gopā and the gopī, the cows and the creepers of Vṛndāvan, also longed."

Sage Śuka continued: These group discussions concerning the glory of Kṛṣṇa and the love that each one had for him had a soul-elevating influence on all. At the same time the foremost among the sages arrived there to meet śrī Kṛṣṇa. As they entered, the kings and the nobles who were there stood up in reverence. Kṛṣṇa and Balarāma welcomed them, washed their feet and after seating them appropriately, worshipped them.

Kṛṣṇa said: We are truly blessed today; for our birth here has attained fruition in that we have been granted the privilege of meeting the great masters of yoga. The sacred rivers, etc., are not the water; gods are not earthen and made of stone—they purify the devotee after a long period of time, but the holy sages purify one by their mere sight. Deities presiding over the fire, the sun, the moon, the stars, the earth and the sky, the vital airs and speech and mind, being tainted by the defect of diversity, cannot purify the heart of man; but the holy sages destroy all sin in the heart of man if he but dwells in their company for a few minutes. He is indeed a donkey who regards the body as his self, wife and others as his, who worships earthly objects and who regards rivers as sacred waters, but who is not devoted to holy ones.

Sage Śuka continued: The holy sages were speechless when they heard the supreme Lord himself extol them in these words. Then recovering their understanding of the truth that the Lord, though transcendent in his real nature, was play-acting as a human being here, they said:

"Lord, who can truly understand you? Though one, you appear as many; even as earth, though one, appears as trees, rocks, etc. You are the changeless substratum of ever-changing phenomena. Though beyond name and form you assume a name and form from time to time for the protection of the good and the destruction of evil. Even as a dreamer is unaware of his true body, being caught in the delusion created by māyā, so too are people not aware of you, though you are ever-present with them. Only they who are solely devoted to you can realise your being. We are indeed blessed today in that we have seen you."

Soon afterwards they wished to leave the place and return to their homes. Seeing this, Vasudeva approached the sages and prayed for instruction: "Kindly tell me how one may free oneself from karma."

Sage Śuka continued: Nārada commented thus on Vasudeva's prayer: "O sages, to Vasudeva, the omniscient Kṛṣṇa is but the son; hence he is directing this question to you. Familiarity leads to under-estimation among people, even as one living on the bank of the Gaṅgā goes to other sacred rivers for self-purification."

In answer to Vasudeva's question, the sages replied: "The only way to overcome karma by activity is to perform all actions as worship of the Lord, who is indeed the goal of all rites and acts of worship. Man here is bound by the threefold attachment or desire: desire for wealth, desire for wife and children, and desire for heaven. One should overcome desire for wealth by worship and charity, the desire for wife and children by a righteous household life, the desire for heaven by realising its impermanence in time. Having thus given up this threefold bondage, one should retire to a hermitage. He falls who renounces the household life without discharging one's debts to the gods, (by performing religious rites), to the holy sages, (by the study and the propagation of scriptures) and to the ancestors (by leaving progeny behind). Hence, propitiate the Lord through religious rites, O Vasudeva."

Immediately acting upon their counsel, Vasudeva performed a religious rite as enjoined by the scriptures and as directed by the holy ones present. At its conclusion Vasudeva gave away rich presents to everyone—even down to the dogs.

Thereafter all the kings and nobles departed and returned to their homes. Vasudeva was exceedingly fond of Nanda and embracing him with supreme friendship, said: "Our friendship is too deep for words, O Nanda! You have always been extremely good to us—though we have been ungrateful to you. When Kaṁsa had imprisoned us we rationalised that we could do nothing for you in return for your great kindness because we were in prison; but even after we had been freed we have failed to express our gratitude to you suitably! Such is the conduct of men in power—they have no use for friendship. Hence, one who aspires for true welfare should shun rulership and positions of power which blind one to friendship and relationship."

Nanda and others prolonged their stay, to enjoy Vasudeva's hospitality. Vasudeva entertained them all in a variety of ways. After a considerable time, Nanda returned to his place. The yādavā returned to Dvārakā.

Sage Śuka continued: As usual, one day Kṛṣṇa and Balarāma went to pay their respects to Vasudeva. Vasudeva remembered the inspiring words of sage Nārada and the eulogistic words in which the sages sang the praises of Kṛṣṇa and Balarāma, whom he had regarded as his sons. Therefore, Vasudeva said to them:

"Kṛṣṇa! You are truly existence-knowledge-bliss absolute. You are the Lord of matter and spirit. You are the Lord of whatever exists at all times, everywhere, brought about by whomsoever or whatsoever cause and for whatsoever reason. You have created the universe out of yourself, and you yourself have entered it, in a manner of speaking, as its very soul and reality. You are the life of the life-force (prāṇa) itself. You are the light in the sun, the stars and lightning; you are the stability of mountains and the qualities inherent in the elements. All the sense-objects, the senses and the power that enables them to function in their respective sense-objects, are all you yourself. You are the buddhi and the faculty that co-ordinates the sense-impressions in the individual. You alone are the tāmasa ego (and the cause of the elements), the rājasa ego (and its effects, the senses) and the sātvika ego (and its effect, the mind). We know that in the case of the created elements the cause inheres in the effect: you, being the causeless cause, exist in all the effects and therefore in all creation. Yet, in truth, they only appear to be in you for the time being: for you are the transcendental being, untouched by the three guṇā (qualities of nature) and therefore by all these modifications of matter. One who does not realise this subtle distinction between your absolute, transcendental nature and the manifestation of the guṇā as this universe, is caught in the cycle of birth and death. You alone are puruṣa (soul or consciousness) and prakṛti (nature or matter): you alone are the efficient and material cause of the universe; the subject and the object— and beyond all these. It was under the influence of your own māyā that, identifying myself with the body, I considered you as my son. I take refuge in you; show me the way out of this cycle."

Thus spoken to by his own father, Kṛṣṇa replied humbly: "I am only your son and you have said all this in order to teach me. I, you, the inhabitants of Dvārakā and all these mobile and immobile creatures are all but the self which is one, self-effulgent, eternal, which even in the modifications caused by the qualities of nature, remains unqualified; and which appears to be diverse in objects apparently created by it." Hearing this, Vasudeva became enlightened.

Arjuna Weds Subhadrā
Book Ten Chapter 85

Sage Śuka continued: Devakī, when she realised the divinity of her son and recalled the cruel murder of her first six children by Kaṁsa, said to Kṛṣṇa:

"Kṛṣṇa, I now know that you are Lord even of the lords of creation. I have heard with wonder how you brought back from the abode of death the son of your preceptor Sāndīpani. I, too, long to be re-united with my children who were cruelly killed by Kaṁsa. Pray, grant this desire of mine."

Kṛṣṇa and Balarāma resorted to their yoga-māyā, and at once transported themselves to the subterranean realm called Sutala. The ruler of Sutala, the great king Bali, was delighted to see the divine brothers enter his realm, and worshipped them. Hugging with great devotion the lotus feet of śrī Kṛṣṇa, Bali spoke to him:

"Lord, beings like us who are demoniacal, entertain hatred towards you; yet we, as well as your great devotees, are close to you, for either through love or through hatred we are constantly united with you. However, even great yogī do not know you in truth. I therefore pray that I may be ever devoted to your lotus-feet which are desired by the desireless, so that I may be freed from this dark pit of worldly existence and may thenceforth roam freely, alone or in the company of those who regard all beings as their friends."

Kṛṣṇa said to him: "O king of demons! The sage Marīci had six sons through his wife, Ūrṇā. When they saw the creator Brahmā approaching his own daughter with carnal intention, they immodestly laughed and earned Brahmā's curse. Consequently they were to be born of Hiraṇyakaśipu, but were however transferred to my mother's womb and so were all killed by Kaṁsa. In order to gladden the heart of our mother we wish to take them back to the land of the living." Bali immediately restored the six children to the two brothers who handed them to Devakī. However, at the very touch of śrī Kṛṣṇa they became enlightened, and immediately ascended to the celestial region. Devakī marvelled at this and did not feel the loss of the children she had just regained from death itself!

He who narrates and listens to these all-purifying stories of the Lord will develop deep devotion to him and attain his abode.

Book Ten Chapter 86

In response to a question from Parīkṣit concerning his grandfather's marriage with his grandmother, sage Suka said: While your grandfather Arjuna was on a pilgrimage, he went to Prabhāsa and there heard of his maternal uncle's daughter Subhadrā. There were rumours that Balarāma was keen on giving her in marriage to Duryodhana. Arjuna disguised himself as a religious mendicant and entered the city. All the citizens were thrilled to see the radiant mendicant, they welcomed him and worshipped him. He decided to spend the four rainy months there, in accordance with the prevailing custom. Balarāma, too, invited the mendicant to his palace, not knowing who he was. Arjuna saw Subhadrā there and promptly fell in love with her. She, too, lost her heart to him. By mutual agreement and with the consent of the elders, one day, when she was going to a temple Arjuna jumped on to the chariot and drove off. Kṛṣṇa and others pacified Balarāma, who thereupon not only consented to the marriage of his sister Subhadrā to Arjuna, but bestowed lavish wedding gifts on them.

In those days there lived in Mithilā a saintly brāhmaṇa called Śrutadeva, who was devoted to śrī Kṛṣṇa with all his heart. The king of Mithilā, too, was devoted to śrī Kṛṣṇa. Intent upon blessing them, śrī Kṛṣṇa, along with holy sages (including myself) went over to Mithilā. Both king Bahulāśva and the brāhmaṇa Śrutadeva were in ecstatic bliss. The Lord, too, went to both the houses simultaneously. In the palace he was welcomed by the king as the self of all beings who, as Kṛṣṇa, had once again demonstrated that he cared more for his devotee than for his brother or consort (a declaration made by lord Rāma). And, in the house of Śrutadeva, the brāhamaṇa and his wife ecstatically worshipped the Lord and the sages. Śrutadeva said: "Ignorant people do not perceive that you are ever present in their own hearts as their very self. You are the sole reality. Even as a sleeping (dreaming) person creates a world within his mind, himself enters into it and becomes aware of it, you have created the whole universe and entered into it."

Śrī Kṛṣṇa revealed: "These holy sages have come to your house with no other intention but to bless you. Indeed, that is the reason why they constantly roam the earth, for the dust of their holy feet purifies the earth. Images of gods, holy places and sacred rivers and lakes purify the devotees who resort to them and are devoted to them for a long period of time; and even this power they derive from holy sages. None, not even my own body, is dearer to me than these holy sages. They are of perverse understanding who worship me in images, etc., and out of jealousy disregard the holy sages who are my own self. Hence, worship them, O Śrutadeva."

Both king Bahulāśva and the brāhmaṇa Śrutadeva attained enlightenment.

Book Ten Chapter 87

In response to another question from Parīkṣit, sage Śuka repeated the following prayer that the vedā offered to the Lord: Victory to you, O invincible Lord! Destroy nescience which, assuming the form of the three qualities of nature, spreads evil, O awakener of souls. Men of wisdom have described this universe to be non-different from the absolute, in as much as the absolute alone remains unchanged before, during and after the appearance of the universe. That again is the reason why the vedā concede that though you are beyond the reach of intellect and speech, whatever the intellect reaches and speech describes is indeed you—just as whatever people may step on, they are stepping on the earth, so you are the ground of all thoughts and all descriptions. Therefore the wise delight in your stories and glories and thus rid themselves of all afflictions. And they who have transcended all limitations and time are devoted to your abode, which is consciousness and bliss absolute.

Only they are alive who tread the path leading to you; others are like breathing objects. You are the life of our life, you animate animate beings, and though you transcend all material substances, they owe their existence and their power to you. Many paths lead to you. People of dense vision are devoted to their bellies (or, meditate upon you in the psychic centres located in the abdominal region). People in whom wisdom has begun to dawn and who possess subtle vision, contemplate on the heart and are devoted to you (or, meditate upon you in the psychic centres located in the heart region). Above that, in the head, is your abode, attaining which one does not return to this mortal existence.

Infinite as you are, you are forever omnipresent; yet, in a manner of speaking you enter into the diverse beings you create. They who live unselfishly in this world, performing all their actions without the least expectation of a reward, recognise your real nature—the indwelling omnipresence.

Book Ten Chapter 87

The Vedā prayed: The scriptures describe the individual soul as part of you; and in this belief the wise develop devotion to your feet. It is then that the course of evolution reaches its culmination. There are some who are tired of the endless wandering in this world of becoming and who, not even desiring liberation, abandon the home-life and live immersed in your stories and glories. It is a pity that having attained this human birth, people do not take delight in loving and adoring you (who are their sole well-wisher, their very self) but tread the path of self-destruction by wasting their life pampering to the whims and fancies of their body and mind, and thus cling to the ever-whirling wheel of birth and death. Constant remembrance of you has redeemed even your enemies!

No created being can possibly know your real nature: you existed prior to all of them. All theories therefore are based on ignorance. Some believe that the unreal comes into being, others that the real perishes; some imagine diversity in the self; and yet others firmly believe in the law of karma (cause and effect)—all these speculations are based upon ignorance and misunderstanding. You are beyond all such speculations, since ignorance cannot exist in you, who are pure knowledge. The universe appears to be real because you (its substratum) are real! Wise men do not reject the world, even as he who seeks gold does not reject ornaments made of gold. But, only he who worships you as the indweller of all beings is unafraid of death and tramples on it. You keep the immature beings bound fast by the word—even if they consider themselves wise. Only they who are devoted to you are freed and free others; not they who have turned away from you.

None is dear to you, nor is anyone your enemy. When you gaze on your own creative power, the individual souls are clothed with a subtle body in accordance with the karma latent in them. These souls are not infinite and eternal as individuals. When matter and spirit are confused with one another the individual is apparently born—just as we speak of the birth of a bubble or a wave. You alone are the reality in them all. This truth is unknown even to those who claim to know it; for all such knowledge is verily imperfect knowledge or mere speculation.

Book Ten Chapter 87

The Vedā prayed: Wise men who realise the impenetrable trick of māyā take refuge in you, who alone can free them from illusion. They alone are able to subdue the impetuous mind which is otherwise unconquerable. Others who battle with their senses and the prāṇa without worshipping the lotus feet of their guru, are therefore a prey to a hundred afflictions. What is the use of wealth, house, wife and children when you who are supreme bliss itself are present in the heart of man? And what is the use of wealth, house, wife and children if man runs after them, unaware of your indwelling omnipresence in which alone he can have eternal satisfaction and security? Even holy men who are devoted to your lotus feet roam about the holy places and sacred rivers, because they have no use for the security and pleasure of the household life.

You alone are existence absolute. The creation did not exist before it came into being, nor will it exist after its dissolution; hence it is non-existent in truth even now. We, the vedā, illustrate this truth by using various earthly and material analogies. Only the ignorant believe that this world is permanent reality. The ignorant man is caught in the wheel of birth and death. You are beyond the reach of the ignorant and even of the pseudo-yogi who is a slave to the senses and the mind.

On the other hand, he who knows you in truth and in essence transcends good and evil which are born of ignorance; he is not bound by the scriptural injunctions, which are meant to govern the conduct of those who are limited by body-consciousness and who, too, will eventually attain final beatitude by constantly hearing the teachings handed down by tradition.

Sage Śuka said: This prayer was repeated by the divine sage Nārāyaṇa to Nārada, who in turn transmitted it to Vyāsa.

Kṛṣṇa Saves Śiva From Vṛkāsura
Book Ten Chapter 88

King Parīkṣit asked: How is it that they who are devoted to other deities (like the ascetic lord Śiva) prosper, while they who are devoted to lord Hari, who is the Lord of the goddess of wealth and prosperity, suffer from poverty?

Sage Śuka replied: Lord Śiva is always united with his śaktī and therefore the three guṇā; he is the deity presiding over the ego. Hence he who propitiates him obtains the objects born of these categories. But, lord Hari is beyond all these and hence it requires renunciation of all worldly goals to worship him. This is what Kṛṣṇa said to Yudhiṣ ṭhira after the aśvamedha rites: "When I wish to bless someone I gradually deprive him of his wealth. This poor man is forsaken by his own kith and kin. Thereupon, in sorrow and despair, he cultivates the company of my devotees. Then I shower my grace upon him, by which he realises the supreme. It is on this account that many people neglect me and seek others. However, even they, once they obtain their desired object, forget even them!"

Lord Śiva is easily propitiated. There are many instances when this led to trouble, even to Śiva himself! There once was a demon by the name of Vṛka. He ascertained from the sage Nārada that lord Śiva could be pleased most easily. He began to perform terrible austerities, finally cutting off his limbs to propitiate the Lord. He was about to cut off his own head when lord Śiva appeared before him and granted any boon of his choice. He prayed: "Grant that he upon whose head I shall lay my hand, shall die." Śiva granted this boon.

Intent as he was on abducting Śiva's consort Pārvatī, the demon rushed towards Śiva himself, to test the boon! Śiva ran, pursued by the demon, but finding no redress in all the worlds, he went to Vaikuṇṭha, the abode of lord Hari. In order to rescue Śiva from the trouble, lord Hari disguised himself as a young brāhmaṇa student and intercepted the demon. "You are obviously in such a great hurry, what is the matter?" he asked the demon, who narrated the whole story with great pride. The young man laughed aloud and said: "Don't you know that Śiva is a leader of ghosts and goblins? How can you believe in his words? I don't think that he really granted you the boon. If you don't trust me, touch your own head with your hand!" Thoroughly confused by the Lord's wit and words, the demon touched his own head and fell dead. Lord Hari then said to Śiva: "No one who wrongs the great can be happy; how can he who offends you prosper?"

He who narrates or listens to this story is freed from fear of enemies.

Bhṛgu Tests the Trinity
Book Ten Chapter 89

Sage Śuka continued: In an assembly of sages a discussion arose as to who should be regarded as supreme among the trinity (Brahmā, Viṣṇu and Śiva). They entrusted the task of determining this to the sage Bhṛgu, one of the sons of the creator Brahmā.

Bhṛgu first went to Brahmā, his father, but failed to show any respect to him! This angered Brahmā, who forgave the sage only because he was his son. Then the sage went to Kailāsa, the abode of Śiva (his own brother). Śiva got up from his seat and came forward to embrace Bhṛgu who, however, pulled himself away in disgust, as it were, saying: "You have violated the injunctions of the scriptures by your conduct; don't touch me." This so angered Śiva that he was about to hit the sage with his trident, but Pārvatī intervened.

The sage then went to Vaikuṇṭha, the abode of Viṣṇu, where lord Viṣṇu was resting on the lap of his consort Lakṣmī. Entering unannounced and abruptly, the sage rudely kicked lord Viṣṇu on his chest. Lord Viṣṇu awoke and at once fell at the feet of the sage and said: "Kindly forgive me for not offering you appropriate welcome, since I was resting. The spot on my chest which your foot touched shall henceforth be the abode of Lakṣmī." The sage was overwhelmed to hear these noble words and he could not utter a word in reply. He returned to the assembly of sages and announced that lord Viṣṇu was the supreme deity.

From lord Viṣṇu proceed dharma, wisdom, dispassion and with it the eightfold manifestation of sovereignty (or affluence) and the glory that wards off the impurities of the mind. He is the supreme goal of sages who are wedded to non-violence, who are tranquil and even-minded and without the least sense of possession. Satva is his form; the holy men are his own deities; and he in turn is worshipped by desireless, peaceful and wise men. Gods, demons and others are born of his own māyā. And, satva alone is the path to attain him.

Meditating upon this truth, the sages attained him.

Brāhmaṇa's Dead Child is Revived
Book Ten Chapter 89

Sage Śuka continued: There was a brāhmaṇa couple in Dvārakā who gave birth to several still-born children. The brāhmaṇa was sore at heart, and one day when Kṛṣṇa and Arjuna were seated in the palace he brought the body of the last dead child and shouted: "Obviously, we have an unrighteous ruler whose sins cause such untimely death of infants." Arjuna was roused to hear this accusation. He bragged: "Is there no warrior in Dvārakā to protect the children of this good man? Indeed, if a ruler permits the holy brāhmaṇa to suffer in his kingdom, he is no ruler but a mercenary who works for his bread! O brāhmaṇa, I shall myself protect your next child. Fear not." But, the brāhmaṇa doubted Arjuna's ability to do so.

As the time for his wife's next confinement drew near, the brāhmaṇa prayed to Arjuna to protect him. Arjuna went over to the brāhmaṇa's house and planted several powerful missiles all around the house, considering the house impregnable thereby. The child was born; it cried for a few seconds and then disappeared bodily. The distraught brāhmaṇa wailed aloud: "What a fool I was to trust the words of this eunuch!" Arjuna's anger was aroused, and he vowed either to bring the child back or commit suicide.

Arjuna went to the abode of Yama, but could not find the child there. He went to heaven and the nether worlds, but could not find the child there. He therefore prepared to jump into the fire. Kṛṣṇa restrained him and, promising to show him the children of the brāhmaṇa, took him along with him. They traversed over many solar systems and realms. They crossed the Lokāloka mountains beyond them. Kṛṣṇa's own radiant light (Sudarśana—perfect insight) showed the way which was otherwise absolutely dark. They went to the end of darkness; beyond that was the realm of light absolute. Beyond that was the region of water, in which there was the thousand hooded snake on whose body lord Viṣṇu lay attended by all the divine powers. Kṛṣṇa and Arjuna bowed to him. He said: "Eager to see you both, I had the children of the brāhmaṇa brought here. You are the sages Nara and Nārāyaṇa and though you have nothing to achieve, you pursue the path of dharma for the welfare of all." Kṛṣṇa and Arjuna bowed to the infinite Lord and said "Yes".

Taking the sons of the brāhmaṇa with them, they returned to Dvārakā and returned the sons to the brāhmaṇa.

Book Ten Chapter 90

Sage Śuka continued: The beauty and the glory of the city of Dvārakā were indescribable. In it the Lord himself dwelt with his numerous consorts, who were intensely devoted to him. They played with him, they teased him, they embraced him. He was their be-all and end-all. They could not bear separation from him even for a moment. Everything in the world reminded them of him. And often they spoke thus to animate and inanimate beings:

"O ocean! We guess that just like us you have got the terrible disease of insomnia and that, like us, you have also been robbed by our Lord of your peace and gravity!

"O cloud! You have the same colour as our Lord. Surely you too constantly meditate upon him, as we do. And like us you think of him again and again and shed tears of love!

"Beloved mountain! You are obviously absorbed in deep thought or contemplation. Surely you fondly hope that our beloved Lord would place his lotus feet on your peak, which resembles our breasts.

"O rivers! How thin you have grown! You are surely deprived of the shower from the clouds, even as we are emaciated when we are deprived of the glances of our beloved Lord."

He whom the adepts in yoga endeavour to attain was the husband of these noble women. O King! The stories and glories of Kṛṣṇa enchant those who hear them: who can then fathom the effect that his nearness had on those who actually lived with him? Who can match the blessedness of those people who actually touched him, pressed his feet, and who had him as their husband?

Śrī Kṛṣṇa demonstrated in his own life that the three goals of life (dharma, artha and kāma) could be had by living the household life; hence he himself adopted that mode of life.

By this time Kṛṣṇa had numerous wives and children. Pradyumna's son, Aniruddha, married the daughter of Rukmī who gave birth to a son, Vajra by name. This boy Vajra was the only one who survived the massacre that destroyed the whole of the yādavā. His progeny, however, continued to grow in time. No one who was born in this family was weak or short-lived. All of them were devoted to God and the holy ones.

Śrī Kṛṣṇa is the only refuge of all beings. He redeemed all: they that loved him, they that hated him, they that played with him and they that treated him as a friend or a lover. Glory, glory to Kṛṣṇa.

Thus did lord Kṛṣṇa live on this earth, exemplifying in himself the ideals of perfect life, for the protection of dharma. Contemplation of the actions of the Lord is capable of wiping out all sins and cutting the bonds of karma. He who wishes to cultivate devotion to him should constantly listen to his stories.

Book Eleven

Yādavā Cursed
Book Eleven Chapter 1

Sage Śuka continued: Śrī Kṛṣṇa's mission on earth, the purpose of his incarnation, had almost been accomplished. The Lord had exterminated the demons and had brought about the destruction of the wicked kings, using the pāṇḍavā as his instruments. Then he thought: "My mission is not yet complete, for the powerful and invincible yādavā are still left behind. They have my protection. They enjoy prosperity, which has created in them a sense of immense power. I myself will have to bring about their extermination before I leave for my realm." With this intention the Lord, who is the indweller of all beings, made the yādavā incur the displeasure of the holy ones, who thereby cursed them, causing their destruction.

King Parīkṣit questioned: How is it possible for the yādavā to be cursed by the holy ones—pray narrate this to me in detail.

Sage Śuka continued: After accomplishing his many-faceted mission on earth, śrī Kṛṣṇa dwelt in the house of Vasudeva. The sages had taken leave of him and gone to Piṇḍāraka. While they were staying there the yādavā youngsters who were roaming that area approached them, wishing to tease them. The bowed to the sages in mock humility. They placed before the sages Jāmbavatī's son Sāmba, whom they had dressed as a woman expecting a child. They questioned the sages: "Holy ones! You know the past, present and the future. This lady who longs for a son wishes to know whether she will give birth to a boy or a girl." The sages were aware of the truth, and they were aware too, that this was the Lord's own will. They replied, as if in anger: "Fools, she will give birth to a pestle which will destroy all of you." Horrified, they disrobed Sāmba and sure enough a pestle dropped to the ground.

The people of Dvārakā, when they heard of the incident, were greatly alarmed. They pulverised the pestle and threw it into the sea—including the last little bit which could not be pulverised—in an attempt to counteract the decree of the sages. A weed known as erakā grew where the particles of iron had fallen. The large bit was swallowed by a fish, the fish was caught by a fisherman, and a hunter who ate the fish, found the iron piece which he fixed to the tip of his arrow. The stage had thus been set for the destruction of the yādavā. This was the divine will.

Sages Discourses to Nimi
Book Eleven Chapter 2

Sage Śuka continued: In Dvārakā the sage Nārada frequently enjoyed the company of śrī Kṛṣṇa. On one such occasion Vasudeva asked Nārada: "Holy men like you move about in this world in order to bring manifold blessings to mankind. What the gods do may be conducive to the happiness or the unhappiness of people; but whatever is done by holy men like you is always conducive to the happiness of people. For the gods bestow on man the fruits of his own past karma; holy men, however, are unconcerned with the karma of others but, being full of love and compassion, shower their love and compassion on all beings. In a previous birth I had prayed to the Lord for a son like him; and he himself was born as my son. Now, tell me of the path by which one may be freed from all fear, and attain final liberation."

Nārada answered: Your question reminds me of the instructions which Nimi the king of the videhā received from the sons of Ṛṣabha. Ṛṣabha's son was Bharata, the sage who had attained the supreme being through the path of renunciation. Ṛṣabha had ninety-nine other sons. Nine became rulers, eighty-one became brāhmaṇā, and nine became sages. They were Kavi, Hari, Antarikṣa, Prabuddha, Pippalāyana, Āvirhotra, Drumila, Camasa and Karabhājana.

Once, during their wanderings on earth, these nine sages went to the land of the videhā where king Nimi was performing a religious rite. Nimi was ecstatically joyful at seeing the sages and said: "Rare indeed is human birth; and in that fleeting birth the company of those who are devoted to the Lord is extremely rare. Even a moment's company with these holy ones is precious and invaluable.

Having obtained such a rich blessing, I pray to you, kindly instruct us in the bhāgavata dharma (the path that leads to the lotus feet of the Lord himself)."

Book Eleven Chapter 2

Sage Kavi said: Whatever path has been laid and whatever practices have been taught by the Lord for the realisation of his being, are all good. But, I believe that worship of the lotus feet of the Lord is the safest, for through that one attains fearlessness immediately. One who follows the path prescribed by the Lord does not go astray, and even if he runs blindfolded he will still reach his destination. He who would truly worship the Lord should offer whatever he does by thought, word or deed, and in accordance with his own nature, to the supreme lord Nārāyaṇa as an act of worship. Thus shall he overcome the sense of duality engendered by body-consciousness, which is the root-cause of fear.

He should see the Lord as his guru and as his own self. Perception of duality is like perception of a dream: it is mental activity. Knowing this, he should free the mind of all conditioning. He will be immediately freed from fear. Freed from all conventions, ever dwelling on the most uplifting pastimes of the Lord, he should roam freely, bowing to all animate and inanimate objects, regarding them as the body of the Lord. Love of God, direct realisation of God and cessation of craving for sensual pleasure manifest in him simultaneously.

Sage Hari said: He who sees all in the self, which is the supreme Lord himself, and the self which is God in all beings, he indeed is the best of the men-of-God. He who is devoted to God, friendly towards his devotees, compassionate towards the ignorant and indifferent to his enemies, is a middling man-of-God. He who worships God only in the images but does not see God in his devotees or others, is the lowest type of a man-of-God.

He who regards the world as the manifestation of the illusory power of the Lord does not get lost in it, though he lives a normal life. Since craving for enjoyment does not arise in him, his actions do not bind him and so he is freed from birth and death. The devotee of the Lord is free from the pride relating to birth (in a wealthy, noble family, etc.); he does not suffer from a sense of possession. Since he constantly remembers the Lord he is freed from the burning illness of ignorance. The name of the Lord enthroned in his heart removes all sins.

Sage Antarikṣa said: Māyā is that energy with the help of which the supreme being, who is absolute consciousness, evolved this creation for the emancipation of souls. Having created diverse beings he himself entered into them—and then evolved the mind and the senses. Through these the indweller enjoys the external world of matter. He conceives a liking for certain experiences and gets attached to them and the objects that made them possible. His actions thenceforward are pleasure-oriented and he is subjected to their consequence. Thus he gropes helplessly in this creation. Towards the end of this world-cycle there arises a drought which lasts a hundred years. This is followed by a cosmic fire which seems to consume all matter. This again is followed by the deluge which inundates everything. Creation is withdrawn, the elements dissolve into their immediate cause and everything ultimately dissolves into nature or māyā. Thus māyā creates, preserves and dissolves this universe.

Sage Prabuddha said: One should see and realise that though one is ceaselessly striving to avoid unhappiness and gain happiness, one is subjected to contrary results! Neither in this world nor in heaven is there the possibility of unalloyed happiness, because the same problems of hate, competition and fear taint life in both these realms. Realising this, a wise man should resort to a preceptor who knows the truth and who is free from attachment and hate. From him the seeker should learn (by devoted service to the guru) the path of God-love, detachment from worldly pleasures and love for God, the right attitude towards human relationship, how to cultivate virtues like self-control and evenness of mind, how to live a simple life, how to see the self or God in all beings, how to offer all his actions (his very life) to the Lord as a self-sacrifice, how to love and lovingly serve the Lord's devotees and everyone in general, and how constantly to narrate and to listen to the glories and the stories of the Lord.

Such a devotee dwells in constant remembrance of the Lord. He sometimes weeps, feeling a sense of separation from the Lord, sometimes rejoices, feeling his nearness, dances and sings and at other times, in self-forgetful realisation of God, remains silent and tranquil. One who thus learns and understands the unpredictable and unconventional ways of his devotee, grows in God-love.

Sage Pippalāyana said: The ever-changing is the form; the changeless is the reality. It is the awareness that remains continuous and unbroken throughout waking, dreaming and sleep (and in the superconscious state of samādhi), just as space remains continuous and unbroken within a house, through the wall and outside the house (and in the sky). It is self-evident like the sun, and even as a spark cannot illumine the fire so that a blind man can see, even so description and speculation cannot enable the spiritually blind to 'see' it. The reality alone was, before the apparent creation; it is then described variously as the three qualities of sattva, rajas and tamas, as the sūtrātman with the potentiality of diversified manifestation, as the cosmic intelligence and as the 'I' of the jīva, as knowledge, activity and its resultant experiences, as the reality and its antithesis (the apparent unreality) and that which is beyond all these—the one infinite reality. This reality is not born nor dos it undergo any change. Its omnipresence lends validity to the belief that it indwells diverse created beings. Only he who has sight can behold the light; only he who is devoted to the Lord with all his being can behold this reality.

Sage Āvirhotra said: Vaidika injunctions concerning prescribed and prohibited action, and its transcendence, are often misunderstood even by the wise. The vedā exhorts man to overcome action by action; and holds out temptations like heaven to lure the fool to pay heed to it. The fool who is ignorant and who ignores the injunctions of the vedā is obviously bound to the unending cycle of action and reaction. But he who performs actions prescribed by the vedā, without attachment and without desire for reward here or in heaven, is liberated. Unto him the vedā and the tantrā prescribe elaborate and effective ways of adoring the Lord. One who has learnt these ways from a guru should worship an image of the Lord according to his choice. Regarding himself as being at-one with the Lord, he should worship the Lord, and after the worship place upon his head the flowers and the water consecrated during the worship. Even so he should worship the Lord in fire, water, sun, in the guest and in oneself, by which he shall soon be liberated.

Book Eleven Chapter 4

Sage Drumila said: This world, the heavens and the nether worlds constitute the Lord's body. He indwells them as their inner ruler and hence he is known as puruṣa. He is the life of all beings. As the rājasa Brahmā he creates; as the sātvika Viṣṇu he protects; and as the tāmasa Rudra he destroys.

For the propagation of the knowledge of the self, the Lord himself manifested as the eternal sage Nārāyaṇa and Nara in days of yore, through Mūrti, the daughter of Dakṣa and Dharma. Indra the god of heaven however, suspected that Nārāyaṇa was engaged in austerities with a view to overthrow him (Indra). As usual therefore he sent Kāmadeva, the god of sensual passion, with a bevy of celestial nymphs to obstruct the sage's austerities. When they tried their tricks on him, the sage smilingly welcomed them without being tempted by them or angered by them. On the contrary, he politely offered them his hospitality. The gods were astounded. At the same time there appeared on the Lord's side a bevy of nymphs of unsurpassable beauty! The humiliated angel and his retinue bowed to the sage and said: "You are beyond delusion and so remain unaffected by our childish pranks. The gods try to obstruct the path of one who endeavours to transcend their realms and thus to reach your abode; they, however, do not do so if one propitiates them at the same time. But nothing daunts your devotee; by your grace he steps on the obstacles and ascends to your feet. There are some who have the power to transcend our messengers like hunger and thirst, cold etc., but fall a victim to anger! Even as a person might cross an ocean but get drowned in a pot-hole. You have shown by your own action that your devotee does not curse even they who obstruct his path." The gods then returned to heaven, taking with them Urvaśī, the foremost among the nymphs attending upon Nārāyaṇa.

The Lord also assumed various other forms for the protection of the good and of dharma, for the destruction of the wicked and the evil. Countless are such manifestations. His glory, his excellences and his qualities are indescribable and infinite.

Book Eleven Chapter 5

Sage Camasa said: From the limbs of the Lord emerged the four classes of human beings—the brāhmaṇā, the warriors, the farmers and the servant class. Whoever among them does not adore the lord Hari forfeits the privilege of human birth and falls into hell. Brāhmaṇā who have access to knowledge of the vedā which is the key to self-knowledge, misread and misinterpret the vaidika injunctions and indulge in drinking wine, animal sacrifice and sexual pleasure. The vedā permitted these as a concession to the ignorant who have no self-control, and even then wine was only to be smelt, the animals should only adorn the ritual site, and sexual enjoyment be indulged in for the sake of progeny only. They who are ignorant of this, haughtily considering themselves wise, kill animals which in turn kill them when they depart from this world. Also, they who hate the devotees of the Lord and the Lord himself and who are at the same time attached to the perishable body—and they who have a theoretical knowledge of truth and who are yet attached to worldly pursuits— fall in the scale of evolution.

Sage Karabhājana said: In the satya age the Lord had a white complexion. Men of even-minded and peaceful disposition adored the Lord through tapas, or austerity. In the tretā age the Lord had a crimson complexion. Men of veda-learning worshipped him by means of vaidika rites. In the dvāpara age the Lord was of dark brown colour. Men worshipped him by vaidika rites and tāntrika rituals. In the kali age the Lord is of a dark complexion. Men adore him by singing his glories: "I take refuge in your feet, O great one! They remove our afflictions and grant our desires. They are the source of sacredness and are adored by the gods. They destroy the devotees' suffering and are a boat to cross this ocean of mundane existence."

In fact, because of the fact that the Lord is so easily accessible to his devotees in this age, wise ones extol the glories of this age when the Lord is attained by singing his names and praises. Southern India will especially produce a great number of devotees of the Lord. These devotees renounce all duties and take refuge in the Lord and they are instantly freed from their obligations to the gods, the ṛṣī and their ancestors. Devotion itself washes away any sin that such a devotee may commit.

Sage Śuka said: Nārada concluded by reminding Vasudeva that the Lord himself was incarnate in śrī Kṛṣṇa. Listening to these words, Vasudeva and Devakī attained enlightenment. He who contemplates on this teaching attains self-realisation.

Book Eleven Chapter 6

Sage Śuka continued: Soon after this, all the gods of heaven, headed by the creator Brahmā, arrived at Dvārakā to see lord Kṛṣṇa. They worshipped him with flowers and sang his praises: "We bow to your lotus feet, O Lord, with our intelligence, our senses, our life-breath, our mind and our speech! For those feet are constantly meditated upon by devotees who aspire for total freedom from the bonds of karma."

Then, Brahmā said: We had begged of you to lighten the burden of the earth, O Lord. And you have completely fulfilled our prayer. You have also established dharma on earth; and the task of its propagation, too, has been entrusted by you to those who are devoted to you. What is more, your glory which destroys the sins of the world has spread throughout the world. You incarnated in the house of

Yadu one hundred and twenty-five years ago. It is time, O Lord, for you to return to your own abode.

Śrī Kṛṣṇa replied: Even so is our intention. The yādavā who have enjoyed my protection so far have grown arrogant and vicious. I have been able to restrain them from breaking the bounds of dharma so far. But no one else will be able to do so. Hence, I have brought about their curse by the brāhmaṇā. As soon as that curse has taken effect, I shall also leave the world.

Soon afterwards, grave evil omens appeared in Dvārakā and śrī Kṛṣṇa advised the yādavā to leave the place and emigrate to Prabhāsa, the holy place which had the reputation of curing even one who suffers from tuberculosis. While the yādavā were making the necessary preparations, Uddhava approached the Lord.

Uddhava said: Lord, it is obvious that you have decided to leave this world. How can we, who have been with you for so long, who have been your constant companions, bear separation from you? Kindly take me also with you. Sages who have renounced everything attain you by prolonged meditation and austerities. Though we are caught in this wheel of karma, we have your stories and glories to ferry us across this ocean of samsāra.

Book Eleven Chapter 7

Lord Kṛṣṇa said: It is true, even as you said, that I am about to leave this earth, as my task has been accomplished and my return to heaven is desired by Brahmā and others. As soon as I depart, the age of kali will begin on earth and people will progressively turn to adharma. Such a world is not fit for you to live in. Give up all attachments. Know that the entire world is but a projection of one's own mind; the appearance itself has no true validity. One who is not inwardly at-one with the reality perceives diversity here; and he is subject to right and wrong action and inaction. Know through yoga self-restraint that the whole world is your own self and has me as its Lord. When you thus renounce all ideas of good and evil, you will not be motivated by good and evil in your actions. You will not refrain from evil because you are afraid of it, nor will you do good because it is more desirable. Your actions will be spontaneous as those of a child. Then you will never fall into error; seeing the whole universe as the self, you will enjoy inner peace as the friend of all.

Uddhava said: Lord! The path of renunciation that you have expounded is impossible for those who have not completely overcome the instinct of pleasure and who are not whole-heartedly devoted to you. Kindly tell me how I can reach such a state of detachment and renunciation. I take refuge in you, O Nārāyaṇa, O true friend of man!

Lord Kṛṣṇa said: In this world, one has to uplift one's own. self by oneself. One is one's own guru, for one discovers the path to supreme blessedness by examining what is perceived and what is inferred. Among all creatures the human being is dearest to me, for he can, by vigilant observation, immediately realise me.

To illustrate this we have the legend of a dialogue between Yadu and an ascetic. Yadu saw a young man of uncouth appearance, but whose face shone with the brilliance of wisdom, roaming the world fearlessly. Approaching him with devotion, Yadu asked him the following question.

Kṛṣṇa's Teaching to Uddhava: The Ascetic and His Twenty-Four Gurū
Book Eleven Chapter 7

Yadu said: What is the source of the wisdom which enables you who are able-bodied to be immune to sensual attractions, and to move about as if you are a child, madman or a ghost?

The Ascetic said: My awakened intelligence received wisdom from twenty-four gurū: earth, air, space, water, fire, moon, sun, dove, python, sea, moth, bee, elephant, apiarist, deer, fish, courtesan Piṅgalā, osprey, infant, young girl, maker of arrow, snake, spider, wasp.

From earth I learnt forbearance on being trodden upon; one should not abandon one's task even if subjected to humiliation, even as earth adheres to its task. The earth, through its trees and mountains, taught me that life is for unselfishly and humbly serving all. Air taught me freedom from being tainted while moving among objects of the world. Air, as life-breath, taught me contentment with what is needed at the moment, and that life is for living and not for sensual enjoyment, so that while one should not starve to death, one should not live to eat. The self is all-pervading and, like space, is unchanged by forms appearing and disappearing. Like water, the yogi should be transparent, sweet and pure. Like fire, he should burn all impurities, and know that like fire the reality is hidden in the appearance. Like fire, too, the yogi who is full of light is not affected by the impurities he might come in contact with. And, like fire, the yogi's real nature is sometimes manifest and sometimes hidden—and he is ever worshipped by all. Waxing and waning of the moon revealed to me that birth and death are not of the self. The sun vaporises water and later showers it as rain without being involved in either; such should be the yogi's activity. I once saw a dove with its mate and offspring living on a tree; when a hunter caught the young ones and their mother in a net, the male also jumped into it, blinded by attachment, and was caught. From this dove I learnt that attachment is blinding darkness.

Book Eleven Chapter 8

The Ascetic continued: Sensual pleasure as well as pain is had in both heaven and hell: hence the wise one should not desire it. Like the python one should be content with what comes unsought. A man of renunciation should be peaceful, calm, unfathomable, impenetrable and as unaffected by the currents of likes and dislikes as the sea. Even as the ocean remains the same whether rivers that flow into it are empty or dry, the ascetic should remain even-minded whether he gets one thing or its opposite. Even as a moth falls into the fire and dies, so the foolish man is attracted by the appearance of a woman and commits spiritual suicide. Even as a bee sits lightly on a flower and collects the nectar without injuring the flower, so the ascetic should gather his alms from the people without troubling them. Again, even as the bee collects nectar from different flowers and makes honey, so the wise man should gather wisdom from several sources and make it his own. On the contrary, unlike the bee, he should avoid hoarding; or else he will perish like the bee which perishes at the hands of the apiarist. A mendicant should avoid all contact with women: the male elephant is caught on account of his desire for the female. A mendicant should not listen to vulgar songs: the deer falls a prey to music. And, dancing in the company of woman, sage Ṛṣyaśṛṅga became a victim of lust. Of all senses, the sense of taste is hardest to control: he who has controlled it easily controls all the others. One who has not controlled his sense of taste is caught, even as a fish is caught on the hook.

There was a courtesan named Piṅgalā. One evening she adorned herself attractively and sat outside her house, waiting for rich patrons. Vainly and anxiously she walked to and fro until midnight when she was tired and dejected. Piṅgalā said to herself: "I am fortunate that my foolish hope has thus been thwarted and I am even more fortunate that at this time my heart and my mind turn towards the supreme Lord. Alas, I have thus far foolishly been running after foul matter clothed in skin and conventionally described as man, to whom I have sold my body for a little money and a lot of suffering. From now on I shall take refuge in the Lord, the beloved of all beings." Thus resolved, Piṅgalā gave up her foolish hope and attained a state of hope-lessness which alone is supreme bliss.

Without experiencing such disgust one will not renounce body-consciousness, and without wisdom one will not give up the sense of possession.

Book Eleven Chapter 9

The Ascetic continued: I saw a powerful osprey attack a weaker one which had meat in its mouth. Even so people harass the man who possesses worldly objects. The osprey dropped the meat and flew happily away—even so the man should renounce worldly objects and remain at peace. Like a child I am free from honour and dishonour, cares and anxieties. Only the innocent child and the child-like sage are happy in this world.

A young girl was attending upon guests who had come with a marriage proposal for her. While she was husking paddy, the bangles on her arms made an unseemly noise. The girl went on breaking them one by one to avoid the noise. Even two made some noise. When she had only one on each hand, there was peace. I learnt from this that where many are gathered, there is chaos; with two, there is gossip. One should therefore remain alone.

One should practise concentration by controlling the breath and the posture, and by dispassion and steady practice, without the least dullness. The arrow-maker was so absorbed in his task that he did not notice the king and his retinue pass by: such should be our concentration. Like a snake, the mendicant should live in dwellings abandoned by others and not waste time building his own. Just as the spider projects the web from itself and withdraws the web into itself, so the Lord creates the universe and withdraws the web into himself: he alone is the reality. Whatever one contemplates with all one's being, either through affection or hate or fear, that one verily becomes; even as a larva stung by a wasp thinks constantly of the wasp, and becomes a wasp.

All these lessons I learnt from my preceptors. I learnt a lot from my body— which belongs to others, not to me. Tormented during his life by the senses dragging him in different directions, his possessions possessing him, he dies after sowing the seeds for his future life. Yet, it was in him that the Lord was pleased after creating all other beings. For, it is the human being alone who can realise the self, and that alone is his special faculty. Unto this end has he taken human birth.

Firm knowledge is not had from one guru alone; the one self is sung variously by different sages.

Śrī Kṛṣṇa said: Hearing this, Yadu was enlightened.

Book Eleven Chapter 10

Lord Kṛṣṇa said: Everyone should do his duty as enjoined by me in the scriptures and by the family traditions, without any selfish desires whatsoever. This purifies the mind. And the purified mind is able to observe life without being involved one way or the other. Wise men suffer and fools prosper in this world; happiness and unhappiness are common to all. Even if a person seems to be happy and healthy, death is unavoidable: and what is happiness when death constantly threatens to wipe everything out? Even as happiness is uncertain and unworthy of our attention here, so happiness in heaven, too, is illusory. One who performs all kinds of religious rites here and thus propitiates the gods, goes to heaven. He moves about in aerial vehicles and is surrounded by beautiful women, himself being healthy and charming, too. But when the merit that earned him this holiday in heaven is exhausted, the jīva returns to mortal existence. When a person is wicked and performs wicked deeds he goes to hell and enters the bodies of lower creatures. As long as the jīva is clothed with a body, and as long as the delusion of diversity lasts, this coming and going continues.

Seeing all this the wise man turns to me. My devotee should engage himself in nivṛtti-karma, i.e., such actions as lead him away from worldliness, and abandon pravṛtti-karma, i.e., worldly actions. When he enters into deeper enquiry concerning me, he should completely ignore all instructions concerning actions. He should at times observe all religious vows and also resort to the guru who is none other than myself. If we can compare them to the churning-rods that are used to kindle fire, the teacher or guru is the lower one, and the disciple is the upper and active one; the latter's enquiry and the former's response is the churning, and it produces the fire of knowledge.

When the disciple who is fully awake and alert obtains the purified knowledge from the guru, he will realise that the diverse appearance is unreal and that oneness is the truth. Diversity is the cause of fear and the realisation of oneness frees one from this fear. He will then know that I alone am known as time, self, scriptures, world, nature and dharma, when the qualities of nature are disturbed and in a state of inequilibrium.

Book Eleven Chapter 11

Lord Kṛṣṇa continued: Bondage and liberation pertain to the guṇā (qualities of nature); since these guṇā are rooted in māyā, there is neither bondage nor liberation in me. Even so, transmigration, karma, pleasure and pain are associates of ignorance, not truth. Yet, ignorance and redeeming knowledge, too, are of me and are beginningless. Hence the jīva considers himself bound till he awakes to the truth that he is ever free. The wise one, though he is embodied, is not bound to the body, like a man who is awake and is freed from dream; the unwise one, though in truth he is not bound, imagines himself bound to the body, as one still in dream-state. The wise man knows that his psycho-physical organism is part of creation and so he is inwardly unaffected by their interaction. His actions are non-volitional. His life-force, senses, mind and intellect are not motivated by selfish thoughts and wishes. He does not react to pain and pleasure, honour and dishonour, nor does he judge others, praise or censure them. A wise man should therefore constantly speak of me. If, however, you are uanble to fix your mind wholly on me, do your duties without selfish interest for my sake; then hear my stories, sing them and have them enacted, and dedicate the pursuit of dharma, of wealth and of enjoyment to me. You will attain me.

Uddhava asked: "What is devotion and what are the characteristics of a devotee?"

Lord Kṛṣṇa replied: A devotee is compassionate, harmless, enduring, truthful, faultless, equipoised, benefactor of all, free from lust, disciplined, tender, pure, poor, passive, moderate in everything, peaceful, firm, devoted to me, vigilant, unperturbed, humble, strong and friendly. Devotion to me consists of: worshipping my images, singing my glories, meditating on me, serving me, celebrating festivals connected with me in temples (with dance, music etc.), pilgrimages, processions, inspiring others to worship me and to install images of me, engaging oneself in social welfare activities incognito, without boasting about them, and offering to me what one likes or cherishes most. Sun, fire, brāhmaṇā, cows, devotees of Viṣṇu, space, air, water, earth, self and all beings are worshipful accesses to me. Through appropriate methods one should worship me through all these. There is no royal road to self-realisation, except devotion to me, preceded by association with the holy ones—satsaṅga.

Book Eleven Chapter 12

Lord Kṛṣṇa continued: None of the following—yoga, sānkhya, dharma, study of scriptures, austerity, renunciation, social welfare work, religious rites, vows, pilgrimages, yama-niyama (disciplines)—pleases me as much as satsaṅga. By satsaṅga (association with devotees) one is freed from attachment. By satsaṅga even demons, animals, birds, celestials, serpents and others have attained me. Without abiding by prescribed rules or acquiring the traditional qualifications, cowherdesses and cows have attained me by utterly self-forgetful love of me. Therefore reject all this talk of scriptural injunctions and prohibitions; take refuge in me alone, for I am the self of all.

Uddhava said: Lord, even after hearing all this my doubts and my ignorance still persist. Kindly dispel them.

Lord Kṛṣṇa continued: The same jīva has entered the secret chambers of one's being through the life-force and, having transformed itself into the mind, manifests as speech. In the same way the different activities of the body, the entire objective universe and the deities presiding over them are all my own manifestations, though I am essentially one and unmanifest. O, Uddhava, give up the false notion that the universe is different from God and that it has an existence independent of God. The universe has no existence apart from God, even as cloth has no existence apart from thread (though the converse is not true). This tree of manifestation is beginningless. It has two seeds (virtue and vice) and innumerable roots (desires and actions). It has the three guṇā for its stalks and the five elements as its boughs. It yields the five afflictions as sap. It has eleven branches (mind and senses) and it harbours two birds (jīva and God). It yields two fruits (joy and sorrow). Worldly men who are slaves to cravings eat one fruit—sorrow. Wise men eat the other—joy.

Only he who, by vigilant observation and instructions of a guru, realises the oneness of the whole creation with me, is able to subdue himself. With your self thus subdued, destroy the root of this diversity born of ignorance with the wisdom born of devotion to the guru; then throw away even this weapon (wisdom) and be free.

Lord Kṛṣṇa continued: By satva (cultivated and strengthened by using what is considered sātvika by wise men in food, scriptures, water, etc.), one should overcome the evil and sinful tendencies which are perpetuated by rajas and tamas. Then by satva itself one should overcome satva. The quality of rajas combines with the false notion of 'I' which is mistaken for the body, etc., and generates craving for pleasure. This leads to motivated activity, which leads to reaction. The wise man, however, observes the evils of such behaviour and by the practice of yoga of meditation (with steady posture, controlled breathing) he gets established in me. This is what I taught to Brahmā and my first disciples, Sanaka and his brothers.

Sanaka and his brothers questioned Brahmā: "The mind ever seeks sensual pleasure which leaves an impression on the mind and which repeats itself endlessly. How can one arrest this degradation?"

Brahmā could not answer this question and so I appeared there in the form of a haṁsa (swan). They asked me: "Who are you?" I replied: "If you are referring to the spiritual unity, how can such a question arise? If you refer to the appearance, the body, then again all our bodies are made of the same substance! Whatever the mind and the senses dwell on, know that to be me in truth. In fact, the sense-objects and the mind and the senses of the jīva constitute an unbroken unity with the body of the jīva which is the 'I'. Realising the truth thus, the jīva should transcend all cravings. Similarly, the jīva underlies all the three states of consciousness—waking, dreaming and sleep: this knowledge will enable one to transcend them. When one realises that identification of the self or the jīva with fragmented consciousness is the cause of all sorrow, one gets established in the unity of consciousness. Diversity (which as fragmentation aids this ignorant identification of the jīva) is unreal. It is like the diversity caused by dream whereas the dreamer (and his dream) is one undivided being. Observing this truth, realise that this diversity here is caused by my māyā and cut the very root of this delusion by the sword of wisdom gained from your association with the wise devotees. Thereafter, though this world might continue to appear as of diverse beings, you will not be deluded any more than one who is awake is deluded by the dream from which he awoke. You will not even be deluded by the body which clothes you, even as a drunkard might be unaware of the dress that clings to his body. One who has experienced the state of samādhi does not experience wordliness any more. His innermost being undergoes a complete mutation. This is the secret teaching of yoga and sāṅkhya. I am the goal of both these.

The doubts of Sanaka and his brothers were dispelled. After being worshipped by them, I flew back to my divine realm.

Book Eleven Chapter 14

Uddhava said: The vedā prescribe many paths and you have laid the path of devotion. Please tell me: is one superior to the other or is each one meant for a particular type of seeker?

Lord Kṛṣṇa said: In the beginning of this age I gave the vedā to Brahmā. He transmitted it to the great sages, from whom the people of all the worlds received it. People, however, interpreted it in their own light: they describe different paths to liberation. Some hold it to be dharma, others consider it to be fame, desire, truth, self-control, tranquillity, selfish endeavour, ruling others, renunciation, self-sacrifice, austerity, charity, vows and virtues. All these practices are conditioned, and hence they who are engaged in them are ignorant and foolish, and the good they may do is trivial and short-lived. None of these, without devotion to me, is of any value whatsoever. He who is devoted to me finds bliss flowing to him from all sides. He who has offered his heart to me longs for nothing else. Nay, I myself run after that devotee in order that the dust of his feet may purify me. The mind of the man who dwells on worldly objects becomes attached to them; the mind of my devotee becomes absorbed in me.

Uddhava prayed: Kindly describe how one should meditate upon you.

Lord Kṛṣṇa said: My devotee should choose a place neither high nor low and sit there in a comfortable posture with his hands placed on his lap, with his body erect and with his gaze directed to the tip of his nose. He should then purify his prāṇa by practising prāṇāyāma with inhalation, retention and exhalation. He should then listen inwardly to the Oṁ-sound emanating from the heart, bringing it up with the prāṇa and then letting it re-enter the heart. He should practise thus, doing ten rounds of prāṇāyāma. If he does this thrice a day he will gain control over prāṇa. Then, he should visualise an inverted lotus in his heart, with eight petals and with the sun, moon and fire on its pericarp. In the centre of the fire he should contemplate my form. Withdrawing all the rays of the mind from their waywardness, he should focus them on me. After thus contemplating the entire form, he should focus his mind on my face alone. When it is thus concentrated he should contemplate my omnipresence as space. At last, abandoning even that, he should not think at all. When the mind is thus completely merged in the self, all misconceptions giving rise to diversity will disappear.

Book Eleven Chapter 15

Lord Kṛṣṇa continued: Siddhī or psychic powers come unsought to the spiritual aspirant or devotee who thus meditates upon me. Eighteen such powers have been described by sages. Of these, ten can be acquired by one who is merely established in satva; while the eight major siddhī seek only my devotee. I shall enumerate them for you.

(1) He who worships me as the subtlest of the subtle, the very soul of the atom, is able to reduce himself to the size of an atom—this is aṇimā.

(2) He who meditates upon me as the greatest of the great (the cosmic illimitable being) and as enveloping each and all of the cosmic elements, acquires the power of magnifying himself to any huge size—this is mahimā.

(3) He who concentrates on me as the indweller of the four elements (excluding space) acquires the power to make himself extremely light—this is laghimā. (The above three powers pertain to the physical body.)

(4) He who meditates upon me as the supreme controller of the ego, born of satva, is able to influence the minds and senses of all beings—this is prāpti.

(5) He who meditates upon me as enveloping the mahat tattva (cosmic intelligence and energy), is able to enjoy any delight—this is prākāmya.

(6) He who meditates upon me as the lord of māyā and the supreme controller of the universe, has control over all beings—this is īśitā.

(7) He who meditates upon me as Nārāyaṇa, or the transcendental principle (beyond the three cosmic principles constituting the totality of physical, astral and causal bodies) known as Bhagavān (one who enjoys a. universal lordship, b. dharma, c. fame, d. prosperity, e. wisdom and f. dispassion) shares my nature and is unattached to anything—this is vaśitā.

(8) He who meditates upon me as Brahman the absolute, attains supreme bliss—this is kāmāvasāyitā.

By means of other practices associated with devotion to me the yogi acquires powers like understanding the language of animals, etc., transporting the body at will, entering into another body and so forth. But all these powers which accrue from birth, drugs, penance and the use of mantrā, are obstacles—in as much as they delay attainment of God-realisation, which cannot be attained except through total devotion to me.

Book Eleven Chapter 16

Uddhava asked: You are indeed Brahman the absolute, O Lord! By means of which of your manifestations can your devotee worship you?

Lord Kṛṣṇa said: Arjuna, too, asked me the same question during the great war. I am the self of all beings, O Uddhava; I am their origin, their existence and their goal. I myself am time, and the state of equilibrium of the guṇā. I am the natural property of all objects. I myself am the mahattattva (cosmic intelligence).

I am the jīva (among subtle principles), Brahmā (the teacher of vedā), oṁ (among mantrā), Bhṛgu (among sages), Nārada (among celestial sages), Prahrāda (among demons), moon (among stars), sun (among sources of light and heat), the king (among men), lion (among animals), the monastic order (among stages of life), the priest class (among classes of men), Gaṅgā (among rivers), the ocean (among lakes), the Himālaya (among places of difficult access), the vow of harmlessness (among vows), air, fire, sun, water and the word (among purifying agencies), samādhi (among limbs of yoga), diplomacy (in those who seek victory), the knowledge of the distinction between spirit and matter (in those who seek a scientific understanding of truth), doubt (in those debating on the theory of perception), the vow of fearlessness (among vows), transcendence of thought-process (among means of attaining fearlessness), silence (among methods of secrecy), time (among those who are unwinkingly vigilant), you (among devotees), Vasudeva (among divine personages), Hanumān (among monkeys), gold (among metals), ruby (among precious stones), lotus bud (among lovely objects), wealth (of whose who seek wealth), gambling (of the cheat), endurance (of the enduring), courage (of the courageous), strength (of the strong) and action (of my devotee). I am the characteristic quality of the earth, water, fire, sun, space, etc. I am the different physical functions of the senses. I am the fundamental nature of the elements, the ego and the mahat-tattva, the three guṇā and Brahman the absolute.

Nothing exists apart from me. I am God and also the jīva, as also all other metaphysical categories. Whatever in this world is glorious, prosperous, famous, powerful, modest, liberal, charming, lucky, energetic, enduring and intelligent—there you find a part manifestation of mine. All this description, however, is a mere play of words. When you restrain your mind and intellect you will realise my omnipresence and the illusion of diversity will vanish.

Book Eleven Chapter 17

Uddhava said: In the previous age, you had taught how people of different occupations and orders of society might attain you. This code of varṇa (caste) and āśrama (order of life) has almost been forgotten. Be pleased to describe it to me.

Lord Kṛṣṇa said: In the satya-yuga all the people were haṁsa, pure, noble, self-restrained and spiritually inclined. In the next, tretā-yuga, the cosmic person evolved the four castes—brāhmaṇa, kṣatriya, vaiśya and śūdra—from his mouth, arms, thighs and feet respectively. The four orders of life (household life, celibate student-life, life of a recluse and order of renunicates) had their abode in my loins, heart, chest and head respectively; from these positions they derived their characteristics and nature.

Self-control, austerity, purity, contentment, truthfulness, compassion and devotion to me form the nature of a brāhmaṇa. Prowess, firmness, valour, endurance, magnanimity, industry and devotion to the supreme being form the nature of a kṣatriya. Faith in scriptures and God, charity, humility, service of the Lord and the holy ones and ambitious pursuit of wealth form the nature of a vaiśya. Service of all the above, of cows and of God, and contentment in what is obtained therefrom, form the nature of a śūdra. Filthiness, falsehood, theft, heresy, hostility, lust and anger form the nature of the casteless. Non-violence, truth, non-stealing, freedom from lust, anger and greed, love and loving service of all beings are universal duties.

The student should enter the preceptor's house and live there a life of rigorous self-control and study, treating the guru as God. If he is not interested in entering the household life he should purify himself by intense austerities and service of the guru and, observing perpetual celibacy, shine as a radiant devotee. On the other hand, one who so desires might, on leaving the guru's abode, get married and lead a simple and divine life. In cases of extreme emergency and adversity one may follow the profession or occupation of the others: but as soon as the emergency or the adversity passes, each should return to his own proper profession.

The householder should constantly beware of getting attached to wife, sons, etc., who are like co-passengers on a long journey, and no more. I am the protector of all beings; and he should therefore not entertain false notions of responsibility towards the family, etc., but regard all his household duties as my worship.

Book Eleven Chapter 18

Lord Kṛṣṇa continued: During the third part of his life the man should retire from the household life—either taking his wife with him or entrusting her to his sons. During this period he should thoroughly break-in the psycho-physical organism that perpetuates ignorance, by undertaking the strictest austerity and total self-control. Summer's heat, the monsoon's rains and the winter's cold should all be directly received by his bare body, which is thus passed through the crucible of self-discipline. No time should be wasted even on keeping the body clean. Food should be minimal and utterly sātvika. Ritual worship of me should, however, be continued.

When the desire for this world or others, earned by religious rites, has dropped away, he should leave the forest and take to a mendicant's life. When one is thus about to renounce the world, the gods (through the instrumentality of his wife, etc.), place obstacles which he should resolutely overcome. The mendicant is not governed by any scriptural code. However, by silence he should govern his speech, by total unselfishness his body, and by prāṇāyāma his mind: merely appearing to be a mendicant does not make one so. With his mind and the senses fully controlled, the mendicant should roam the earth. He should beg for his food and take what is just enough to keep body and soul together. If he has not been instructed in spiritual truth he should resort to the feet of a guru whom he should serve and worship as God himself, and receive the spiritual truth from him. He who has such knowledge should wander the earth, with his mind unattached to the world which he knows to be a mere appearance. Though enlightened, he should behave as a child; though proficient and efficient, he should behave like a fool; though highly learned, he should speak as if he is mad; and though he is well versed in the scriptures, he should behave like an animal. He should not react to honour and dishonour. He should not annoy anyone, nor be annoyed by whatever others may do to him. He should never cultivate the enmity of anyone.

He adheres to even these rules as if in sport. For there is no ignorance in him, nor perception of diversity. He continues to be aware of the world-appearance by force of past habit, till the death of his body. Thereafter he is totally united with me—his non-existent ego (which was but a shadow) having vanished.

Everyone performing his duties unselfishly and as an offering unto me will attain me.

Book Eleven Chapter 19

Lord Kṛṣṇa continued: Neither austerity, pilgrimage, prayer, charity or other means of self-purification enable one to reach perfection as even a ray of knowledge does. Therefore equipped with such knowledge, worship me, for men of wisdom are devoted to nothing but me.

Uddhava said: Pray explain to me in detail the nature of devotion, of wisdom and of virtue and vice.

Lord Kṛṣṇa replied: After the termination of the great war, Yudhiṣṭhira asked these very questions of Bhīṣma. I shall relate to you the gist of the latter's answers. Jñāna or wisdom is a thorough understanding of the nine fundamental principles (prakṛti, puruṣa, mahat, ahaṁkāra, and the five subtle elements), the eleven evolutes (the ten sense-organs and the mind), the five gross elements, the three guṇā (which permeate the entire creation) and also the one absolute being which indwells all these as their sole reality. Vijñāna is that by which one does not perceive the diversity at all, but is aware of the unity which alone exists eternally and therefore should be considered as real. Only that is real which existed in the beginning, in the middle and the end (past, present and future), though it undergoes evolutionary transformations in the middle. The testimony of sages, direct perception, tradition and inference reveal this unity.

Now hear the aids to devotion: faith in my stories, singing my glories, dedication to my worship, hymns and prayers, eagerness to serve me, prostrating to me, worship of my devotees, and most important, seeing me in all beings, doing everything for my sake, offering of one's mind to me, desirelessness, renunciation of wealth, pleasure and enjoyment for my sake, and performing all religious activities for my sake. Supreme love for me manifests in the hearts of those who practise these. Once you have this love nothing more remains to be achieved or is worth achieving.

Non-injury, truth, non-stealing, non-attachment, modesty, non-hoarding, faith, continence, silence, firmness, forgiveness, fearlessness, purity, japa, austerity, fire-worship, dedication, hospitality, worship of me, pilgrimage, selfless service, satisfaction, service of the guru—these are yama and niyama.

Hating none is the highest charity. Courage is self-discipline. He who regards the body as the self is a fool. The man of virtue is rich. The discontented man is a destitute. Vain is discussion of virtue. To consider the merits and demerits of others is error; not to look into the merits and demerits of others is virtue.

Book Eleven Chapter 20

Uddhava said: You yourself have said (in the vedā) that one should constantly discriminate between good and evil; and now you yourself say that such discussion is vain. Pray, clear up this confusion.

Lord Kṛṣṇa said: Three paths to yoga (union with me) have been laid by me—jñānam, karma and bhakti. Jñāna is suited to one who is not interested in rituals. Karma is for one who has faith in them. One, in whom a taste for hearing my stories and glories has been awakened, takes to devotion.

One should continue to perform his duties as ordained by the scriptures so long as he has desire for sensual enjoyments and has not developed exclusive taste for my stories and glories. In course of time his heart will be purified and wisdom or devotion will arise in it. Even while performing his duties he should wean his mind away from such enjoyment, nay even enjoyment in heaven. If he longs for a birth in heaven or hell or even in this world, he will be attached to embodiment and will stray from the path. He commits suicide if he, having obtained this human birth and the blessings of a guru and my grace, does not endeavour to cross this ocean of saṁsāra.

When his duties drop away from him he should learn the art of concentration and meditation. He may use the method of conciliation (calculated compromise), at the same time controlling the prāṇa and his senses, and increasing satva. But he should never allow the mind to function unobserved. By dwelling on the processes of evolution and involution, too, the mind is weaned away from its wickedness. Once concentration is achieved he should engage himself in enquiry into the self, or in worship of me.

Should a yogi commit a sin by neglect, he should counteract it by the practice of yoga alone. One-pointedly pursuing one's set course is virtue. Deviation from it is a fault or error. He who has developed a taste for my stories but still longs for pleasure, should worship me, and enjoy sense-pleasures while condemning them as sources of pain. I am present in his heart; and I will remove all the obstacles for him. All the cravings that dwell in his heart will disappear. When I am seen by him, then the knot of ignorance is cut and all his karma and doubts are destroyed.

They who are devoted to me long for naught else, not even for liberation which I gladly bestow upon them. He who follows the path set out above will soon realise the supreme being, known as Brahman.

Book Eleven Chapter 21

Lord Kṛṣṇa continued: Devotion to one's own duty is generally acclaimed as virtue; whatever is contrary to this is regarded as evil. Hence what is virtue for one is not so for another. This paradox has been deliberately introduced in order to create a healthy doubt in regard to good and evil, virtue and error, thereby keeping one alert and enquiring. Other definitions of good and evil are meant to preserve social solidarity and to lay down patterns of conduct for the masses to adopt. Such definition becomes necessary in order to guide those who are charged with the maintenance of law and order.

All creatures in this world are constituted of the five elements and the jīva, and are therefore non-different. The vedā classify them into brāhmaṇā etc., and in order to point out the best way to reach perfection, prescribe certain duties. In fact, the vedā (which is my own word) even attribute good and evil to space (place) and time! Thus, certain places are considered holy and others are not. And, certain periods are considered auspicious and others not. Certain objects coming into contact with certain other objects polluted; and their purification is also brought about by purifying agents like earth, water, fire, air and the passage of time. Beings endowed with the ego-sense are purified of pollution by bathing, charity, penance and rituals, and above all by remembering me.

The vedā itself declares that what is good is evil in certain circumstances, and vice versa, in order to make it clear that these values are not absolute. For instance, by considering something or some action as good, man gets attached to it; from such attachment comes desire which leads to a quarrel with others, then comes anger, and then delusion which obscures wisdom—and this is evil! Such non-vigilant and mechanical adherence to goodness defeats its purpose.

The vedā seems to encourage performance of certain duties and rites for attaining heavenly enjoyments. Knowing the evanescence of the latter, how could the vedā do so? Nay, it is only to wean people away from sensuous life and then to direct them to God. The utterances of the vedā are hard to comprehend. The articulate sound of the mantrā alone is not the truth. The real meaning of the vedā is hidden and is known only to me. Therefore, only he who is solely devoted to me, can grasp it.

Book Eleven Chapter 22

Uddhava asked: How many fundamental principles are there in truth, O Lord? You yourself referred to them as twenty-eight. Other sages have different reckonings. Who is right, who is wrong?

Lord Kṛṣṇa replied: Whatever the holy ones have said in this connection is supported by reason and is therefore reasonable! They are all engaged in this verbal wrangling, telling each other: "I am right, you are wrong" because these principles, which are but the manifestations of my nature or power, are essentially beyond their grasp or understanding. Every effect is inherent in its cause and vice versa, and hence each one determines what he would accept as fundamental and what as the effect or secondary principle. Hence this diverse description, which is reasonable. Only when the senses have been subdued and the mind controlled will the truth concerning them be realised.

Some sages feel that the individual soul cannot liberate itself and so introduce another category called god; others assert that the distinction between soul and God is arbitrary, that God is what is mistaken as the soul, and that therefore an additional category is unwarranted. Therefore, according to some the categories are twenty-six, and to others twenty-five.

When I mentioned twenty-eight categories I took the guṇā separately; but others find them redundant after prakṛti has been mentioned, and so they get twenty-five. Some reduce the whole list to seven; the five elements, the consciousness (soul) and the substratum of both these. Some reduce it to six: the five elements, and consciousness (or the supreme being). Others omit space and air and reduce the number to just four.

Some others adopt a list of seventeen categories: the elements, the senses, mind and ātman. Some omit the mind, which is included in the ātman, and so describe sixteen categories. Some accept thirteen categories: the five elements, the five senses, the mind, the jīva and the supreme spirit. Those who take the mind and the jīva to be included in the supreme spirit accept only eleven. There is another classification which admits of only nine categories: the five elements, mind, intellect, ego and consciousness. Thus all these are valid and reasonable reckonings. Such diversity of schools of thought is not unbecoming of learned and wise men.

Book Eleven Chapter 22

Lord Kṛṣṇa continued: When the equilibrium of the three guṇā is disturbed, diversity as well as the perception of that diversity is brought into being. Infinite though this diversity is, it is viewed as falling into three categories: adhyātma, adhibhūta and adhidaiva. Take the sense of sight for example: the faculty itself is adhyātma, the colour of the object is adhibhūta, and the cognitive principle that relates one to the other is adhidaiva. Even so with the other aspects of one's personality. The ātman is of course consciousness itself, the substratum of all these. The futile polemics of whether the ātman exists independent of these or not, will not cease so long as the disputants turn away from me, their own self.

Uddhava asked: Kindly tell me how the omnipresent ātman enters and leaves successive bodies.

Lord Kṛṣṇa continued: It is the mind of the jīva that moves from one body to another. On account of total identification with the new body (which constitutes its birth) it completely forgets the old one. The complete cessation of identification with the body (on account of the exhaustion of the karma connected with it) constitutes its death. When such a birth takes place, the threefold distinction already described comes into being and consequently the perception and the experience of diversity. In fact, beings undergo birth and death all the time; but on account of the speed and subtlety of time, this is not so perceived. Just as the flame of a candle is constantly renewed and the waters of a stream are continually changed—and yet people regard them as the same flame and the same stream—even so with the body. Again, the jīva neither takes birth nor dies: fire exists for ever though it seems to appear and disappear. Conception, gestation, birth, infancy, childhood, youth, middle age, old age and death are the nine states of one's being. He who is completely identified with the body undergoes pain and pleasure etc., and is deluded, and he revolves on the wheel of karma. If he had cultivated satva he goes to the realm of the gods on leaving his body; rajas takes him to another human birth; and tamas to the realm of the spirits or of sub-human creatures. All this is the result of attachment to the body. A wise man should therefore disentangle himself from this delusion, and whatever may happen to his body and whatever ill-treatment it may be subjected to, he should be totally indifferent, and not react.

Book Eleven Chapter 23

Lord Kṛṣṇa continued: It is easier to bear physical injury than insult. A good man is deeply hurt by insults hurled at him by wicked people. There is a story to illustrate this:

There was a brāhmaṇa in Avanti. He was a very rich miser, hence his own close relations and even the gods, the ancestors, holy men, human beings and animals turned against him, as he failed to perform the five great daily sacrifices enjoined upon a householder. Hence, all his merits exhausted, the wealth (in the acquisition of which he had exerted so much) left him. His relations took a portion, robbers another and the rest was lost either by accident, taxation or by being corrupted by time.

Now a destitute, the brāhmaṇa grew despondent and cursed himself: "What a dreadful thing this wealth is! It is the root-cause of all evil and of all sin and suffering in this world. Theft, cruelty, falsehood, pride, lust, anger, arrogance, hypocrisy, disharmony, hostility, mistrust, love of gambling and misery—these are all evils which arise directly from wealth. Hence one who aspires for final beatitude should never aspire for wealth (artha) which is truly evil (anartha). Wealth estranges friends and close relations and transforms them into enemies. I have wasted my life and energy in amassing and hoarding this mortal enemy, while death is forever knocking at my door. Yet, I am sure I have the supreme grace of śrī Hari on account of which I have grown despondent and also wise, before it is too late. Whatever time is left for me on this earth I shall devote to the adoration of the Lord. It is not impossible for me to attain his feet: Khaṭvāṅga attained it within a very short time by whole-hearted devotion."

Immediately he took to the mendicant order of life. With mind and senses fully controlled, with the knots of egoism and mineness undone, he wandered about as a mendicant. People, however, did not understand him. Some took him for a mad man, some for a hypocrite, and, to prove their contention, hit him, spat on him, caged him and tortured him. Whatever sufferings (natural, divine or physical) came to him, he cheerfully welcomed them as his lot.

The Brāhmaṇa said to himself: Neither these people, nor a god, nor the self, nor the stars and planets, nor karma, nor time is responsible for my pleasure or pain; mind alone is the cause, for it is the mind that keeps this wheel of birth and death revolving. The mind activates the three guṇā and from them proceed different kinds of actions and their consequent reactions (involving one in repeated birth and death). The Lord who is seated in my heart is a pure witness of all this. He is my true friend; but I, the jīva, get involved in the modifications that the mind undergoes and hence become bound. They extol virtues like charity—but if one's mind is tranquil, what does he achieve by means of charity, and if his mind is uncontrolled, what does he gain by charity, and so on? He who is unable to control his greatest enemy (his own mind) treats others as friends and enemies!

If another person is held responsible for my sorrow, does it not imply that one body is hurting another body; if the teeth bite the finger, who is to be blamed? Even so, if a god is held responsible for one's sorrow, the god inflicts pain on himself (as he presides over the different organs of the body), not on the atman, which is distinct from the mind and the senses. If one's own soul, the ātman, is responsible for one's sorrow, then where is the sense in rebelling against one's own nature? The stars and planets can exert their beneficent and malefic influence only on the physical body, so why should I, the soul, get angry with them? Even so, karma affects only the body which the karma gave birth to. Body is material and the soul is pure consciousness. If karma means action (and its consequent reaction), such a thing possibly does not exist in reality, as neither a material substance nor pure consciousness can act. If time is held responsible for our sorrows it incurs no blame either, for the soul and time are identical with the supreme being. Hence, the ātman which is omnipresent and therefore not limited, which is pure consciousness and therefore not subject to materiality, has nothing whatsoever to do with sorrow. Only the illusory ego-sense is subject to sorrow. He who has realised this truth is never afraid of any being. Firmly established in this realisation I shall shake off the illusion of samsāra, by the grace of the lord Kṛṣṇa.

Lord Kṛṣṇa continued: Even so, with your whole being focused on me, control your mind. This indeed is the highest yoga. He who contemplates this sublime and inspiring narrative of the Avanti brāhmaṇa is not affected by dualities like pleasure and pain, happiness and unhappiness.

Book Eleven Chapter 24

Lord Kṛṣṇa continued: I shall now declare to you that knowledge which frees one completely from ignorance, delusion and sorrow.

Before this creation the one absolute Brahman alone existed. In this infinite being there arose the mysterious māyā with its potential duality. This duality became actual with the emergence of prakṛti (nature) which was sub-divided into cause and effect, and of puruṣa (consciousness). As time, I myself continued to disturb the equilibrium of prakṛti from which the three guṇā—satva, rajas and tamas—were evolved. From these were evolved the cosmic sūtrātman (one with the potentiality of plurality of jīva) and mahat (cosmic intelligence). From mahat was evolved ahaṁkāra (cosmic ego sense), which was divided into three: sātvika, rājasa, and tāmasa.

From sātvika ahaṁkāra the deities were evolved, from the rājasa ahaṁkāra the senses were evolved, from tāmasa ahaṁkāra the root-elements evolved. This ahaṁkāra is therefore regarded as both spiritual and material, the link between the two.

All of them together formed the cosmic egg which lay on the cosmic waters. I emerged from it as Nārāyaṇa. From my navel was born Brahmā the creator. He evolved the entire universe in three spheres—bhūr-loka (the earth and the subterranean regions) bhuvar-loka (intermediary space) and svar-loka (the heavenly spheres). In these the human, superhuman and sub-human beings worked out their karma. Beyond svar-loka were the mahar-, jana-, tapo-, and satya-lokā which are reached through yoga, austerity and renunciation. Beyond them all is my own realm, which can be reached solely by devotion.

The entire creation is a manifestation of prakṛti and puruṣa, because only these two existed before creation began and only they will exist after dissolution. Hence, the truth is that only they exist even now. When the time for the dissolution of the creation arrives, all living creatures enter the earth, earth dissolves in water, water merges in fire, fire in air and air disappears in space—each one with its natural quality. The effects merge in their original cause. Thus, all these merge in ahaṁkāra, ahaṁkāra in mahat-tatva, mahat-tatva (as the three guṇā) in prakṛti, prakṛti and puruṣa in the cosmic person, the director of māyā—and these latter in me. This knowledge of the sāṅkhya expounded by me destroys doubt and delusion, the root-causes of sorrow.

Book Eleven Chapter 25

Lord Kṛṣṇa continued: Uddhava, I shall now tell you how the guṇā influence man. Each guṇā produces a distinct reaction which manifests as a quality. Satva manifests as self-control, endurance, austerity, truthfulness, compassion, awareness, satisfaction, renunciation, non-attachment, faith, modesty and delight in the self. Rajas manifests as lust, selfish activity, arrogant obstinacy, craving, pride, hope, unwise discrimination, pleasure-seeking, impetuosity, ebullience, hankering for fame, complacency, immodest laughter, energy, strength and endeavour. Tamas manifests as anger, greed, falsehood, violence, begging, hypocrisy, languor, discord, sorrow, delusion, drowsiness, expectation, sleepiness, hope, fear and laziness.

The guṇā are often mixed up in their manifestation in various proportions and hence the nature and the behaviour of men manifests a mixture of the different qualities mentioned above. A man may be devoted to religious practices, with the hope of obtaining a reward, and thus reveal the mixture of two or more guṇā.

All substances in this world—places, fruits, time, knowledge, action, the doer of action, faith, states of consciousness, birth, destiny—are classified into sātvika, rājasa, tāmasa. These three qualities are constantly revolving and overwhelming one another. Hence sometimes one and sometimes the other prevails and the others are temporarily subdued.

In general, satva elevates the soul and takes it closer to me in pure devotion, without expectation of an earthly or heavenly reward. Rajas disturbs the peace of the person and keeps him actively pursuing pleasure and profit on the human level. Tamas, on the other hand, drags him down to lower states of existence and consciousness, nature and behaviour. One's future birth is determined (naturally) by the nature of one's being at the time he leaves the present body.

One should study the nature and operation of the three guṇā very carefully and choose the sātvika in everything and thus overcome rajas and tamas. Then he should overcome satva by satva itself; and by disentangling himself from the subtle body, attain me. For satva is not the goal of life. Even if in one's daily life and actions one offers everything to me and lives for my sake, he shall go beyond the influence of the three guṇā. One who thus transcends the very concept of jīva and the guṇā neither goes outside nor inside: he lives in me constantly.

Book Eleven Chapter 26

Lord Kṛṣṇa continued: The heart of the wise man who is devoted to me 'does not go out'. He is able to pierce the veil of māyā and realise that the perception of pleasure in the objects of the senses is false. He who cultivates such devotion would do well to avoid the company of women or people who are fond of sensual enjoyment. The latter are blind to the reality, and anyone associated with them will also fall into blinding darkness.

You know how Purūravā lived with Urvaśī, how he was abandoned by her and how he tried again to win her over. When she abandoned him he ran after her, naked, shouting: "Wait, wait a moment." Then, despondent, he said to himself:

"Terrible and exceedingly powerful is this infatuation. Under its influence I have wasted years and years of my precious life, which have passed unnoticed. Look at me—though I am a mighty emperor of eternal fame, I am shamelessly running after a woman, naked and demented. Of what use is knowledge, austerities, renunciation, vaidika study, seclusion or silence to him whose heart has been stolen by a woman? I am indeed pitiable. I am unaware of my real interests. I consider myself learned and wise, but I am a fool. I have gained great power but I am overpowered by women. Even after years of enjoyment, sensual craving has not abated; on the contrary, it has only become more intense. Only the Lord can save me from this hell. What is the sense in blaming a woman: it is not the fault of the rope that a fool mistakes it for a snake, even so it is the passion in man that causes his downfall.

"All, for the sake of this body. Whose body is this—who knows? Does it belong to the parents, one's wife, the employer, fire, dog, vulture, one's own self or one's friends? Who knows? Believing the body to be himself, man seeks objects that produce pleasurable sensations to the body. If the mind is not directed towards objects of sense-indulgence it will become (and remain) tranquil. The wise man should never trust his mind and senses. He should avoid the company of women and those who are fond of women." Thus resolved Purūravā fixed his heart on me and attained me. A wise man should by all means avoid evil company and cultivate the company of devotees and sages, who are like a ship to take one across this ocean of saṁsāra. Food is vital to living beings; I am the sole refuge of the afflicted; dharma is man's only wealth; and even so, company of holy men is the only resort for those who aspire for liberation.

Book Eleven Chapter 27

Uddhava said: Sages have repeatedly proclaimed that kriyā yoga is the path to man's highest good. Kindly instruct me in kriyā yoga.

Lord Kṛṣṇa said: I shall describe kriyā yoga in brief. There are three ways to worship me—the vaidika, the tāntrika and a combination of both. One can adopt whatever mode he likes.

On awaking in the morning a man should clean his teeth and purify his body. After smearing his body with clay etc., he should take his bath. Without neglecting his worldly and religious duties he should then duly worship me, using any of the eight kinds of images—stone, wood, metal, clay, sandal-paste, paint, sand, precious stone—or an image conceived in his mind, of either the movable or the immovable type. In those images I should be offered appropriate worship: the image in the heart is of course worshipped with love alone. The devotee should sit facing the east or the north or the image itself and offer me a seat, a bath, clothes, ornaments, food-offerings and so on, all the time feeling that his own body is permeated by my living presence.

After this, he should worship me in the sacrificial fire, into which he should pour oblations of ghee (clarified butter) with the appropriate mantrā. Having thus worshipped me and the fire, he should repeat his own basic mantra, contemplating on me as being the infinite Nārāyaṇa. He should then sing my glories with popular hymns or the hymns found in the various purāṇā (legends), and repeatedly pray: "O Lord, save me, protect me." Holding my feet he should fall flat in front of me and pray: "Save me from this ocean of samsāra." My devotee can worship me whenever he likes and through whatever image he likes most.

He who can afford it should build a temple for me. By doing so he earns great merit.

Book Eleven Chapter 28

Lord Kṛṣṇa continued: The wise man, realising that oneness alone is the truth, should neither praise nor condemn anything in the world.

Diversity is the result of the soul's sleep, or ignorance! It is a long dream. When such is the case, what is good, what is evil? Whatever is described by speech and whatever is thought of by the mind is all false.

Uddhava submitted: Then, O Lord, what is the entity that transmigrates?

Lord Kṛṣṇa answered: So long as the sleeping soul dreams this world of diversity and gets involved in the senses and their objects, and the mind and its modifications, it dreams that it is getting in and out of embodiment. The inner soul that identifes itself with the body, the senses, life-force and the mind is the jīva. It is this jīva in its unenlightened state that feels sorrow, etc., whereas it is in truth not subjected to such sorrow. When one develops keen discrimination, in the light of which one realises the complete non-involvement of the self in the changes that the body and the world of matter undergo, one is freed from bondage and delusion and roams about the world, rid of all craving and sorrow.

Duality is untenable. I alone existed before creation and shall exist after dissolution; hence I alone exist even now by whatever names and forms I may be thought of. Gold is gold always, both before and after its transformation into what is known as ornament, for even an ornament is gold only. One should therefore cultivate the keenest discrimination or understanding, by which one is able to rise above the mist of dualities and bask in the eternal sunshine of self-knowledge. Till then of course the deluded jīva will undergo transmigration. Nothing short of perfection, which is the realisation of the self, or unity, can bestow liberation on you. Till that is achieved the lusts and cravings that are the offering of this perception of diversity will return again and again like improperly treated illness.

If the yogi, while striving for perfection, experiences obstacles on the path of yoga, he should overcome them: some by the practice of concentration; some by yoga postures performed with inner concentration; others through austerities, herbs or repetition of mantrā; others through my worship and singing of my names and glories; and yet others by the devoted service of masters of yoga. He who practises yoga, depending upon me, is never baffled by obstacles but soon attains enlightenment.

Book Eleven Chapter 29

Uddhava said: Lord, the yoga you have taught me is extremely difficult, for to control the mind is difficult and without control of mind one cannot practise this yoga. Kindly point out an easy way to achieve this.

Lord Kṛṣṇa replied: I shall tell you what I consider to be the greatest form of yoga, that practice which pleases me most and which is the best way to attain immortality. One should offer his whole mind to me, his heart to me, and with his whole being devoted to me, do all actions for my sake. He should see me alone in all beings and thus cultivate equal vision towards all beings–from the high-born and learned brāhmaṇa and devotee to the lowest and meanest of creatures. By this incessant practice he will overcome the spirit of rivalry, of finding fault with others and of contempt—all of which are associates of self-conceit. Without the least sense of shame and without regard for the opinions of others he should prostrate himself like a falling piece of wood before all, even to animals like the donkey.

In this way he comes to regard everything as Brahman the infinite. This indeed is the greatest of spiritual disciplines, the greatest yoga and the quickest way to self-knowledge. There is no loss at all in this path and nothing but spiritual gain; as this practice has been ordained directly by me it is beyond the operation of the three guṇā. All actions dedicated to me are also beyond the operation of the guṇā, and hence conducive to liberation.

What I have told you thus far contains the quintessence of the knowledge of vedānta. I shall confer my own self on him who propagates this knowledge. He who listens to this dialogue of ours will develop supreme devotion, and is not bound by karma.

Uddhava said: The darkness of ignorance that clouded my understanding has been dispelled by your teaching. Bless me, so that unceasing love for you may fill my heart.

Sage Śuka said: Lord Kṛṣṇa then instructed Uddhava to go to Badarikāśrama and there engage himself in constant remembrance of the Lord. Uddhava bowed to the Lord and, departing from that place, proceeded towards Badarikāśrama. There he practised the yoga taught by the Lord, and attained union with him.

Kṛṣṇa's Ascent to Heaven
Book Eleven Chapter 30

Sage Śuka continued: As I told you already, when śrī Kṛṣṇa noticed evil omens portending calamities he advised his relations and friends to leave Dvārakā and migrate to Prabhāsa. He advised them to send away the women, children and aged men to Śaṅkhoddhāra and the younger men to Prabhāsa. This they did.

There in Prabhāsa, with their minds deluded by the curse of the holy brāhmaṇā and their evil destiny clouding their intelligence, they drank strong liquor known as maireyaka, which further impaired their discrimination. There followed arguments, quarrels and fights among the yādavā themselves. Soon they started hitting one another with clubs, maces, arrows and even bows. Brothers hit brothers, sons fought with their fathers. They hit one another with swords and anything that came in handy. When all these were exhausted they pulled out the erakā weeds that grew on the seashore; these erakā weeds had the pulverized pieces of the iron pestle born of the brāhmaṇā's curse. As they wielded these weeds and hit one another they began to fall dead. Such was the brāhmaṇā's curse; such was Kṛṣṇa's will. When Balarāma and Kṛṣṇa tried to intervene the yādavā turned against them! They considered Balarāma and Kṛṣṇa as their enemies. What could delusion and perversion not do!

With their total destruction, śrī Kṛṣṇa decided that his mission (destruction of all the wicked people on earth) had been fulfilled. He was ready to leave, too. In the meantime Balarāma, contemplating the supreme being, ascended to his realm. Śrī Kṛṣṇa walked over to a peepul tree and sat under it, leaning against its trunk. He shone like a smokeless fire. Just then a hunter named Jarā fixed an arrow to his bow and shot Kṛṣṇa's foot, which resembled the mouth of an antelope. That arrowhead had the last remnant of the iron pestle for its tip!

Horrified to discover the real victim of his arrow, the hunter cried aloud in agony: "Lord, kill me and relieve me of this sin." But the Lord full of love, said to him: "Fear not, Jarā, you have done what I desired; you will ascend to heaven, the abode of the righteous." After bowing to Kṛṣṇa, Jarā went up to heaven in an aerial vehicle. Dāruka, Kṛṣṇa's charioteer, had arrived there in the meantime with the chariot. Kṛṣṇa said to him: "Go back to our women, children and aged men and tell them what happened here. I shall presently leave the earth and Dvārakā will be engulfed by the sea. Our parents, children and ladies should leave for Indraprastha. As for you, be devoted to me and you will surely attain me." As he was saying this, the chariot rose to heaven.

Book Eleven Chapter 31

Sage Śuka continued: The gods headed by Brahmā the creator, the celestials, the sages and others, reached Prabhāsa eager to witness the Lord's ascent to his own abode. They worshipped him with a shower of flowers. The Lord looked at Brahmā and, withdrawing his self into the self, he closed his lotus eyes. By practising the yoga method called agni-dhāraṇā he did not burn (or burnt, if the word is taken as dagdhvā) the body which had delighted the hearts of all people and which, when meditated upon, confers all auspiciousness on the devotee; he then entered his own realm. Some of the spectators witnessed this wonderful phenomenon; others could not. After this, the gods retired to their own spheres.

O Parīkṣit! All this is mere sport for the Lord. He creates, preserves and sustains. He himself puts on the appearance of a human being and plays his role in this world. All this is mere sport. Forever he remains established in his own glory, which is not diminished in the least by this divine sport. Though the Lord is omnipotent and is able without any other aid to create, sustain and dissolve everything, he did not wish to preserve his body in this world, in order to bring home to people that it is not worth preserving a perishable body forever—though he could have, if he had wished to. He who every morning recites the story of Kṛṣṇa's ascension will himself ascend to the Lord's abode.

Dāruka went back to where Kṛṣṇa's people were and narrated everything to them. the Lord's earthly parents on hearing this gave up their lives.The womenfolk embraced their dead heroes and ascended the pyre along with their husbands. Even so, the wives of Balarāma, embracing his body, burnt their own bodies. Kṛṣṇa's wives, too, left their mortal coil, meditating upon him.

Arjuna, sore distressed at heart and unable to bear separation from Kṛṣṇa, recalled Kṛṣṇa's teaching, the Bhagavad Gītā. He departed from Indraprastha, escorting the women and others who had survived the holocaust. He crowned Vajra, the only surviving son of Aniruddha, as the king. Thereafter the pāṇḍavā left for the Himālaya, crowning you king.

He who narrates or listens to this auspicious story of lord Kṛṣṇa will develop supreme devotion to the Lord.

Book Twelve

Book Twelve Chapter 1

King Parīkṣit asked: After the departure of śrī Kṛṣṇa, who ruled the earth?

Sage Śuka continued: A dynasty of five kings known as the Pradyotanā will rule for a hundred and thirty-eight years. The next will be the Śiśunāga dynasty who will rule for three hundred and sixty years. The last of them will be Mahānandi whose son Mahāpadma will be born of a śūdra woman, and who will establish a mighty empire. Mahāpadma and his sons will rule for a hundred years; this will be known as the Nanda dynasty. From your birth to the coronation of Nanda would be one thousand one hundred and fifteen years. Cāṇakya will bring this dynasty to an end and will install Candragupta Maurya on the throne. The Mauryā will rule for a hundred and thirty-seven years.

Bṛhadratha Maurya will be assassinated by his army chief Puṣyamitra Śunga, who will establish the Śunga dynasty of ten kings, who will in all rule for more than a hundred years. The immortal Devabhūti of the Śunga dynasty will be assassinated by his minister Vasudeva who will found the Kaṇva dynasty, which will reign for three hundred and forty-five years. Suśarmā, the last of the Kaṇvā will be assassinated by his servant Bali. Bali and his descendants (thirty in all) will rule for four hundred and fifty-six years.

Then there will be seven Ābhīra kings, ten Gardabhī, sixteen Kankā, eight Yavanā, fourteen Turuṣkakā, ten Guruṇḍā, and then eleven Maunā will rule for a total period of one thousand three hundred and ninety-nine years. After this Bhūtananda and his descendants will rule for a hundred and six years. Then will come the Bāhlikā, Puṣpamitra and Durmitra.

An evil-minded ruler known as Purañjaya The Second will convert all his subjects into mlecchā, exterminate the kṣatriyā and rule from the city of Padmāvatī, the stretch of land on the bank of the Gaṅgā down to Prayāga. Śūdrā, fallen brāhmaṇā and all manner of unrighteous men will rule over the banks of the Sindhu and Candrabhāgā, and also the region of Kāśmīr. These kings will kill women, cows, children and brāhmaṇā and adopt diabolical ways of living. Devoid of righteousness, their actions characterised by rajas and tamas, they will enslave their own people and torture them. Their subjects, too, will follow the rulers example, exploiting one another, and thus rushing headlong towards utter ruin. He who exploits others for the sake of his body is unaware of his own true welfare. Great rulers who have aspired to possess the earth have passed away. They are but names in stories narrated today.

Description of Kali Yuga
Book Twelve Chapter 2

Sage Śuka continued: Kali yuga commenced when Kṛṣṇa departed from this earth. In this yuga, day after day righteousness will decline, along with the health, strength and longevity of the people. Wealth alone will be the criterion for the worth of one's birth, conduct and character. Strength alone will determine who is righteous and just in his dealings. The relationship between husband and wife will depend on mutual liking. Cheating will be common business practice. Masculinity and femininity will be judged by sexual efficiency. Brāhmaṇā will be distinguished only by a thread they may wear. Even the administration of justice will be perverted by bribery and corruption. Hairstyles will determine beauty. Vehemence of speech will determine truth! People will do good to society only in order to gain fame. The four stages of life (celibate-student, etc.), will all become one household life!

During this period the good people will flee the corrupt cities and isolate themselves on mountains and in forests, being content to live on roots, fruits and honey. Elsewhere, people will be overtaken by famine, pestilence, drought and storms. Their wealth drained by taxation and robbery and their energy depleted by their own unrighteous living, they will die young. Even trees will become stunted on account of their ruthless exploitation by unrighteous men. Cows will become emaciated and will yield very little milk.

At this time, the Lord will incarnate in a brāhmaṇa family in the village known as Śaṁbhala, and will be known as Kalki. With unequalled splendour he will fly swiftly across the sky, destroying million of robbers in the disguise of rulers. Then will the next satya yuga commence—an age of righteousness and holiness. Satya yuga will commence when the sun, the moon and jupiter rise together in the same house, and the puṣya constellation is in the ascendant.

Devāpi, brother of Śantanu, and Maru of the Ikṣvāku dynasty will continue to live in the village of Kalāpa. They will be alive when the satya yuga commences, in order to teach mankind the essence of dharma.

Book Twelve Chapter 3

Sage Śuka continued: The good earth pities insolent kings and, as it were, says: "How foolish of man to think he can conquer me! Often man imposes self-control upon himself and then conquers other people, with his ambition to conquer continually expanding! How short-sighted, for self-control is meant only for attaining self-knowledge. Why does he not see that death is ever waiting to devour him. So many great kings have endeavoured to conquer me, and I have had the last laugh. They have disappeared, leaving only a story behind." I have narrated the stories of some of them, Parīkṣit, only to create disgust in you for such life. For only the stories concerning the Lord are fit to be heard and meditated upon.

King Parīkṣit asked the sage to describe the dharma relating to each yuga, in answer to which sage Śuka continued: In satya yuga dharma had all its four legs—truth, compassion, asceticism and loving service of all creatures. In tretā yuga a quarter of all the four feet was destroyed by the power of adharma. Half of all the four feet was destroyed in dvāpara yuga. In the kali yuga three-fourths has gone, and the other quarter too, is steadily declining. In satya yuga, satva prevailed. In tretā yuga, rajas prevailed. In dvāpara yuga, rajas and tamas prevailed. In kali yuga, tamas predominates. Hence, women become unchaste. Even men of religion are after pleasure and wealth. Women become unsexed and harsh in their behaviour. Servants are disloyal to their masters who, in their turn, mercilessly dismiss incapacitated servants, Even so, barren cows are starved. Unqualified people masquerade as hermits, to earn their livelihood.

People who are ignorant of religion preach it. People kill one another for a petty sum of money. Greedy fathers disown their sons; and ungrateful sons fail to maintain their aged parents. And, worst of all, people do not worship lord Viṣṇu, the highest object of adoration in the universe. Only when the Lord is enthroned in people's hearts will the evils of kali yuga disappear from there. If a dying man even helplessly utters his name, the Lord takes him to his own realm.

But, there is one great redeeming feature in kali yuga. One can reach the supreme by merely singing the names of Hari. What was possible only by meditating upon the Lord in satya yuga, by the performance of religious rites in tretā yuga and by unselfish service in dvāpara age, one can easily attain by singing the Lord's names in kali yuga.

Book Twelve Chapter 4-5

Sage Śuka continued: I shall now describe the different forms of dissolution of the universe, O Parīkṣit. A thousand cycles of the four yugā constitutes a day of the creator, a kalpa. At the end of this kalpa there is a pralaya (dissolution) of an equal duration, during which the creator sleeps. This is known as naimittika pralaya (occasional dissolution) when both the lord Nārāyaṇa and the creator Brahmā sleep, the creation having been withdrawn into themselves. But at the end of the lifetime of Brahmā, the causal principles (mahat, ahaṁkāra and the subtle elements) are dissolved in prakṛti: and hence this is known as prākṛitika pralaya. This is preceded by exceptionally long drought, followed by fierce heat both from the sun and from subterranean sources and cosmic storms which reduce the entire universe of matter into the primordial element, which is the cosmic egg; and this cosmic egg floats on the casual waters. Prakṛti (unmanifest nature) and the supreme person are withdrawn into cosmic consciousness, beyond description and beyond expression.

Whatever is, has been and will be, is cosmic consciousness alone. There is nothing apart from it. The intellect, the senses and their objects are all rooted in consciousness; the three states of waking, dreaming and sleep are based on this consciousness. Just as clouds form and vanish in the sky, so this universe appears and disappears in the infinite being. Even as the cloud born of the heat of the sun veils the sun from our eyes (which are presided over by the sun), even so the ego, born of consciousness, veils that very consciousness. When the cloud disperses the sun is seen: when the ego is dismissed Brahman is seen. This is known as ātyantika pralaya, final dissolution of ignorance of the self. In addition sages declare that everyone experiences perpetual dissolution—nitya pralaya—inasmuch as there is continuous creation and dissolution of the elements that constitute this universe, like sparks in a flame, or waters of a river.

Give up the foolish notion that you were born and that you will die. All this takes place in the dream state of the ignorant jīva, not in truth. Mind alone creates, perpetuates and dissolves; and mind is a product of māyā. The body, its birth and its death are all illusory projections of this māyā. Remain established in this truth: "I am Brahman the infinite, the supreme abode, I am Brahman the highest goal."

Thus have I narrated to you, my own self, the holy actions of lord Hari: what else is there worth hearing?

Parīkṣit is Killed by Takṣaka
Book Twelve Chapter 6

King Parīkṣit said: I am perfect and I am blessed, having heard from you who are the very embodiment of supreme compassion, the accounts of the eternal Hari. I am not afraid of the serpent Takṣaka at whose hands my death has been ordained; I am not afraid of death itself. I am one with the infinite being, I have reached the fearless state, thanks to your teaching.

Sūta said: After being thus glorified and worshipped by king Parīkṣit, the sage Śuka departed from that place. The king sat in deep meditation on the bank of the holy Gaṅgā, and merged in the infinite. Soon after, the serpent named Takṣaka, who had been instigated by the brāhmaṇa's curse to bite and kill Parīkṣit and who could assume any guise he desired, appeared as a brāhmaṇa and proceeded to where Parīkṣit was. On the way he met Kaśyapa, who knew the secret of counteracting the poison; he bribed Kaśyapa, to prevent him from coming to the aid of the king. Approaching the king who was in deep meditation (having already attained union with the supreme) Takṣaka bit his body and reduced it to ashes.

Seeing this, the king's son Janamejaya was greatly angered. With the help of some brāhmaṇā he commenced a holy rite invoking the destruction of all serpents. Takṣaka immediately sought Indra's asylum, which was granted. Failing to find his father's killer, Janamejaya questioned the brāhmaṇā and found out the truth. "Let us pour oblations into the sacred fire with the invocation that Takṣaka and all those who harbour that criminal—Indra and others—should perish in this fire," said Janamejaya. When this was done, the very throne of Indra began to shake. Bṛhaspati thereupon interceded and counselled Janamejaya: "You have destroyed many innocent snakes in this fruitless rite. Takṣaka has quaffed some nectar and so cannot be killed. Beings suffer the consequences of their own action: the mode of one's death is determined by one's own karma. So, please stop this malevolent rite." Janamejaya did so.

Action and reaction, pleasure and pain and such others are in the realm of māyā. The Lord is beyond all these. He who would attain the abode of Viṣṇu should rise above the notions of 'I' and 'mine' which are associated with the body and house, etc., and not react to any situation that may arise as a consequence of such notions.

Salutations to lord Kṛṣṇa, by the grace of whose lotus-feet I learnt this most glorious scripture.

Book Twelve Chapter 6

Śaunaka asked: Tell us about the origin of the vedā and their classification.

Sūta said: Brahmā the creator conentrated his mind and focused it on the self. He then heard in the cavity of his own heart a sound-vibration which is capable of being experienced when the mental modifications are tranquillised. By adoring that sound vibration the yogī purify themselves of the impurities caused by material substances, actions and forms, and attain immortality. That sound vibration was heard as the OM with its three divisions of A U M, and which is the indicator of the supreme being.

The three division of this monosyllable represent the three qualities (guṇā), the three vedā, the three spheres and the three states of consciousness. From these the creator then evolved the complete set of alphabets. Exercising these alphabets, with his four faces and mouths Brahmā gave expression to the four vedā—ṛk, yajus, sāma and atharva. Brahmā taught these vedā to his sons, the mind-born sages, who in their turn passed them on to others. Thus the vedā continued to be 'heard' by successive generations of sages.

During the present cycle a part of the Lord incarnated as the son of the sage Parāśara and Satyavatī, with the auspicious name Vyāsa. It was he who classified the vedā, dividing them into four groups. He taught the ṛg-veda to Paila, the yajus to Vaiśampāyana, the sāma to Jaimini and the atharva to Sumantu. They in their turn passed it on to their pupils, dividing and sub-dividing the vedā into many more branches.

Yājñāvalkya, a pupil of Vaiśampāyana, had through insolence in connection with an expiatory rite earned the wrath of his preceptor, who made him 'vomit' the knowledge he had imbibed. The vomited knowledge was picked up by other sages who had assumed the form of partridges, and hence came to be known as Taittirīya. Yājñāvalkya himself worshipped the sun-god who, pleased with him, assumed the form of a horse and imparted knowledge of portions of the yajur-veda which had not been learnt by others. This came to be known as vājasani.

Thus the vedā continued to be propagated from generation to generation.

Book Twelve Chapter 7

Sūta continued: Trayyāruṇi, Kaśyapa, Sāvarṇi, Akṛtavraṇa, Vaiśaṁpāyana and Hārīta were the six expounders of the purāṇā (legends), All of them learnt one collection from my father: I learnt all from them. The purāṇā have ten characteristics—creation, manifestation, preservation, protection, the world-cycle, dynasties, accounts connected with these dynasties, dissolution, cause and the substratum. Some sages are content with five, the others being included in them.

Sarga (creation) is the evolution of the subtle elements, consequent upon the disturbance of the equilibrium of the guṇā.

Visarga is the further creation of the mobile and the immobile creation, in all its diversity, and the interpenetration of all this by the supreme being himself, giving rise to the self-perpetuation of all the species of creation.

Vṛtti is the description of the means of subsistence for all living beings, and how they live.

Rakṣā is divine protection in the shape of the Lord's own periodic descent into his own creation in order to restore the balance, and thus to enable the created universe to progress to its proper destination.

Antarā are the 'manvantarā' (world-cycles) over each of which a manu presides, assisted by gods and sages, as has already been described.

Vaṁśa refers to the dynasties of rulers over the earth whose exploits are described in the purāṇā.

Vaṁśānucarita is the narration of the exploits of the rulers which illustrate certain spiritual truths, the most important being that all pursuits in this world, except the attainment of self-knowledge, are futile and foolish.

Saṁsthā is dissolution—the fourfold dissolution of the creation which has already been mentioned.

Hetu is the cause of creation; and apāśraya is the substratum for the entire creation, which is the supreme being.

Such purāṇā are eighteen in number: Brāhma, Pādma, Viṣṇu, Śiva, Linga, Gāruḍa, Nārada, Bhāgavata, Agni, Skānda, Bhaviṣya, Brahma-vaivarta, Mārkaṇḍeya, Vāmana, Vāraha, Mātsya, Kūrma and Brahmāṇḍa.

Mārkaṇḍeya
Book Twelve Chapter 8

Śaunaka said: Some people say that the sage Mārkaṇḍeya lived through a pralaya (dissolution) without being affected by it. Yet we know that he lived in this very world-cycle which has not yet passed through a dissolution. How shall we reconcile this contradiction?

Sūta said: Mārkaṇḍeya was duly invested with the holy thread, after which he acquired the knowledge of the vedā and practised asceticism. He had undertaken the vow of lifelong celibacy and engaged himself in intense penance and devotion to the Lord, śrī Hari, at the same time worshipping the guru, the sun and the sacred fire. Thus meditating upon the Lord for a very, very long time Mārkaṇḍeya had conquered all the enemies of spirituality—lust, anger, greed, ego and ignorance, and had overcome even death.

Six manvantarā, or world-cycles, had passed in this manner. During the seventh manvantara, Indra the king of the gods became anxious lest Mārkaṇḍeya should, as a fruit of his unprecedented austerities, win the throne of Indra for himself. Hence, as was his custom, Indra deputed a bevy of celestial nymphs and other suitable accompaniments in the form of musicians and Cupid himself, to disturb the sage's penance.

Cupid and the nymphs went to the northern slopes of the Himālaya where the sage was meditating. They tried their best to disturb the heart of the meditating sage, but to no avail. Thoroughly defeated in their attempt they returned to Indra, crest-fallen.

In the meantime, highly pleased with the sage's penance, lord Hari in the twin-form of Nara-Nārāyaṇa appeared before him. Seeing them the sage fell on his face and worshipped them. He stood up, and bowing deeply to them, offered his heartfelt prayer to them:

"Lord, this twin-form of yours is manifest here in this world solely for the redemption of all the beings of the three worlds. I take refuge at your feet which free the devotee once and for all from the operation of the guṇā. Even the mighty time, Kāla, is nothing more than the play of your eyebrows. When such is the case, what is the value of other worldly objects and what is the use of being attached to this perishable body and all that is related to it? Hence, I turn away from all that and take refuge in you."

Book Twelve Chapter 9

The glorious Lord said: I am highly pleased with your lifelong discipline and unequalled asceticism, and your utter devotion to me. Choose any boon from me.

Mārkaṇḍeya said: Lord, what greater boon shall I choose, having by your grace seen you face to face? Yet, if you would like to bless me, I would like to see the power of your māyā.

Sūta continued: "Be it so" said the Lord and returned to his abode. And the sage carried on his life as before, contemplating the meaning of the Lord's māyā. His devotion to the lotus feet of the Lord grew to such intensity that he sometimes forgot to worship the Lord. One day, as he was worshipping him on the bank of the river Puṣpabhadrā, a violent storm shook the whole place, followed by unprecedented rain. It rained so heavily that the whole place was flooded; and it looked as though the oceans had swollen and had almost submerged the whole earth.

The sage Mārkaṇḍeya was anxious: he saw waves rising sky-high all round. All living beings had been wiped out. He was the only living person, somehow borne on this terribly rough ocean. It was totally dark. He could not even tell in which direction he was facing. He felt as though millions of years passed in this predicament. He thought it was the universal dissolution.

After what appeared to be a long, long time, the sage saw the prominence of a piece of earth. On it stood a banyan tree. On one of the leaves of that tree lay a naked babe, exceedingly charming to look at, of dark-green complexion, holding its foot with its hands and putting that foot into its coral-lipped mouth. The sage, who had been tormented by the deluge for a very long time, felt that the very sight of that babe had relieved him of his fatigue and despair. He went near it. With its inhaled breath he entered into the body of the baby; and within its belly he saw everything—the whole universe—with the Himālaya, his āśrama and himself! With its exhaled breath he was thrown out.

Astounded by this experience he rushed once again towards the baby in order to embrace it. But before he could touch the baby it had disappeared, the waters had disappeared, the earth stood as before and he was standing on the bank of the river near his hermitage.

Book Twelve Chapter 10

Sūta continued: Realising that this was the experience of the Lord's māyā which he had asked to see, the sage Mārkaṇḍeya contemplated the Lord and once again offered him a heartfelt prayer.

One day, lord Śiva and Pārvatī were flying over the sage's hermitage when Pārvatī looked at the sage sitting absorbed in contemplation, and prayed to lord Śiva to reveal the sage's supreme devotion for the emulation of devotees. Śiva said: "Sages like him will not think of seeking any boon from any divinity, as you will see." Having said so, Śiva descended and stood in front of the sage.

Completely absorbed in his contemplation of the Lord, the sage did not notice lord Śiva standing in front of him. Thereupon lord Śiva entered the heart of the devotee. It was only then that the sage noticed him. He worshipped the Lord and Pārvatī and sang the Lord's praises.

Lord Śiva said: The trinity—Brahmā, Viṣṇu and myself—grant boons to our devotees: so, O sage, choose any boon you like. All the gods and we three (Brahmā, Viṣṇu and myself) salute and adore the holy sages who are ever peaceful, unattached to anything and full of love for all creatures, who are exclusively devoted to us, who are free from hostility and who are endowed with equal vision. They do not make any distinction between me, lord Viṣṇu and Brahmā, or between us and other beings in the universe. Hence we adore people like you. By merely hearing about you the worst sinners are purified. How much more glorious it is to see you and to be with you.

Mārkaṇḍya said: Lord, who can fathom your glory and your actions? Your actions are meant only for the emulation of people. Glory, glory to you, O Lord. The only boon I ask from you is this: may my devotion to lord Hari, his devotees and to you, grow forever and ever.

Lord Śiva said: Be it so, O sage. Furthermore I confer another boon on you. May your fame endure till the end of this world-cycle. May you enjoy radiant health and complete immunity from death. May you be established in self-knowledge. May you teach a purāṇa, to be named after you.

Thus did Mārkaṇḍeya experience the mystery of the Lord's māyā and feel that he had survived a dissolution. He lived in a state of mahāyoga and attained the supreme.

Śaunaka asked: O Sūta, kindly describe the Lord's person to us, to enable us to meditate upon him with the right attitude.

Sūta said: The cosmic egg has been described to consist of the nine fundamental principles (prakṛti, mahat, sūtra, ahaṁkāra and the subtle elements) and the sixteen modifications (mind, ten senses, five gross elements). This is presided over by the cosmic being or puruṣa. The divinities that dwell in the various limbs of the puruṣa have already been narrated to you.

Consciousness that is the jīva is the kaustubha gem on his chest, whose splendour is the śrīvatsa. The guṇā constitute the flower garland. The vedā are the golden linen around his loins. Oṁ is the sacred thread (A U M are the three strands). Sāṅkhya and yoga are his ear-rings. Brahma-loka itself is his crown. The unmanifest is his serpent couch. Satva is his lotus-seat. Prāṇa is his mace. Conch represents water, and the discus fire. The sword is space and the bow is time. The quiver contains the karma of all jīva. Mind is his chariot.

Worship the Lord in the orb of the sun, for the worship itself destroys all sins.

The Lord carries a lotus representing the six lordly attributes of Bhagavān. Vaikuṇṭha is his umbrella. His vehicle Garuḍa is the vedā. He himself is yajña. the spirit of sacrifice. His own power is Lakṣmī. Viṣvaksena, his chief attendant, is the tantra or mode of his worship. The divine powers appear as his attendants. He himself is conceived of as having four forms, as Vāsudeva, Saṅkarṣaṇa, Pradyumna and Aniruddha, which are viśva, taijasa, prājña and turīya (representing the four states of consciousness).

Though he has been variously described, he is one—and he is the very self of his devotee. If early every morning his devotee repeats the verse: "Kṛṣṇa, friend of Arjuna, best among Vṛṣṇī, Govinda, who is the destroyer of wicked rulers, whose power is infinite, whose glory is sung by cowherdesses and others, protect your devotees," he will realise the supreme being in his heart.

Śaunaka said: Tell us about the sun-god who is śrī Hari himself.

Sūta said: Though one and a manifestation of lord Hari himself, the sun-god has been described by the sages under different names. Though one, śrī Hari has been described as time, space, activity, doer, instrument, work, scripture, material substance and fruit. As time, the Lord himself appears as the sun-god, and courses through the twelve zodiacal signs, month after month, with twelve groups of attendants.

Book Twelve Chapter 12

Sūta said: I salute dharma; I salute Kṛṣṇa; I salute the holy ones. I have narrated to you the story of lord Viṣṇu, which is excellent, even as you have requested me to. In this the Lord's glory has been sung. In this has been brought out the infinite being and its secret wisdom, along with the enunciation of direct realisation. In this has been brought out the yoga of devotion and vairāgya (dispassion).

We narrated the story of Parīkṣit and the curse upon him. We recounted the dialogue between Vidura and Uddhava and the dialogue between Vidura and Maitreya. This was followed by the story of creation and evolution, and a description of time.

We have also given a full account of the Lord's incarnation as Kapila and his instructions to his mother Devahūti, containing the highest wisdom. The Lord's other incarnations have also been dealt with.

An account of the division of the universe into different spheres has been given. The story of Ajāmila, then of Dakṣa and his daughters, from whom various creatures were born, have also been given in detail.

You have also heard the account of the different dynasties—the manvantarā— the solar and the lunar dynasties. It was in the latter that the Lord himself was born as Kṛṣṇa.

You have heard of lord Kṛṣṇa's childhood and youthful pastimes, as well as the great deeds he performed during his divine life on earth. You know how playfully he accomplished the formidable task of the extermination of the evil forces on earth, and how he granted salvation to all those who were devoted to him, either out of love, out of fear or out of hate. You also heard how he brought about the destruction of his own people, instructed Uddhava in the highest wisdom and then departed for his own realm. Finally, you also heard how king Parīkṣit attained the supreme, and left his body.

He who utters the holy words: 'Haraye namaḥ' (salutations to Hari) even unwittingly, is redeemed. The only worthy occupation here is to sing his names and glories. You are all highly blessed in that you are all so devoted to him. I, too, am blessed in that I have been able to narrate this supreme Bhāgavata Purāṇa in your presence. He who reads or listens to it is instantly purified of all sins.

Book Twelve Chapter 13

Sūta continued: Salutations to the Lord, whom Brahmā, Varuṇa, Indra, Rudra and the wind-gods praise with divine hymns, whom the psalmists praise with the vedā; whom the yogī, immersed in the state of deep meditation with their hearts entered into him, perceive; and yet whose 'measure' even the gods and the asurā do not know. The Lord, assuming the form of the divine tortoise, felt sleepy on account of the sensation of scratching which the mountain Mandara (which he supported) produced on his back; and he gently breathed in and out. May his inhalation and exhalation protect you. How mighty they are! They disturbed the ocean and thus were the waves generated—and the waves continue to arise in the ocean even today!

You have heard that there are eighteen purāṇā on the whole. Altogether they comprise four hundred thousand couplets, of which the Bhāgavata Purāṇa alone has eighteen thousand couplets.

This Bhāgavata Purāṇa was revealed by the Lord himself to Brahmā, the creator; hence it is known as *Bhāgavataṁ*, the Book of God. And it is Bhāgavataṁ because it is entirely devoted to the Lord and his glories. It is the essence of the Upaniṣad and has the infinite absolute being (Brahman) for its subject matter.

He who gives away a copy of the *Bhāgavataṁ* on the day of the full moon in the Bhādrapada month attains the highest goal.

The other purāṇā shine only so long as one has not heard the *Bhāgavataṁ*. Even as Gaṅgā is the foremost among rivers, Viṣṇu among the manifestations of the Lord, Śiva among the devotees of the Lord, even so *Bhāgavataṁ* is the foremost among the purāṇā. It is dearest to the devotees of Viṣṇu and to the ascetics of the highest order. He who listens to or reads it and contemplates it is liberated.

Salutations to lord Kṛṣṇa. Salutations to śrī Vyāsa. Salutations to sage Śuka and to king Parīkṣit. Salutations to Hari, chanting whose names frees one from all sins and sorrow.

Printed in the United States
19666LVS00003B/1-30